Biomedical Informatics

Jules J. Berman

JONES AND BARTLETT PUBLISHERS

Sudbury, Massachusetts

BOSTON   TORONTO   LONDON   SINGAPORE

World Headquarters

Jones and Bartlett
  Publishers
40 Tall Pine Drive
Sudbury, MA 01776
978-443-5000
info@jbpub.com
www.jbpub.com

Jones and Bartlett
  Publishers Canada
6339 Ormindale Way
Mississauga, Ontario L5V
1J2
CANADA

Jones and Bartlett
  Publishers International
Barb House, Barb Mews
London W6 7PA
UK

Jones and Bartlett's books and products are available through most bookstores and online booksellers. To contact Jones and Bartlett Publishers directly, call 800-832-0034, fax 978-443-8000, or visit our website, www.jbpub.com.

Substantial discounts on bulk quantities of Jones and Bartlett's publications are available to corporations, professional associations, and other qualified organizations. For details and specific discount information, contact the special sales department at Jones and Bartlett via the above contact information or send an email to specialsales@jbpub.com.

Copyright © 2007 by Jones and Bartlett Publishers, Inc.

All rights reserved. No part of the material protected by this copyright may be reproduced or utilized in any form, electronic or mechanical, including photocopying, recording, or by any information storage and retrieval system, without written permission from the copyright owner.

Production Credits
Acquisitions Editor, Science: Cathleen Sether
Acquisitions Editor, Science: Shoshanna Grossman
Managing Editor, Science: Dean W. DeChambeau
Editorial Assistant, Science: Molly Steinbach
Production Director: Amy Rose
Production Editor: Tracey Chapman
Marketing Manager: Andrea DeFronzo
Manufacturing Buyer: Therese Connell
Composition: Northeast Compositors
Cover Design: Timothy Dziewit
Cover Images: © Betrand Collet / ShutterStock, Inc.; Bruce Rolff / ShutterStock, Inc.
Printing and Binding: Courier Stoughton
Cover Printing: Courier Companies

Library of Congress Cataloging-in-Publication Data
Berman, Jules J.
    Biomedical informatics / Jules J. Berman.
        p. cm.
    Includes bibliographical references and index.
    ISBN-13: 978-0-7637-4135-8 (pbk.)
    ISBN-10: 0-7637-4135-3 (pbk.)
    1. Bioinformatics. 2. Biomedical engineering. 3. Medical informatics.
    I. Title.
    [DNLM: 1. Medical Informatics. 2. Computational Biology.
3. Medical Records. 4. Biomedical Engineering.   W 26.5 B516b
2007]
    R856.B47 2006
    610.28—dc22

                                                    2006015061

6048

Printed in the United States of America
10 09 08 07 06   10 9 8 7 6 5 4 3 2 1

Author Biography

Jules Berman, PhD, MD is a pathologist with an eclectic technical background that includes a bachelor's degree in mathematics from MIT. He was Program Director for Pathology Informatics in the Cancer Diagnosis Program in the U.S. National Cancer Institute for a period that spanned two millennia (1998-2005). He has first-authored more than 100 scientific articles. Currently, he is President of the Association for Pathology Informatics.

Table of Contents

Preface

Biomedical informatics is the branch of medicine that combines biology with computer science. The purpose of all medical disciplines is to advance medical progress and to eliminate diseases. In the field of biomedical informatics, this is done by integrating biological information with medical information using computational techniques. The purpose of this book is to provide the reader with tools and strategies for obtaining, organizing, and analyzing biomedical data.

LIST 0.0.0. WHAT EVERY DETERMINED READER WILL LEARN FROM THIS BOOK

- How to acquire and organize biomedical data even when the data are received in the form of unstructured text
- How to merge and share biomedical data even when the data are confidential or come from seemingly incompatible sources
- How to write your own programs in Perl that will allow you to perform common informatics tasks with just a few lines of code
- How to automatically index biomedical text and code text using freely available biological and medical nomenclatures
- How to use metadata to provide structure and meaning to biomedical datasets
- How to use confidential medical data while obeying current law and protecting patients
- How to reduce the complexity of biomedical data and biomedical software
- How to evaluate ethical problems related to intellectual property, privacy, **human subjects research**, **data sharing**, and software development

Because so many different kinds of people need to use biomedical data, this book is directed at a diverse readership.

LIST 0.0.1. PEOPLE WHO WILL BENEFIT FROM READING THIS BOOK

- Bioinformaticians
- Biomedical scientists
- Clinical trialists
- Computer scientists who need cross-over skills in the biomedical sciences
- Government officials at any of the health-related federal agencies
- Healthcare graduate students and professionals who use large biomedical datasets, who need to have data/software interoperability, or who need to comply with federal, state, or institutional data requirements
- Hospital staff, including medical students, physicians, nurses, technicians, hospital administrators, and information officers
- Lawyers who handle **intellectual property** cases related to biomedicine
- Library scientists
- Medical ethicists
- Medical software developers and vendors
- Medical transcriptionists
- Members of IRBs (**Institutional Review Boards**) and **Privacy Boards**
- Privacy experts who work with medical scientists

No book on biomedical informatics would be complete without some instruction in computer programming. So as not to discourage nonprogrammers, the book is organized so that all of the programming instruction is found in Chapters 5 and 6. In later chapters, snippets of Perl code may occasionally intrude, but the chapters can be read and appreciated by nonprogrammers. Readers may choose to skip Chapters 5 and 6 and return to them if they ever feel the urge to learn Perl programming.

The field of biomedical informatics is quite different from the field of bioinformatics. As used herein, "bioinformatics" is a field within biology that uses computers to study biomolecules (primarily DNA, RNA, and proteins). Curious bioinformaticians will want to expand their expertise into the medical domain. Once the function of a macromolecule or molecular pathway is understood, the next obvious question relates to the role of these findings in human diseases. This book describes, in some detail, the practical opportunities (and impedimenta) for bioinformaticians who choose to cross into the world of medical research. In addition to a new set of scientific tools and questions, bioinformaticians will also face a new set of legal and ethical dilemmas. Chapter 16, "A Practical Approach to Ethics for Biomedical Informaticians," should be required reading for anyone using confidential medical records.

To the best of my knowledge, Chapter 17, "Grantsmanship for Biomedical Informaticians," has no counterpart in any other informatics text and will be of enormous value to every student and researcher. Biomedical informatics is an incredibly important field. At this moment, the large funding agencies share this opinion and have launched many initiatives in this direction. Though the field of basic (i.e., non-patient-oriented) bioinformatics is progressing rapidly, the field of biomedical informatics (where biology data meet clinical records) is lagging behind. After seven years as Program Director for Pathology Informatics within the National Institutes of Health, and over 30 years as a biomedical researcher, I have a sense of the common mistakes and the uncommon wisdoms that rattle the research process. Chapter 17 provides some suggestions and reflections for hopeful scientists.

Contributors to the field of biomedical informatics may notice that their important contributions have been omitted from relevant chapters. This is because the text emphasizes the fundamental questions (not solutions) in the field of biomedical informatics. The problems that we face today are likely to be with us for a few more decades. The solutions will come and go. I hope to foster self-reliance by providing a set of open source tools and methods that readers will use to suit their own circumstances.

Because this book emphasizes basic skills, I avoid reference to commercial software. An extensive appendix lists and describes 48 free and open source software tools and resources. The cost of biomedical informatics projects would be drastically reduced if everyone in the field availed themselves of these accessible no-cost utilities. The software included in the appendix were chosen for their enduring popularity, the ease with which they can be downloaded and installed, and their particular utility in the field of biomedical informatics. Readers will find this book's appendix to be indispensable (unlike the dispensable vermiform appendix that protrudes from the cecum).

It is impossible to write a general text on biomedical informatics without including terms that might be new to some readers. A glossary is included, and new terms introduced in the text are set in boldface type.

There is an extensive reference section with 180 references. Each reference is appended with a comment explaining its significance. Many of the references are important sources of standards, data, or software. Knowing that references have little value if they cannot be easily retrieved, I tried to cite manuscripts that are accessible on the Internet. The majority of references have a formal literary citation plus a web address.

Lists are an excellent way of distilling knowledge. The book contains over 240 lists. The "Index of Lists" is included in Chapter 21. Readers may find it useful to include some of these lists in their own teaching seminars, and they have the publisher's permission to do so.

Special thanks go to Dr. Milton Datta who participated in the formative discussions that preceded work on this book. Dr. Datta was the primary reviewer and contributed many suggestions that have been written into this final version. Also, this book could not have been written without the support of my family. The process of writing a large technical tome seldom endears an author to his loved ones. I am eternally grateful to my dear wife and daughters who tolerated my frequent mental absences with grace and humor.

CHAPTER

1

What Are Biomedical Data, and What Do We Do With Them?

1.1. BACKGROUND

Biomedical informaticians (sometimes called informaticists) integrate large biologic and medical datasets for the purpose of conquering diseases and improving human health. Because medical data are often extracted from private and legally protected medical records, people who work with medical data must be versed in the legal and ethical issues related to human subject protections. Because biological data, particularly experimental biological data obtained from human tissue specimens, are sometimes owned and sold, people who work with biological data must also be versed in issues related to intellectual property. Because large **heterogeneous data sets** (such as experimental data and medical data) cannot be effectively merged and analyzed unless all of the diverse data sources conform to standard methods of organizing and representing data, biomedical informaticians must understand the principles of data standardization. In fact, biomedical informaticians are expected to have deep knowledge that extends to many different fields (List 1.1.1).

LIST 1.1.1. ROLES OF THE BIOMEDICAL INFORMATICIAN

- Biologist
- Healthcare professional
- Lawyer
- Software programmer
- Computer scientist
- Cryptographer
- Metadata expert
- Linguist
- Statistician
- Diplomat

Most importantly, biomedical informaticians are expected to take all diverse data sources and somehow translate the data into some clinically useful result.

1.2. THE CHALLENGE OF TRANSLATIONAL RESEARCH

Translational research is a relatively new term that seems to have arisen from a growing sense of frustration in the biomedical community. Translational research is the process whereby a scientific discovery is developed into a procedure, test, treatment, device, or process that improves patient care and treatment outcome.

There is a growing perception that the stunning scientific discoveries of the past half century have produced only incremental improvements in the overall health and longevity of mankind. Most of the high-impact advances in medicine that have brought improved health and longer life were introduced prior to 1955 (List 1.2.1).

LIST 1.2.1. PRE-1955 BIOMEDICAL ADVANCES RESULTING IN INCREASED LONGEVITY IN MANY DEVELOPED COUNTRIES

- Antisepsis
- Refrigeration of food
- Standards for the hygienic preparation of food
- Eradication of insect vectors for yellow fever and malaria
- Potable public drinking water
- Antibiotics effective against many bacterial infections including syphilis, gonorrhea, and tuberculosis
- Vaccines against smallpox, polio, diphtheria, pertussis, and tetanus
- The virtual elimination of iodine-deficiency associated goiter
- The near elimination of vitamin deficiency diseases
- The marked reduction of cervical cancer in women thanks to cytologic screening of cervical smears
- The prevailing blood tests and quantitative blood cell analyses used to monitor deviations from normal function
- The correction of diabetic hyperglycemia with insulin
- The introduction of radiologic imaging
- The treatment of hypertension with a variety of effective drugs
- The recognition of the association between cigarette use and cancer
- The role of diet and of cigarettes in the progression of vascular diseases

Some would suggest that the last 50 years have been plagued by stunning failures in public health (List 1.2.2).

LIST 1.2.2. MEDICAL SETBACKS SINCE 1955

- The global spread of AIDS
- Diminished access to potable water in much of the world population
- The emergence of multiple antibiotic resistant strains of *Staphylococcus aureus* and other previously treatable organisms
- Increased number of cancer patients due primarily to an absolute increase in the number of senior citizens at highest risk for cancer
- The re-emergence of tuberculosis
- The re-emergence of insect and other vectors carrying viral and parasitic diseases
- The astronomical costs of new, effective medications for chronic diseases, including cancer
- High quality, long-term health care attainable for only a small fraction of the earth's population
- The rising incidence of obesity and sequelae disorders, worldwide
- The rapid geographic spread of outbreaks of new strains of influenza and other evolving viruses, including HIV and hemorrhagic fever viruses
- The threat of destructive and pathogenic species of plants, insects, and animals that have been introduced to new habitats through acts of human negligence or error
- Weakening of the earth's ozone layer, increasing human exposure to ultraviolet radiation
- The political uses of toxic agents, endemic diseases, and public health infrastructures

A recently issued white paper from the Food and Drug Administration (FDA) suggests that the pace of medical progress is slowing (1). The FDA report notes that despite many achievements in genomics, proteomics, and nanotechnology, there has been a downturn in medical product applications at the FDA. Furthermore, the number of new, approved medical diagnostics in the United States has declined to just one per year on average. The report also asserts that products recently approved by the FDA have not yet had much impact on patient care. Likewise, a review of serum-based diagnostics by Anderson et al. reported that despite rapid advances in the field of proteomics, few new serum proteins are currently used in routine clinical diagnosis (2). Their study indicates the rate of introduction of new protein tests has declined over the last decade. In the breast cancer field, according to Benowitz, only one marker has appeared in the last decade that has modified breast cancer treatment (i.e., Her2 for some cases of breast cancer) (3).

Just a few years ago, the expectation of therapeutic options based on genotyping individual patients promised a new era of personalized medicine. The new era of pharmacogenomics has been slow in coming. In a 2005 review of pharmacogenomics from the Royal Society, the authors reached the conclusion that pharmacogenomics is unlikely to revolutionize or personalize medical practice in the near future (4). Aside from the enormous data issues related to cataloging genetic variations that predict drug reactions, there are a number of practical clinical limitations. Many of the factors related to ineffective or adverse drug effects are simply caused by misdiagnosis, prescription errors, or patient noncompliance with therapeutic recommendations. Worldwide, the major cause of patient noncompliance relates to the prohibitive cost of pharmaceuticals. Pharmacogenomics is a field that may have advanced to a place that lies outside the realm of practical implementation.

Advances in medical science do not necessarily result in improved methods for preventing, detecting, or treating disease. History is replete with stories of unimplemented scientific breakthroughs.

1.3. DISASTERS IN TRANSLATIONAL RESEARCH

For hundreds of years, scurvy was a terrible peril of oceanic exploration. In 1497, Vasco da Gama sailed from Lisbon to Calcutta around Africa. His adventure was the first recorded voyage sufficiently long to induce scurvy, killing three fifths of his men. Their deaths were ghastly, characterized by swollen bodies covered by purple blotches. Their teeth would loosen, falling out of their sockets with any sudden shake of the head. Frequently, victims would die suddenly, in mid-sentence, from intracranial hemorrhage.

In 1593, Sir Richard Hawkins cured scurvy with oranges and lemons. In 1597, a type of salad cress, aptly named scurvy grass, was shown to cure scurvy. In the 1600s, captains of the Dutch East India Company noticed that scurvy only occurred when the navy diet lacked fruits and vegetables (5). The Dutch East India Company planted citrus orchards at port islands and prevented the disease. All of these successful measures were abandoned over time. In 1747, James Lind (1716–1794) determined that citrus prevents scurvy. Fifty years passed before Britain enacted antiscorbutic measures to protect her navy. On April 22, 1848, the exploring ships Erebus and Terror, on their way to find the Northwest Passage to the Pacific Ocean, were trapped in ice. One hundred and five men reached shore, but they neglected to carry lemon juice. The men died of scurvy. The Eskimos related stories of encountering enfeebled white men bleeding from the mouth (6). Over the centuries, thousands of men died of scurvy while a simple and effective preventive measure was ignored over and over and over again.

Scurvy was not the only example of a lost translational opportunity. Body temperature was studied as a monitor of human health and disease by Galileo Galilei (1564–1642) and by his contemporary, Sanctorius (1561–1636) (7). In 1683, Robert Boyle dismissed body heat measurements as "a work of needless curiosity." The value of temperature measurement was re-established nearly 2 centuries later in Carl Wunderlich's 1868 publication, *Das Verehalten der Eigenwarme in Krankheiten* (7). At about the same time, a clinical thermometer, small enough to fit in a patient's mouth without discomfort, was finally engineered.

Dr. Ignaz Philipp Semmelweis (1818–1865) worked at the Vienna General Hospital (1847) where women died after childbirth at an appalling rate from puerperal fever. Through no small effort, Semmelweis forced medical students to wash and scrub their hands. The mortality rate in the medical students' section of the maternity clinic fell dramatically. The subsequent events were unimagined by Semmelweis, another example of the law of unintended consequences (List 1.3.1).

LIST 1.3.1. IMMEDIATE CONSEQUENCES OF SEMMELWEIS'S PREVENTION OF PUERPERAL FEVER DEATHS

- The medical students were opposed to being forced to wash their hands.
- Semmelweis's superior, Johann Klein, was likewise opposed, considering the clinical trial a criticism of his performance.
- Other obstetricians agreed that Semmelweis's measures were an attack on their professional conduct.
- The maternity patients were opposed as well, interpreting sanitary measures as a criticism of their personal hygiene.

Semmelweis's handwashing measures were quickly abandoned. Nearly 20 years later, Lister introduced antisepsis into medical practice, with somewhat more success. One hundred and fifty years later, a 2001 Johns Hopkins Hospital study paired house staff with unidentified observers who recorded their handwashing habits. Overall handwashing rates were low (44%). Physicians were the least likely to comply, handwashing 15% of the time, compared with 50% handwashing rate for registered nurses (RNs) (8). Today, soap applied with water remains the most effective preventive measure against infection, but we cannot implement this simple procedure sans duress.

In 1928, Alexander Fleming made the observation that penicillin mold inhibited the growth of staphylococci. At the time, Fleming did not imagine that his observation would have clinical utility. Twelve years later, Howard Florey read Fleming's research and understood its translational importance. Within 18 months, Florey refined the mold and injected it into a patient, but Florey had not succeeded in cultivating and purifying the antibiotic in sufficient quantity to meet the demand (primarily World War II combatants). Americans grew the mold in brewers' vats, and the supply of penicillin was adequate for the 1944 D-Day invasion of Europe (6). How can we account for the 16-year lapse between the discovery and the translational implementation of penicillin?

In the case of scurvy, antisepsis and antibiotic treatment, opportunities were lost because gained knowledge was either forgotten, lost, disbelieved, or unexploited. Biomedical informatics is based on the (unproven) assertion that as we integrate immense biological and clinical data sets, the advance of medical science will rapidly accelerate. The important data produced in clinics and laboratories will not be neglected or lost if we can somehow collect and organize everything. With sufficiently powerful techniques, biomedical informatics will ensure that laboratory discovery will be ineluctably linked to clinical implementation. At least, that is the idea. Translational efforts will require public confidence that the underlying beliefs fostered by biomedical informaticians will work as claimed (List 1.3.2).

LIST 1.3.2. BELIEFS HELD BY BIOMEDICAL INFORMATICIANS

- Medical progress requires the integration of biological data and clinical data.
- Aggregate clinical data have value beyond their use in guiding the treatment of individual patients.
- Researchers need methods to acquire clinical data without harming patients.
- To be useful, biological and clinical data need to be organized in a standard manner that permits **seamless data integration**.
- **Classifications** drive down the complexity of clinical and biological data.

- Important new testable hypotheses may derive from pre-existing biological and clinical datasets, but only if the datasets are made available to scientists.
- The primary data that support scientific assertions should be made publicly available, whenever feasible.
- Data analysis is an inexpensive pursuit if you know how to program.

1.4. THE ROLE OF BIOMEDICAL DATA IN TRANSLATIONAL RESEARCH

Lessons learned from molecules, cells, and laboratory animals do not always extend to humans. Someone needs to validate experimental hypotheses directly in humans before a research finding has medical value. For this to happen, researchers must have access to research data, medical records, clinical trial data, and human tissue specimens. The data must be collected in a manner that protects human subjects. The collected data must be organized and annotated. All this needs to be done openly so that scientific results can be validated and extended. All of this work falls under the aegis of biomedical informatics.

It is my perception that throughout history, translational research was hampered by limitations in data access, data organization, and data analysis. Today, we have the technical means to rapidly translate basic biomedical discoveries into important medical advances. There are, however, some impediments that we must first overcome (List 1.4.1).

LIST 1.4.1. SOME IMPORTANT BOTTLENECKS IN TRANSLATIONAL RESEARCH

- Access to clinically annotated tissues collected from human subjects
- Access to electronic medical records and other electronic archives of human clinical data
- Methods to organize data in a manner that permits the data to be meaningful and comparable from laboratory to laboratory and from institution to institution
- Methods to draw clinically valid conclusions from large datasets containing heterogeneous types of data (e.g., molecular data and clinical test data)

Modern biomedical research is **data-intensive**. The typical biomedical experiment may result in many thousands of individual measurements on each sample tested (e.g., **gene expression arrays**). Often, the collected data from experiments does not consist of simple numeric datatypes. Instead, biological data often come in the form of an image or a collection of images (e.g., **tissue microarrays**). When dealing with multiple images collected on many different specimens, involving many different observational parameters, and extending over multiple time-points, it becomes easy to see that a single experiment may yield terabytes of data. Furthermore, clinical trials and **clinical validation studies** are typically performed on large numbers of human subjects or large numbers of human tissues, geometrically expanding the size of datasets.

Society is just now learning how to cope with the problem of integrating biological data with clinical data. Before much progress is made, biomedical informaticians must develop a wide range of tools and techniques, and these will be discussed in later chapters.

1.5. EXPERTISE IN BIOMEDICAL INFORMATICS

Biomedical informatics skills can be separated into basic and advanced categories (Lists 1.5.1 and 1.5.2).

LIST 1.5.1. BASIC SKILLS AND ACTIVITIES IN BIOMEDICAL INFORMATICS

- An understanding of a computer's file and subdirectory system
- The ability to download, install, and use popular software applications and utilities
- An awareness of the differences between structured and unstructured data
- Basic understanding of **XML** and metadata annotation
- Basic appreciation of computer algorithms
- Some familiarity with data privacy rules and how these rules relate to the research uses of medical data. Most countries have such privacy regulations for biomedical data. In the United States, this would be the HIPAA privacy rules (9), and in the United Kingdom, it would be the Data Protection Act (10).
- A general understanding of concepts of medical record de-identification
- Familiarity with the publicly available biological search engines, databases, and tools, including PubMed and GenBank

LIST 1.5.2. ADVANCED SKILLS AND ACTIVITIES IN BIOMEDICAL INFORMATICS

- Programming at a moderate level in at least one programming language
- Experience choosing and implementing a laboratory or hospital information system
- Knowledge of regulations pertaining to the use of identified medical data in research
- Participation in an effort seeking FDA approval for a device or technology developed from a biomedical informatics effort
- Participation on a standards committee
- Intermediate level understanding of XML
- Basic understanding of **RDF** (Resource Description Framework)
- Experience as a member of an IRB or privacy board
- Competing for funding for a biomedical informatics grant or contract

1.6. THE GOOD NEWS: NO-COST TOOLS

Readers who are familiar with the IT (information technology) industry are well aware of the enormous sums of money spent each year by hospitals and academic centers on IT support. Surely, biomedical informatics, which is closely tied to institutional IT services, must also be an expensive proposition. Not necessarily. Much of biomedical informatics relies on the pre-existence of large biomedical datasets. How those datasets came into being (acquisition issues) is less of an issue to the biomedical informatician than are issues of how the information is organized and accessed. In addition, much of the data, methods, and tools in this field have been made available at no cost.

It is the author's opinion that biomedical informatics is the second-best bargain in the world of science (the first being a public library card). All of the programming languages, all of the software utilities, and all of the software applications you will ever need to be an expert in biomedical informatics are available immediately and at no cost. In addition, an enormous volume of biological data, **medical ontologies** and nomenclatures, epidemiologic records, census data, and disease-related datasets are also available for free download from the Internet.

Every tool and dataset described in this book is available at no cost and can be easily downloaded from the Internet (see Appendix). Commercially available items are intentionally omitted from discussion.

Readers who freely use available open source tools and who learn to create their own software utilities will be in a position to complete projects quickly and at enormous savings.

1.7. THE BAD NEWS: THE HIGH COST OF HUMAN COOPERATION

If the software, methods, tools, and much of the data of biomedical informatics are free, then where is the money spent? Data acquisition and organization accounts for the greatest cost in the field of biomedical informatics.

Data miners can learn a lesson from gold miners. What does one really pay for when one purchases a quantity of gold metal? The gold itself was not created by the seller. The gold was simply waiting in the ground. When one buys gold, one is paying for the effort of buying the land that holds the gold, securing mining rights, locating the gold, removing it from the ground, refining the substance, certifying its purity, transforming the substance into a standard shape and weight, and transporting the substance to the buyer.

The data that biomedical informaticians need to obtain from hospital information systems is just sitting and waiting in some database. It was collected to make a specific medical decision for a specific patient. Once the medical decision was made, the data became history. In order for the data to become useful to the biomedical informatician, the data miner follows the same steps as the gold miner (List 1.7.1).

LIST 1.7.1. STEPS IN GOLD MINING (OR DATA MINING)

- Obtain physical access to a mine
- Obtain legal rights of access to mine
- Acquire tools to find desired items in mine
- Acquire tools to extract desired items from mine
- Acquire tools to refine desired items
- Acquire tools to certify the purity and quantity of desired items
- Transform the desired items into a standard format
- Transport the desired items to an intended recipient
- Arrange payment for the desired items
- Store the desired items
- Protect the stored items

Obtaining high-quality medical data can be hideously expensive. In many cases, the bulk of the research dollars spent on a bioinformatics project are devoted to the costs of obtaining consents from human subjects and the costs of manually collecting data from different sources and compiling the data into a format and quality suitable for the particular study.

One of the goals of this book will be to provide an approach to data procurement that reduces the costs incurred by funding agencies and medical institutions.

1.8. REALISTIC OPPORTUNITIES FOR BIOMEDICAL INFORMATICIANS

The biomedical informatician needs to understand biological data and medical data and must have the computational skills to integrate and interrogate both types of data sources. Mastering these disparate fields is not, however, the greatest challenge to biomedical informaticians. It is the author's opinion, based on many years of interactions with biomedical scientists, that the greatest challenge is discerning the important questions that can be answered with available tools and data.

Sometimes, even a young scientist needs to be reminded that life is short and training is long. A typical scientist may expect only a few decades of productive years following a graduate-level education and postdoctoral training. During the time available, biomedical informaticians must choose key questions that will form the focus of their professional lives. These questions should lead to clinically valuable results and must be answered with available data and tools (Lists 1.8.1 and 1.8.2).

LIST 1.8.1. REALISTIC USES OF BIOMEDICAL INFORMATICS

- Store, share, search, retrieve, and analyze heterogeneous data sources. This entire process is vastly enhanced by our current ability to send any type of data anywhere at anytime cheaply.
- Create large comprehensive databases (millions of cases) that allow you to ask questions that could not be asked of small or noncomprehensive databases
- Drive down the complexity of biomedical data by using data specifications and classifications
- Track data collected in hospital information systems and dispatch automatic clinical alerts when data values fall outside an expected

range of behavior or when values violate the expected properties of data classes

- Develop new hypotheses by examining and correlating biological and clinical observations
- Validate new clinical tests and treatments by examining the correlations between test values, treatment choices, and clinical outcomes

LIST 1.8.2. UNREALISTIC USES OF BIOMEDICAL INFORMATICS

- Replace physicians with computers: Doctors are trained to make diagnoses, and they don't desire or use software that purports to do this for them.
- Create superdoctors through the use of computer tools: The practice of medicine is learned through personal experiences. Doctors seldom need simulations of reality.
- Vastly improve upon books and traditional teaching strategies: Books are an adequate method of conveying knowledge. Computers can certainly provide some improvements to book learning, but there is no reason to think that a system of learning based on printed literature, that works perfectly fine, can be vastly improved.
- Solve subtle or complex problems via the use of medical ontologies: Complex systems are inherently chaotic, and inferences reached through a logical ontology modeling a complex system are likely to be misleading.
- Create, within the next decade, comprehensive medical records for all US citizens that can be accessed and annotated by all authorized caregivers: This holy grail of US medical informatics is a worthy long-term pursuit, but there is no reason to expect that it can be achieved within a decade or even two decades.

Forecasts of what is and is not scientifically feasible are notoriously inaccurate and should only be used to roughly indicate where current trends seem to lead. Readers may be interested in knowing my prediction that the field of biomedical informatics will be focused for the next decade on the fundamental issues of data access, data representation, and data sharing. These three issues will recur throughout this book. In the author's opinion, major medical and public health breakthroughs will be slow in coming until the research community masters the techniques of acquiring and sharing well-described and well-organized biomedical data.

The Data of Biomedical Informatics

2.1. BACKGROUND

Hospitals hold an enormous amount of data related to clinical encounters. Nobody has measured the total amount of archived clinical data, but the author has heard representatives of large health care organizations speak of terabytes of data collected weekly by their concerns. Pathology, pharmacy, and radiology contribute the vast majority of data collected in hospital information systems. A typical pathology department renders data on about 5,000 biopsies and more than a million clinical laboratory tests each year. With well over 5,000 hospitals in the United States, these activities provide approximately 25 million biopsy results each year and about twice that number of cytology reports (11).

At greater than 1 million laboratory tests per hospital, the number of tests conducted each year in the United States easily exceeds 5 billion. Each laboratory test may be accompanied by a host of ancillary data items, including patient identifiers, identifiers of the physician who ordered the test and possibly the names of ward personnel responsible for entering the test order, transaction details (when the specimen was received, who logged in the received specimen, when the test was conducted, quality control data), and finally the results, which may include normal ranges. So-called reflex data may be included when the value of the test result prompts an action (such as phone notification of the ordering physician or a request for a re-test).

US pharmacists are kept occupied filling 3.27 billion prescriptions each year in the United States (12). Pharmacy orders may contain transaction data, quality control data, and reflex data (e.g., drug interaction warnings).

Structured data are collections of simple data points (lab test values; alphanumerics, such as dates and hospital identifiers; transaction codes and control words, such as names of persons and types of tests).

Unstructured data are narrative text, also known as free-text, such as may appear in surgical pathology reports, autopsy reports, operation notes, and nursing notes.

Unstructured data may also encompass complex datatypes that require expert interpretation and that cannot be represented as a simple **character string**. Examples are telemetric data (such as EKG traces and spirometric charts), images (such as radiologic films, histopathology consultations, and endoscopic photographs), sound recordings (such as a speech pathology session), or even movies (from patient sessions). In the past, this kind of data was summarized with a few words (e.g., sinus tachycardia) and only the summary was retained as the patient's electronic record. More recently, methods have been introduced that capture raw medical data in digital form. These methods generate **binary data objects** that are now the focus of biomedical analysis (e.g., radiology images, photomicrographs, EKG traces, Doppler readings, and spirometry tests).

2.2. DATA FILES AND DATABASES

The electronic data collected by hospitals need to be stored. Basically, there are two ways of storing electronic data: as data files or as databases. Data files are the simplest way of holding electronic data and consist of collections of sequential listings of data in a named file that can be opened and examined by a computer or by a person. Data files can be easily copied and transported from computer to computer and from place to place. It is easy to determine exactly what is contained in any data file. You can add, delete, or change information in a data file using a simple **text editor** (see Appendix).

Databases are software inventions that store data in structures that can be quickly retrieved by the software but cannot be directly read by humans. A database is not a readable file. It is typically a complex software environment, with all the data kept in assigned memory locations. The memory locations that hold the data are held somewhere on a disk or a tape or in volatile memory, but these locations are assigned by the database application and are not sequentially stored in a named file. When you need a record, you query the database, and it quickly provides the record. The advantage of databases over data files is related to the speed with which records can be created, deleted, modified, or retrieved by the database software. In fact, the essence of any database application is its ability to create new records and store them in a data structure from which they can rapidly be retrieved.

I liken the differences between a database and a data file to the differences between dining at a fine restaurant and dining at a smorgasbord. In the former, you never get to see the full repertoire of the chef, but if you know what you want and you know how to order, then you will get the professionally prepared dinner that you requested. In a smorgasbord, you get to see everything all at once, and if you have the appetite, then you can sample and evaluate all the items. There is nobody to serve you or to recommend the best items, but you get to choose from what you see.

When are databases preferred over data files? In the past, databases were preferred over data files for issues of speed. A database query could retrieve records essentially instantaneously. In contrast, queries over files were slow. A typical data file consists of a sequential set of data records with one record per line. Sets of sequential records in a file are called "flat files," indicating that the file consists of one record following another without the benefit of multidimensional pointers capable of connecting keyed elements from different records (as might be found in a database structure). A query conducted over a flat file would entail a sequential search through every record in the file, assessing each record to determine if it matched the search criteria. Also, the addition, deletion, or modification of records is much slower in flat files than in databases.

For these reasons, researchers have traditionally favored databases over flat files. In the past few years, a number of advances have made the choice of database over flat file much less clear-cut. Computers have gotten much faster and can now be loaded with much more RAM (Rapid Access Memory) than ever before, and data storage has become easy and cheap. XML has emerged as a standard method for data representation, and XML data is packaged in simple alphanumeric files. Many programmers now prefer to work with files rather than databases because fast data file searches are now feasible, and some programmers may prefer the accessibility and flexibility afforded by data files (List 2.2.1). The use of database technology, in many instances, has become an issue of personal preference rather than an issue of necessity (List 2.2.2).

LIST 2.2.1. WHEN ARE DATA FILES PARTICULARLY USEFUL?

- When the dataset is relatively stable
- When the data structure is relatively instable (i.e., when the fundamental model of the data records changes)
- When XML is the native method of data representation
- When the computer staff (responsible for the data) prefers to work with data files

LIST 2.2.2. WHEN ARE DATABASES PARTICULARLY USEFUL?

- When the stored data are complex (e.g., hospitals and academic centers)
- When the basic data structure is constant (i.e., when the model of the data records does not change)
- When there are continuous real-time additions, deletions, and modifications of records by multiple users
- When the computer staff (responsible for the data) prefers to work with databases

2.3. MEDICAL DATABASES AND HOSPITAL INFORMATION SYSTEMS

It is difficult to determine the moment in history when hospitals became generators of large data collections. Some might argue that hospital data collections became seriously large in 1760, when Giovanni Battista Morgagni published the results of 640 autopsies. This prodigious effort to collect patient-based observations had enormous significance, which marked the genesis of modern pathology, but it did not produce datasets of well-defined data elements. Rene-Theophile-Hyacinthe Laennec (1781–1826) is credited with inventing the stethoscope. Laennec's 1816 invention was soon followed by his 900-page Traite de l'Auscultation Mediate (1819). Laennec's meticulous observations brought us closer to hospital data collection techniques, but if fell short of a modern approach to data representation (7).

Karl Vierordt's 1854 sphygmograph (pulse recorder) was designed for routine monitoring of patients. However, it did not generate a historical dataset that can be studied today.

My personal nomination for the beginning of modern hospital data collection goes to Carl Wunderlich's 1868 publication, *Das Verhalten der Eigenwarme in Krankheiten* (1868), which collected body temperature data on approximately 25,000 patients (7). Wunderlich associated peaks and fluctuations of body temperature with 32 different diseases. Not only did this work result in a large collection of patient data, it also sparked considerable debate over the best way of visualizing datasets. Competing suggestions for the representation of thermometric data (as it was called) included time interval (discontinuous) graphs and oscillating realtime (continuous) charts. Shortly after body temperature measurements became widely popular, sphygmomanometry (blood pressure recordings) was invented (1896). With bedside recordings of pulse, blood pressure, respirations, and temperature (the so-called vital signs), the foundations of modern medical data collection were laid.

According to the American Hospital Directory and the American Hospital Association, there are about 6,000 hospitals in the United

States (13). These medical centers handle nearly 37 million admissions each year (14). With few exceptions, the data created by all these admissions are captured in computers.

Modern medical centers put their collected data into Hospital Information Systems (HISs). HISs are multifaceted databases that create records for all the transactions of the medical center, including medicine, surgery, pharmacy, and billing. In addition to their database functionality, HISs provide a sophisticated graphic user interface that supports data entry from many points in the medical system and data access by a wide variety of hospital personnel. The HIS typically formats its collected data in a variety of ways to accommodate the needs of many specialized users (e.g., operating room schedules, clinic lists, and billable procedures).

Within a hospital, there may be specialized information systems that reside outside the HIS. Examples are laboratory information systems (for pathology data) and PACS (Picture Archiving Communication Systems) typically used as databases for digitized radiology images.

A first principle of HISs is that data collection proceeds in a consistent and organized manner that facilitates staff access to patient records. In the 1980s and 1990s, the focus of all HISs was to store medical reports (e.g., radiology reports, lab tests, and surgical pathology reports) that could be retrieved for a patient. Concentrating as they did on the task of creating and retrieving reports, some early hospital systems gave insufficient consideration to issues related to data integrity and data modeling (i.e., the way that data is structured in the database). Many of the problems associated with modern databases stem from three inescapable properties of reality (List 2.3.1).

LIST 2.3.1. THREE PROPERTIES OF REALITY RELEVANT TO HOSPITAL DATABASES

- Database records can be designed in such a manner as to corrupt the integrity of the database.
- Databases do not care if their integrity is corrupted.
- Modifications to the basic structures of database records almost always have negative (sometimes catastrophic) consequences.

Hospital databases typically ignore cautionary lessons in biomedical informatics that will be explained and repeated in later chapters (List 2.3.2).

LIST 2.3.2. COMMON WEAKNESSES OF SOME HOSPITAL DATABASES

- Inability to guarantee that every patient is uniquely identified within the database
- Inability to classify types of data into groups with shared properties
- Inability to extend data records to include data elements linked to other databases
- Inability to organize data as simple collections of meaningful statements
- Inability to produce self-describing data records (i.e., including in data records all the data necessary to fully describe the meaning of the data record)

Every hospital database should conform to a set of desired features (List 2.3.3).

LIST 2.3.3. DESIRED FEATURES FOR HISs

- Every patient must be uniquely identified within the system
- Every report must be uniquely identified and associated with one patient
- Data items contained in reports must be entered into reports once only
- Data items must be well defined and used in a consistent manner throughout the system
- Data values must be bound to a **unique identifier** and associated with a unique report
- All data entered should be technically retrievable
- Someone must have the authority to retrieve any and all data in the hospital information system
- Data, once entered, should not be corrected or modified in any way without creating a visible transaction record of the modification
- All electronic data related to an electronic medical record in the hospital information system should be included in the hospital information system

The failure to implement sensible data acquisition techniques that reliably identify data and bind medical data observations to unique patients has been the bane of medical informatics for decades.

HISs installed in large medical centers may cost in excess of $100 million. Annual operational costs are enormous. When installed HISs are evaluated, many fail to meet expectations. HISs are expected to increase the efficiency of the medical center, to improve patient care, and to provide a return on investments. Biomedical informaticians need to be aware of the critical role of HISs in hospitals and academic medical centers. The success of these expensive systems is largely dependent on having a highly trained staff who understand the fundamental principles of data representation and data integrity. Biomedical informaticians must be prepared to constructively participate in institutional committees that deploy hospital information systems that serve translational research activities.

2.4. EVERY PATIENT MUST BE UNIQUELY IDENTIFIED WITHIN THE SYSTEM

In many early hospital information systems, data entry procedures did not ensure that patients were entered into the system once and only once under a unique identifier that persists when the patient changes her name or address. A patient new to the dermatology clinic may have been registered with a new hospital identifying number. The same patient may show up at the gynecology clinic a week later and be provided with a second hospital identifying number by the admitting staff. This surprising scenario might happen again and again. Why? Sometimes the patient is asked, "Have you ever been here before?" and answers no, because she has never been to that particular clinic. The admitting desk may have intended to inquire whether the patient had ever been to the hospital. A simple misunderstanding can easily result in double registration for the same patient. Sometimes the clinic will try and fail to find a registered patient in the system. They may have misspelled the patient's name or incorrectly entered some identifier, such as a social security number, or the patient may have actually changed her name (because of marriage, divorce, or personal choice) in the interim between visits. A mother with a child patient may have provided her own name instead of the child's name. The result of all these misunderstandings and lax patient registration procedures is a system wherein a single patient may have multiple registrations under different hospital identifiers.

Why is it bad to have multiple registrations for a patient? A single person may have several different types of bank accounts at a single bank and may have accounts at multiple banks, all using different identifiers. This does not cause any harm to the person or to the bank because the accounts (not the account holders) need to have a unique identifier.

In a medical setting, serious problems arise when a single person has multiple registration numbers. Searching for reports under a single registration number will not retrieve reports attached to another registration number held by the same patient. Knowing that a patient may have multiple registrations, a physician who needs to access a patient's reports may prefer to find all the reports associated with a patient name, thereby bypassing the problem of retrieving reports by registration number. The problem with this approach is that many different patients in a large medical facility are likely to have the same name. Thus, a search for Mary Williams' cervical Pap smear may retrieve reports on several different persons named Mary Williams.

Because very few early implementations of HISs ensured the unique identification of patients, much of the legacy data from the 1980s and 1990s is tainted. One of the thorniest issues in medical informatics is the reconciliation of patient identities in data stored within an institution and across different institutions (15).

The task of uniquely identifying patients has been a persistent problem in medical informatics. Its solution is usually achieved by having a dedicated registrar responsible for registering every patient into the hospital system and ensuring that the patient is uniquely identified, and by prohibiting registration by anyone other than the registrar. This solution to the problem is an example of an implementation enforced through policy, not by software. It exemplifies an often-made observation in medical informatics: that software implementation requires a deeper understanding of human psychology than of software design.

Readers from outside the United States are probably wondering why the United States agonizes over the problem of patient identification. In many other countries, individuals are given a unique national identifier, and all medical data associated with the individual are kept in a central data repository under the aegis of the government's health service. A single, permanent identifier is used by a patient regardless of the hospital, clinic, or doctor's office that she visits.

In the United States, there has been fierce resistance to the idea of national patient identifiers. The drive for a national patient identification system is raised from time to time. The benefits to patients and to society are many. Regardless, US citizens are reluctant to have an identifying number that is associated with a federally controlled electronic record of their private medical information. In part, this distrust results from the lack of any national insurance system in the United States. Most health insurance in the United States is private, and private insurers have the right to refuse enrollment to new clients. There is a fear that if there were a national patient identifier with centralized electronic medical records, prospective insurers may stop high-risk individuals from buying insurance. Because the cost of US medical care is the highest in the world, medical bills for uninsured patients can quickly mount, impoverishing individuals and families. Many in the United States fear that a system that facilitates access to private health information will be used to deny them medical insurance. It will be interesting to see whether current US government interest in a national patient identifier system will produce a record system that protects the insurability of citizens.

2.5. ALL DATA ENTERED SHOULD BE RETRIEVABLE

HISs are complex databases and are designed to enter and retrieve a wide variety of medical information. Because patient care is an individualized process, HISs are customized to create and retrieve individual reports. HISs are not designed to collect multiple reports on multiple patients at once. HISs do not generally perform database queries that require analysis of a subset of data elements distributed across many different patients. In most medical centers, staff are limited to queries that collect reports on one patient at a time, or perhaps a small subset of patients seen in a scheduled clinic. Regardless of the practical and ordinary uses of an HIS, hospitals should have a way of retrieving any and all information residing within the hospital information system and should not be reliant solely on the selective query modules built into the system by the software vendor.

2.6. ENTERED DATA SHOULD ONLY BE MODIFIED WITH GREAT CAUTION

The author has personally observed HISs that permit personnel to blithely alter medical history by deleting a data entry and replacing data values or narrative text with modified information. The problem with this is that once data is released into the system, people may start to act on the data, unaware that it will be replaced with better data sometime in the future. Nothing could be more damaging in a legal case against a hospital than two printed versions of the same report, each containing different information. It is the computer equivalent of being caught in a lie. Because electronic data can be easily modified, it is very important for hospitals to have in place a system whereby all entries of data are **time-stamped** (see Appendix) and kept as part of the permanent medical record. Modifications to records must be identifiable as modifications and must not have the appearance of an original report. Hospital staff should be notified of any modifications in their patients' reports, and a record of the notification should be included as an addendum to the report.

2.7. THE GOVERNMENT AS A SOURCE OF BIOMEDICAL DATA

Governments are among the largest suppliers of biomedical data. In the United States, the government printing office (founded 1813) was created to disseminate to Americans information emanating from the three branches of government. With few exceptions (e.g., security concerns or concerns related to the welfare of individuals), the works produced by US government employees cannot be copyrighted. Government works usually belong to the **public domain**. The specific exception of greatest relevance to biomedical informaticians is the enormous amount of patient-related data collected by government health care facilities (such as Veterans Administration Medical Centers). Patient-related medical data collected by the US government is fully protected from distribution to the public.

2.8. YOUR RIGHT TO OBTAIN GOVERNMENT DATA—FREEDOM OF INFORMATION ACT

Many countries have passed Freedom of Information laws to ensure that citizens can request the government to provide unpublished government data.

The US Freedom of Information Act (1966) (FOIA, pronounced Foy-a and rhymes with LaToya) has been used by biomedical scientists in highly innovative ways to obtain research data, medical data, and biomedical software.

As an example, the Veterans Administration HIS, VISTA, used by approximately 160 hospitals, was developed as a government work. This software, worth millions of dollars, is available for the asking. Anyone can request a copy of the VISTA hospital information system through the US FOIA office (16).

Stories of controversial FOIA requests are many. Dr. George Kurzon submitted a FOIA request to the NIH in 1999. He sought the names and addresses of all NIH grant applicants who had failed to get funding in the May 1999 National Institutes of Mental Health Council round. The term "applicant" was interpreted to mean the principal investigator, not the applicant institution. The NIH FOIA office denied the request, arguing that this would be an invasion of the privacy of the investigators. Dr. Kurzon proceeded to file a lawsuit against the NIH. In July 2001, the district court judge in New Hampshire ruled that the privacy interests of the grant applicants was outweighed by the public interest in making the information available through the FOIA request. The NIH subsequently released the list of applicants (17).

In the United States, individual states may have FOIA laws similar to the federal FOIA. The *Southern Illinoisan*, a newspaper, requested state health department documents relating to the incidence of neuroblastoma from 1985 to 1997. The state health department denied the request, arguing that although the documents were stripped of identifying information, it may be possible for a determined person to discover the identifies of the patients using demographic and other information contained in the records.

The Illinois court ruled in favor of the *Southern Illinoisan* and against the state health department, ruling that:

"Public health data collection is a worthwhile cause in the name of reducing morbidity and mortality. Although the strict confidentiality of health data is a noble cause and is worthy of statutory protections, ultimately a balance must be struck between public health concerns and privacy concerns" (18).

In this case, the balance struck on the side of the public's interest in having access to a medical data collection.

2.9. ACCESS TO RESEARCH DATA DISCOVERED UNDER US GRANTS

The federal government spends billions of dollars each year on research grants. Does the public have access to the information obtained through taxpayer-funded grants? In some cases, yes, under a 1999 Amendment to Circular A-110 of the Freedom of Information Act.

The 1999 Amendment extended the FOIA provisions to cover, in some instances, research data collected under federal grants, even when the research was conducted by nongovernment workers. It applies to data collected by institutions of higher education, hospitals, and nonprofit institutions that receive grants and other financial assistance provided by federal agencies. It does not apply to data collected by commercial organizations. It does not apply to most data collected by state and local governments.

The 1999 FOIA extension does not apply to data collected under contracts. Contracts are a funding mechanism that differ from grants. In contracts, unlike grants, there is a specific deliverable product (tangible or intangible) that the government receives from the contractor. Because the government, following a contract, often holds the data produced under the contract, contract data often can be accessed through the regular FOIA route. Amendment A-110 applies only to data produced with federal support that are cited publicly and officially by a federal agency in support of an action that has the force and effect of law. So, amendment A-110 has a very narrow scope. Still, it serves to make available research data that have an impact on public health. Such data is of special interest to biomedical informaticians.

2.10. GRANTEES STRIKE BACK: THE UNITED STATES BAYH-DOLE ACT

Under the Bayh-Dole Act, US federal grantees have the right to elect title to inventions and other intellectual property developed under their grants. Investigators and institutions may seek appropriate intellectual property protection (e.g., copyright or patent), and these rights extend to both software and data. As a general rule, the federal government has the right to use inventions developed under a federal grant, but this right of use does not usually extend to the public.

The Bayh-Dole Act (officially named The Patent and Trademark Amendments of 1980, PL 96-517) has been a boon to many funded researchers. It has allowed grantees to develop commercial applications for works produced under federal awards. This act has made grants much more attractive by expanding the use of grant research findings beyond the narrow realm of government interest. The legislation reduces the problem of abandonware (software developed under a grant and abandoned the moment funding expired; see Glossary) by encouraging grantees to profit by commercializing their software. The 1980 Bayh-Dole Act covered universities, nonprofit organizations and small businesses. In 1983 President Reagan extended the Bayh-Dole Act to cover large companies.

The downside of the Bayh-Dole Act is that grantees who may have opted to donate their grant-supported software and datasets to the **public domain**, may now prefer to hold onto the products of their labor in hopes of using the intellectual property in a future commercial venture. Institutions may have policies and contracts in place that prohibit staff from releasing software and data to the public, so as not to jeopardize future opportunities to profit under Bayh-Dole.

2.11. INTELLECTUAL PROPERTY

The "dark matter" of the biomedical informatics universe lies within the realm of protected intellectual property. It is assumed that there is much more proprietary software and data than free and open source software and data. Although there is no way to determine the quantity of proprietary intellectual property, we may learn something of its size by looking at the money spent to obtain and license patents. It is estimated that more than $4.5 billion is spent each year in the United States to pay for legal services and fees for patent registration. In 1999, the royalties collected on US patents exceeded $110 billion (19).

Intellectual property usually refers to proprietary methods, software, data, or text that is owned by an entity, with the rights of ownership preserved by some legal instrument.

In the distant past, the most popular method of holding something proprietary was to keep it a secret. If nobody knew your secret, then your exclusive use of the property could be leveraged to your financial advantage.

When a medical method is kept secret, few people benefit from its invention. In addition, if the person who knows the secret dies before passing the secret onto another person, the value of the secret is lost until another person rediscovers the invention.

Paul Strathern relates the curious history of a coveted piece of intellectual property, the delivery forceps (5). Circa 1570 William Chamberlen, a surgeon, invented or acquired the design of a cupped delivery forceps (tongs with large curved grasping handles that can be pressed together with a scissors action). The forceps was highly profitable to William and to his sons. His son Peter became the attending physician to Queen Anne, the wife of James I, and to Queen Henrietta Maria, the wife of Charles I. The forceps kept the Chamberlen family in riches for over a century. A descendant fell upon hard times and sold the secret of the forceps in 1720 to Dutch surgeons. The secret of the forceps ended when several of the new owners published the design. But the world really paid no notice until the highly influential William Smellie published a description of an improved model of the forceps in 1750. Because an intellectual property was kept secret, the world was deprived of a life-saving medical advancement for approximately 180 years.

Today, there is nothing to stop intellectual property holders from keeping their advances secret. Though depriving society of a medical advance is not a crime, few holders of intellectual property resort to secrecy nowadays. Governments provide two mechanisms whereby intellectual property can be made accessible to the public while still protecting the property holder's right to profit. These mechanisms are copyright and patent.

A patent is a property right (lasting 20 years) given by a government to an inventor (List 2.11.1).

LIST 2.11.1. GENERAL CLASSES OF PATENTS

- Utilities—new and useful methods, machines, items, or chemical compounds
- Designs—a new appearance for a manufactured article
- Plants—the invention or discovery of a plant variety that can be asexually reproduced

Patent means "open," so named because the patent process opens the invention to scrutiny. All of the US patents and all of the pending patent applications in the Patent and Trademark office are available for search and review at: http://www.uspto.gov/

The right to patent is sometimes referred to as the right to sue patent infringers. The idea is that patents are made public. Users of patented inventions must pay the patent holder a royalty. In return for a royalty, the patent holder refrains from taking legal action against the user.

Copyright is another intellectual property device that is usually applied to books and other bodies of text. Copyright protection extends to the form and content of the text and images and does not apply to particular ideas that might be expressed in the copyrighted work. Copyright protection lasts much longer than patent protection. The Copyright Term Extension Act of 1998 extended copyright terms in the United States by 20 years. Now copyright lasts until 70 years after the death of the author. Copyrights for corporate authorship last 95 years. Copyrights may apply to software and other digitized works (20).

When a patent or copyright has expired, the work falls into the **public domain** and can be used freely.

Though controversial, the US Patent and Trade office grants patent protection to items of paramount importance to biomedical informaticians: genes and software (21). Jensen and Murray reported in 2005 that 4,382 of 23,688 human genes in National Center for Biotechnology Information had been patented (22). Many scientists are confused and outraged by this policy, which seems to counter the long-held principle that "ideas" are not patentable. Software developers argue that new software is built from recycled algorithms whose original sources are lost to techno-history. Developers understand that all software contains bits of code that might be included in the listed claims of a registered patent. Many software developers live in fear that a snippet from their code or a brief algorithm they may have included in a complex software application will infringe on one or more software patents. The ever-present risk of patent infringement is a major problem for the software industry.

Organizations that develop new software standards and new methods to ensure **software interoperability** are worried that a patent owner will pop up and claim that a minor component of their standard contains a patented algorithm. Such considerations are not without precedent. Several years ago, there was concern among members of the World Wide Web Consortium (W3C) that the ISO (International Standards Organization) would charge fees for the commercial use of ISO codes (e.g., ISO 639 language codes, ISO 3166 country codes, and ISO 4127 currency codes) included as metadata standards within Internet protocol recommendations (23).

In a recent meeting with representatives of the US Patent and Trademark Organization, open source software developers voiced their concern that software patents were being awarded for so-called "prior art." The term "prior art" refers to inventions and processes that were known to the public prior to a patent application. Patents should not be awarded for processes that are already known (i.e., prior art). At this time (2006) discussions are underway between software developers and the US Patent and Trademark Organization. These discussions may lead to a process by which interested parties can notify the Patent office of prior art that would disqualify certain pending software applications.

2.12. FAIR USE AND OTHER ACADEMIC PRIVILEGES

Academic researchers have traditionally assumed that they may freely use patented intellectual property without paying royalties. Courts have a long tradition of protecting academics from copyright and patent infringement lawsuits through the application of "fair use." The long-held judicial concept of "fair use" was formally entered into law in the 1976 Copyright Act (List 2.12.1). Fair use, as written for copyrighted works, is generally thought to extend to patented works.

LIST 2.12.1. COPYRIGHT ACT OF 1976, TITLE 17, U.S. CODE, SECTION 107. LIMITATIONS ON EXCLUSIVE RIGHTS: FAIR USE

- Notwithstanding the provisions of sections 106 and 106A, the fair use of a copyrighted work, including such use by reproduction in copies or phonorecords or by any other means specified by that section, for purposes such as criticism, comment, news reporting, teaching (including multiple copies for classroom use), scholarship, or research, is not an infringement of copyright. In determining whether the use made of a work in any particular case is a fair use, the factors to be considered shall include:
    - the purpose and character of the use, including whether such use is of a commercial nature or is for nonprofit educational purposes;
    - the nature of the copyrighted work;
    - the amount and substantiality of the portion used in relation to the copyrighted work as a whole; and
    - the effect of the use upon the potential market for or value of the copyrighted work.
- The fact that a work is unpublished shall not itself bar a finding of fair use if such finding is made upon consideration of all the above factors (24).

Basically, the idea behind "fair use" is that copyrights and patents are devices that allow the intellectual property holders to seek profit. Neither copyright nor patent laws were intended to give intellectual property holders the right to keep their discoveries secret. If an academic uses the intellectual property in a way that benefits society and that does not reduce the value or profitability of the property, then "fair use" might apply. For a long time, it was assumed that "fair use" automatically extended to academic researchers. Madey versus Duke may have changed this notion forever.

2.13. MADEY VERSUS DUKE AND THE EROSION OF ACADEMIC PRIVILEGE

The case of Madey versus Duke casts doubt on the honored tradition of academic protection from patent infringement prosecutions.

John Madey was a Duke University lab director who was terminated from his position. Madey owned patents that were obtained prior to his appointment at Duke. Duke University used these patents without paying royalties. Madey sued Duke for patent infringement. Duke argued that the patents were being used on government contracts. The government was exempted from patent royalties for these particular patents, and Duke asserted that the protection should extend to government-funded contractors. Also, the University asserted that the work fell under the "experimental use" protection.

The district court upheld Duke's positions, but the federal court reversed the district court decision in favor of Madey (25). The federal court decided that although the work was done under a government contract, this did not necessarily mean that the work was done for the United States. The federal circuit court held that the research was done to further the interests of the University and was not motivated by scientific curiosity. Successful research projects help universities attract future funding and enhance the overall status of universities. Those who work in academic centers understand that biomedical research is an industry, even when it occurs in academia. Translational research almost always promises financial reward. Often, the researchers and their institutions have a monetary stake in the success of the research. The Madey versus Duke decision seems to signal a growing disenchantment with quaint notions of academic altruism.

2.14. FURTHER CAUTIONS ON THE USE OF PROPRIETARY SOFTWARE AND DATA

When something is proprietary, that means it is owned by a legal entity, usually a person or a corporation, and is protected by legal constructs such as patent or copyright. When someone pays to use proprietary software or data, she is typically paying for a license indicating that the owner of the intellectual property will allow certain specified uses of the property. In the case of software and data, the license may stipulate that the property cannot be copied or used on multiple computers or at multiple sites. The license may specify that certain types of profit deriving from the use of the property are subject to future royalties owed to the proprietor. Royalties or other payments attached to unspecified future income received by the licensee are sometimes referred to as "reach-through." The proprietor, as if by magic, reaches through into the future and seizes a share of the licensee's profits.

A software proprietor may choose to organize software output into a specific type of data structure and may stake a proprietary claim to the format in which the data is packaged. For example, several image formats are proprietary and cannot be used without violating patents. The popular GIF image format makes use of the LZW compression algorithm, which is covered by several patent claims owned by UNISYS and IBM. By most accounts, the last patent claim on GIF will expire in 2006. For years, millions of Web enthusiasts have created and exchanged GIF images with very little concern that they may be infringing someone's patent. Others have been more circumspect. The PNG image standard was created as a nonproprietary GIF surrogate that does not use the patented LZW compression algorithm.

As an exercise in paranoia, let us suppose that you are a researcher and you would like to archive your work on an institutional Web site. The work was created with proprietary software and produced a dataset in a format that was copyrighted by the company that created the software application. The dataset contains the primary data that supports the conclusions of your work, along with binary data inserted by the **software application**. The inserted binary data provides formatting information ensuring that the primary research data can be visualized with the proprietary software viewer. You are eager to make your primary data available to your colleagues. The software license indicates that the software application and any derivative works cannot be distributed by the licensee.

Can you safely distribute the dataset to your colleagues, and can you safely post the dataset on the Web? These questions are asked every day, and the author of this book has sought guidance and advice from scientists and legal experts. I have been informed that despite keen interest among scientists, there is precious little legal precedent to provide a good answer. Some have offered the opinion that scientists are protected by "fair use" provisions of the Copyright Act. Others have warned that software companies are itching to find a deep-pocketed institution to sue as a test case. Some have opined that when infringement is in widespread use, and the software company has not exercised its intellectual property claims, a credible claim for tort damages would be untenable.

In a sense, the question posed can be re-stated as, "When is it acceptable to cheat a little bit?" It is difficult to produce a satisfactory answer. It may just depend on how an institution gauges the risks, costs, and benefits of functioning in a data-centric universe.

Proselytizers of free distribution of data and software must remember that many of the advances in science and medicine in the past several decades have come from proprietary methods and proprietary software applications. If software developers had no way of receiving monetary compensation for their efforts, then there would be no software development and no software developers. Perhaps the best way to deal with proprietary restrictions on data sharing is to have a clear understanding of the roles of free and open source software and to have access to methods ensuring that any shared data and software is legally unencumbered. These methods will be discussed in later chapters.

2.15. THE OFTEN MISUNDERSTOOD CONCEPT OF PATIENT DATA "OWNERSHIP"

Who owns confidential medical data? Is it owned by the patient? Is it owned by the medical center? Actually, nobody owns medical data; however, the law recognizes that different entities have specified rights to use the data that nobody seems to actually own.

Ownership is a mercantile concept meaning the right to sell. If someone owns a cow, that means that they have the right to sell the cow. If I own my house, even if I have a huge mortgage that I must pay, then I have the right to sell the house. In law, there does not seem to be anyone who is legally assigned the right to sell human tissue specimens and human medical records. Even the patient has no established right to sell her own tissues. Most countries have deferred assigning legal rights of sale on private medical items for fear of establishing precedents for trade-in-flesh.

Simply because nobody owns medical records does not mean that entities cannot be assigned rights to their use. Patients have the right to ask hospitals to send their medical records to other medical centers or to themselves. Hospitals are expected to archive tissues, medical reports, and patient charts to serve the patient and society. State health departments, the Centers for Disease Control and Prevention (CDC), and cancer registries all expect medical centers to deliver medical reports on request. All of these customary activities proceed without an assignment of ownership.

Both the HIPAA and Common Rule Federal Regulations stipulate that research using medical records has societal value. Quite independent of "ownership," researchers can be provided access to medical records and human tissue specimens when an IRB determines that the research has value and that the research can be conducted without harming patients (9, 26).

Problems may arise, however, when institutions seek to sell records and tissues to research organizations or to tissue repositories. In both cases, an argument can be made that records and tissues can be transferred from a medical institution to a third entity when the entity has demonstrated that the items will be used for societal benefit and when it can be shown that individual patients will not be harmed by the transaction.

In many instances, stored surgical tissues have no value to patients and are typically destroyed (List 2.15.1). If hospitals routinely dispose of tissue, then why can hospitals not transfer the tissues (that would otherwise be destroyed) to a third entity (i.e., a party that is neither the patient nor the medical care facility that excised the tissue) (List 2.15.2)?

LIST 2.15.1. TISSUES THAT ARE ROUTINELY DESTROYED BY PATHOLOGY DEPARTMENTS

- Institutions regularly dispose of tissues removed during surgical procedures. When a large specimen, such as a colon, is received in a pathology department, samples are routinely embedded in paraffin and saved for at least 5 years. The unsampled colon (the bulk of the specimen) is saved for several weeks, sufficient time to ensure that the pathologist has rendered a final diagnosis on the specimen, and then the specimen is discarded.

- Institutions regularly dispose of archived paraffin-embedded tissues. Most institutions archive paraffin-embedded tissues for at least 5 years. At that time, some medical centers conclude that the tissues are no longer of any importance to the patient. To avoid the expense of continued storage, some institutions simply dispose of archived material after 5 years.

LIST 2.15.2. QUESTIONS THAT INSTITUTIONS SHOULD ASK BEFORE TRANSFERRING TISSUES AND MEDICAL RECORDS TO AN EXTERNAL TISSUE REPOSITORY

- Would the transfer to a third party constitute a sale of human tissue?
- Would the transfer to a third party harm any of the patients from whom the tissue was excised?
- Would the transfer to a third party benefit society?
- Do any of the institutional staff encouraging the transfer of tissues and data have relevant conflicts of interest?

When tissue samples are transferred from a medical center to a private or public tissue bank, there is a considerable amount of work that goes into retrieving the tissue specimens, annotating the specimens with de-identified clinical information, and ensuring that the quantity and quality of the archived tissues is sufficient for the intended uses of the tissue. Money transferred from a tissue bank to a medical facility offering human tissues compensates a wide range of professional services. The transfer of money from the third entity to the medical center may not constitute a purchase of tissues.

When tissues and medical records are destroyed, the risk to patients from loss of confidentiality or privacy is finally ended. If the tissues and records are transferred to a third party, then the risks are extended and transferred as well. Medical institutions that transfer tissues and records to a third party are obligated to protect their patients, and this is typically done by anonymizing the transferred materials. An institutional privacy board or an IRB may seek to verify that the transfer of human subject material (tissues and records) is conducted in a manner that protects patients from harm and provides a societal service. IRBs may also determine whether any of the medical center staff have conflicting interests in the transaction (e.g., they are employed by the third entity or are likely to profit directly from the arrangement). The purpose of most tissue repositories is to facilitate translational research that will benefit society. There is ample reason to support efforts to build a translational research infrastructure that does not harm patients.

2.16. SHARING DATA

How has society benefited from data sharing? Basically, all scientific advancement is built on the cumulative work of predecessors. If we did not have journal articles that carefully described experiments and observations, then scientific progress would be quite slow. Much has been written about the millennium in Europe known as the Dark Ages (circa 450 A.D. to 1450 A.D.). Europe in 1450 A.D. was scarcely more advanced than Greece, Egypt, or China in 200 B.C. People blame the plagues, superstitious thinking, and poor leadership. I like to think that poor data sharing policies played a role.

Tycho Brahe (1546–1601) was a meticulous scientist who kept careful records throughout his adult life of the positions of the planets in the sky. He had a long-standing argument with his junior colleague, Johannes Kepler (1571–1630). Brahe thought that the earth was the center of the universe. Kepler favored a heliocentric system. Despite their professional differences, Tycho Brahe, upon his death, shared all his data with Kepler. Kepler, depending entirely on Brahe's data, charted the elliptic orbits of planets around the sun. Kepler's charts were used later by Isaac Newton (1642–1727) to develop the mathematical laws that govern the paths of planets and pebbles. Had Brahe not shared his data with his intellectual competitor, our understanding of physics may have been delayed by many decades.

Johann Jakob Balmer (1825–1898) was a mathematics teacher in Switzerland. In 1885, Vogel and Huggins published the primary observations of the emission spectrum of hydrogen (i.e., the hydrogen spectrum). From these published numbers, and to the surprise of the physics community, Balmer found a formula that predicted the frequencies using whole numbers and a mathematical constant. Niels Bohr, in 1913, discovered Balmer's formula and re-interpreted formula and spectrum in terms of energy emissions between discrete electron orbits. This marked the birth of modern quantum physics.

These two examples of data sharing were chosen, from among many, because the original data was collected without any understanding of how the data would be used by other scientists. Even the scientists who first used the shared data (Kepler and Balmer) could not have anticipated how their work would underpin advances of even greater scope and importance (i.e., Newton's laws of physics and Bohr's quantum physics).

Despite the historical imperative of data sharing, the field of medicine has been slow to adopt data sharing policies. In the past, the value of observational data ceased once the data was summarized and the summary was recorded as a hospital record or as a manuscript. A manuscript might contain a table in which the data from a large experiment were summarized in a single sentence. "One thousand patient records were reviewed, and 298 patients had glucose values exceeding 120, while the average blood glucose of the population was 83." Assuming that the data was reviewed for the purpose of determining the prevalence of patients with elevated glucose levels, a single sentence would suffice to encapsulate the data. This concise approach to data representation worked very well for journals and other printed works. What would otherwise require pages and pages of mind-numbing numerics was now replaced by a succinct statement that could fit into a short manuscript. If someone questioned the validity of the statement, they could just repeat the study, using another set of glucose levels measured on a different set of patients.

The old paradigm of a medical experiment was that data existed only for the purpose of establishing a generalizable statement. Once the scientific statement was made and accepted, the data served no further purpose. This paradigm has much less validity in our modern data-intensive world.

Modern medical science often involves immense datasets created by large teams of scientists. In a sense, the data in many scientific projects

Figure 1   Manuscripts are satellites revolving around a data-centric mass.

is the most valued product of the scientific investigation. Manuscripts may be thought of as secondary events or as editorials that comment on the dataset.

This is certainly true of most bioinformatics projects. When dozens of scientists pool their talents to sequence the genome of a pathogenic organism, the achievement is certainly not the manuscript that announces the achievement. The achievement is the sequence database, which will serve as the focus of hundreds and possibly thousands of additional manuscripts that derive some clinically useful lessons from the gene sequences. We are undergoing a major paradigm shift directly analogous to the shift away from thinking of the earth as the center of the universe. People think of a publication as the center of the universe and all supplemental files as objects that orbit the published article. The new paradigm places data, at the center of the universe, with manuscripts as derivative works orbiting the data. Large datasets, such as gene array data and tissue array data, should have our central focus. A large dataset may grow, link with other datasets, and may have many different scientific articles in its orbit.

In the data-centric view of the universe, datasets are the primary product of research and must be made available to the public. In fact, a variety of inducements are now in place to improve the public's access to research data (List 2.16.1).

LIST 2.16.1. RECENT DEVELOPMENTS THAT HAVE ENHANCED ACCESS TO EXPERIMENTAL DATASETS

- Online journals that invite authors to submit data files
- Editor policies that require the submission of data files supporting assertions made in manuscripts
- Technical ease of storing large datasets on publicly available servers
- Technical ease of downloading large datasets from servers via the Internet
- Data sharing requirements issued by biomedical funding agencies
- Expansion of the Freedom of Information Act
- Greater involvement of informaticians in biomedical research
- Scientific advancements using publicly available datasets
- Stunning power and scope of publicly available search engines, including Google (Internet documents) and PubMed (medical abstracts)

Thanks largely to computers, data sharing has become feasible. Thanks to funding agencies, data sharing is occasionally mandatory. The NIH policy on data sharing took effect October 1, 2003 (27). The policy specifies that "all investigator-initiated applications with direct costs greater than $500,000 in any single year will be expected to address data sharing in their application." The reasons for this policy appeared in the following NIH statement:

"Sharing data reinforces open scientific inquiry, encourages diversity of analysis and opinion, promotes new research, makes possible the testing of new or alternative hypotheses and methods of analysis, supports studies on data collection methods and measurement, facilitates the education of new researchers, enables the exploration of topics not envisioned by the initial investigators, and permits the creation of new datasets when data from multiple sources are combined. By avoiding the duplication of expensive data collection activities, the NIH is able to support more investigators than it could if similar data had to be collected de novo by each applicant."

The US National Research Council has issued its own recommendations, endorsed by many research journals. Authors should include with their articles all of the data that is needed to support the central assertions in the paper (28). Research agencies, aware of the need for data-sharing protocols, are awarding grants for the purpose of developing new ways to safely share medical research data.

The ancient Sumerians used clay tablets to record their data. Three millennia later, these same clay tablets can be read. Gilgamesh was a king in Babylonia (now, geographically, Iraq) who lived around 2700 BC. An epic story depicting the life of the king was written about 2000 BC. The amazing tale of an antediluvian king, and the clay tablets on which the story was written, have survived to modern times. Compare and contrast this account with some of your personal data recordings made on 5.25" magnetic disks, or entrusted to Beta videotape. Early computer users may have manuscripts composed in a long-abandoned word processing format or may have saved their data on a now-obsolete tape medium. Libraries still use microfiche to archive journals, but most of us prefer to read journal articles online. The microfiche viewer will soon be obsolete, and microfiche reels will become an archiving problem, rather than an archiving solution. Most of the data collected by modern man has already been lost to future generations. The Codata working group on archiving scientific data said, "A general problem amongst disciplines is the relatively low priority attached to data management and archiving. Archiving is often viewed as something that happens after the research is completed, and is done by someone other than the researcher" (29).

Long-term data archiving is of particular importance to biomedical informatics because the electronic medical histories of patients extend over many decades. A person who lives 100 years accumulates 100 years of personal medical data. If a patient's electronic records date back only a few years, then the bulk of the person's medical history is excluded from review. If society places scientific, medical, social, and historic value on the life-long medical histories of individuals, then there will certainly be a need to develop methods for collecting, organizing, and permanently archiving medical data accrued over the many decades of a person's life.

2.17. LEGACY DATA

Legacy data are the contents of databases that have been replaced by new databases. Hospital databases often have highly structured ways of storing data, including proprietary data dictionaries and rules for binning particular data elements in particular locations in database memory. Newly implemented HISs are not always capable of porting legacy data into their systems. For this reason, it is common for legacy data to be orphaned.

The common practice of abandoning legacy data is a betrayal of patient trust. When a patient receives care, she is seldom provided with the records of lab tests, a listing of her medications, or a copy of the notes summarizing the visit. When a patient leaves the care of a hospital, she is almost never provided with a comprehensive summary of her care.

Patents entrust their cumulative data records to the hospital. The hospital is expected to archive the patient's medical record so that it can be accessed when needed. In the past, hospitals kept each patient's cumulative record in a physical folder (chart) archived in the medical records room. With the advent of hospital information systems, many patient transactions have achieved a pure digital existence. When legacy data is orphaned, the entrusted patient data may simply vanish into a binary void.

The aggregated legacy data for thousands of patients may contain scientifically important trends in outcome followed over many years. Hospitals anticipating the benefits of next-generation hospital information systems should remember that five-year outcome measurements on a treatment initiated today will require five years to collect. Treatment encounters held in a legacy database will typically contain more than five years of outcome data. To a biomedical informatician, legacy data is often much more valuable than current data because its chronologic range permits the association of medical interventions with clinical outcomes. Health professionals should strive to save legacy data whenever feasible.

2.18. FREE, OPEN SOURCE, AND PROPRIETARY SOFTWARE AND DATA

Biomedical informatics is an integrative science. It often makes use of tools and data from several different disciplines in order to solve a particular problem arising in the course of a designed experiment. A **gene expression study** may yield a candidate gene of special interest. The researcher may want to find information about the gene and might need to have a resource that specifies all the different names that gene may have. Having all the names for the gene, the researcher may want to review prior studies of the gene (under any of its names), particularly studies that associate a biological trait with the expression level of the gene.

Most efforts of the biomedical informatician will require an array of software tools, databases, nomenclatures, trial results, and published reports. Many of these resources will have costs, restrictions, royalties, reach-through provisions, and a variety of intellectual property encumbrances. Some of these encumbrances may limit a researcher's access to materials. Others may limit the ability of a researcher to profit from her research discovery, to receive due professional credit for the discovery, or to distribute her findings to the scientific community.

To reduce intellectual property encumbrances, it makes sense to use free or open source material whenever feasible. The terms free and open source can apply equally well nowadays to software, data, and data standards. Today, virtually all biomedical informaticians will choose to program using a free programming language, such as Perl or Java or C. They will use public domain databases and datasets offered by the US National Center for Biotechnology Information

(NCBI), and conduct literature searches through a public biblio-graphic site (PubMed). Within a few years, most biomedical infor-maticians will use XML and other open standard metadata constructs (discussed in Chapter 12) to organize their data into self-describing documents. It is important that biomedical informaticians know which components of their datasets are free or open source, and which components are proprietary, or otherwise encumbered by restrictions on their use (List 2.18.1).

LIST 2.18.1. SOME DEFINITIONS OF TERMS RELATED TO THE OPEN SOURCE MOVEMENT

- Free software—The concept of free software, as popularized by the Free Software Foundation, refers to software that can be used freely, without restriction, and does not necessarily relate to the actual cost of the software. The generally acknowledged father of the free software movement is Richard Stallman, an MIT visionary who has led an energetic and unwavering campaign to create and freely dis-tribute some of the most valued software applications in use today. The free software movement is similar to the open source software movement, but some of the features of free software (ability to mod-ify and re-distribute software in a prescribed manner as discussed in the software license) are not always guaranteed in open source software.
- Open source—The Open Source Software movement is an off-spring of the Free Software movement. The reason that the open source movement was created was, in part, to placate developers who wanted to sell software and felt the term "free" as in "free soft-ware movement," would be misconstrued by prospective cus-tomers to mean that the developer requires no remuneration. Although a good deal of free software is no-cost software, the intended meaning of the term "free" is that the software can be used without restrictions. The term "open source" obviates the need to draw this distinction. The Open Source Initiative posts an open source definition (30) and a list of approved open source licenses (31).
- Open access—In general, open access applies to text and data the same way that open source applies to software. In general, open access biomedical data is retrievable (i.e., you can find it by using a PubMed search or through a search engine), and once you have found it, you can download it and read it. There are several closely related consensus statements on the meaning of open access (32, 33).

- Open source software license—The Open Source Initiative has an approval process for open source licenses. Software distributed under an approved license can include a declaration that the software is "OSI Certified Open Source Software." The GNU copyleft licenses have been certified as open source software licenses.

- Patented software—Few subjects incur more heated debate than software patents. In the United States, the patent and trade office (USPTO) grants patents for software and software methods that meet the general terms of patentability that apply to tangible inventions. New patents have a term of 20 years.

- GNU software licenses—The GNU organization publishes two licenses, used for software produced by GNU and by anyone who would like to distribute their software under the terms of the GNU license. They are referred to as "copyleft licenses," because they primarily serve the software users, rather than the software creators. One of the GNU licenses, the General Public License, covers most software applications. The GNU Lesser General Public License, formerly known as the GNU Library General Public License, is intended for use with software libraries or unified collections of files comprising a complex application, language, or other body of work (34, 35).

- Free software license—Virtually all free software is distributed under a license that assigns copyright to the software creator and protects the creator from damages that might result from using the software. Software sponsored by the Free Software Foundation, and much of the software described as either free software or open source software, is distributed under one of the GNU software licenses.

- Free Software Movement v Open Source Initiative—Beyond **trivial semantics**, the difference between free software and open source software relates to the essential feature necessary for "open source" software (i.e., access to the source code) and to the different distribution licenses of free software and open source software. Most informaticians use the two monikers interchangeably and do not seem to suffer for the oversight. In practice, there is very little difference between free software and open source software. Richard Stallman has written an essay that summarizes the two different approaches to creating free software and open source software (36).

- FOSS—Free and open source software. This term encompasses both free and open source software and can be used to placate sticklers who distinguish between the two related movements. Another term sometimes encountered is FLOSS (Free Libre Open Source Software), which holds international appeal.

- Public domain software and data—If an intellectual property is available to the public and has no copyright or other intellectual property assignment, then it belongs to the public domain. Anyone who obtains a public domain document can use it without restriction. Although the creator of public domain material has no special property rights, that does not mean that the creator is non-existent. A large portion of the public domain material is produced by governments or government employees (who cannot claim copyright). Another source of public domain material are old works for which the copyright or patent has expired. A smaller source of public domain material is gifts from authors who donate their creations de novo into the public domain. Users of public domain software or data should always attribute authorship of the software or data to the creator. Failure to do so is plagiarism.

2.19. UNDIFFERENTIATED SOFTWARE

Software developers sometimes speak of undifferentiated software and of differentiated software. Undifferentiated software comprises the basic algorithms that everyone uses and re-uses in the process of developing new software applications (Lists 2.19.1 and 2.19.2). All software developers have reasons to keep this basic kind of software free, because nobody knows who developed the algorithms originally, and nobody wants to devote their careers to prosecuting or defending tenuous legal claims over the ownership of the fundamental building blocks of computer science.

LIST 2.19.1. EXAMPLES OF UNDIFFERENTIATED SOFTWARE

- Basic algorithms
- Fundamental laws of physics, chemistry, mathematics, and biology
- Free, cross-platform programming languages
- TCP/IP Internet protocol
- HTML and XML

LIST 2.19.2. EXAMPLES OF UNDIFFERENTIATED DATA

- Human genome
- Standards documents
- Nomenclatures
- Biological classification systems

Differentiated software is developed for a specific use and is often commissioned by a specific user (Lists 2.19.3 and 2.19.4). An example would be a hospital information system designed to meet the needs of a specific facility and to interface with the equipment held at the facility. The same vendor's hospital information system might be sold to many other medical centers, but each local implementation of the software would require additional work and re-engineering of the basic software product.

There is broad sentiment that it is unwise to patent or copyright so-called undifferentiated software and data. Doing so would result in an endless spectacle of acrimonious and exhausting lawsuits and counter-suits. There is also general agreement that developers and scientists have the right to claim as intellectual property those scientific advancements that result directly from their own labors.

Proprietary software generally builds upon free and open methods, adding particular value that buyers will pay for. GenBank may be freely available to the world, but a software developer may provide an application that mines specific types of data from GenBank and correlates GenBank data with a proprietary dataset produced at great expense by a pharmaceutical corporation. This illustrates the complementary roles of public data and proprietary data in biomedical research.

LIST 2.19.3. EXAMPLES OF DIFFERENTIATED SOFTWARE

- Programming languages with special features such as easy-to-use interfaces or integrated environment, or a specialized purpose
- Neural network programs designed for specific types of data input
- Complex software designed to support commercial devices, such as CT scanners
- Most hospital information systems and laboratory information systems

LIST 2.19.4. EXAMPLES OF DIFFERENTIATED DATA

- Lexis/Nexis and other legal databases
- Subscription journals
- Codes for billable procedures
- Science Citation Index
- Chemical Abstracts (R) database

2.20. WHAT ARE SOME OF THE OPEN ACCESS BIOMEDICAL DATABASES?

The creation and organization of biological information is one of the most active areas of biomedical research. Most of the available bioinformatics databases are described in the yearly, **open access** database issue of Nucleic acids (37). Of the hundreds of databases discussed, perhaps the most relevant to the field of biomedical informatics are the databases related to specific human diseases and genes (List 2.20.1).

LIST 2.20.1. A FEW OF THE HUMAN DATABASES THAT HAVE BEEN DESCRIBED IN THE NUCLEIC ACIDS RESEARCH DATABASE ISSUE

- Androgen Receptor Gene Mutations Database
- Atlas of Genetics and Cytogenetics in Oncology and Haematology
- Atlas of Genetics and Cytogenetics in Oncology and Haematology
- BGED—Brain Gene Expression Database
- Cancer Chromosomes
- Cancer gene databases
- CGED—Cancer Gene Expression Database
- Collagen Mutation Database
- COSMIC—Catalogue of Somatic Mutations in Cancer
- Cypriot National Mutation Database
- Cytokine Gene Polymorphism Database
- Cytokine Gene Polymorphism in Human Disease
- Database of Genomic Variants
- Database of Germline p53 Mutations
- EICO DB—Expression-based Imprint Candidate Organiser
- EpoDB—Erythropoiesis Database
- ERGDB—Estrogen Responsive Genes Database
- Gene-, system-, or disease-specific databases
- General polymorphism databases
- GOLD.db—Genomics of Lipid-associated Disorders
- GRAP Mutant Databases
- HAGR—Human Ageing Genomic Resources
- HCAD—Human Chromosome Aberration Database
- HemoPDB—Hematopoietic Promoter Database

- HERVd—Human Endogenous Retrovirus Database
- HGMDr—Human Gene Mutation Database
- HORDE—Human Olfactory Receptor Data Exploratorium
- HPMR—Human Plasma Membrane Receptome
- Human p53, human hprt, rodent lacI and rodent lacZ databases
- Human PAX2 Allelic Variant Database
- Human PAX6 Allelic Variant Database
- IARC TP53 Database
- Imprinted Gene Catalogue
- IPD—Immuno Polymorphism Database
- Lowe Syndrome Mutation Database
- MTB—Mouse Tumor Biology Database
- NCL Mutation Database
- OMIM—Online Mendelian Inheritance in Man
- Oral Cancer Gene Database
- PTCH1 Mutation Database
- RB1 Gene Mutation Database
- RTCGD—Retroviral Tagged Cancer Gene Database
- SNP500Cancer
- SV40 Large T-Antigen Mutant Database
- T1DBase—Type 1 Diabetes Database
- The Autism Chromosome Rearrangement Database
- The Lafora Database
- The SNP Consortium Database
- TPMD—Taiwan Polymorphic Microsatellite marker Database
- Tumor Gene Family Databases (TGDBs)

2.21. OPEN ACCESS MEDICAL TERMINOLOGIES

Medical terminologies are essential tools for organizing, indexing, and retrieving medical data (38). When a scientist conducts a PubMed medical literature search on the term "renal cell carcinoma", the search software retrieves all the manuscripts that contain the concept of "renal cell carcinoma" under any of its synonymous terms (including carcinoma of kidney, rcc, Grawitz tumor, adenocarcinoma of kidney). This is very important because manuscript authors will use different names for the same concept. The list of different terms for a concept come from large, curated nomenclatures.

By far, the largest medical nomenclature is the US National Library of Medicine's Unified Medical Language System Metathesaurus (UMLS Metathesaurus), which contains several million terms grouped under about a million concepts. The UMLS is comprised of over 100 individual **thesauruses**, many of which are contributed by efforts funded by the US government. The UMLS metathesaurus can be acquired at no cost from the National Library of Medicine (see Appendix).

Anyone wishing to obtain the UMLS metathesaurus must obtain and sign the UMLS License Agreement and register as a UMLS user. The UMLS metathesaurus, the UMLS License Agreement, and detailed instructional documents are available from the following URLs:

License Agreement: http://www.nlm.nih.gov/research/umls/
  license.html

Current version of Metathesaurus: http://www.nlm.nih.gov/research/
  umls/

The UMLS License Agreement contains specific language describing usage restrictions that pertain to the individual thesauruses contained in the metathesaurus. The thesauruses are classified according to the category of restrictions that encumber their use. The highest category of restrictions effectively prohibits using UMLS-annotated datasets for any of the following purposes: 1) distribution to colleagues, 2) posting on a publicly available site (such as an Internet Web site), 3) submission to shared dataset repositories, or submitted as supplemental data in support of research articles, and 4) submission to scientific journals.

The least restrictive license category within UMLS is usually referred to as category 0. The category 0 vocabularies prohibit users "from distributing the UMLS products or subsets of these products." This is a reasonable condition, enforcing the National Library of Medicine's role as the sole **curator** and distributor of UMLS. However, The UMLS License stipulates an exception when the subsets are "an integral part of computer applications developed by LICENSEE for a purpose other than redistribution of data contained in the UMLS products." When a researcher includes a UMLS term in a dataset and distributes the dataset to a colleague, the purpose is to disseminate her research. In this case, annotation terms are integrated into the data and do not appear as complete source vocabularies or as subsets of the UMLS that would be suitable as a medical vocabulary (see Glossary). Therefore, distributing datasets annotated with category 0 terms would not violate the UMLS License Agreement.

For the most part, the category 0 terms have been contributed directly by US federal agencies or by organizations that receive US federal funds for the purpose of creating publicly available vocabularies. MeSH (Medical Subject Headings) is probably the largest and most useful category 0 vocabulary found in the UMLS methathesaurus.

2.22. MESH (THE NATIONAL LIBRARY OF MEDICINE'S MEDICAL SUBJECT HEADINGS)

One of the most important nomenclatures within UMLS is the US National Library of Medicine's Medical Subject Headings (MeSH).

MeSH is used by the National Library of Medicine to index all biomedical abstracts included in MedLine, and has been used to index medical terms found throughout the Internet. MeSH is a mature, well-curated, large, comprehensive, and publicly available nomenclature. MeSH alone is a sufficient medical vocabulary for many indexing purposes. MeSH can be downloaded at no cost (see Appendix).

2.23. TAXONOMY

One of the best examples of a large **taxonomy** is `taxonomy.dat`, which attempts to list the living organisms of earth. So thorough is `taxonomy.dat` that it not only lists all known variations of an organism's name, but it also lists commonly used misspellings of an organism (List 2.23.1).

LIST 2.23.1. A RECORD IN TAXONOMY

- ID: 50
- PARENT ID: 49
- RANK: genus
- GC ID: 11
- SCIENTIFIC NAME: Chondromyces
- SYNONYM: Polycephalum
- SYNONYM: Myxobotrys
- SYNONYM: Chondromyces Berkeley and Curtis 1874
- SYNONYM: Polycephalum Kalchbrenner and Cooke 1880
- SYNONYM: Myxobotrys Zukal 1896
- MISSPELLING: Chrondromyces

A recent version of `taxonomy.dat` is dated June 20, 2004 and is 55,233,858 bytes in length. It has 246,800 entries. The `taxonomy.dat` file is available for public download through anonymous ftp at ftp://ftp.ebi.ac.uk/pub/databases/taxonomy/. Information about the `taxonomy.dat` file is found at http://www.ebi.ac.uk/msd-srv/docs/dbdoc/ref_taxonomy.html.

2.24. DISEASE DATA AND EPIDEMIOLOGIC DATA

Much of the epidemiological data available to biomedical informaticians is made freely available by government agencies.

In the United States, sources of epidemiologic data are the CDC (Centers for Disease Control and Prevention), the National Cancer Institutes SEER (Surveillance, Epidemiology, and End Results) project, the US census, the US Department of Vital Health Statistics, and the CMS (Centers for Medicare and Medicaid Services) public use data (see Appendix).

2.25. THE IMPACT OF FREE AND OPEN SOURCE DATA AND SOFTWARE ON BIOMEDICAL INFORMATICS

The free software movement and the open source initiative bring some measure of order and uniformity to the field of computer science and its ancillary interests (e.g., biomedicine). Both movements provide a way in which users have open access to the software and the data that must be used by everyone in the field to perform common tasks.

In Chapter 12, we will see that the distinctions between data, software, and standards have all but disappeared. Free and open source standard methods for creating and describing interoperable data and software are the most important contributions of the free software movement.

Confidential Biomedical Data

3.1. BACKGROUND

Until recently, many researchers who collected confidential or proprietary data had a heavy-handed way of dealing with confidentiality issues: They denied everyone access to their data. As a result, the scientific community had no way of verifying, replicating, or extending research conducted by their colleagues. The U.S. National Institutes of Health (NIH), sensing that data hoarding had become an impediment to medical progress, published its policy on data sharing in 2003 (27).

"NIH reaffirms its support for the concept of data sharing. We believe that data sharing is essential for expedited translation of research results into knowledge, products, and procedures to improve human health. The NIH endorses the sharing of final research data to serve these and other important scientific goals. The NIH expects and supports the timely release and sharing of final research data from NIH-supported studies for use by other researchers. Starting with the October 1, 2003, receipt date, investigators submitting an NIH application seeking $500,000 or more in direct costs in any single year are expected to include a plan for data sharing or state why data sharing is not possible."

Research societies requested that NIH develop techniques for data sharing that protect confidential information. In particular, concern was expressed that methods for keeping data confidential must conform to the HIPAA privacy standards. In this chapter, the central problems related to sharing confidential data are discussed. In Chapters 10 and 11 we will discuss technical approaches to data sharing.

3.2. HUMAN SUBJECT RISKS

Patient risks imposed by medical research fall into one or more of four categories (List 3.2.1).

LIST 3.2.1. THE TYPES OF HUMAN SUBJECT RESEARCH RISKS

- The risk to life and health as a direct result of a medical intervention
- The risk of loss of database functionality
- The risk of loss of confidentiality resulting from participation in a medical study
- The risk of loss of privacy resulting from participation in a medical study

3.3. THE RISK TO LIFE AND HEALTH AS A DIRECT RESULT OF A MEDICAL INTERVENTION

Two recent examples are the cases of 18-year-old Jesse Gelsinger, who died of liver failure September 17, 1999, four days after receiving a viral inoculation in a gene transfer experiment conducted at the University of Pennsylvania (39); and Ellen Roche, a 24-year-old healthy volunteer who died from lung failure on June 2, 2001, several weeks after inhaling hexamethonium as part of a Johns Hopkins asthma study (40). Death resulting from interventional medical research is the most serious of human subject risks, and special measures are taken to ensure that interventional studies adhere to safe protocols. For interventional studies, patients must give written consent for participation in the experiment. The consent document must inform the patient of all the risks (adverse consequences) that might result from participation in the study. The patient signs the consent form to indicate that she understands the risks and that she consents to participate in the study despite the risks.

3.4. THE RISK OF LOSS OF DATABASE FUNCTIONALITY

Sometimes researchers may inadvertently disrupt HIS (hospital information system) services when they try to modify the system to accommodate their research objectives. An example may be to enhance a server to function as a peer in a peer-to-peer network that receives and exchanges data records with other institutions participating in a data mining project. When researchers modify an HIS to suit their needs, there is some risk that they will impair or disable the HIS, resulting in interruptions in the health care delivery. IRBs (institutional review boards) should be cognizant of this problem and should develop protocols to assess these kinds of risks, which are sometimes omitted from IRB proposals. Investigators and hospital information officers should work together to develop methods to eliminate or reduce vulnerabilities in HISs that may arise in the course of research activities.

3.5. THE DIFFERENCES BETWEEN CONFIDENTIALITY AND PRIVACY

Privacy, security, and confidentiality are related but distinct conditions.

Confidentiality is broken when an authorized (trusted) holder of private medical information gives the information to an unauthorized person.

Loss of privacy relates to adverse or unwanted intrusions into the private life of a person by the person or entity that was entrusted with the private information.

Security is lost when an unauthorized individual gains access to patient records or an authorized individual uses patient records for an unauthorized purpose. Entrusted holders of confidential patient information are expected to take reasonable measures to protect data security. In general, data security extends to all aspects of hospital activities (not just research).

3.6. EXAMPLE: LOSS OF PRIVACY RESULTING FROM PARTICIPATION IN A MEDICAL STUDY

Members belonging to an extended family consent to have their blood samples used in the study of a familial disease. In the course of research, a husband is informed by the research team that an examination of blood samples had determined that one of his children is not his biological progeny. Unless he had given specific consent to have this kind of information brought to his attention, this would be an action that violates his privacy. Another example of loss of privacy may occur when a person who has participated in a completed study is pursued by the medical researcher for permission to obtain additional samples of blood for a second project.

Both examples describe unanticipated intrusions into a person's life that occurred after the researcher was given private information about the research subject. In general, privacy issues arise from all studies that create patient data, because new data on a patient may potentially have an impact on a patient's health.

Privacy issues are almost always pertinent to heritable genetic studies, even when the study does not involve the creation of new experimental data, because studies that review data records of many members of a family may uncover information related to the likelihood of disease in individual members of the family.

In general, studies that have privacy risks will require individual consent from all of the people whose data records are used in the study. Assuming that the only risk for the study participants would be loss of privacy, the consent form would need to clearly delineate the conditions under which study participants would be contacted by the researchers.

3.7. LOSS OF CONFIDENTIALITY

Although there have been reported instances of hospital employees releasing patient records for malicious or mischievous purposes, I know of no instances where this occurred during a research study. Based on many conversations with scientists and scientific administrators with expertise in the area of human subject protections, it would appear that researchers have done a remarkably good job at guarding patient confidentiality.

In the United States, restrictions on the research uses and electronic transfer of confidential medical records are covered by two federal regulations: the Common Rule (45 CFR 46, Protection of Human Subjects) and the Standards for Privacy of Individually Identifiable Health Information, Final Rule (usually referred to under the broader act, the Health Insurance Portability and Accountability Act, HIPAA) (9, 26).

The Common Rule describes the responsibilities of researchers and institutions to ensure human subject protections. When a patient's record is used in a research project, the patient is considered a participant in the research, and the research project is classified as human subject research. The Common Rule provides some relief to biomedical informaticians by permitting the unrestricted use of patient records that contain no information that associate a particular person to the patient record. Another way of looking at it is that if a record has no patient, then it is not a "patient record." In addition, the law suggests several ways of disassociating patients from their records: **anonymization** and **de-identification**. These two processes of rendering patient data harmless to patients can be discussed as computational algorithms and fall under the purview of biomedical informaticians.

The Common Rule also specifies that institutions receiving US federal research support must have an IRB to insure that all human subject research performed within the institution is conducted in a manner that protects human subjects.

HIPAA is the 1996 Health Insurance Portability and Accountability Act. As the result of that act, HHS (Health and Human Services) has issued

45 CFR Parts 160 and 162, the Final Rule of the Health Insurance Reform: Standards for Electronic Transactions (9). Although the HHS Final Rule is a small part of HIPAA, common parlance refers to the Final Rule as "HIPAA." The HIPAA guidelines place certain requirements on entities that hold and transfer electronic medical records. Specifically HIPAA applies to health plans, health care clearinghouses, and to any health care provider who transmits health information in electronic form. Entities that are not one of the previously mentioned entities are not subject to HIPAA regulations.

3.8. THE RESPONSIBILITIES OF BIOMEDICAL INFORMATICIANS TO HUMAN SUBJECTS

Federal laws applying to the research uses of medical data permit the unlimited and unburdened use of patient records provided that the records are anonymized (as described by the Common Rule (26)) and de-identified (as described by HIPAA (9)). Researchers do not need to obtain patient consent for the use of de-identified patient records. Large-scale biomedical informatics research can be accomplished with anonymized or de-identified patient records that have been obtained from institutional databases via authorized data transfers.

In the United States, confidentiality issues for biomedical informaticians will distill to a few items (List 3.8.1).

LIST 3.8.1. CONFIDENTIALITY ISSUES FOR BIOMEDICAL INFORMATICIANS

- Demonstrating to the hospital's **IRB** that the chosen methodology for anonymizing or de-identifying records is safe and reliable
- Demonstrating to the hospital's IRB and to the hospital's information officers that the anonymization and de-identification processes can be performed automatically, without giving the informatician any access to the primary patient record and without opening any HIS vulnerabilities when data is transferred out of the system

3.9. PATIENT RECORD ANONYMIZATION

The term "anonymization" is an informal term used in the United States to embody the language contained in Exemption 4 of the Common Rule (26) (List 3.9.1).

LIST 3.9.1. EXEMPTION 4 (E4) OF 45CFR46 PERMITTING UNCONSENTED RESEARCH ON DE-IDENTIFIED MEDICAL RECORDS

"(4) Research involving the collection or study of existing data, documents, records, pathological specimens, or diagnostic specimens, if these sources are publicly available or if the information is recorded by the investigator in such a manner that subjects cannot be identified, directly or through identifiers linked to the subjects."

Anonymization usually involves stripping patient identifiers (name, address, social security number, hospital record number, etc.) from records or substituting a false identifier for the real identifier. Once anonymized, even the researcher has no way of determining the patient based on inspection of the patient record. The researcher is NOT permitted to create a table that maps the real identifiers to the false identifiers.

Research conducted with E4-exempted material is considered harmless under the Common Rule and can be used ad libitum without obtaining patient consent. There are several points that the biomedical informatician must understand.

In most institutions, the IRB will need to review any anticipated E4-exempted research to determine whether the research actually satisfies the E4 exemption. This requirement irks researchers who complain that if their research is exempted from IRB approval, then they should not need any IRB review. Most institutional assurance documents stipulate that IRBs review all institutional research, if only to determine that the research satisfies the E4 exemption and does not need to undergo the IRB approval process.

If the research records are "public" (e.g., found in a published book or excerpted from a Web site), then exemption is virtually non-contestable under statute. However, an institution may have compelling ethical reasons to suspend research on publicly available data that has been obtained illegally (e.g., Nazi medical experiments on concentration camp prisoners).

If the data is to be rendered anonymous through a computational algorithm exercised over each record, then researchers may need to prove that the algorithm actually works and that the process does not require human review. If the process removes a patient's name from an identifier field but neglects to remove the name from a section of text buried in a surgical pathology report, then the anonymization algorithm has failed. If the anonymization algorithm needs to be developed by taking a set of identified reports (training set) and visually comparing them with an output (typically repeating the process with test sets), then someone needs to have direct access to identified patient reports, and this access may violate the E4 exemption under the Common Rule.

As commonly interpreted, the anonymization process precludes the ability to re-identify patients, even when the research uncovers information that may have critical importance to the patient. Consequently, anonymization often removes the opportunities to check data integrity by reviewing the primary patient data record and to add data to the patient record (i.e., follow-up clinical data is disallowed).

Protocols have been proposed that functionally anonymize data using an encryption broker. The broker receives encrypted identifiers in medical data sent by an institution. The broker encrypts the identifiers one more time and passes the data (now with doubly encrypted identifiers) to the researcher. The data has been made functionally anonymized in that no single entity can link the medical data to a patient. However, if the original institution, the researcher, and the broker all agree to re-identify the data, then they may do so. Re-identification would only be done with IRB approval. This type of protocol is somewhat inaccurately referred to as an "honest broker" transaction. In fact, the broker can be dishonest, and the protocol will still succeed. The protocol fails when all three of the participants are dishonest.

HIPAA permits unrestricted research use of electronic patient records that have been de-identified (9). De-identification is subtly different from anonymization. In de-identification, a record may actually be prepared in a manner that allows an authorized person to re-link a patient with her research record. However, a de-identified record must contain no information that will allow an unauthorized person to infer a patient's identity using clues from the data elements. For instance, if a data record contains zip code, gender, date of birth, and ethnicity of a patient (common demographic elements), along with diagnostic information, then a malicious individual could identify the patient using public records (such as birth records, the telephone book, or any lists of residents of an area along with non-medical demographic data). If a medical record set indicates that a person with a particular disease is a Hispanic male of a certain age living in a specified zip code, then obtaining the individual's identity might be easy for someone with a list of area residents along with non-medical demographic data (age, address, ethnicity).

Even when a study has been exempted under the Common Rule, the use of patient data may still be restricted under other federal regulations (e.g., HIPAA), or it may fall victim to restrictions in applicable state laws.

An example of an activity that is allowed under the Common Rule but that is restricted under HIPAA is the unconsented use of autopsy material and data. The Common Rule is designed to protect human subjects from research-related harm. Under the Common Rule, a human is defined as a live person. Under the Common Rule, deceased persons are excluded from protection, and researchers can use any autopsy tissues without restriction.

Under the HIPAA Privacy Rule, deceased individuals are protected (List 3.9.2).

LIST 3.9.2. SECTION 164.502(f) OF THE HIPAA PRIVACY RULE— DECEASED INDIVIDUALS

- "We proposed to extend privacy protections to the protected health information of a deceased individual for two years following the date of death. During the two-year time frame, we proposed in the definition of 'individual' that the right to control the deceased individual's protected health information would be held by an executor or administrator, or other person (e.g., next of kin) authorized under applicable law to act on behalf of the decedent's estate. The only proposed exception to this standard allowed for uses and disclosures of a decedent's protected health information for research purposes without the authorization of a legal representative and without the Institutional Review Board (IRB) or privacy board approval required (in proposed Sec. 164.510(j)) for most other uses and disclosures for research."
- "In the final rule (Sec. 164.502(f)), we modify the standard to extend protection of protected health information about deceased individuals for as long as the covered entity maintains the information. We retain the exception for uses and disclosures for research purposes, now part of Sec. 164.512(i), but also require that the covered entity take certain verification measures prior to release of the decedent's protected health information for such purposes (see Secs. 164.514(h) and 164.512(i)(1)(iii))."
- "We remove from the definition of 'individual' the provision related to deceased persons..."

The stark difference between the Common Rule and the HIPAA privacy act in their protections of autopsy data give biomedical informaticians some pause. These differences notwithstanding, researchers can have access to autopsy data under HIPAA section 164.512, if some safeguards are taken. These are discussed in Chapter 17.

3.10. PATIENT RECORD DE-IDENTIFICATION

Latanya Sweeney was an early proponent of technical approaches to medical record de-identification and has published extensively on the subject (41, 42, 43). Her work formed the foundation for current multi-step approaches to de-identification encompassing five tasks (List 3.10.1).

LIST 3.10.1. FIVE REQUIREMENTS FOR DE-IDENTIFYING MEDICAL RECORDS

- De-identification of data fields that specifically characterize the patient (name, social security number, hospital number, address, age, etc.)
- Free-text data scrubbing, removing identifiers from the textual portion of medical reports
- Free-text data privatizing, removing any information of a private nature that may be contained within the report
- Rendering the dataset ambiguous, ensuring that patients cannot be identified by data records containing a unique set of characterizing information
- Rendering the data noncomplementary, ensuring that the data cannot be combined with data from other databases or from multiple searches of the same database that can lead to the identification of records

For almost all research conducted on large databases of preexisting pathology reports, methods that can reliably de-identify medical records are essential. Some of these methods will be discussed in Chapter 10.

HIPAA and the Common Rule also permit IRBs to waive consent requirements when the research risks to the patients are negligible and the benefits to society are large. This low-risk, high-benefit situation sometimes applies to medical database studies where patient confidentiality is partly protected, but not protected to an extent that would exempt the study from HIPAA or Common Rule regulations (9, 26).

3.11. AN EXAMPLE OF THE LAW OF UNINTENDED CONSEQUENCES

A special problem is encountered with tissues from Native Americans. Certain Native American nations believe that removed tissues should be returned to the patient (or patient's family), so that the buried remains of the patient comprise a complete body. Complying with this particular religious requirement is a major concern for biomedical informaticians and for tissue bankers. It requires a system in place to identify patients who may elect to opt out of a protocol that de-identifies a dataset of patients and their **tissue blocks**. The act of specifically identifying patients based on ethnicity, preparatory to de-identifying the same set of patients, creates a new set of human subject risks. When a dataset is reviewed for the purpose of identifying a subset of patients, the review process threatens patient confidentiality. It becomes the task of the biomedical informatician to conduct the review in a manner that protects the confidentiality of all patients and protects subsets of patients (in this case, Native Americans) who may otherwise suffer a direct harm based on personal religious beliefs.

3.12. VIOLATIONS AGAINST THE COMMON RULE (IN THE UNITED STATES)

The Common Rule applies to federally funded agencies. Violations of the Common Rule may result in adverse consequences (List 3.12.1).

LIST 3.12.1. SOME POSSIBLE CONSEQUENCES OF COMMON RULE VIOLATIONS

- The loss to the institution of its funding for the grant in question
- The loss to the institution of its Federal Assurance. The Office of Human Research Protections issues assurances (currently called Worldwide Federal Assurances or WFAs) to institutions that have in-place processes for IRB reviews of research and for maintaining research standards. An institution must have an assurance registered with OHRP in order to receive federal funding for human subjects research.
- An institution-wide suspension of human subject research efforts
- The imposition of grant-related restrictions imposed on the investigators (e.g., a prohibition from applying for federal grant funding)

Needless to say, violating the Common Rule is not recommended as a wise career move for would-be biomedical informaticians.

3.13. VIOLATIONS AGAINST HIPAA (IN THE UNITED STATES)

HIPAA contains language describing penalties for the misuse of identified patient information (List 3.13.1).

LIST 3.13.1. SECTION 1177 OF THE ACT ESTABLISHED CIVIL AND CRIMINAL PENALTIES

- "Civil Money Penalties. HHS may impose civil money penalties on a covered entity of $100 per failure to comply with a Privacy Rule requirement. Pub. L. 104-191; 42 U.S.C. 1320d-5. That penalty may not exceed $25,000 per year for multiple violations of the identical Privacy Rule requirement in a calendar year. HHS may not impose a civil money penalty under specific circumstances, such as when a violation is due to reasonable cause and did not involve willful neglect and the covered entity corrected the violation within 30 days of when it knew or should have known of the violation."

- "Criminal Penalties. A person who knowingly obtains or discloses individually identifiable health information in violation of HIPAA faces a fine of $50,000 and up to one-year imprisonment. Pub. L. 104-191; 42 U.S.C. 1320d-6. The criminal penalties increase to $100,000 and up to five years imprisonment if the wrongful conduct involves false pretenses, and to $250,000 and up to ten years imprisonment if the wrongful conduct involves the intent to sell, transfer, or use individually identifiable health information for commercial advantage, personal gain, or malicious harm. Criminal sanctions will be enforced by the Department of Justice."

3.14. TORT AND VIOLATIONS AGAINST INDIVIDUALS

Violations of either the Common Rule or HIPAA do not preclude (and may well enhance) claims against institutions and researchers arising when individuals (or groups) are harmed.

In general, harm befalling patients falls in the realm of tort law. A tort is a damage or wrongful act done in which there is liability. When an entity is held liable for a tort, the entity is typically expected to provide compensation sufficient to restore the damaged person(s) back to a pre-damaged state. If it is established that the tort was committed in a willful or negligent manner (i.e., not just bad luck), then the court may award punitive damages to the complainant.

Everyone has heard of enormous awards against hospitals and physicians in tort cases. Hospitals stand to lose much more in tort cases than in HIPAA prosecutions.

3.15. WHAT CONSENTS DOES THE PATIENT HAVE ON RECORD?

A patient may have consented to many studies over many visits to the hospital. The consents may apply to certain specimens/data and not to others, and to certain uses of specimens/data and not to others. Once a consent form is signed, institutions have a host of data tracking responsibilities (List 3.15.1).

LIST 3.15.1. QUESTIONS RELATED TO CONSENT TRACKING THAT INSTITUTIONS MUST BE ABLE TO ANSWER

- Does each consent form have an identifier and a locator, a study number, and a data element indicating that the consent form itself was approved by an IRB?
- If needed, could you put your hands on the physical consent document?
- Does your database indicate the specific study for which consent was approved?
- Was the consent form sufficiently detailed, allowing the patient to approve certain uses of specimens/data and to decline other uses?
- Is each consent tagged with tracking data?
- Was the consent approved or declined?
- What day was the consent signed?
- Does the institution have a policy that applies to situations wherein a subject cannot provide an informed consent (e.g., infants, patients with dementia)?
- If the institution has a policy of excluding certain classes of patients from providing informed consent, has the institution received approval for the policy from its IRB?
- For children and challenged subjects, was the informed consent document signed by a surrogate?
- For children and challenged subjects, how is it determined who may act as a surrogate, and how is the identity of the surrogate recorded and tracked?
- Did the consenting subject change her mind and withdraw consent after consent had been approved?
- If consent was withdrawn, on what date did this occur?

- If consent was withdrawn, was consent withdrawn for a particular use of a specimen/data, or for all purposes described by the consent document?
- If consent was withdrawn, does the withdrawal of consent apply to more than one consent form?

The costs of consented research usually exceed projections. It is the opinion of the author that consent activities inflate grant budgets without producing any societal benefit. An informatician clever enough to devise a strategy that avoids consent while protecting human subjects from research risk has done a very good thing.

3.16. CONSENTED VERSUS UNCONSENTED HUMAN SUBJECT RESEARCH

Many people seem to think that consented research (research performed on human subjects who have expressly consented to the research) is a morally superior way of conducting research than unconsented research. People do not like it when scientists assume that they can use medical records without permission.

The biomedical informatician knows that a lot of data is better than a little data. Informaticians prefer large clinical datasets, with millions of patient records. The problem is that it is not feasible to obtain patient consents on millions of records. This means that biomedical informaticians will almost always take the "low road" to unconsented records, if they can.

To close this chapter, I would like to leave the reader with the contrarian assertion that unconsented human subject research is actually okay. Unconsented human subject research on medical records has many practical advantages (List 3.16.1) and can be done in an ethical manner that protects patients.

LIST 3.16.1. ADVANTAGES OF UNCONSENTED MEDICAL RECORD RESEARCH

- Unconsented research saves money and time by eliminating the tedious and expensive process of obtaining individual consents.
- Unconsented research sometimes is favored by patient advocacy organizations, who see unconsented research as a way of expediting medical progress and improving the chances of survival of the patients in their disease constituencies.

- De-identification requirements for most unconsented patient record research essentially guarantees that no harm will come to the patient.
- De-identified unconsented databases can be shared and used for multiple scientific efforts. Consented databases, in most cases, can be used only for the purposes specified in the consent form.
- Archived de-identified unconsented databases pose no particular threat over time to patients. Consented databases often contain patient identifiers and may pose a confidentiality and privacy threat long after the consented research is concluded.

Standards for Biomedical Data

4.1. BACKGROUND

No topic has been so frustrating, contentious, and yet tedious as the subject of data standards. Standards can be divided into three major classes: natural standards, dealt standards, and common standards (author's terminology). Natural standards relate to immutable properties of reality that exist with or without human participation. The speed of light, Avogadro's number, and the diameter of the earth are all natural standards. Natural standards are usually reached by a commission composed of reputable scientists who approve and oversee some measurement task and then accept a number that serves as the natural standard.

Isaac Newton (1642–1727) is best known for explaining the universal laws of physics in mathematical terms, co-inventing calculus, and unraveling the basic mysteries of light and optics. In 1705, Newton was knighted, but his knighthood had nothing to do with his fundamental discoveries into the nature of the universe. Isaac Newton was knighted to honor his work as Master of the Mint, in which capacity he standardized the way we measure the purity of gold. This just goes to show that the universe may conform to Newtonian laws, but much more importantly, the earth conforms to Newtonian standards.

Not all standards relate to physical constants. A dealt standard is "dealt out," much as cards are dealt in a poker game. Users learn to live with the hand they are dealt (List 4.1.1).

LIST 4.1.1. EXAMPLES OF DEALT STANDARDS

- The permitted levels of toxic substances in foods
- TCP/IP (Transmission Control Protocol/Internet Protocol), the Internet specification
- IEEE 802.11, the wireless data transfer standard
- Longitude and latitude assignments
- Divisions of time (days, hours, minutes, and seconds)
- Statutes governing medical privacy

In the United States, the HIPAA Privacy Regulations (9), and the Common Rule (26) are dealt standards. They were created by people, not by nature, but they impose a version of reality to which everyone must adhere. Dealt standards typically tell us what we can and cannot do.

Common standards are ways of doing or saying things that meet a certain level of acceptance by a domain of interested users. Languages, nomenclatures, classifications, ontologies, schemas, namespaces, and markup languages are all examples of common standards.

Common standards are by far the most difficult kind of standard to promulgate. They are not tethered to fundamental universal constants and are not enforced by laws or statutes. For instance, several computer languages have been standardized (e.g., C, ADA, and BASIC). When a language is made a standard, criteria are established for the behavior of the language, particularly the operations and functions that characterize the language. When a commercial version of a language satisfies all the tests for a language's standards of behavior, it can be marketed as standard C or standard ADA or standard BASIC. A company may simply find that it is in their best interests to modify the language to provide features that best fit long-term marketing strategies. If there is no pressure from software consumers to comply with the standard, then the market may become saturated with commercial versions of the language that are incompatible with the original standard.

Medical nomenclatures are another example of malleable common standards. Buyers of hospital information systems may insist on having a licensed version of a standard medical nomenclature bundled into their software to facilitate coding of their diagnoses, procedures, and transactions. The vendor may find it advantageous to truncate the nomenclature that is used in their information system. This decision may be based on the vendor's determination that the entire nomenclature may slow the performance of the system, or the vendor may determine that most of the terms in the nomenclature are unnecessary. The vendor may also

provide the option for institutions to add their own terms to the nomenclature ad libitum. This means that as time progresses, an institution's
hospital information system may lack many of the terms of the standard
nomenclature and may contain many terms not found in the standard
nomenclature.

In fact, most voluntary standards organizations have no mechanism to
ensure that their standards are implemented correctly. As time goes by,
there is a tendency for implementers to drift away from the original standard, creating a system that works locally, but which would be incompatible with systems in use in other institutions.

Common standards have long been plagued by noncompliance or (more
frequently) under-compliance. Unfortunately, virtually all standards
within the domain of biomedical informatics are common standards.
When common standards are ignored or poorly implemented, the fabric
of space and time is not torn asunder, but efforts to achieve cross-insti-
tutional data integration become difficult.

The purpose of this chapter is to provide a background to the topic of
standards in biomedical informatics. This chapter will prepare readers
for a semantic approach to providing standard data representations that
confer meaning and interoperability to hospital information.

4.2. THE CRITICALITY OF COMMON STANDARDS

In England a billion is a million million, whereas in the United States a
billion is a thousand million. So long as everyone uses scientific notation to signify numbers (i.e., 10 to the ninth power in the United States
and 10 to the twelfth power in England), no problems should arise. But
once Americans and Britains start using words to describe quantities,
the likelihood of miscommunication increases.

The probability of disaster grows when data is exchanged with numerics unaccompanied by datatype. The number 3 means one thing when it
is 3 cm and another thing when it is 3 inches. An interval of 3 ms only
has meaning when all parties agree that "ms" represents a millisecond
and not a microsecond.

There are countless examples of catastrophic errors resulting from non-
standards, conflicting standards, or standards ineptly executed on
exchanged data. Some of the saddest seem to occur in outer space,
where errors seldom provide latitude for correction.

On September 23, 1999, the United States-launched Mars Climate
Orbiter (MCO) crashed into Mars. Just seven weeks later, the official
investigation reported that the crash occurred due to a software glitch

that arose when English units of measurement were used in the software when Metric units were supplied as input (44).

"The MCO MIB (Mars Climate Orbiter Mishap Investigation Board) has determined that the root cause for the loss of the MCO spacecraft was the failure to use metric units in the coding of a ground software file, "Small Forces," used in trajectory models. Specifically, thruster performance data in English units instead of metric units was used in the software application code titled SM_FORCES (small forces)."

The Mishap Investigation report is particularly interesting because it does not stop at reporting the error. The investigation details a variety of system errors that contributed to the occurrence of the error. The report also reviews events that occurred during the flight of the MCO that may have presaged the impending disaster, and the report included steps to reduce the likelihood of future disasters.

In 1995, ADA 95 became an ANSI/ISO standard programming language, a distinction held by only a few languages. The U.S. National Institute of Standards recommended that ADA be used by federal departments and agencies in software applications that involve control of real-time or parallel processes, very large systems, and systems with requirements for very high reliability (45).

On June 4, 1996, the maiden flight of the French Ariane 5 launcher ended 40 seconds after initiation. At an altitude of about 3700 meters, the launcher exploded. An official investigation report followed (46).

"The internal SRI software exception was caused during execution of a data conversion from 64-bit floating point to 16-bit signed integer value. The floating point number which was converted had a value greater than what could be represented by a 16-bit signed integer. This resulted in an Operand Error. The data conversion instructions (in ADA code) were not protected from causing an Operand Error, although other conversions of comparable **variables** in the same place in the code were protected."

ADA is a fine programming language, but this standard language was not implemented correctly, and nothing in ADA prohibited an unprotected data conversion.

Probably the most famous medical software disaster involved the Therac-25 (47). Between 1985 and 1987, at least six patients received massive overdoses of radiation due to a software error in a radiation therapy device. A review of the incidents uncovered numerous errors in the engineering and in procedures for detecting and correcting software problems.

Software errors are not rare. The FDA analyzed 3140 medical device recalls conducted between 1992 and 1998 and revealed that 242 of them (7.7%)

were attributable to software failures. Of those, 192 (or 79%) were caused by software changes made after the software's initial production and distribution (48).

The nonstandard use of medical **terminology** can lead to medical errors, as indicated by the U.S. Joint Commission on Accreditation of Healthcare Organization's recent ban on certain common medical abbreviations (49). This action was taken to reduce the occurrence of medication errors that result when nonstandard abbreviations are interpreted differently by different people. The U.S. Institute of Medicine has advocated standardized methods for collecting codified diagnostic data as a strategy for reducing medical errors (50).

In the field of biomedical informatics, a wide variety of problems relate to inadequate standards (List 4.2.1).

LIST 4.2.I. SOME CAUSES OF MEDICAL ERRORS IN THE FIELD OF BIOMEDICAL INFORMATICS

- Absence of standards (for describing clinical data)
- Inadequate terminologies
- Poorly written text
- Inadequate object identifiers (e.g., identifiers for names, tests, reports)
- Poor interoperability of software tools
- Poor integration of biomedical databases
- Poor documentation (of software, of medical devices, of protocols)
- Poor annotation (of medical encounters and transactions)
- Inadequate data structuring (of reports)
- Sloppy data representation

One of the most important types of standards in biomedicine are terminologies. Medical terminologies provide a common language for indexing narrative text. Unfortunately, medical terminologies are replete with examples of minor term modification that can result in treatment error. One example is the "carcinoid tumor of appendix." Carcinoid tumors of the appendix are typically indolent. When the primary tumor is localized and resectable, 5-year survival rates are very high. There is a variant of appendiceal carcinoid known as the goblet cell carcinoid of appendix. Someone uninitiated in tumor biology may infer that the goblet cell carcinoid is a morphologic variant of an indolent neoplasm undeserving of any special designation. Actually, the goblet cell carcinoid of appendix is a highly malignant tumor that has a completely different clinical course and a different recommended treatment than the carcinoid of appendix (51). If a neoplasm nomenclature were to omit the term "goblet cell carcinoid of appendix," someone encountering the term in a pathology report may mistakenly code the subsumed term, "carcinoid of appendix." Alternately, if the curator of a nomenclature is unaware of the distinction between the two tumors, he or she may mistakenly assign the same code to both terms. In either case, mistaking a carcinoid of the appendix with a goblet cell carcinoid of appendix could result in harm to the patient.

A biomedical standard will result in medical errors when the standard is incomplete or is implemented incorrectly. Biomedical standards are intended to keep us safe and to maximize the value we receive from biomedical databases (List 4.2.2). Nonetheless, biomedical informaticians must understand some of the known pitfalls in standards creation and standards implementations.

LIST 4.2.2. PURPOSES OF DATA STANDARDS

- Enhance interoperability of software
- Enable data integration
- Increase the efficiency of medical services
- Increase the speed of medical research
- Reduce medical errors

4.3. THE NONROLE OF GOVERNMENT (IN THE UNITED STATES) IN STANDARDS-MAKING

It is natural for people to think that standards come from governmental agencies. After all, the role of government is to make policies and laws that apply to everyone. Governments are always forcing standards on their citizens. For the most part, government standards relate to methods that ensure that laws and policies are applied the same way to everyone. Standards for driving, standards for flying, standards for using the rivers and coastal oceans, and standards for trade are all government-created methods intended to ensure uniform compliance with government policies and laws.

But when it comes to common standards, the federal government prefers that they be developed by nongovernmental bodies. This principle is specified by the National Technology Transfer and Advancement Act of 1995 (NTTAA), Public Law 104-113 (52). This act directs federal agencies to use standards developed by private standards development organizations, instead of government agencies, whenever feasible.

Furthermore, it may be possible for individuals to sue the government for violations of NTTAA. In an opinion published by the Center for Regulatory Effectiveness:

"Unless there is 'clear and convincing' evidence that Congress intended to preclude judicial review under a statute, persons adversely affected or aggrieved are entitled to seek redress for federal agency violations of that statute under the APA (Administrative Procedure Act)" (53).

There are practical reasons for governments to leave standards development to private interests (List 4.3.1).

LIST 4.3.1. WHY GOVERNMENTS MAY CHOOSE TO AVOID CREATING BIOMEDICAL STANDARDS

- Private entities that use a standard may be in the best position to create the best possible standard.
- Private entities that use a standard may be willing to pay for the standards development process.
- Private entities are more likely to adopt a new standard if they had a part in developing the standard.
- Governments may be unwilling to accept the responsibility of promoting a new standard.
- Governments know that many standards are never adopted by the public and do not want to waste their resources on a standard that will be ignored.
- Governments may be reluctant to face criticism for standards that may adversely affect certain segments of its population.

4.4. THE HAZARDS OF CREATING A NEW STANDARD

Few people think of the standards development process as a very risky business. The author cannot cite instances where standards developers have gotten into any legal trouble. Still, the potential for mischief is undeniable.

When creating a standard, it should be remembered that every design element can potentially benefit one group of people and harm another group of people. This is why the standards process can be contentious.

Though it seems outrageous, the author has personally been involved in discussions wherein the U.S. RICO laws are invoked as a potential concern for standards developers. RICO is the Racketeer Influenced and Corrupt Organizations Act, U.S. Code Title 18, Part 1, Chapter 96 (54). RICO has sections that pertain to specific types of relevant misconduct. A RICO section potentially applicable to standards is found in List 4.4.1.

LIST 4.4.1. EXCERPT FROM RICO THAT MAY BE APPLICABLE TO STANDARDS DEVELOPERS

- "1951. Interference with commerce by threats or violence
  - (a) Whoever in any way or degree obstructs, delays, or affects commerce or the movement of any article or commodity in commerce, by robbery or extortion or attempts or conspires so to do, or commits or threatens physical violence to any person or property in furtherance of a plan or purpose to do anything in violation of this section shall be fined under this title or imprisoned not more than twenty years, or both.
  - (b) As used in this section-
    - (1) The term 'robbery' means the unlawful taking or obtaining of personal property from the person or in the presence of another, against his will, by means of actual or threatened force, or violence, or fear of injury, immediate or future, to his person or property, or property in his custody or possession, or the person or property of a relative or member of his family or of anyone in his company at the time of the taking or obtaining.
    - (2) The term 'extortion' means the obtaining of property from another, with his consent, induced by wrongful use of actual or threatened force, violence, or fear, or under color of official right."

The point to remember is that whenever a group of people conspire to interfere with commerce under color of official right, their activities may fall under RICO. The standards development group would be (in a worst-case interpretation) the conspirators. The "official right" (section (b)(2)) would be the standard. The imposed burden of complying with the standard (resulting in the obstruction or the delay of commerce) would be the extortion.

The threat of RICO prosecution is not the only danger that standards developers fear. Developers must also guard against the inadvertent inclusion of protected intellectual property within their standard. If a standard contains protected intellectual property, then every user of the standard may be obligated to pay applicable royalties. If the standards developers create the impression that the standard can be used freely, and at no cost, then the results for the unwary user may be catastrophic. As an example of the concern that this issue has raised among standards developers, the OMG (Object Management Group) has included the following cautionary language in a specification released in 2004 (55) (List 4.4.2).

LIST 4.4.2. DISCLAIMER AGAINST HIDDEN PATENTS WITHIN STANDARDS

- "The attention of adopters is directed to the possibility that compliance with or adoption of OMG specifications may require use of an invention covered by patent rights. OMG shall not be responsible for identifying patents for which a license may be required by any OMG specification, or for conducting legal inquiries into the legal validity or scope of those patents that are brought to its attention. OMG specifications are prospective and advisory only. Prospective users are responsible for protecting themselves against liability for infringement of patents" (55).

These points are only offered to indicate that standards development is serious business (List 4.4.3). It is not unusual for standards development groups to have legal counsel present during their meetings.

LIST 4.4.3. PERCEIVED RISKS OF DEVELOPING A NEW STANDARD

- The standard may inadvertently contain intellectual property (particularly patented methods) resulting in a legal complaint against the creators of the standard.
- The standard may create loss of revenue or property to certain entities, resulting in legal actions taken against the creators of the standard.
- The standard may result in medical errors, resulting in injury to patients and subsequent legal actions taken against the creators of the standard.
- The standard may have been developed in a manner that excluded participation by an entity, resulting in a legal action.

4.5. OVERVIEW OF STANDARDS DEVELOPMENT

Before beginning any standards effort, those involved should pose several questions to themselves (List 4.5.1).

LIST 4.5.1. QUESTIONS THAT SHOULD BE ASKED PRIOR TO DEVELOPING A NEW STANDARD

- Is there a preexisting standard that covers the same technology?
- If there is a preexisting standard, then can it be enhanced or modified to provide a desired functionality?
- How much will it cost to develop the standard?
- How long will the standards development process take?
- Will the intended beneficiaries of the standard pay for the standards development process?
- Who will develop the standard? Are the selected developers competent to produce an adequate standard?
- Are any of the developers conflicted? Do they stand to profit if the standard is developed in a specific way?
- Do any of the developers have proprietary software or data that they may wish to include in the standard?
- Are the expected developers committed to work through the duration of the standards development process, and are they committed to providing all of the time and energy needed to develop the standard?
- Will there be a mechanism whereby drafts of the standard are reviewed openly by the public? Will the minutes of the working committee be made public? Will public comments be used to modify successive drafts of the standard?
- Will the standard have dependencies on other standards? If so, are there intellectual property issues that must be resolved before development begins? Will these issues require licenses or royalty agreements from the standards developers or the standards users?
- Once created, is the standard likely to be adopted? Is the anticipated standard easily implemented?
- Who will be the adopters of the standard? Are the expected standard adopters included in the development process for the standard?
- Will the standard benefit a range of users beyond the standards developers?
- What are the hazards that the standard may produce, and who might be hurt by the standard? In particular, will any entities be disadvantaged if they cannot readily adopt the standard?
- Is it necessary to have the standard approved by an external organization?

- If so, who will pay for the extra costs of obtaining approval from an external standards organization?
- Will the standard need to be continuously updated and modified? Is there a planned process for producing multiple versions of the standard?
- Is it really important to have the standard? Is it worth the effort?

Assuming that every question is answered in an encouraging manner, the standards effort can begin—if you can afford the price. The costs of standards development should not be underestimated. **HL7** is one of the best known of the biomedical standards development efforts. In 2005, HL7 reported more than 2200 individual members and more than 530 organization members (56). Taking into account registration/member fees, travel, lodging and salary time, the costs to corporations may easily exceed $15,000 per year per member. The costs mount when the participation of a single employee ($15,000) is multiplied by the number of delegates from the company and by the number of different standards efforts that the company may choose to join. Of course, these are just the costs of participation by a single company. A standards effort (such as HL7) may involve the toil of thousands of people extended over several decades. The final outcome of all this human activity may be a few paltry pieces of paper containing a list of terms, codes, and format requirements.

4.6. HOW ARE STANDARDS DEVELOPED, APPROVED, AND ADOPTED?

Any person, company, organization or association can develop a standard. The tired joke is that people enjoy standards so much that everyone wants to have one of their own. The term "standard" has no specific legal meaning, other than indicating that a certain item has generally acknowledged features that others can use to compare or replicate items.

In the biomedical informatics field, a standard is often a protocol, specific data format, information structure, or agreed way of representing data. All of these types of standards are reached through a consensus process.

Standards are developed by standards development organizations composed of members who have an interest in using the standard or who have an interest in ensuring that others (such as software vendors) use the standard in a way that will benefit the standards developer.

In the United States, there are hundreds of standards development organizations devoted to the field of biomedical informatics. These organizations create thousands of consensus reports and other documents. The most common standards activities involve issues of data integration and software interoperability.

In the United States, standards developers can use the services of a facilitating organization that has a set of procedures for standards development that ensure that the standards are developed fairly and in a manner that will be acceptable to an organization that certifies standards (List 4.6.1).

LIST 4.6.1. ORGANIZATIONS ACTIVE IN THE FIELD OF BIOMEDICAL STANDARDS

- ASTM, American Society of Testing and Materials
- **ANSI**, American National Standards Institute
- HISB, Health Information Standards Board
- IEEE, Institute of Electrical and Electronics Engineers, Inc.
- ACR/NEMA, American College of Radiology (ACR) and National Electrical Manufacturers Association (NEMA), which oversees the DICOM (Digital Imaging and Communications in Medicine) image standard
- NCPDP, National Council for Prescription Drug Programs, Inc.
- NIST, National Institute of Standards and Technology
- ISO, International Organization for Standardization
- IEC, International Electrotechnical Commission

In the United States, the most active standards facilitating organization is ANSI (American National Standards Institute) (57). ANSI is a private, non-profit organization that provides coordination for the United States voluntary standards efforts. It provides procedures for establishing consensus among qualified groups. It ensures that standards are developed in a manner that ensures consensus, balance, transparency, due process, and openness. ANSI does not approve standards. It accredits the participants and the process by which the standard is created. The finished standard is an American National Standard, signifying that it was obtained through ANSI-compliance. The ANSI process does not ensure that the standard meets any particular set of performance characteristics.

ANSI coordinates approval of American National Standards by international standards organizations. ANSI works with ISO and/or IEC when the standards developers in the biomedical field seek certification from a standards authority. ISO and IEC certification can strengthen a standard by providing international stature and increasing the chances that the standard will be used by governmental agencies (List 4.6.2).

LIST 4.6.2. SOME AMERICAN NATIONAL STANDARDS PROGRAMMING LANGUAGES

- Mumps (ANSI approval 1977)
- BASIC (ANSI approval 1978)
- ADA (ANSI approval 1983)
- C (ANSI approval 1989)
- Common Lisp (ANSI approval 1994)
- ADA 95 (ANSI approval 1995)
- Smalltalk (ANSI approval 1998)
- C++ (ANSI approval 1999)

4.7. THE UTILITY OF NONSTANDARDS

It can be overwhelming to think about all the things that should be standardized. The biomedical informatics community needs to have standard ways of reporting the data produced by every new technology that generates biomedical data (List 4.7.1).

LIST 4.7.I. NEW AND FUTURE TECHNOLOGIES THAT CREATE BIOMEDICAL DATA

- **Gene Expression arrays**
- Proteomic arrays
- Tissue microarrays
- Metabolomic arrays
- Image morphometric arrays

Considering the expense, effort, tedium, and ultimate risk of total failure faced by any standards effort, one may wonder if there may be some alternative approach that is a little less awful.

4.8. THE NONSTANDARD PRESENT—SPECIFICATIONS AND UNIQUE OBJECTS

The terms "standard" and "specification" are considered synonymous by many. For the purposes of this book, a distinction is drawn between the terms.

- Standard—A standard is a uniform way of manufacturing, measuring, or describing objects. The items of a standard are approved by a standards developing organization. Objects that are manufactured, measured, or described to identical specifications of the standard should be identical or near-identical objects.

- Specification—A specification is a common way of describing something using well-defined descriptors and well-defined units of measurement, and organizing the descriptive data in a manner than can be unambiguously understood.

As defined here, the difference between a standard and a specification is much like the difference between an obligation and an option. A standard obligates you to manufacture, measure, or describe objects using the rules encompassed by the standard. A specification provides you with the option to describe things using defined words and a common syntax for organizing the items in your description.

It is my perception that the need to have uniform ways of creating and understanding data is outpacing our ability to create new data standards. Those who work on standards committees may disagree, noting that the level of participation in standards development committees has never been higher. Perhaps this is so, but there are dilemmas faced by standards developers that cannot be solved by recruiting additional committee members. As new standards are created, old standards are revised. When an old standard is revised, database managers must adopt the new standards and retroactively modify the existing data records stored in the now-obsolete format. This can create a never-ending game of catch-up that is only exacerbated by the creation of new standards.

The biomedical informatics community faces a host of intractable problems stemming from the standards development process (List 4.8.1).

LIST 4.8.1. PROBLEMS CREATED BY THE INTRODUCTION OF NEW STANDARDS

- New classes of data objects require a new standard for the new object class (e.g., Tissue Microarray data, Gene Expression Array data).
- New standards require new implementations.
- Existing data standards require revision.
- Revisions of existing standards require retroactive implementation in data records conforming to the prior version of the standard.
- New data standards require harmonization with other existing standards. Otherwise multiple standards may compete for the stan-

dards-based data structures and data descriptors applicable to data elements common to multiple standards.
- Because standards often become the intellectual property of the standards development organization, new standards cannot include parts of standards developed by other organizations. This means that redundant standards may describe the same objects.

4.9. THE NONSTANDARD FUTURE—DATA SEMANTICS

Postel's Law was defined in RFC 793 as "be conservative in what you do, be liberal in what you accept from others."

Consider the following imaginary scenario. I go to the store and buy an assortment of standard-sized PVC tubes (the round plastic pipes often used in house plumbing). I also buy a bunch of polyvinyl chloride (PVC) joints that can connect to PVC pipes at varying angles. Each pipe comes in a standard length and diameter, and the joints meet standards for PVC joints.

I use these pipes and joints to build a chair. I do not need to cut down any of the pipes or add any additional materials. When I finish, I have a sturdy structure that I can sit on comfortably. On a piece of paper, I list the PVC pieces that I used, and I describe how the chair can be assembled from the pieces.

Have I just created a standard chair? I think so. I've used standard construction materials, with each piece listed and described in the PVC industry catalog. Furthermore, the assembly of the chair is described in an easy-to-understand file that lists the component parts and the relationships between each of the parts.

My neighbor happens to be an active member of the (fictitious) International Furniture Standards Board. At my invitation, he examines my new chair and informs me that 1) the structure does not comply with the construction standards issued by the International Furniture Standards Board; 2) the materials used are not listed in the Standard Materials catalog endorsed by the International Furniture Standards Board; 3) the structure does not look like any of the chairs listed in Furniture Standards Listing, and 4) the structure that I have created is not a chair. My neighbor pronounces these judgments oblivious to the fact that he is sitting in my new chair.

This story draws the distinction between a specification and a standard. I may have created and specified a new object (something akin to a chair), but I have not created a standard chair. Does my specification have any real value? Yes. The specified chair can be re-created

Figure 2 A specified chair.

by following the instructions included in the specification. The specified chair can be distinguished from any different kind of chair that was built with a different set of specifications. The specification permits the description of fundamental advances in chair design that were neither anticipated nor accommodated by a furniture standard. The fundamental properties of a specification are quite simple (List 4.9.1).

LIST 4.9.1. FUNDAMENTAL PROPERTIES OF A SPECIFICATION

- The object specified must be defined and distinguished from all other objects (i.e., one object cannot have two nonequivalent specifications and one specification cannot apply equally to two nonequivalent objects).
- The description must be organized in a way that is understandable and unambiguous.

- The descriptors must be well defined in the context of the specification and not confused with descriptors of the same name but different meaning that may appear in other specifications (e.g., a "date" may be a calendar notation in one standard and a type of dried fruit in another specification).
- The measurements and descriptor values must be well defined and not confused with measurements and values of the same alphanumeric value but different meaning that may appear in other specifications (e.g., 10 lbs is not the same as 10 Kg).
- The specification must describe itself and include information pertaining to its purpose, its creator, its ownership, any restrictions on its uses, and any instructions necessary to interpret the specification.

Specifications are different from standards (List 4.9.2).

LIST 4.9.2. LOGISTICAL ADVANTAGES OF SPECIFICATIONS OVER STANDARDS

- A specification need not be developed through a standards development process. A specification is basically a descriptive document and only requires fully unambiguous language. An individual can create a specification that everyone in the world can understand and use.
- Specifications do not require approval by any federal agency or organization. Standards have almost no meaning unless they are approved. In some cases, standards are enforced by authority of law.
- There are usually many different ways of specifying things. The same object can be described by different specifications. Standards tend to impose monolithic implementations.
- A specification is a general way of describing things and can be used for many different and new types of things. Standards are typically developed for specific items and cannot accommodate new items without pursuing a development and approval process through a standards development organization.

Biomedical informaticians who use research data will almost certainly find that existing standards will not keep pace with the arrival of new techniques and data objects. The chair shown (see Figure 2) is a specified image created with Pov-Ray, a free, open source rendering program (see Appendix). It was created using a .pov file, which is a plain-text set of instructions written for the rendering application.

List 4.9.3 is an example of part of the .pov file used to create the chair.

LIST 4.9.3. SNIPPET FROM chair.pov RENDERING SPECIFICATION, MODIFIED FROM MATTHIAS OPITZ'S PUBLIC DOMAIN SCENE FILE USED TO CREATE FIGURE 2

```
-plane [ {
-    y, -40
     pigment { color rgbf<0.7, 0.7, 0.7 0.1>}
     normal { ripples 10.0 frequency 1 scale 5}
     finish {
-          reflection 0.1
-          ambient 0.3
          }
     }
```

Pov-Ray has its own language for specifying how images are rendered. Basically, the scene is broken down into objects (planes, spheres, cylinders, cones, light sources, camera), and objects are given properties (location, size, color, texture, etc.). The collection of fully specified objects compose the elements of a scene. The Pov-Ray application renders the specified scene as a 3-D image. A high resolution 3-D image may have a size of several megabytes, while the specification for the image may be as small as a few hundred bytes. The chair in Figure 2 was specified in a little more than 4 Kbytes. Pov-Ray was developed through a cooperative effort of many different programmers, but it is not a standard.

The biggest mistake an informatician can make is to collect and store data that has been inadequately specified. Collections of inadequately specified data tend to have limited scientific utility and often have detrimental consequences.

The following sections will discuss two of the basic elements of a data specification: **unique object** identifiers and logical statements that have meaning. The subject of data specifications will be visited again in a later chapter, after the reader is introduced to computer programming and to XML.

4.10. UNIQUE IDENTIFIERS

Thoughts of unique identifiers in medicine always turn to patient identifiers. Every hospital has non-unique names in their patient databases (e.g., John Smith, Frank Johnson, Tom Rice). A common remedy is to identify patients by their social security number. Unfortunately, even if social security numbers are unique (an assertion that has been challenged), they certainly are not used in a manner that ensures the unique identification of patients. Many patients provide false social security numbers, either through error or through deception.

Wikipedia.com recounts a story that dates back to 1938. The E. H. Ferree Company manufactured wallets and decided that it would be good business to promote its product by showing how a social security card would fit into its wallets. A display social security card, containing the social security number of an employee, was placed in each wallet sold. Though the display cards were printed in red (the real card is printed in blue), were half the size of real social security cards, and had "Specimen" printed across the front, many people utilized the card as their own social security number. Over time, the display number was claimed by over 40,000 people. As late as 1977, the number was still being used by 12 individuals.

4.11. LIFE SCIENCE UNIQUE IDENTIFIERS

The OMG has developed a standard for uniquely identifying biomedical data objects (55). A Life Science Identifier (LSID) conforms to the URN (Uniform Resource Name) standards defined by the IETF (Internet Engineering Task Force). Every LSID has up to five parts, which are separated by a colon (Lists 4.11.1 and 4.11.2) (58).

LIST 4.11.1. PARTS OF AN LSID, FROM THE LSID RESOLUTION PROTOCOL PROJECT

- Network Identifier (NID)
- Root DNS name of the issuing authority
- Namespace chosen by the issuing authority
- Object ID unique to that namespace and assigned locally
- Revision ID for storing versioning information (optional)

LIST 4.11.2. EXAMPLES OF LSIDS, FROM THE LSID RESOLUTION PROTOCOL PROJECT

- urn:lsid:pdb.org:1AFT:1 This is the first version of the 1AFT protein in the Protein Data Bank.
- urn:lsid:ncbi.nlm.nih.gov:pubmed:12571434 References a PubMed article.
- urn:lsid:ncbi.nlm.nig.gov:GenBank:T48601:2 Refers to the second version of an entry in GenBank.

Though the LSIDs may contain a server address, the server addresses are not required to be active links to a URL. The identifier has one purpose, to provide a unique name for a unique object. Two objects identified by the same LSID must be identical to each other. If an object changes (e.g., if a file identified by an LSID is modified), then it can no longer be identified by the same LSID.

4.12. HL7 UNIQUE IDENTIFIERS

An enterprise can obtain an OID (Object Identifier) at http://www.iana.org/cgi-bin/enterprise.pl

For example, the University of Michigan OID is: 1.3.6.1.4.1.250.

The enterprise OID serves as a prefix for unique data objects within an institution. Are HL7 OIDs always unique (59)?

"Though HL7 shall exercise diligence before assigning an OID in the HL7 branch to third parties, given the lack of a global OID registry mechanism, one cannot make absolutely certain that there is no preexisting OID assignment for such third-party entity. Also, a duplicate assignment can happen in the future through another source. If such cases of supplicate assignment become known to HL7, HL7 shall make efforts to resolve this situation. For continued interoperability in the meantime, the HL7 assigned OID shall be the preferred OID used."

4.13. UNIQUE PROBLEMS ASSOCIATED WITH UNIQUENESS

The problem of unique object identifiers is that it may be very difficult to guarantee uniqueness for identifiers. A fascinating discussion of biomedical uniqueness is provided by Peter Kuzmak and coworkers (60). Kuzmak studies the problem of duplicate unique identifiers for hospital-acquired radiologic images archived using the DICOM (Digital Imaging and Communications in Medicine) image standard. The same observations may apply to HL7, LSID, and other unique object assignment services.

DICOM uses UIDs (Unique Identifiers) to identify different instances of clinical information objects. When a duplicate UID is generated, different studies or different images are assigned the same UID value, and it is possible to associate the study or image with the wrong patient. It is estimated that the frequency of occurrence of duplicate UIDs in DICOM is approximately one in a thousand. Kuzmak further estimates that the number of DICOM images archived world-wide is approximately one billion. This means that one million DICOM images may have duplicate identifiers.

Vendors of medical imaging devices implement private methods for assigning unique identifiers. A common flaw involves generating primary keys from nonconstant attributes. For instance, an institute may consecutively number its images by attaching consecutively numbered suffixes to the unique identifiers of the institution and the radiology department.

Image 3345-21-6690

In this case, 3345 is the institution identifier, 21 is the department identifier, and 6690 is the image number.

It is a safe bet that every institution that uses a similar scheme will have an image number 6690, but the prefix numbers (institution identifier and department identifier) will provide uniqueness to the image identifier.

A problem arises if the institutions merge, the image service is assigned to another department in the institution, departments split, or another department in the same institution is reassigned the number 21. What sometimes occurs is that the image number stays the same, but the prefix assigned to the image changes. Suddenly image 6690 is assigned the same "unique" number as another image 6690 in a different institution or department.

Sometimes unique numbers are assigned based on an incrementing feature of the space-time continuum. The simplest approach is to use an infinite counter. Every new object is assigned an increasing identifier number. The problem with this approach is that counters can be reset, broken, replaced, ignored, or duplicated. If there is more than one counter, then the problems of assigning consecutive identifiers can be intractable.

Sometimes identifiers are determined by event timing. Problems occur when the clock is set back, moved forward, or broken. If the branches of an institution are dispersed across time zones, a single time identifier can be assigned to different objects.

The worst situation occurs when multiple devices built by the same vendor deploy the same method of identifier assignment at many locations throughout an institution. This can easily result in the appearance of multiple "unique" identifiers in a single medical center.

Another problem occurs when an object is purposefully provided with multiple different unique identifiers. This may occur when an image study is ported to a device that is programmed to assign a unique identifier to all imported images (even if the image already has a unique identifier). This seems like an absurd situation, but this kind of software design serves to relieve vendors from assuming the uniqueness of identifying data received from another vendor. A vendor may be highly motivated to create software that insulates itself from flaws in an external software system, even at the expense of interoperability.

DICOM is not the only standard with a unique identifier issue. Although the HL7 organization maintains a central authority for distributing unique identifiers to institutions, assignments of unique identifiers to the data objects created and stored by the institutions are local implementations, subject to the same flaws as seen in DICOM.

The basic principles of unique object identification can be summarized in three principles (List 4.13.1). Implementing a unique identification protocol is not particularly difficult, but it requires careful planning, oversight, and testing.

In practical terms, biomedical institutions should have an office that is responsible for maintaining all the unique identifiers employed by the institution. This office would be responsible for registering the institution with external services that supply unique identifiers (List 4.13.1). The office would ensure that different unique objects cannot be assigned the same identifiers.

LIST 4.13.1. PRINCIPLES OF UNIQUE OBJECT IDENTIFICATION

- A unique object can be distinguished from all other unique objects.
- A unique object cannot be distinguished from itself.
- A class (or collection) of instances can be unique.

On occasion, one unique object will be assigned multiple unique numbers. This will be the case when external agencies provide identifiers for objects within an institution (List 4.13.2). The office would need to maintain a list of equivalencies for multiple unique numbers assigned to a unique object. The office would be responsible for maintaining a smooth transition for uniquely identified legacy data when new information systems are deployed within the enterprise system. Institutions that simply ignore the problem will have corrupted databases.

LIST 4.13.2. SOME REGISTRIES THAT CONTINUALLY ASSIGN UNIQUE IDENTIFIERS TO REQUESTING ENTITIES

- DOI (Digital Object Identifier)
- PMID (PubMed Identification) Number
- LSID (Life Science Identifier)
- HL7 OID (Health Level 7 Object Identifier)
- DICOM (Digital Imaging and Communications in Medicine) identifiers
- ISSN (International Standard Serial Numbers)

- Social Security Numbers (for U.S. population)
- NPI (National Provider Identifier) for physicians
- Clinical Trials Protocol Registration System
- Office of Human Research Protections FederalWide Assurance number
- Data Universal Numbering System (DUNS) number (61)
- DNS (Domain Name Service)

Unique object registries serve a very important purpose, particularly when the object identifiers are persistent and used by many different people. It makes sense to have a central authority for Web addresses, library acquisitions, and journal abstracts. There are occasions when it is impractical to obtain unique identifiers from a central registry. This is certainly the case for ephemeral transaction identifiers such as the tracking codes that follow a blood sample accessioned into a clinical laboratory. The Network Working Group has issued a fascinating protocol for a Universally Unique IDentifier (UUID, also known as GUID) that does not require a central registrar. A UUID is 128 bits long and reserves 60 bits for a string computed directly from a computer time stamp (62). UUIDs, if implemented properly, should provide uniqueness across space and time. UUIDs were originally used in the Apollo Network Computing System and were later adopted in the Open Software Foundation's Distributed Computing Environment.

The following is an example of the string representation of a UUID as an Internet-compatible Unique Resource Name (62):

urn:uuid:f81d4fae-7dec-11d0-a765-00a0c91e6bf6

By deploying UUIDs, institutions can deploy millions of unique identifiers. The reader may be wondering if data object uniqueness is worth the effort. If one thinks about the computer-based databases that really seem to work well, one finds that they all have a system of unique object identifiers (List 4.13.3).

LIST 4.13.3. DEPENDABLE COMPUTER SYSTEMS THAT RELY ON UNIQUE OBJECT IDENTIFIERS

- Google (relies on URLs)
- PubMed (relies on PubMed identifiers)
- Libraries (rely on ISSN, DOI)
- Swiss banks (rely on unique account numbers)

If one thinks about the common errors of the medical world, how many relate to identification errors (List 4.13.4)?

LIST 4.13.4. SOME MEDICAL ERRORS RELATED TO MISIDENTIFICATION

- Correctly identified medication provided to incorrectly identified person
- Incorrectly identified medication provided to correctly identified person
- Incorrectly identified dosage of correct medication provided to correctly identified person
- Blood transfused provided to incorrectly identified person
- Report sent to incorrectly identified physician
- Report identified with wrong person's name
- Bill sent to incorrectly identified person
- Report provided with diagnosis intended for different person
- Wrong operation performed on incorrectly identified patient
- Incorrectly identified patient treated for another patient's illness

---

We will see in the next section, and again in Chapter 12, that unique identification is absolutely essential for all meaningful data acquisition in biomedicine.

4.14. SPECIFYING INFORMATION: DO YOU HAVE THE TIME?

When you specify information, you provide a full description that distinguishes the described item from all other nonequivalent items. A specification consists of the defined vocabulary needed to describe objects and a syntax that organizes the descriptors in a manner that can be understood.

Consider the statement, "We will have our meeting next Tuesday." Does this mean that the meeting will occur on the first occurring Tuesday? Or does it mean that the meeting will occur on the Tuesday following the first occurring? Can the rules change depending on the day that the statement is uttered? For instance, if the statement is made on a Monday, most people would tend to think that the meeting will occur 8 days hence (a week after the first occurring Tuesday). If the statement is made on a Wednesday, many people may think that the meeting will be held 6 days hence (on the first occurring Tuesday). In both instances, two people may pick the same date, while following totally different logic rules. The phrase "next Tuesday" does not adequately specify a date. Consider the statement, "The meeting will occur on Tuesday, January 24, 2006 at 2:00 PM." This is better, but you really need to indicate the time zone. As the world turns, 2:00 PM will occur at 24 different moments on any given day. The phrase "January 24, 2006 at 2:00 PM" does not specify a time, because there are 24 alternate times that can be represented by the same phrase.

In hospitals, specified time is used for many different purposes. It can be used to establish time of birth, time of death, time of receipt of perishable biological materials, time when confidential material was accessed on a computer, and so on. The value of the time can be used in a mathematical algorithm that produces an identifier for a report or a transaction. Because time is so important, there is an ISO standard, 8601, that specifies the date and time. The standard arranges named time intervals by decreasing length.

Year, month, day, hour, minute, second; YYYY-MM-DD; hh:mm:ss

When listing date and time, the preferred representation is:

<date>T<time>Z

A "T" separates date and time, and a "Z" specifies the default time zone, UTC. UTC stands for Coordinated Universal Time and is equivalent to the time at the prime meridian, Greenwhich Mean Time, world time, or Zulu time.

Other time zones can be used, but they are specified by their offset from Zulu time. An American time of 3:00 PM with a 6 hour offset from Zulu time would be represented as:

2006-01-24T15:00:00-06 This is equivalent to: 2006-01-24T21:00:00Z

Data must be fully specified before it can be usefully parsed and analyzed. Much of the work of biomedical informaticians will require developing the specifications for information found in different knowledge domains.

4.15. INTRODUCTION TO MEANING

Consider the statement, "He has a blood glucose of 85." The statement has no particular meaning because "he" can refer to approximately half of the world's population. If the statement were, "John Smith has a blood glucose of 85," then the statement has somewhat more meaning. However, if there is more than one person named "John Smith," then the statement would be meaningless. Some might argue that if the clinic had only one person registered in its database named "John Smith," then the statement would have meaning. A counter-argument would hold that another patient of the same name might register in the clinic the next day, retroactively obfuscating the meaning of the statement. Or the clinic may need to merge its data with the data from other clinics, yielding multiple "John Smith" entries.

Actually, the statement "John Smith has a blood glucose of 85" has no meaning in the "informatics" sense (List 4.15.1).

LIST 4.15.1. INFORMATION DEFICIENCIES IN THE STATEMENT "JOHN SMITH HAS A BLOOD GLUCOSE OF 85"

- No unique patient identifier (many people are named John Smith)
- No unique time identifier (indicating when the test was performed and distinguishing the test results from other blood glucose values obtained from the patient at other times)
- No unique test identifier (indicating the specific protocol used to measure blood glucose in this instance)
- No unique identifier for the units of measurement
- No unique report identifier (indicating that the report itself is a unique laboratory object that can be archived and retrieved)

A set of meaningful statements related to John Smith's blood glucose might appear in several short assertions:

P-554993 is patient John Smith.

P-554993 has laboratory test T-443921.

T-443921 is type "glucose test; (CP-443664)."

T-443921 performed September 02, 2006.

T-443921 measured in units of mg/dL.

T-443921 has value 85.

Believe it or not, this series of assertions speaks to the heart of biomedical informatics. In the first assertion, we are informed that our patient, John Smith, has been assigned the unique patient identifier P-554993. In a well-organized medical center, no other person, including no other persons with the name, "John Smith" will be assigned the P-554993 identifier. Whenever our specific "John Smith" comes to the medical center, he will be identified by P-554993. Looking at the list of assertions, does P-554993 (John Smith) have a blood glucose value of 85? No. The blood glucose value is a property assigned to test T-443921. Isn't this quibbling? The test was performed on John Smith, so wouldn't the glucose value belong to John Smith? If we associate the blood glucose value directly with the patient, then the patient record will have multiple values of glucose taken during the course of the patient's life. It does little good to know that a patient had glucose values of 85, 129, 82, 300, and 40, without a better understanding of the relationship between the glucose values over time and treatment. By associating the glucose value with a uniquely identified test, we gain the knowledge conveyed by the attributes attached to the test.

In this case, the unique identifier for the test is assigned the name of the patient, the date of the encounter, the measured value, and the measurement units. In America, glucose is measured in milligrams per deciliter (mg/dL). In England, glucose is commonly measured in millimoles per liter (mmol/L). The type of test is assigned a unique laboratory identifier. If we were to look up CP-443664 in the hospital information system, we would likely find that this is a test for glucose in blood (not urine), and we may find a complete protocol for the glucose test as well as quality assurance studies done by the hospital and a normal range for the results of the test. If we were to look up P-554993 in the hospital information system database, we would probably find the name, date of birth, and address of the patient.

In informatics, "meaning" is achieved when a property and a value are bound to a fully specified object (List 4.15.2).

LIST 4.15.2. THREE CONDITIONS FOR A MEANINGFUL ASSERTION IN INFORMATICS

- There is a specified object about which the statement is made. When the object is a unique object (such as a patient), the object must be specified in a manner that distinguishes the object from all other objects, and this is typically done with a unique object identifier.
- There is data that pertains to the specified object.
- There is metadata that describes the data (that pertains to the specified object).

For example, consider a uniquely identified glucose test report:

T-443921 (unique object) performed on (property) Sept. 02, 2006 (value).

Statements of meaning can be merged without losing meaning. For instance, I could look through a thousand databases, pulling all statements of meaning that begin with any unique object, and I would learn

Figure 3 The meaning of meaning: a subject encases data held by metadate

more and more with each added record. If I collected every record that began with P-554993, I might end up with a small database:

- P-554993 is patient John Smith.
- P-554993 has laboratory test T-443921.
- P-554993 has city_address Philadelphia.
- P-554993 has state_address Pennsylvania.
- P-554993 has radiology test R-995121.
- P-554993 has radiology test R-396331.
- P-554993 has genetics lab test G-5588300.

Each piece of information has meaning (Figure 3). Since the radiology, lab, and genetics tests all have unique identifiers, I can search these in the hospital information system and find information about each test.

Readers will need to accommodate themselves to the idea that many of the numbers that we thought we owned are actually just borrowed. Suppose you are 35 years old. You may think that being 35 is a property that describes you. But last year, you were 34 years old, and next year you will be 36 years old. The age of a person constantly changes and has no permanent value in a medical record. An invariant property of any patient is the birthdate. Encounters are recorded events such as inoculations, blood tests, x-rays, and so on. Each medical encounter after birth has a date, and the patient has numerous calculable ages at these different encounters (date of encounter minus date of birth). In order to track the patient, we need to know only the unique identifier of the patient, some invariant properties of the patient, and the identifiers of the patient encounters, which should include the dates of the encounters.

The informatics-based concept of binding specified objects to a described value in an assertion is often lost on research biologists, who are devoted to discovering generalities about nature. In biology, physics, and chemistry, statements attain value only when they are generalizable (List 4.15.3).

LIST 4.15.3. GENERALIZABLE SCIENTIFIC STATEMENTS

- f = ma: Force equals mass times acceleration.
- If a gas is held at constant temperature, then its volume is inversely proportional to its pressure (Boyle's law).
- Ontogeny recapitulates phylogeny: fetal development follows the evolutionary path of the species (a false assertion).
- There are 10 types of people, those who use binary notation and those who do not.

It is not surprising that biologists, who are trained to find general rules that make sense of a complex universe, are prone to ignore the importance of data uniqueness. Nonetheless, generalizations drawn from biomedical data require us to distinguish one observation from another.

The biologist might argue that she does not need to know the name of the person who has brown eyes. The name of the patient is something that might be required for a medical report but not for a scientific study. Unfortunately, life is not that simple. Though the biologist may not need to know who has brown eyes, she will still need to distinguish all the different people who have reported eye color. Suppose John Public has an eye color observation made on two separate occasions at institution A, and has an eye color observation made at institution B. If both institutions stripped patient names and merged their observational datasets, this would create three de-identified patient records for one person. This appearance of multiple de-identified records for a single individual can quickly invalidate the scientific value of a database. The only way of avoiding this problem is to somehow maintain the identity of records in merged databases without violating patient confidentiality.

The term "identifier" as used is somewhat imprecise. An identifier does not tell you the name or characteristics of the object that is uniquely identifies. At best, the purpose of an identifier is to tell you that whenever the identifier is encountered, it refers to the same unique object, and whenever two different identifiers are encountered, they refer to different objects. Strangely, one of the most important functions of an "identifier" is to "de-identify" the object by permitting unique objects to be distinguishable without divulging the name of the object (List 4.15.4).

LIST 4.15.4. ALGORITHM FOR DE-IDENTIFYING WITH AN IDENTIFIER

- Collect data on unique object. "Joe Public has brown eyes."
- Assign a unique identifier. "Joe Public has unique identifier, 77300183."
- Substitute name of object with its identifier.
- Consistently use the identifier with data. "77300183 has brown eyes."
- Do not let anyone know that Joe Public is 77300183.

At this point, it should be clarified that most hospital information systems fail to provide unique object identifiers, fail to provide a data element **dictionary** with defined unique objects, and fail to create data records that can be parsed as statements of meaning (specified objects followed by defined properties and values). One of the primary challenges of biomedical informaticians is to transform hospital and biological data into a form that permits the integration of information held in diverse databases. This task requires some familiarity with the concept of "meaning" as used by informaticians.

4.16. WHAT HAVE WE LEARNED?

In general, files that comply with a standard are rigidly organized and can be easily parsed and manipulated by software specifically designed to adhere to the standard. For instance, it is relatively easy to write software that manipulates DICOM medical images, because the standard requires the fields of the image to occur at prescribed byte locations in the file. The downside is that files that conform to the standard are inde-cipherable by software that is not specifically written for the standard.

Files that comply with a specification are typically self-describing doc-uments that contain within themselves all the information necessary for a human or a computer to derive meaning from the file contents. In the-ory, files that comply with a specification can be parsed and manipu-lated by generalized software designed to parse the markup language of the specification (e.g., XML, RDF) and to organize the data into data structures defined within the file. The downside is that the software and the files must be cleverly written. A recurring theme throughout this book is that informaticians may achieve the functionality of a standard, without going through the standards process, through a disciplined approach to data organization and data description.

We will see in Chapter 12 that when informaticians collect data in mean-ingful statements, their datasets can be transformed (into different types of data structures), integrated (with other datasets), queried (searched using algorithms designed for parsing meaningful statements), and understood (annotated with descriptive information that describes the aggregate dataset in addition to describing each data element within the dataset).

Just Enough Programming

5.1. BACKGROUND

If you have read the first four chapters, then you have learned something about the different kinds of biomedical data and how data can be acquired and organized.

Before beginning this chapter, you should know that it is not essential that you know how to program. You can be a leader in the field of biomedical informatics without acquiring programming skills. However, you will probably find that learning to program is easier than you had imagined, and that writing your own programs is a source of great intellectual pleasure. If you would like, you can skip this chapter and return to it when the mood suits you.

The remainder of the book deals with techniques for organizing, indexing, searching, retrieving, and integrating biomedical data. These common tasks use basic programming skills. In this chapter, the reader is given just enough programming exposure to appreciate the algorithms and simple program scripts that will appear in Chapters 6–17.

5.2. WHY YOU SHOULD LEARN SOME FUNDAMENTAL PROGRAMMING

People do not seem to mind learning how to use popular computer applications. It may take many hours to learn the intricacies of a word processor, a spreadsheet, or an imaging program. For each new application, the learning process needs to be repeated. The same people who willingly master several proprietary software applications are often unwilling to learn a programming language. There is a prevalent opinion that the difference between using a software application and writing a software application is like the difference between listening to music and composing music. This is not strictly true.

What is the difference between a software application and a programming language? Software applications can best be thought of as purposefully hobbled programming languages. Imagine working on a word processor application and deciding that you would like to create a complete index of the words in the current file with all their file locations. Or suppose that you would like to know the frequency of occurrence of each of the words in the file, or that you would like a list of words that are longer than 10 characters. Suppose you need a comparison between the current file and 100 other text files issued the same date in order to ensure that all of the dates included within the files are written in a consistent format. Or perhaps you need a list of all of the names of diseases that were mentioned in the file. Your word processor, as powerful and complex as it may be, prohibits modifications. A few lines of code added to the application may have provided your desired functionality.

What does a biomedical researcher do if she needs software functionality that is not provided by a proprietary software application? Does she shop for another software application that can do the job? Where does she find the time to search for new software, the money to purchase the software, and the energy to learn the new application? After a long search, what does she do if no existing software application will suffice? Does she hire a programmer to write an application just for her? Or does she simply give up and look for some other project?

Software programming languages, unlike software applications, are designed to do everything. Software languages support all kinds of file input and output operations. Programming languages let you create and manipulate data. The astonishing thing about programming languages is that they do absolutely everything you can think of doing with data. Most tasks will require just a few lines of software code (List 5.2.1). It would be difficult or impossible to find software applications with similar flexibility. Most importantly, it is sometimes easier to learn a programming language than to learn a software application.

LIST 5.2.1. SOME QUESTIONS THAT CAN BE APPROACHED WITH SHORT PROGRAM SCRIPTS

- Strip all the private identifiers from a medical record.

- Find all the surgical procedures included in the dataset of surgical post-op notes, and annotate each procedure with its frequency of occurrence in the dataset.

- Index a book with the page location of all terms that are names of diseases.

- Find all the palindromes in a gene sequence database and arrange them by frequency of occurrence.

- Find the most common occurring sequence of octamers in the human genome database.

- Find all octamers that occur only once in the human genome database.

- Rank sequences from a gene expression array experiment based on levels of expression.

- From a patient database, find the diseases that have a chronologic relationship with another condition (e.g., chicken pox never occurs after shingles).

- Find all tumors associated with a gene fusion mutation.

- Collect 100 histopathologic images of liver disease from the Web.

One of my former math professors at MIT (Gian Carlo Rota) once said that every mathematician gets by on three chosen tricks. Once mastered, mathematicians approach all problems in terms of their three tricks. There is some truth to this. For my own part, most of the software programs that I have written are composed of 5 to 25 lines of code and use three little tricks (List 5.2.2). I have used many different programming languages. Whenever I need to program in a new language, I quickly search for the basic language tools that support my favorite three tricks, ignoring everything else in the language. I can usually create simple programs within a few hours of encountering an unfamiliar programming language.

LIST 5.2.2. THE THREE PROGRAMMING TRICKS IN MEDICAL INFORMATICS

- File parsing (opening a file and examining the contents of the file, one line at a time)

- Pattern matching (finding a fragment of parsed text that matches a word, a phrase, or a character pattern of interest)

- Assigning data structures to hold numbers or textual data that can be operated on by Perl commands

With very few exceptions, every biomedical computer task can be described as an exercise in these three tricks. Here is an example, written in pseudocode (List 5.2.3). Pseudocode programs are algorithms (the logical steps in a program) expressed in narrative text, rather than in the structured coding syntax of a programming language.

LIST 5.2.3. PSEUDOCODE TO COLLECT ALL THE LINES FROM A FILE THAT CONTAIN THE PHRASE "BIOMEDICAL INFORMATICS"

1. Open a file for reading. (Verbose equivalent: Get a file from the hard drive that has a particular name and prepare it so that the data in the file can be extracted and put into holders in the computer's memory.)

2. Parse the lines of the file. (Verbose equivalent: Grab the characters from the first line of the file and put it into a data holder that occupies a specific place in computer memory. Be prepared to repeat this for all the lines of the file.)

3. Collect all the lines that contain the phrase "biomedical informatics." (Verbose equivalent: As each line is placed in a holder in computer memory, determine whether the line contains the string "biomedical informatics" and if it does, add the held data to a structure called an array, which can hold many character strings, in sequence.)

4. When the file is exhausted, empty all the matching lines into an external file, opened for writing. (Verbose equivalent: At the end of the file parsing loop, take the array structure and transfer all the character strings from the array, in sequence, into a newly created file that has been prepared to accept data.)

This pseudocode uses all the tricks that you will need for 90% of your programming tasks: file parsing, pattern matching, and using a data structure (in this case, an array).

There are lots of excellent programming languages. Perl is popular among bioinformaticians for a variety of reasons (List 5.2.4), but other languages (Python, Ruby, Java) would be just as good. All the Perl scripts included in the book are very short, stressing a few lines of code that implement a specific algorithm. Python and Ruby programmers will have no problem reading Perl code and converting the short scripts to their preferred languages.

LIST 5.2.4. REASONS TO PROGRAM IN PERL

- Perl can be obtained at no cost.

- Perl is available for virtually every operating system and comes bundled into Unix and Linux distributions.

- Perl is extremely popular among bionformaticians.

- It takes just a few hours to learn enough Perl to write your own biomedical informatics programs.

- Perl programs tend to be much shorter and easier to understand than programs written in C or Java.

- A Perl script written for your computer will probably work on any other computer loaded with a Perl interpreter, even if the other computer has a different operating system.

- Unlike C, Perl comes with native pattern matching commands (so-called regular expressions) that are used in virtually every program in the field of biomedical informatics.

- There are many thousands of freely available Perl tools that perform a wide range of useful operations to extend the functionality of your own programs.

- Perl code can be written in a manner that looks much like simple narrative text (if you make the effort), making it easy for others to read.

- Once you have learned Perl, you can migrate to almost any other programming language with ease.

This chapter is written for people who do not know any programming language and who need a basic introduction to Perl.

5.3. JUST ENOUGH PERL

The purpose of this section is to provide you with just enough knowledge about Perl to create simple scripts for common tasks in biomedical informatics. Most readers will be able to do all their Perl programming by cutting and pasting lines from the example scripts into their own programs.

We will not be covering many of the programming skills that advanced programmers would deem essential (scoping, referencing, debugging, or object-oriented programming). There are innumerable books and online resources for the serious scholar. We will also omit discussion of good programming technique (e.g., using pragmas, distinguishing local and global variables, and optimizing code). The enthusiastic programmer should look elsewhere to improve his or her programming technique.

5.4. DOWNLOADING PERL

ActiveState currently has the most current Perl versions for many popular operating systems. Other sites offering free Perl downloads are www.perl.com and www.cpan.org. CPAN (Comprehensive Perl Archive Network) is an incredible resource for all Perl-related things, including new Perl modules. Perl interpreters for dozens of different operating systems are available from CPAN at http://www.cpan.org/ports/.

Installation procedures can vary greatly. Most installation procedures are easy and have Web-based instruction.

5.5. FILE OPERATIONS

For the biomedical scientist, perhaps the most fundamental programming task is to open a file and display its contents. Surprisingly, virtually all commercial word processors fail at this simple task. If you do not believe this, just try opening a 1 Gigabyte text file in your favorite word processor. Biomedical informaticians routinely need to open and read very large files composed of sequential plain-text records.

Perl excels at file manipulation. In a few lines of Perl, you can open a file of almost any size and directly access chunks of data from any location within the file (random file access). Perl will let you open multiple files at once, and it will let you iterate through all the files on a drive or on a network. Perl will let you extract and analyze data from a text file or a binary file. Perl will do these tasks very quickly and with just a few lines of code.

Why are file routines so important? Most biomedical data is accessible in file form. Virtually all genome, proteome, and array datasets are available as simple text files. The data elements are typically separated by commas or by tabs or (in the case of sentences) periods (List 5.5.1). We will see how Perl can quickly search through a file of 20 or 30 megabytes, look for string matches, and return all of the matching strings in about one second.

LIST 5.5.1. SAMPLE CONTENTS OF A TYPICAL FLAT-FILE, "TAXO.TXT" EXTRACTED FROM "TAXONOMY"

- SYNONYM: Bacillus aegyptius

- SYNONYM: Haemophilus aegyptius

- SYNONYM: Hemophilus conjunctivitidis

- SYNONYM: Haemophilus influenzae aegyptius
- SYNONYM: Bacillus conjunctivitidis
- SYNONYM: Bacterium aegyptiacum
- SYNONYM: Bacterium conjunctivitis
- SYNONYM: Bacterium pseudo conjunctivitidis

A short Perl script, open1.pl, opens a text file and prints the content, line by line (Lists 5.5.2 and 5.5.3).

LIST 5.5.2. PERL SCRIPT, OPEN1.PL, TO OPEN A FILE AND READ A FILE

```
#!/usr/bin/perl
open(FILE, "taxo.txt");
$line = " ";
while ($line ne "")
{
$line = <FILE>;
print $line;
}

exit;
```

LIST 5.5.3. OUTPUT OF OPEN1.PL

- C:\ftp>perl open1.pl
- SYNONYM: Bacillus aegyptius
- SYNONYM: Haemophilus aegyptius
- SYNONYM: Hemophilus conjunctivitidis
- SYNONYM: Haemophilus influenzae aegyptius
- SYNONYM: Bacillus conjunctivitidis
- SYNONYM: Bacterium aegyptiacum
- SYNONYM: Bacterium conjunctivitis
- SYNONYM: Bacterium pseudo conjunctivitidis

Your first Perl script opens and reads through a text file named `taxon.txt`. This output shows 8 lines from `taxonomy.dat`, a large data file exceeding 36 megabytes. We will be looking at `taxonomy.dat` later in the book. In the next few section, we will look more closely at our first Perl script.

5.6. PERL SCRIPT BASICS

The Perl script (named `open1.pl`) demonstrates the basic structure of every Perl program. First, notice that the Perl program is itself a text file and consists of character text. There is no special programming "environment" in Perl. You can use any text editor to create a Perl file. Notepad will work fine. If you use a word processor, you need to avoid the proprietary mark-up that word processors include in their documents. Make sure that you save the file as a plain-text file. Perl scripts should be given filenames that end with a ".`pl`" file extension.

When you want a Perl script to run, you simply call it from the command line.

A typical invocation of a Perl script may look like: `c:\>perl open1.pl` (followed by the return key).

Actually, in most systems, you do not need to type in the word "perl," because the system knows where the Perl executable is located and also knows that files ending in .`pl` are interpreted by the Perl executable. You may only need to enter the name of the script (followed by the return key), and your program will run (execute):

`c:\>open1.pl`

The opening line of the Perl script (`#!usr/bin/perl`) in the Unix/Linux environment lists the directory path to the Perl interpreter. Perl scripts downloaded from the Web may have all sorts of variations of the first line, depending on where the author's Perl script resides (e.g., `#!perl`, `#!user/local/bin/perl`, `#!usr/perl`).

If the Perl script does not reside in the same directory as your Perl interpreter or in your PATH (list of directories that your system searches to find Perl), then you may start your program from the Perl interpreter subdirectory and include the full path to the script, for instance:

`c:\perl>perl c:\scripts\open1.pl`

If this is not clear to you, please read the next few paragraphs, which are written for non-Linux users who are new to or unfamiliar with command-line instructions executed via a DOS prompt.

5.7. THE DIRECTORY PATH TO PERL

For non-Linux computers, command lines can be invoked through the MS-DOS shell. A command line is also available through the "Run" dialog box available by clicking on the "Start" button.

When your Perl interpreter is in the same subdirectory as your Perl script, your script will execute when you invoke "perl <name of script>" from the Perl subdirectory command prompt. It may prove impractical to always place your Perl scripts in the same directory in which your Perl interpreter resides. In the DOS system, there is an internally stored list of paths that the operating system searches whenever an executable program is invoked from the command line. You should add the directory in which your Perl interpreter resides to your operating system's path list, usually achievable by simply adding the path to Perl in the "path" statement of your system's autoexec.bat file. When the directory in which the Perl interpreter resides is listed in your system's Path, you can call the Perl interpreter from any directory or subdirectory on your hard drive, and your system will find Perl.

So, if your Perl script (anything.pl) is kept in the anywhere subdirectory, then you can execute the script with:

```
c:\anywhere>perl anything.pl
```

5.8. ACCESSING FILES

In order for the open1.pl program to work, there must be a file taxo.txt and, in this simple case, the taxo.txt file must reside in the same directory as the open1.pl Perl script.

The output of the file, appearing on the computer screen, consists of a copy of the original taxo.txt file.

5.9. THE OPEN1.PL SCRIPT, LINE BY LINE

Let's look at the open1.pl script (vida supra). The first line of the script has a specific format, consisting of the pound sign, followed by an exclamation point, followed by the directory path leading to the subdirectory in which the Perl interpreter resides. Think of this line as a header that reminds the computer that it is reading a Perl script. The meaning and the syntax requirements of the header line are somewhat platform-dependent. To make every system happy, be sure to include a header line in each script, and make sure that the header line begins with #! (so-called shebang—sharp or pound sign plus exclamation point) and has the word "perl" somewhere in the line. Many Perl programmers add optional switches to the top line of their Perl scripts that can change the behavior of the Perl compiler and enforce good coding technique.

The script begins with a command to open a file for reading:

```
open(FILE, "taxo.txt");
```

This simple command is one of the most powerful and useful Perl commands. When Perl encounters this command, it searches the current directory for the file named "taxo.txt". If it finds the file, then it assigns the file a filehandle, which is Perl's internal identifier for the file. In this case, the filehandle name is FILE. You should always choose filehandle names in uppercase. The file is set to begin reading at the beginning of the file and is ready to accept a variety of file operations, including reading a single line of text (using the <> notation), or moving to different locations in the file. These operations must be called using the assigned filehandle name, not the name of the file as it occurs in its directory. Notice that the line ends with a semicolon. Perl command statements always end with a semicolon. The most common error in writing any Perl script is the omission of the obligatory semicolon.

Although Perl provides a variety of parameters that alter the OPEN command, examples of the three most useful are:

```
open(HANDLE, "some.txt")
```

This opens the named file, "some.txt", for reading, assigning the supplied filehandle, "HANDLE".

```
open(OUT ">other.txt")
```

This opens the named file, "other.txt", for writing (file writing is determined by the ">" parameter), assigning the supplied filehandle name, "OUT", and setting the first write operation for the beginning of the file. Writing to the beginning of a file will overwrite any preexisting text in the file.

```
open(FUN ">>third.txt")
```

This opens the named file, "third.txt", for appending (file appending is determined by the ">>" parameter), assigning the supplied filehandle name, "FUN", and setting the first append operation for the end of the file.

The next line of the script is:

```
$line = " ";
```

This command creates a new **string variable**. We arbitrarily name the variable "*$line*" and assign it the space character (i.e., the character created whenever you push the keyboard's space key). We could have chosen almost any character other than the empty character ("") to initialize the variable. The beginquotes and endquotes are Perl's way of delineating a string. In Perl, the "=" operator assigns whatever is on the right side of the operator to the variable on the left side of the operator. In Perl, every variable begins with the "$" sign. The second most common error when writing Perl files is to forget to put a "$" sign in front of every named variable.

The next line is:

```
while ($line ne "")
```

This is a conditional statement. The word "while," followed by an expression enclosed by a set of parentheses, constitutes a conditional expression. This tells Perl to evaluate the expression inside the parentheses to determine whether it is true or false. The "while-block" is entered only if the expression is evaluated to true. Otherwise, Perl skips to the next command following the while-block. Perl knows where the block starts and ends by looking for the paired curly brackets designating the beginning "{" and ending "}" of the block. The while-block will loop forever until the while statement becomes false or until some instruction within the while-block tells Perl to exit the block.

In later sections, we will learn several other forms of conditional blocks in Perl, and we will learn several easy ways to gracefully exit an otherwise endless loop. We will also learn that blocks can be nested (conditional statements within conditional statements). The most common mistake when writing a Perl script is to have unbalanced sets of curly brackets surrounding blocks. A consistent programming style (e.g., indenting curly brackets and allowing a separate line for each bracket) will reduce such errors.

The expression within the parentheses is:

```
$line ne ""
```

Perl has several string comparison operators: ne, eq, lt, and gt. These stand for not equals, equals, less than, and greater than. These should not be confused with Perl's numeric comparison operators: ==, >, <, >= and <=. A common mistake for new Perl programmers is to use a string comparison operator (ne, eq, lt, gt) on numeric variables or to use a numeric comparison operator (==, >, <, >= or <=) on string variables. The use of "ne" tells Perl to determine whether the two string variables flanking the "ne" operator are "not equal" (i.e., contain different strings). If they are not equal (i.e., their inequality evaluates to true), then Perl proceeds to evaluate the command statements within the block.

The "" represents the empty string (i.e., a variable that contains nothing between the quotes). We know that the first test of the while condition will evaluate to "true" because we initiated the variable *$line* by making it nonempty (placing a "space" character into the variable). Since *$line* is not equal to the empty string, Perl will proceed to evaluate the commands in the while-block.

The first command statement in the block is: `$line = <FILE>;`

The equals sign in Perl is not a logical test for equality (for that, you will use the == sign). Remember, the "=" operator tells Perl to take the value on the right and put it into the variable on the left. In this case it takes whatever is in `<FILE>` and puts it into *$line*. When Perl sees `<FILE>` it automatically reads from the file referred to by the file-handle `FILE`, returning one line, the next line from the file. In this case, a line is removed from "`taxo.txt`" and put into the variable *$line*. Perl has now advanced one line in the file and is ready to read the next line. When Perl takes a line from the file, the file is not altered in any way. Reading a line from a file is like reading a line from a book.

The next line is:

```
print $line;
```

This tells Perl to take the contents of *$line* (containing a line from the file `taxo.txt`) and display it in the default output device, your computer monitor. In the next section, we describe how you can easily instruct Perl to send the variable to another file.

The next line is the end-loop curly bracket ("}"). This marks the logical end of the loop and tells Perl to go back up to the loop-initiating line (in this case the while condition) for evaluation. If the while condition evaluates as true, then the loop is entered again.

In this program, the while loop is entered again and again, as long as there are lines remaining in the file `taxo.txt`. When the file has been entirely read, the block puts the empty string into the *$line* variable. Finally, the while loop evaluates as false because when the file is empty, the statement that *$line* is not equal to the empty string becomes false. When the while condition becomes false, the program bypasses the while loop and goes to the line that follows the loop, in this case, the "`exit;`" line. This tells Perl that the script has finished.

5.10. AN 8-LINE PERL WORD PROCESSOR

Now that we have slogged through the preliminaries, let us try a more ambitious, but equally brief, Perl script, `mywp.pl`. This short program takes your keyed-in screen input and puts it into two different files, one line at a time (List 5.10.1).

What are the two files that the program creates? One file is named mynew.txt. This file contains only the text that you entered during the current session of the mywp.pl script. If there was any text in the mynew.txt file when you invoked the mywp.pl script, then that text will be lost forever.

The other file is named mycumu.txt. This file contains the accumulated input of everything you have ever entered using the mywp.pl script. Even if you have started the script every day of your life and typed all day each time you have used the script, all your typed words over your entire lifetime will be in the mycumu.txt file. Try doing that with a word processor!

LIST 5.10.1. MYWP.PL, A RIDICULOUSLY SHORT TEXT EDITOR IN PERL

```perl
#!/usr/bin/perl
open (OUT, ">>mycumu.txt");
open (NEW, ">mynew.txt");
$line = " ";
until ($line eq "\n")
{
$line = <STDIN>;
print OUT $line;
print NEW $line;
}

exit;
```

How does the mywp.pl script work? The first two lines of the script create the cumulative file mycumu.txt.

```perl
open (OUT, ">>mycumu.txt");
```

This tells Perl to open a file called mycumu.txt as an "append" file, a type of file whose prior contents are not lost when the file is opened for writing. If the file does not already exist, then Perl will create the file for you. The file is assigned the OUT filehandle.

The next line is:

```perl
open (NEW, ">mynew.txt");
```

This opens a file for writing. Any preexisting text in the "mynew.txt" file will be lost. Perl will create a new file named "mynew.txt" if one does not already exist.

With the files created and waiting for your input, the script creates an until loop that will accept keyed input forever or until you press the return key twice (List 5.10.2).

LIST 5.10.2. UNTIL LOOP IN PERL

```
$line = " ";
until ($line eq "\n") #loop stops when all you've entered is
    #the return key
{
$line = <STDIN>; #waits for the next line of input
print OUT $line; #appends to the cumulative file
print NEW $line; #writes to the current script-session file

}
```

You are finished. In a few lines of Perl, you have made a powerful word processor that will continue adding text to the mycumu.txt file, regardless of the size of the file. Perl will open the file and be ready instantly for your input, even if the file is a Gigabyte in length. The word processor can be invoked just by typing "perl mywp.pl" at the command prompt. It will even keep a current session file for you in case you only want to review the most recent script session.

List 5.10.2 introduces another Perl device, the "#" comment. When a "#" occurs on a command line, Perl ignores the line-text that follows. This device allows Perl programmers to add comments within scripts, without confusing the Perl interpreter.

5.11. DO NOT PANIC—PERL WILL FORGIVE YOU

Though Perl is a forgiving language, some scripts occasionally "hang" (fail to execute) and leave you waiting for a screen that does not respond to plaintive mouse clicks and pathetic jabs at the return key. Do not worry. Your computer is fine. Pressing the control-key and the break key together (control-break) tells Perl to give up and returns you to the command prompt. Sometimes it takes a few seconds for Perl to realize that it must stop, but this technique almost always works. If all else fails, control-alt-delete will take you out of the DOS environment.

You may notice that when you compose a Perl script, it may often fail to compile the first time you try to execute the program. This is okay. Perl begins each execution of a program by interpreting your script. If there are syntax errors, then Perl exits the script and indicates the error. Typically, the Perl error explanation is sufficient for you to go back into the script and correct the problem. It has been my experience that a few types of errors account for the bulk of script failures (List 5.11.1). Perl has an assortment of tricks that make it easy to track and debug errors, and these methods are described in most Perl books. Because the purpose of this section is to teach readers how they might write simple and short Perl scripts, the standard error messages displayed by the Perl interpreter will suffice.

LIST 5.11.1. COMMON ERRORS IN PERL SCRIPTS

- Perl blocks must be balanced with curly brackets. Every block (e.g., while, if, for, unless, foreach) must have a beginning curly bracket,"{" and a balanced closing curly bracket, "}". This can become hairy in scripts that have multi-nested blocks.

- Command lines must end with a semicolon.

- String variables must be pre-pended with a "$", as in *$date.*

- Spelling is important. Perl cannot interpret a misspelled command or variable.

- An uppercase character has a different ASCII value than its lowercase equivalent. With few exceptions, you will find it useful to maintain case consistency in Perl scripts.

- Characters that serve as reserved Perl symbols must be backslashed if they are used as string characters. For example, use \. \/ \\ \$ if you want to use ./\ or $ as characters. There are exceptions to this rule: \n,\d, and \w are reserved symbols and never refer to the letters n, d, and w. The strange and nonintuitive use of backslashes in Perl takes some mental adjustment and accounts for the "leaning toothpick syndrome" in Perl scripts. Complex regular expressions often resemble toothpicks tossed amidst string characters.

- Certain operations must be enclosed by parentheses (e.g., if (1 == 2), not (if 1 == 2).

- The "=" operator assigns a value and does not test for equality. To test for equality, use "==" if you are comparing two numbers and

> use "eq" if you are comparing two strings. Remember that string comparison operators (eq, ne, lt, gt) are different from number comparison operators (==, >, <).
>
> • Do not use an "=" operator when you really want to use the regex comparison operator, "=~".

What have we learned so far (List 5.11.2)?

LIST 5.11.2. SUMMARY OF THE FIRST PERL PROGRAMMING SECTIONS

- Perl scripts are simple text files.

- Perl scripts should be named using the .pl extension.

- Perl is a quintessential command-line language. At the command prompt, run your scripts by typing perl, then the name of the script, then the return key (on some systems, you needn't include the name perl).

- Perl scripts start off with a header line.

- Perl commands end with a semicolon.

- Perl blocks are delineated by curly brackets ({ }).

- You can assign strings to variables by using the assignment operator, "=".

- You can read, write, or append to files after using the "open" command.

- You can add comments to script lines, after a "#" sign.

5.12. PSEUDOCODE FOR A GENERAL BIOMEDICAL INFORMATICS PROGRAM

Virtually every program I write has a common structure (List 5.12.1) and length (10–40 lines). My programs tend to take named files as input and produce named files as the output. The input files can be narrative text or arrays of data, or sequential records. The files are usually found on my computer's hard drive, but I occasionally write programs to parse through files scattered across the Internet. With the exception of the actual values of variables, most of my programs can be constructed from bits and pieces of my previously written programs. The generalizability of scripted code and the ability to accomplish most tasks in a few lines of code are compelling reasons to learn programming.

LIST 5.12.1. PSEUDOCODE THAT OUTLINES THE GENERAL CONSTRUCTION OF A PERL SCRIPT

```
header (shebang) line;
input something;
  if (something evaluates to true)
    {
    do something;
     for or while (some condition)
       {
       do something;
       }
    do something;
    do something;
    }
  for or while (some condition)
    {
    do something;
      if (something evaluates to true)
        {
        do something;
        do something;
        do something;
        }
    output something;
      }
exit;
```

5.13. INTERACTIVELY READING LINES FROM A FILE

Opening large text files in word processors is always a frustrating experience. Depending on your system memory and your word processor, trying to open a large (many megabyte) file can crash or stall your software. Many of the files used in biomedical research exceed 100 Megabytes and cannot be opened by word processor applications.

Perl can read any file and has rapid access to any location in the file. Just use the open command to open a file and use seek() to move to any byte location in the file. Follow that with a read() command and Perl will promptly export a specified length of text into a variable or file or display the text on your screen.

When I have downloaded a large file, the first thing I like to do is to read a few pages starting at the beginning. The bigread.pl Perl script will open any file and put the first 20 lines on your monitor (List 5.14.1). Every time you press the return key, another 20 lines will display. You can key through the whole file if you like.

5.14. SCANNING ENORMOUS FILES QUICKLY

LIST 5.14.1. PERL SCRIPT BIGREAD.PL

```perl
#!/usr/bin/perl
#This script lets you page through enormous files,
#20 lines at a time, with no file load time.
print "What file do you want to read?";
$filename = <STDIN>;
chomp($filename);
open (TEXT, $filename)||die"Can't open file";
$line = " ";
while ($line ne "") #comment: while $line is not equal to empty
    {
    for ($count = 1; $count <= 20; $count++)
    {
    $line = <TEXT>;
    print $line;
    }
    print "Type QUIT if you want to quit. Otherwise press
any key\n";
    $response = <STDIN>;
    if ($response =~ /QUIT/i)
      {
      last;
      }
    }
exit;
```

LIST 5.14.2. PARTIAL OUTPUT OF FILE-READING SCRIPT,
BIGREAD.PL

```
C:\ftp>perl bigread.pl
What file do you want to read?e:\omim.txt
*RECORD*
*FIELD* NO [100050 [*FIELD* TI [100050 AARSKOG SYNDROME
[*FIELD* TX [Grier et al. (1983) reported father and 2 sons
with typical Aarskog [syndrome, including short stature,
hypertelorism, and shawl scrotum. [.
    .

    .

sons and that this suggested autosomal dominant inheritance.
Actually, the mother seemed less severely affected, compat-
ible with X-linked

Type QUIT if you want to quit. Otherwise press any key
```

How does the bigread.pl script work? The first two lines simply prompt the user for the name of the file to be opened (List 5.14.2).

```
print "What file do you want to read?";
$filename = <STDIN>;

chomp($filename);
```

The print command tells Perl to put the argument string into the standard output (STDOUT), which is your computer screen.

Look at the next line. STDIN is Perl's name for the standard input, your keyboard. This statement tells Perl to wait for input keyed into your monitor. Perl is prepared to wait forever for you to reply to the "What file do you want to read?" prompt. Type in the name of a file and then press the return key. The command line tells Perl to take whatever is keyed into the monitor and put it into the variable *$filename*. When you press the return key, the text passed to STDIN is automatically appended with a newline character. In many instances, you do not really want the newline character to be attached to your string, so Perl provides a simple way to cut the newline character from the end of a character string (if there is one). It is called chomp.

The next few lines of the script are:

```
open (TEXT, $filename)||die"Can't open file";
$line = " ";
```

```
while ($line ne "")
{
for ($count = 1; $count <= 20; $count++)
{
$line = <TEXT>;
print $line;

}
```

Perl opens the file that you provided in response to the prompt (now placed in the variable *$filename*) and assigns it the filehandle TEXT. When Perl opens a file, it is ready to start reading from the first byte in the file.

We will make a new variable, *$line*, that will hold the lines from the file. We will need to be able to read the file line by line until there is nothing left in the file. We will use the "empty" condition for *$line* as the conditional test that we have not yet reached the end of the file. A variable is empty when it contains nothing. The string representation of empty is "", indicating that there is nothing between the beginning and the end of the string. Because we will stop reading lines when *$line* is empty, we must initialize *$line* with a nonempty value. We assign " " (a space character) as the initial value of line. We could have chosen any character.

Next, we begin a nested conditional block.

We want to read only twenty lines at a time. We use a for-loop to restrict iterations to a set of conditions.

The syntax of the "for" loop is:

- for (*expression*1; *expression*2; *expression*3)

- *expression*1 is the index variable that marks the first iteration (usually 1)

- *expression*2 is the index where the iterations stop

- *expression*3 is the expression that indicates how the index will be incremented

In the example:

```
for ($count = 1; $count <= 20; $count++)
```

Set the index to one, and increment the value of the index by 1 with each iteration, but stop the loop when the index exceeds 20.

Note that $count++ is just a Perl shortcut for indicating that the value in *$count* should be incremented by 1, and is equivalent to the assignment:

```
$count = $count +1;
```

So, for twenty loops, the program takes a line of text from the file whose filehandle is TEXT, and displays that line of text in the standard output (the computer screen).

Needless to say, this loop executes instantaneously in Perl. Once the loop is completed and 20 lines are shown, the for loop finishes and the next line of Perl is interpreted and executed.

The Perl script advances to:

```
print "Type QUIT if you want to quit. Otherwise press any key\n";
    $response = <STDIN>;
    if ($response =~ /QUIT/i)
      {
      last;
      }
    }

exit;
```

A line of text appears on the screen, prompting the user to press a key (to see more text) or to exit the program by typing QUIT (followed by the return key, of course).

The line

```
$response = <STDIN>;
```

tells Perl to wait until the user responds to the prompt. When the user types a response, the typed character string is assigned to the *$response* variable.

Then Perl performs a pattern match on the character string containing the user's response.

```
if ($response =~ /QUIT/i)
```

Perl evaluates the if expression (the stuff in parentheses) to determine its truth. In Perl, an expression is true if it does not evaluate to 0 or False. Had we simply written "if (5)", Perl would evaluate the if expression as true (because 5 is never 0 or False). In this case, Perl needs to evaluate the pattern `/QUIT/i` to determine whether the pattern matches the variable *$response* (the variable containing the user's reply to the screen prompt).

In Perl, patterns are typically represented as regular expressions delimited by slants:

```
/EXPRESSION/
```

The simplest pattern is a character string. In this case, we use the word "QUIT". If the string "QUIT" is contained in the variable response, then the if expression will evaluate to True and the if block will begin.

Notice that the pattern is followed by the letter i. The i tells Perl that the pattern match is case-insensitive:

```
~ /QUIT/i,
```

The following items will match the pattern expression.

QUIT quit Quit quiT fjsdaklaQuitasdklaf aasquiTasklfafsd

All of these items contain QUIT (case-insensitive).

In this case, the if block would instruct the program to end the loop (using the "last" command). Because the loop is finished, Perl advances to the next line after the loop, which is the exit command. The exit command, as you might expect, ends the program.

What have we learned in this section (List 5.14.3)?

LIST 5.14.3. SUMMARY OF THE SECOND PERL PROGRAMMING SECTION

- Conditional tests
- How to prompt a user for input
- Looping using for() and while() blocks
- Constructing if() blocks
- Simple pattern matching

5.15. GETTING JUST WHAT YOU WANT WITH PERL REGULAR EXPRESSIONS

Regular expressions add enormous power to Perl scripts (List 5.15.1).

LIST 5.15.1. THINGS YOU CAN DO WITH A ONE-LINE REGULAR EXPRESSION

- Collect the lines from a file that contain a specific word, phrase, number, or character pattern

- Rearrange the content of lines based on matching words, phrases, numbers, or character patterns

- Substitute any alphanumeric character string for any other, for the entire file

Perl programmers pride themselves on what they can do with a single regular expression (regex, for short). Regular expressions can vary from the simple (e.g., matching a specific character string) to the ridiculously obscure. Most Perl language primers cover regular expressions extensively, and at least one book has been devoted exclusively to regular expressions. For the purposes of biomedical informatics, we will describe the rudiments of regular expressions and provide some of the most useful patterns for matching, substituting, rearranging, and extracting data (Lists 5.16.1 and 5.16.2).

5.16. PSEUDOCODE FOR COMMON USES OF REGEX (REGULAR EXPRESSION PATTERN MATCHING)

LIST 5.16.1. USING THE MATCH OPERATOR WITH REGULAR EXPRESSIONS

- for all the lines of a given file:

    {

    put the next line from the file into some variable;

    check the line to see if it matches your regular expression;

    {

- if the line matches the regular expression

    {

    do something with it, like put it into another file;

    or do an operation on the matching value;

    }

LIST 5.16.2. USING THE SUBSTITUTION OPERATOR WITH REGULAR EXPRESSIONS

- for all the lines of a given file:

  {

  put the next line from the file into some variable;

  do a substitution on all of the parts of the line that match your regular expression;

  do something with the revised line, like rearranging it and then putting the rearranged line into another file;

  }

Though simple-minded, the list describes a scripting process for the most common tasks performed by Perl scripts. That is why Perl is called the "Practical Extraction and Report Language." If you can understand the basic scripting model for parsing files and extracting or substituting text elements based on regular expression matches, then you will have the basic set of Perl skills used in biomedical informatics.

5.17. REGULAR EXPRESSION SYNTAX

LIST 5.17.1. PATTERN MATCH OPTIONS

- g Match globally, (find all occurrences)

- i Do case-insensitive pattern matching

- m Treat string as multiple lines

- o Compile pattern only once

- ^ Match the beginning of the line

- . Match any character (except newline)

- $ Match the end of the line (or before newline at the end)

- | Alternation, accepts either of the patterns flanking the "|" character

- () Grouping, designates a segment of the matching term that can be assigned to a variable. Groups are assigned variables $1, $2, $3 sequentially as they appear in the regex expression.

- [] Character class, tells Perl to look for a match to any of the characters included within the square brackets

- * Match 0 or more times

- + Match 1 or more times

- ? Match 1 or 0 times

- {n} Match exactly n times

- {n,} Match at least n times

- {n,m} Match at least n but not more than m times

- \n newline character

- \W Match a nonword character

- \s Match a whitespace character

- \S Match a nonwhitespace character

- \d Match a digit character

- \D Match a nondigit character

The example below uses a public domain text from Project Gutenberg. Project Gutenberg is a highly successful effort to create plain-text electronic files of many classic novels. Novels that have outlived their copyright protection fall into the public domain. Edward Gibbons (1737–1794) wrote a fascinating and erudite account of ancient Rome in "The History of the Decline and Fall of the Roman Empire." This public domain text can be downloaded at no cost from:

http://www.gutenberg.org/dirs/etext96/1dfre10.txt

For the example below, we use Volume 1, with filename, 1DFRE10.TXT, size 1,656,383 bytes. We will use this file for other scripts, but any large plain-text file will suffice.

We will now write a practical Perl script. In the field of machine translation, narrative text must be parsed into sentences, and the sentences become the grammatical units that are interpreted by translation software. We will write a simple program that takes narrative text and breaks the text into discrete sentences, assigning each sentence to a line of an output file. To write a sentence parser in just a few lines of Perl, we will utilize everything we have learned about Perl pattern matching.

The following 7-line script (sentence.pl) parses through the text file "1DFRE10.TXT" producing an output file named "1DFRE10.OUT". The output file lists the sequentially occurring sentences from the text file on separate lines (List 5.17.2).

LIST 5.17.2. SENTENCE.PL **PERL SCRIPT, WHICH CREATES A FILE WHEREIN EACH NEW SENTENCE BEGINS ON A NEW LINE**

```perl
#!/usr/local/bin/perl
open (TEXT, "1DFRE10.TXT")||die"Can't open file";
open (OUT,">1DFRE10.OUT")||die"Can't open file";
undef($/);
$string = <TEXT>;
$string =~ s/[\n]+//g;
$string =~ s/([^A-Z]+\.[ ]{1,2})([A-Z])/$1\n\n$2/g;
print OUT $string;

exit;
```

The first command of sentence.pl opens a file for reading, and the second command opens a file for writing.

By default, when Perl reads a line of text, it accepts characters until it comes to a newline character, marking the end of a line. Perl allows the programmer to define (or undefine) the character that signifies the end of a line by modifying the built-in record separator, $/. By using the undef operator on $/, Perl is deprived of an endline indicator, so Perl slurps the entire file into a variable when it comes upon the <TEXT> (line assignment) command:

```perl
undef($/);

$string = <TEXT>;
```

The next line deploys the substitution operator, which has the following syntax:

```perl
$string =~ s/<pattern that you match>/<replacement pattern>/options;
```

In this command, every newline character is replaced by a space. The g option at the end of the command ensures that Perl will repeat the substitution for every instance of a pattern match:

```
$string =~ s/[\n]+/ /g;
```

This ensures that the file contained in *$string* no longer contains any line breaks.

Next, every occurrence of a succession of characters that are not uppercase letters, followed by a period, followed by 1 or 2 spaces, followed by an uppercase letter, is replaced by a string consisting of the value of the first matched parenthetical expression, ([^A-Z]+\.[ ]{1,2}), which Perl designates as $1, followed by two newline characters, \n, followed by the second matched parenthetical expression ([A-Z]), which Perl designates as $2:

```
$string =~ s/([^A-Z]+\.[ ]{1,2})([A-Z])/$1\n\n$2/g;
```

This regex command is very powerful. It takes the entire file held in the *$string* variable (which contains no line breaks) and inserts two line break characters at patterns that are likely to occur at the ends of sentences.

Think about what constitutes a good marker for the end of a sentence by observing the transition between sentence 1 and sentence 2 from the previous paragraph:

```
"werful. It tak"
```

You find that lowercase letters are followed by a period, followed by two spaces, followed by an uppercase letter. This is the kind of pattern generalized by the regular expression.

This script is not foolproof. But it does a fair job of converting a text into a list of sentences, each separated by two newline characters.

5.18. REMOVING PERIODS THAT DO NOT DELINEATE SENTENCES

As an exercise, let us try to find a way to eliminate the periods in sentences that do not signify the end of a sentence (Lists 5.18.1 and 5.18.2). You may find this example very difficult. It is easy to write regular expressions that are opaque to casual inspection. However, if you can understand the regular expression used in this example, then you will be well prepared for any free-text parsing.

LIST 5.18.1. `PERIODS.PL,` A PERL SCRIPT FOR REMOVING PERIODS THAT DO NOT DELINEATE SENTENCES

```
#!/usr/bin/perl
#replaces periods with *, except when period marks end of
#sentence
$k = "Mr. P.I.N. Ph.D. M.D. 0.3 .4 5. 4.6.7.8.9 end_of_sen-
tence. Hello";
$firstvalue = $k;
$k =~ s/\b([\w\d]*)\.+(?=[\w\d]*)(?! [A-Z])/$1\*$2/g;
print "$firstvalue =>\n$k";

exit;
```

LIST 5.18.2. OUTPUT OF `PERIODS.PL`

- `C:\ftp>perl disbrev2.pl`

- `Mr. Dr. P.I.N. Ph.D. M.D. 0.3 .4 5. 4.6.7.8.9 end_of_-`
  `sentence. Hello =>`

- `Mr* Dr* P*I*N* Ph*D* M*D* 0*3 *4 5* 4*6*7*8*9 end_of_-`
  `sentence. Hello`

Here are some additional commonly used regular expressions. Readers are encouraged to study these or to include them in short Perl test scripts to see how these regex expressions perform on sample text (List 5.18.3).

LIST 5.18.3 SOME REGEX (REGULAR EXPRESSION) OPERATIONS

- $string =~ s/^ +//o; removes leading spaces from a character string

- $string =~s/ +$//o; removes trailing spaces from a character string

- $string =~s/ +/ /g; changes all sequences of one or more spaces to just a single space

- $string =~s/\n//g; gets rid of newline (sometimes called line-break) characters in your string

- $string =~s/\b(\w+\.[ ]{1,2})([A-Z])/$1\n$2/g; finds the most common sentence delimiter (a word followed by a period followed by one or two spaces, followed by an uppercase letter) and substitutes a newline character so that the new sentence begins on a new line. $1 is the text that matches the first parenthesized expression. $2 is the text that matches the second parenthesized expression.

- $string =~ tr/A-Z/a-z/; converts every uppercase letter to a lowercase letter using the translate operator (tr/a-z/A-Z/ does the opposite)

- $string = lc($string); converts every uppercase letter to a lower-case letter using the lc operator (uc($string) does the opposite)

- $string =~s/\<[^\<]+\>//g; removes angle-bracketed expressions, such as HTML or XML markup

5.19. COUNTING ALL THE WORDS IN A TEXT FILE

Let us try another Perl script, this time using the `split()` command and introducing the concept of a Perl array. The script `wc.pl` counts the words in a text file (List 5.19.1).

LIST 5.19.1. WC.PL PERL SCRIPT, WHICH COUNTS THE WORDS IN A FILE IN FIVE COMMANDS

```perl
#!/usr/local/bin/perl
open (TEXT, "1DFRE10.TXT");
undef($/);
$all_text = <TEXT>;
@wordarray = split(/[\n\s]+/, $all_text);
print scalar(@wordarray);

exit;
```

The text of Volume 1 of "The History of the Decline and Fall of the Roman Empire" is opened for reading and assigned a handle name, "TEXT":

```perl
open (TEXT, "1DFRE10.TXT");
```

The line delimiter is undefined, so that when a line is called by Perl, the entire file is slurped into the variable:

```perl
undef($/);

$all_text = <TEXT>;
```

The next line uses a new command, the `split()` operator:

```perl
@wordarray = split(/[\n\s]+/, $all_text);
```

Split takes a character string, splits it at each matching instance of a pattern, and puts the fragments into an array.

For example, the following command line splits a word at every occurrence of the character "i":

```
@array = split(/i/,"Mississippi");
```

@array becomes a list of ordered items:

```
M
```

```
ss
```

```
ss
```

```
pp
```

In this case, @array = ("M","ss","ss","pp"). Perl starts counting items at zero, so "M" is the zeroth element of the array named @array. Notice that "ss" appears as two different array elements (the first and the second elements of the array).

In the script, Perl is commanded to split the character string that holds the entire text of Volume 1 of "The History of the Decline and Fall of the Roman Empire" and to split the string wherever there is one or more occurrences of a linebreak (the \n character) or a space:

```
@wordarray = split(/[\n\s]+/, $all_text);
```

This creates an array of all the words in the text. The scalar operation returns the size of the array. The size of the array is simply the number of words in the text.

5.20. FINDING THE FREQUENCY OF OCCURRENCE OF EACH WORD IN A TEXT FILE (ZIPF DISTRIBUTION)

George Kingsley Zipf (1902–1950) gave us Zipf's law, asserting that in a text corpus, the frequency of any word is roughly inversely proportional to its rank in the frequency table (63). This means that the second most frequently occurring word in a text might occur about half as frequently as the first most frequently occurring word in a text.

A practical way of interpreting Zipf's law is that a small amount of words account for most of the occurrences of words in any text. A Zipf distribution is a listing of the different words in a text, in the descending order of their occurrences. The Zipf distribution of this paragraph is shown in List 5.20.1.

LIST 5.20.1. THE ZIPF DISTRIBUTION OF THE PRIOR PARAGRAPH

- `c:\ftp>perl zipf.pl`
- 00007 of
- 00005 a
- 00004 the
- 00003 words
- 00003 is
- 00003 in
- 00002 zipf
- 00002 text
- 00002 occurrences
- 00002 distribution
- 00001 zipf's
- 00001 way
- 00001 this
- 00001 their
- 00001 that
- 00001 small
- 00001 shown
- 00001 see
- 00001 practical
- 00001 paragraph
- 00001 order
- 00001 most
- 00001 listing
- 00001 list
- 00001 law
- 00001 interpreting
- 00001 for
- 00001 different

- 00001 descending

- 00001 any

- 00001 amount

- 00001 account

Notice that Zipf's law was not strictly obeyed. The second most frequently occurring word, "a," occurred at nearly the same frequency as the most frequently occurring word. Zipf would surely have insisted that his law is tuned to large texts. A few sentences cannot serve to test Zipf's law.

When the Zipf script parses the entire text of Volume 1 of "The History of the Decline and Fall of the Roman Empire," the first 10 lines of output are shown in List 5.20.2. Zipf's observation that the ranked frequency of occurrence of words in a text drops inversely to its rank seems to hold.

LIST 5.20.2. THE FIRST TEN ITEMS IN THE ZIPF DISTRIBUTION OF "THE DECLINE AND FALL OF THE ROMAN EMPIRE"

- 26856 the

- 18032 of

- 09136 and

- 06026 to

- 04654 a

- 04155 in

- 03170 was

- 03081 his

- 02815 by

- 02391 that

Computational linguists rely on Zipf distributions to identify high frequency, low information words that delimit phrases of high information content. Zipf distributions are used to build nomenclatures and indexes. They can be useful for tracking the occurrence of misspelled words. Zipf distributions can be used as a "signature" for a text and as part of methods to detect plagiaristic text or to rank textual concepts.

With Perl, a Zipf distribution for text files of any size can be created with just six command lines (List 5.20.3).

LIST 5.20.3. `ZIPF.PL`, **A PERL SCRIPT THAT CREATES A ZIPF DISTRIBUTION IN SIX COMMANDS**

```perl
#!/usr/local/bin/perl
open (TEXT, "1DFRE10.TXT");
open (OUT, ">1DFRE10.OUT");
undef($/);
$all_text = <TEXT>;
$all_text = lc($all_text);
$all_text =~s/[^a-z\-\']//g;
@wordarray = split(/[\n\s]+/, $all_text);
foreach $thing (@wordarray)
   {
   $freq{$thing}++;
   }
#The Zipf list finished. The next lines just display the
#distribution.
while ((my $key, my $value) = each(%freq))
   {
   $value = "00000" . $value;
   $value = substr($value,-5,5);
   push (@termarray, "$value $key")
   }
@finalarray = reverse (sort (@termarray));
print join("\n",@finalarray);

exit;
```

This script works very much like our previously described word counting script. The brunt of the computational work occurs when the text is split into individual words that are ported into an array variable.

```perl
$all_text = lc($all_text);
$all_text =~ s/[^a-z\-\']//g;

@wordarray = split(/[\n\s]+/,$all_text);
```

Perl has a simple command for converting strings to lowercase, `lc()`, the lowercase operator. Not surprisingly, Perl has an uppercase operator, `uc()`, for converting all the characters of a string to uppercase. In this case, the lowercase operator is applied to the entire text held in the variable *$all_text*.

Also, we are only interested in words, not punctuation. The substitution operator, s/[^a-z\-\']/ /g, removes all characters that are not lowercase a through z, a hyphen, or an apostrophe (i.e., removes all characters that are not found in words). Remember that the caret in an expression block forces negation on the expression. So [^a-z\-\'] matches everything that is NOT lowercase a through z, a hyphen, or an apostrophe.

The next three lines of the script count the frequency of occurrence of each word in the array, using a foreach block:

```
foreach $thing (@wordarray)
    {
    $freq{$thing}++;

    }
```

The foreach block moves sequentially through an array, item by item for each loop, assigning each encountered item to the $thing variable for each loop.

The $freq{$thing}++ introduces a new type of data structure that Perl and many other programming languages use extensively—the associative array. Associative arrays are also known as dictionaries, keyed lists, or hashes (not to be confused with one-way hashes, which will be discussed in Chapter 11).

An associative array consists of an unordered collection of key/value pairs. An example of items in a Perl associative array follows in List 5.20.4.

LIST 5.20.4. EXAMPLE OF AN ASSOCIATIVE ARRAY, %PATIENT_WEIGHT

```
$patient_weight{"John Public"} = 155;
$patient_weight{"Mary Smith"} = 110;
$patient_weight{"Jules Berman"} = 195;

$patient_weight{"Jules Berman"}++; #evaluates to 196
```

In the example, there is an associative array of key/value pairs, and the name of the associative array is %patient_weight. Perl requires a "%" prefix to designate an associative array (e.g., %patient_weight). Perl assigns the individual key/value elements of an associate array with a specific syntax (e.g., $patient_weight{"Jules Berman"} = 195;). "Jules Berman" is the key, and "195" is the value. Once a key/value pair is assigned, a key's value can be accessed (e.g., $patient_weight{"Jules Berman"} will evaluate to 195). Notice that while the name of the associative array is prefixed with a "%" sign, the name of a key/value pair contained in the array is prefixed with a "$" sign. This is because associative array members are strings.

The last line of the list applies Perl's "increment" operation to the value of the array key:

```
$patient_weight{"Jules Berman"}++;
```

This operation takes the value of $patient_weight{"Jules Berman"} and increments it by one, yielding 195 + 1 = 196. Once this operation is completed the value of $patient_weight{"Jules Berman"} is modified, and future invocations of $patient_weight{"Jules Berman"} will evaluate as 196.

Returning to the Zipf script, we can see that one line of Perl is sufficient to transform an array of items (some repeated) into an associative array wherein the value of each key is the number of times that the key occurs in the original array.

```
foreach $thing (@wordarray)
    {
    $freq{$thing}++;

    }
```

As each array item is parsed, it is assigned to the variable, *$thing*, and looped through the list of instructions for the loop block. In this case, the array that is being parsed is the sequence of words appearing in Volume 1 of "The History of the Decline and Fall of the Roman Empire."

The loop itself contains just one instruction:

```
$freq{$thing}++;
```

This line creates an associative array element, with a key of the string variable *$thing* (corresponding to an occurrence of a word in the text) and a value corresponding to an incremented count of the number of times that the word has been looped through the block. If the loop encounters a word for the first time, Perl implicitly increments from zero, and assigns a value of one to the associative array key corresponding to the word. The next time the word is encountered in the loop block, the value will be incremented by one. In this way, every word in the text is assigned an item in the %freq associative array, with the word serving as the item key and the number of occurrences of the word as the item value.

Once every word in the array of words from the text has been looped through the block, the associative array is complete.

The next lines simply format and print the items from the %freq associative array, producing a Zipf distribution in descending order of word frequency in the text:

```
while ((my $key, my $value) = each(%freq))
    {
    $value = "00000" . $value;
    $value = substr($value,-5,5);
    push (@termarray, "$value $key")
    }
@finalarray = reverse (sort (@termarray));

print join("\n",@finalarray);
```

A while block is created to loop through each member of the %freq associative array. This loop command has many applications, and its syntax should be studied:

```
while ((my $key, my $value) = each(%freq))
```

A string of five 0s is prefixed to the each value in the %freq associative array, using the Perl string concatenation operator, ".":

```
$value = "00000" . $value;
```

This reformats the number of occurrences of each word in the text. For example, "33" would become "0000033".

The next line truncates the string, using Perl's substr() operator. This ensures that every value consists of a total of exactly five digits front-justified with 0s:

```
$value = substr($value,-5,5);
```

So, "0000033" becomes "00033".

As each transformed value is created, it is immediately added to a new array (named @termarray), using Perl's push() command. The push() command takes a variable and adds it to the end of an array, as shown:

```
push (@termarray, "$value $key")
```

By turning every value in the %freq array into a number that is exactly five digits in length, and front-justified with 0s, the newly created array of values can be sorted using Perl's built-in sort function.

In the next line, the 5-digit values corresponding to the number of occurrences of words in the text file are sorted, then reversed to provide a descending array of word frequencies:

```
@finalarray = reverse (sort (@termarray));
```

This reverse-sorted array can be printed to the monitor. The `join()` operator creates a string consisting of each member of the array joined by a chosen string (in this case the newline character). This produces a list wherein each member of the array appears at the beginning of a new line.

```
print join("\n",@finalarray);
```

What have we learned in this section (List 5.20.5)?

LIST 5.20.5. SUMMARY OF THE THIRD PERL PROGRAMMING SECTION

- Creating and interpreting complex regular expressions
- Looping through arrays with foreach blocks
- Looping through associative arrays with while blocks
- New Perl operators and commands `split()`, `push()`, `lc()`, `sort()`, `join()`, `substr()`, `scalar()`, `undef()`, incrementing values, and concatenating strings
- Advanced pattern substitution and substitution options

5.21. CREATING A PERSISTENT DATABASE OBJECT

Until now, we have studied scripts that take text files as input and create text files as output. In Chapter 2, we discussed the differences between data files and databases. Databases, unlike data files, create data structures that are optimized for retrieving records. Databases are applications that contain binary data structures and cannot be opened and read like a flat file.

In Perl, most data structures (strings, arrays, and associative arrays) created in a script will vanish once the script has executed. A persistent object is stored in an external file that exists even after the Perl script that created the object has finished executing. You can copy and distribute the persistent object just like any other file, and you can write specialized Perl scripts that retrieve or modify data held by the persistent object.

Perl has a built-in module that permits you to create a persistent database object that is stored as an external binary file. You can write additional Perl scripts to retrieve records from the (persistent) external file. This database functionality in Perl is very useful when you have millions of records.

The following Perl script creates an external database file from the MeSH flat file (Lists 5.21.1 and 5.21.2).

LIST 5.21.1. A SAMPLE MESH RECORD

- *NEWRECORD

- RECTYPE = D

- MH = Heparin

- AQ = AA AD AE AG AN BI BL CF CH CL CS CT DF DU EC GE HI IM IP ME PD PH [PK PO RE SD SE ST TO TU UL UR

- PRINT ENTRY = Heparinic Acid I T118 I T121 I T123 I

- NON I EQV I UNK (19XX) I 800523 I abbbcdef

- PRINT ENTRY = alpha-Heparin I T118 I T121 I T123 I NON I NRW I

- UNK (19XX) I 800523 I abbbcdef

- ENTRY = Liquaemin I T118 I T121 I T123 I TRD I NRW I UNK (19XX) I 861029 I abbbcdef

- ENTRY = Sodium Heparin I T118 I T121 I NON I NRW I UNK (19XX) I 830330 I abbcdef

- ENTRY = Heparin, Sodium

- ENTRY = alpha Heparin

- MN = D09.698.373.400

- PA = Anticoagulants

- PA = Fibrinolytic Agents

- EC = antagonists & inhibitors:Heparin Antagonists

- MH_TH = BAN (19XX)

- ST = T118

- ST = T121

- ST = T123

- N1 = Heparin

- RN = 9005-49-6

- MS = A highly acidic mucopolysaccharide formed of equal [parts of sulfated D-glucosamine and D-glucuronic acid with

- sulfaminic bridges. The molecular weight ranges from six to [twenty thousand. Heparin occurs in and is obtained from liver,

- lung, mast cells, etc., of vertebrates. Its function is unknown, [but it is used to prevent blood clotting in vivo and vitro, in

- the form of many different salts.

- PM = /therapeutic use was HEPARIN, THERAPEUTIC 1965

- HN = /therapeutic use was HEPARIN, THERAPEUTIC 1965

- MED = *1635

- MED = 3275

- M90 = *2406

- M94 = 4517

- MR = 20040707

- DA = 19990101

- DC = 1

- UI = D006493

LIST 5.21.2. CREATING A PERSISTENT DATABASE OBJECT FROM THE MESH FLAT-FILE

```perl
#!/usr/bin/perl
use Fcntl;
use SDBM_File;
tie%item, "SDBM_File", 'mesh', O_RDWR|O_CREAT|O_EXCL, 0644;
untie%item;
open (TEXT, "d2002.bin")||die"Can't open file";
$/ = "*NEWRECORD";
$line = " ";
while ($line ne "")
    {
    tie%item, "SDBM_File", 'mesh', O_RDWR, 0644;
    #use the created persistent database object file
      $line = <TEXT>;
      @linearray = split(/\n/,$line);
      foreach $piece (@linearray)
        {
        if ($piece =~ /MN =/)
```

```
            {
            $meshno = $';
            }
        if ($piece =~ /ENTRY = /)
            {
        $entry = $';
        if ($entry =~ /\|/o)
            {
            $entry = $';
            }
        $entry =~s/s\b//g;
        $entry = lc($entry);
        push (@synonyms, $entry);
            }
        }
    foreach $term (@synonyms)
        {
        $item{$term} = $meshno;
        }
    undef $meshno;
    undef @synonyms;
    untie%item;
    }
undef(%item);
close TEXT;

exit;
```

The first lines of the script tie a Perl associative array to a persistent database object:

```
use Fcntl;
```

This command tells Perl to use the built-in Perl module, Fcntl (file control) because you will be creating a file using the Fcntl syntax.

```
use SDBM_File;
```

This command tells Perl to use the built-in Perl module SDBM_File, because you will be creating a database object.

```
tie %item, "SDBM_File", 'mesh', O_RDWR|O_CREAT|O_EXCL, 0644;
```

This line does not need to be explained. It is simply Perl's special syntax for creating an external database object file (mesh) and "tying" it to the associative array %item. From this point on, you can use the associative array, %item, just like any Perl associative array, but the data structure will be automatically encapsulated in the external file, "mesh." Actually, Perl creates two files, `mesh.pag` and `mesh.dir`. Both of these files are binary files. They can be accessed for read/write operations by tying them back to an associative array (next script).

```
untie %item;
```

You can untie the associative array from the database object, and you can tie them back together again when you need to read or write data.

```
open (TEXT, "d2006.bin")||die"Can't open file";
```

`d2006.bin` is the MeSH (see Appendix) flat file. We could have chosen any file. We will parse data elements from the MeSH flat file and assign them to the %item associative array.

```
$/ = "*NEWRECORD";
```

The records in the MeSH `d2005.bin` file are multi-line and each record begins with "*NEWRECORD" string. By assigning "*NEWRECORD" as the line delimiter, a line-read operations will place an entire multi-line MeSH record into a variable.

The remainder of the Perl script is straightforward, and we will only discuss the first few lines of the while loop.

```
while ($line ne "")
   {
   tie%item, "SDBM_File", 'mesh', O_RDWR, 0644; #use the
   #created file
   $line = <TEXT>;
   @linearray = split(/\n/,$line);
```

This line once more ties the %item associative array to the already-created persistent database, named "mesh." The persistent database is set to read/write access.

```
$line = <TEXT>;

@linearray = split(/\n/,$line);
```

During each loop, one record in the MeSH flat file is moved into the *$line* variable. Then *$line* is split into an array, where each item in the array is a line of the multi-line MeSH record.

The next lines of the script parse the record into data elements. The important step comes when the %item associative array is built:

```
$item{$term} = $meshno;
```

As each key and value is added to the %item associative array, the tied persistent database object is likewise built.

Finally, after all the parsed MeSH elements are added to the associative array, the persistent database object can be untied:

```
untie %item;
```

The purpose of the script was to build a persistent external database object. When the script ends, all nonpersistent items vanish into the bit-void. This includes string variables, like *$line*, and associative array variables, like %item. But the persistent database object now exists as two portable files (mesh.pag and mesh.dir), containing the MeSH terms and numbers, that can be directly accessed without rebuilding their data structures. In the next script, we will show how the persistent object can be used to retrieve data.

5.22. RETRIEVING INFORMATION FROM A PERSISTENT DATABASE OBJECT

LIST 5.22.1. RETRIEVING A PERSISTENT DATABASE OBJECT FROM THE MESH FLAT-FILE

```
#!/usr/bin/perl
use Fcntl;
use SDBM_File;
tie%item, "SDBM_File", 'mesh', O_RDWR, 0644;
while(($key, $value) = each (%item))
    {
    print "$key => $value\n";
    }
untie%item;

exit;
```

Once built, accessing the data in a persistent database object is easy and fast (List 5.22.1).

We use the now-familiar syntax to tie the created data file, "mesh" to a Perl associative array, %item:

```
use Fcntl;
use SDBM_File;

tie%item, "SDBM_File", 'mesh', O_RDWR, 0644;
```

Perl looks for "mesh" in the external files `mesh.pdg` and `mesh.dir`, which should be located in the current directory. Once tied, %item becomes the same as the external mesh database object (i.e., the files `mesh.pag` and `mesh.dir`).

```
while(($key, $value) = each (%item))
    {
    print "$key => $value\n";
    }
untie%item;

exit;
```

The while(($key, $value) loop prints all of the key value pairs in the %item associative array.

5.23. VALIDATING XML TAGS USING REGULAR EXPRESSIONS

It is rare to find a Perl script that has no regular expressions. Almost all script inputs (even lists of numbers) need to be validated. Is 1,000,000 acceptable when your mathematical operator is expecting 1000000? Is .5 acceptable when your subroutine is expecting all numbers to begin with an integer followed by a decimal?

Let us look at two examples where Perl regular expressions are used to validate XML markup tags and parse free-text sentences.

We will be learning a lot about XML in a later chapter. For now, suffice it to state that XML tags are angle-bracketed descriptors of the information that exists between the start and end of the tag; for example: `<name>`Jules Berman`</name>`

XML tags (also known as markup) must satisfy other requirements (List 5.23.1).

LIST 5.23.1. SYNTAX RULES FOR VALID XML TAGS

- XML tags, like Perl variables, are case-sensitive ("Name" is different from "name"). Parsers must preserve character case.

- Letters, underscores, hyphens, periods, and numbers may be used in a tag.

- Only letters and underscores are eligible as the first character.

- Colons are allowed, but only as part of a declared namespace prefix. For all practical purposes, this means that only one colon is allowed in a tag, and the colon must appear in an internal location in the tag (not at the beginning or the end of a tag).

LIST 5.23.2. TAGCHECK.PL, A PROGRAM THAT VALIDATES XML TAGS

```perl
#!/usr/bin/perl
@elements = qw (gene 4gene gene:ncbi gene-autry ge::ne
          gene&autry -gene _gene gene- gene:
          :gene ge:n:e ge:ne: ge,ne ge.ne);
foreach $value (@elements)
    {
      if ($value =~ /^[a-z\_][a-z0-9\-\.\_]*{\:]?[a-z0-9\-
\.\_]*$/i)
        {
        print "$value is good\n";
        }
      else
        {
        print "$value is bad\n";
        }
    }
exit;
```

Reviewing the requirements for a valid XML tag, we can see that the tagcheck.pl script correctly classified tags in every instance (List 5.23.2). Can you see why the invalid terms were rejected by the script?

Let us look at how the tagcheck.pl script works. The first step in the script is to prepare an array of would-be gene tags:

```perl
@elements = qw (gene 4gene gene:ncbi gene-autry ge::ne
          gene&autry -gene _gene gene- gene:
          :gene ge:n:e ge:ne: ge,ne ge.ne);
```

The qw operator is a handy device that accepts array lists without commas or string quotes. This operator was made for lazy Perl programmers who do not want to worry about properly "commifying" a list.

Each member of the array is examined (in a foreach loop) for a pattern match to a regular expression that embodies every criteria for a proper XML tag:

```perl
if ($value =~ /^[a-z\_][a-z0-9\-\.\_]*[\:]?[a-z0-9\-\.\_]*$/i)
```

What does this regular expression do? It requires that the string begins with one letter between a and z or an underscore. The ^ symbol appearing at the beginning of a pattern expression indicates the beginning of the string. A block, "[..]", indicates a permitted match to any of the characters listed in the block. The first character of a proper XML tag must be a letter between a and z, or the underscore character. The characters following the first letter must be a letter between a and z, a number character (0–9), a hyphen, an underline character, or a period. It may also be the colon prefix, but if it is a colon prefix, then it can occur only once. The colon prefix is put into its own block. The "?" after a block indicates that that the contents of the block (the colon character in this case) can occur zero times or one time. Following the colon, if it occurs, can be any number of occurrences of a letter of the alphabet, an underscore, a period, or a hyphen. At the end of the pattern holder (/...../) is the letter "i" indicating that the match pattern can be either uppercase or lowercase letters of the alphabet. Review the output from the `tagcheck.pl` script to show yourself that it really works (List 5.23.3).

LIST 5.23.3. OUTPUT OF TAGCHECK.PL

- `c:\ftp>perl tagcheck.pl`

- gene is good

- 4gene is bad

- gene:ncbi is good

- gene-autry is good

- ge::ne is bad

- gene&autry is bad

- -gene is bad

- _gene is good

- gene- is good

- gene: is good

- :gene is bad

- ge:n:e is bad

- ge:ne: is bad

- ge,ne is bad

- ge.ne is good

5.24. WHAT HAVE WE LEARNED?

LIST 5.24.1. WHAT WE HAVE LEARNED SO FAR

- The =~ operator tells Perl to look for the pattern that follows the operator in the variable that precedes the operator. Regular Expressions are Perl's way of describing a pattern.

- You can create most of your patterns by following a few simple rules and by "borrowing" regular expressions from published listings.

- The most common usage for regular expressions are in scripts that examine a line (or all the lines) from a file and that perform a substitution or rearrangement or other operation on the line, based on the results of the pattern match.

- Regular expressions are powerful and fast tools for modifying text or data records, or for finding exactly what you want in any text.

- Perl associative arrays can be tied to an external database object that persists even when the Perl script has finished executing.

CHAPTER

6

Programming Common Biomedical Informatics Tasks

6.1. BACKGROUND

In my experience, the most common biomedical informatics tasks involve transforming text or datasets from one format into another (so-called data munging). Mathematical operations on data are called data crunching. Perl can munge and crunch data to your heart's content (see List 6.1.1).

LIST 6.1.1. SOME BIOMEDICAL INFORMATICS TASKS THAT CAN BE ACCOMPLISHED WITH PERL

- Statistics
- Mathematical computations
- Mathematical modeling
- Web protocols (e.g., http and ftp)
- Cryptographic techniques
- Integrating data
- Glue functions (e.g., calling subroutines written in C)
- Digital Signal Processing (including image analysis)
- Bioinformatics methods (e.g., interfacing to Blast)
- Database interfaces
- Remote procedure calls and distributed computing
- **Middleware** (see Glossary)
- **Software agents** (via Web services, **GRID**, **SOAP**, or related protocols)
- Transformations to and from XML
- XML data queries
- Logical annotation of data (e.g., RDF)

In this chapter, we review some uses of Perl in biomedical informatics. The purpose of this chapter is to persuade readers that they can perform many kinds of tasks without relying on commercial software products.

6.2. COMPUTING A ONE-WAY HASH FOR A WORD, PHRASE, OR FILE

A one-way hash is an algorithm that transforms a string into another string in such a way that the original string cannot be calculated by operations on the hash value (hence the term "one-way" hash). These popular algorithms are discussed in HIPAA where they are referred to as HMACs (Hashed Message Authentication Codes). Examples of public domain one-way hash algorithms are MD5 (64) and SHA, the Standard Hash Algorithm (65). These differ from encryption protocols that produce an output that can be decrypted by a second computation on the encrypted string.

The resultant one-way hash values for text strings consist of near-random strings of characters, and the length of the strings (i.e., the strength of the one-way hash) can be made arbitrarily long. Therefore name spaces for one-way hashes can be so large that the chance of hash collisions (two different names or identifiers hashing to the same value) is negligible. We will be discussing the many uses of one-way hash algorithms in later chapters. For now, you need only know that Perl is distributed with modules (external programs that can be called from Perl scripts) that will create one-way hashes for any character strings and for whole files, as shown (List 6.2.1).

LIST 6.2.1. CREATING AN MD5 ONE-WAY HASH VALUE FOR ANY PROVIDED STRING

```
#!/usr/local/bin/perl
use MD5;
print "What words would you like to digest?\n";
$holdstring = <STDIN>;
chomp;
$hexhashstring = MD5->hexhash($holdstring);
print "md_5 hexhash =>$hexhashstring\n";
exit;
```

This simple script invokes the Perl MD5 module:

```
use MD5;
```

This command line instructs Perl to use the MD5 one-way hash module that is bundled in standard Perl distributions.

The next line prompts the user to provide a character string. The user enters any string, and the script uses the chomp command to cut off the newline character at the end of the input string.

The script next calls the MD5 module's hexhash method:

```
$hexhashstring = MD5->hexhash($holdstring);
```

How did we know the correct syntax for using the MD5 hexhash method to create a one-way hash from a string variable parameter?

We did not. At least, we did not know how to use the MD5 module until we looked inside the module documentation, which is in the same file that holds the Perl source code for the module. In fact, the hundreds of modules distributed with Perl and the thousands of public Perl modules obtainable from the Comprehensive Perl Archive Network contain usage instructions in all module files.

The MD5 module file is MD5.PM and can be found in the /site/lib subdirectory of the Perl distribution files.

A usage statement in the file indicates how to call the hexhash method to transform a scalar into a one-way hashed output string in hex notation:

```
$string = MD5->hexhash(SCALAR);
```

Hex notation is base-16 ASCII, and it uses an alphabet of composed of (0,1,2,3,4,5,6,7,8,9,a,b,c,d,e,f).

The output of the MD5 algorithm for two rounds of input using the same character string, "Jules Berman" is shown in List 6.2.2.

LIST 6.2.2. THREE EXECUTIONS OF THE MD5 ALGORITHM

- Execution 1:
  - c:\ftp>perl md5_word.pl
  - What words would you like to digest?
  - Jules Berman
  - md_5 hexhash => 0ab7ad79962fd2ea036cc8dbaade6f2a
- Execution 2:
  - c:\ftp>perl md5_word.pl
  - What words would you like to digest?
  - Jules Berman
  - md_5 hexhash => 0ab7ad79962fd2ea036cc8dbaade6f2a

- Execution 3:
  - c:\ftp>perl md5_word.pl
  - What words would you like to digest?
  - Jules J. Berman
  - md_5 hexhash => b59d141b7962b930e7a803bbaa451ddf

The first two executions demonstrate that when an input string is hashed, it produces the same output with each execution of the script. The third execution shows that if any characters of an input string are changed, it produces a completely different one-way hash output.

One-way hashes are useful for authenticating files. A file can be hashed, just as a character string can be hashed, to produce a string of characters that is virtually unique for the file. If a single byte in the file is changed, then the one-way hash for the file is completely changed. If a file always produces the same one-way hash value, then it is a safe bet that the file has not been modified. The Perl MD5 module has a method for producing one-way hashes on files (List 6.2.3).

LIST 6.2.3. CREATING AN MD5 ONE-WAY HASH FOR A FILE

```perl
#!/usr/local/bin/perl
use MD5;
print "What file would you like to digest?\n";
$holdfile = <STDIN>;
chomp;
open (TEXT,"$holdfile");
$context = new MD5;
$context->addfile(TEXT);
$digest = $context->digest();
print (unpack ("H*", $digest));
exit;
```

6.3. SIMPLE STATISTICS

There are many excellent statistics packages available to researchers. In the past few years, the R statistical programming language has emerged as a popular and versatile tool for biomedical informaticians (see Appendix). However, those who prefer to program their own methods in Perl will find that common statistical methods can be readily implemented.

The easiest and most fundamental statistical tests involve computing the mean of a population (List 6.3.1).

LIST 6.3.1. SIMPLE PERL SCRIPT FOR COMPUTING THE MEAN FROM AN ARRAY OF NUMBERS

```
#!/usr/bin/perl
@numbersarray = (1,2,3,4,5,6,7,8,9,10);
$arraysize = scalar(@numbersarray);
print "The number of elements in our array is
$arraysize\n";
$sum = 0;
foreach $value(@numbersarray)
    {
    $sum = $sum + $value;
    }
$mean = $sum / $arraysize;
print "Your population number is $arraysize\n";
print "The array mean is $mean\n";
exit;
```

This simple program takes an array (provided in the script code) and prints the mean (average) of the array (sum of elements divided by the size of the array). Perl has several ways of determining the size of an array. The easiest is to force an array into scalar context, using scalar(@array). This returns a string variable containing the number of elements in the array. To determine the sum of all the elements in the array, we loop through the array, adding the value of each element to a summation variable. The mean is determined by dividing the sum of the elements by the number of elements, using the division operator, "/".

In practice, you will be computing the mean from files containing lists of numbers. Assuming that your file consists of records containing numbers, you would build the array using an algorithm such as the one in List 6.3.2.

LIST 6.3.2. GENERAL METHOD OF BUILDING AN ARRAY THAT CAN BE USED IN A STATISTICAL OR MATHEMATICAL PERL ROUTINE

- Open the file containing your records.
- Go through the file, one line (record) at a time.
- From a complex record, pick out the number you want using Regex.
- Add that number to your array variable (using the Perl push command).
- Calculate the mean (or any other statistical test) on the array variable.

Or, you may want to collect numbers directly from the keyboard. The next script, `mean2.pl`, prompts you to start entering numbers, pressing the return key after each number. If you press the return key without entering a number, the script assumes you have finished your numbers and produces an output that contains the list, along with the computed mean (Lists 6.3.3 and 6.3.4).

LIST 6.3.3. COMPUTING THE MEAN OF AN ARRAY ENTERED AT THE KEYBOARD

```perl
#!/usr/bin/perl
#mean2.pl
#computes the mean of an array of numbers entered at
#keyboard
print "Type a bunch of numbers, pressing the return key\n";
print "after each number. Decimal numbers are
allowed\n\n";
$number = " ";
until ($number eq "")
    {
    $number = <STDIN>;
    $number =~ s/\n//o; #deletes the newline character
    if ($number eq "")
      {
      next;
      }
    if ($number !~ /[0-9]+/) #the entry must contain at
#least one digit
      {
      print "You're only allowed to enter numbers...";
      print "We just won't count this entry\n";
      next;
    } if ($number !~ /^[0-9 *[\.]?[0-9]*$/)
                    #checks that the entry was a number
      {             #by passing anything that contains
                    #characters other than digits and
                    #the decimal point
      print "You're only allowed to enter numbers...";
      print "We just won't count this entry\n";
      next;
      }
    push(@numbersarray, $number);
    }
$arraysize = scalar(@numbersarray);
```

```
$sum = 0;
foreach $value(@numbersarray)
   {
   $sum = $sum + $value;
   }
$mean = $sum / $arraysize;
print "@numbersarray\n";
print "Your population number is $arraysize\n";
print "The population mean is $mean\n";
exit;
```

LIST 6.3.4. OUTPUT OF MEAN2.PL

- C:\ftp>perl mean2.pl
- Type a bunch of numbers, pressing the return key after each number. Decimal numbers are allowed
- 11 12 13 11.111 12.33345 10 109hello12435
- You're only allowed to enter numbers... We just won't count this entry 10
- 11 12 13 11.111 12.33345 10 10
- Your population number is 7 The population mean is 11.3492071428571

The mean2.pl script permits the user to enter numbers via the keyboard. After each entry, it determines

1. Whether or not anything was actually entered (pressing the return key without entering anything is the signal to compute and display the mean).
2. Whether or not the entry was a valid number (zero or more digits separated by zero or one decimal point followed by zero or more digits).

It is interesting to note that a simple decimal point unaccompanied by digits on either side meets criterion 2 for a valid number. We do not want this to happen, so we add the additional requirement that entries must contain at least one digit.

```
if ($number !~ /[0-9]+/)
```

6.4. INVOKING STATISTICAL TESTS THROUGH PERL MODULES

Although it is possible to write simple Perl scripts for any statistical test, the author cautions against this practice. It is simply too easy to make a mistake when writing your own statistical scripts, and it is altogether too difficult to find script errors. It is much easier to use well-tested statistical modules that can be easily called from your scripts (List 6.4.1).

LIST 6.4.1. SOME OF THE AVAILABLE PERL STATISTICS MODULES[66]

- Statistics-Basic
- Statistics-ChiSquare
- Statistics-ConwayLife
- Statistics-Frequency
- Statistics-RankOrder
- Statistics-ROC
- Statistics-Table-F
- Statistics-TTest
- Statistics-Contingency
- Statistics-Descriptive
- Statistics-Distributions
- Statistics-LineFit
- Statistics-LogRank
- Statistics-RankCorrelation
- Statistics-Regression
- Statistics-SerialCorrelation

Before you can use these tests, you must download the appropriate module into your Perl installation. A sample installation of Statistics-Descriptive (by Colin Kuskie, Andrea Spinelli, and Jason Kastner), through the ActiveState package manager is shown:

```
ppm> install statistics-descriptive
Install 'statistics-descriptive' version 2.6 in ActivePerl
5.8.7.815.
Downloaded 10294 bytes.
Extracting 5/5: blib/arch/auto/Statistics/Descriptive/.exists
Installing
```

```
C:\activepl\html\site\lib\Statistics\Descriptive.html
Installing
```

```
C:\activepl\site\lib\Statistics\Descriptive.pm  Successfully
installed
```

```
statistics-descriptive version 2.6 in ActivePerl 5.8.7.815.
```

Only the first line is the user's input: ppm> install statistics-descriptive

The remaining lines are package manager output. The installation usually takes a few seconds. Once installed, the Statistics-Descriptive package can be called from a Perl script (Lists 6.4.2 and 6.4.3).

LIST 6.4.2. PERL SCRIPT FOR CALCULATING VARIANCE

```
#/usr/local/bin/perl
use Statistics::Descriptive;
$stat = Statistics::Descriptive::Full->new();
$stat->add_data(1,2,3,4,5,6,7,8,9,10);
$mean = $stat->mean();
$var = $stat->variance();
print "mean $mean\nvariance $var\n";
exit;
```

LIST 6.4.3. OUTPUT OF STATISTICS SCRIPT

- c:\ftp>perl stat.pl
- mean 5.5
- variance 9.16666666666667

Similarly, Statistics-ChiSquare (by Jan Orwant) can be downloaded and invoked from a Perl script (Lists 6.4.4 and 6.4.5).

LIST 6.4.4. PERL SCRIPT FOR COMPUTING THE CHISQUARE STATISTIC

```
#!/usr/bin/perl
use Statistics::ChiSquare;
print chisquare([1, 9, 1, 15, 4, 7]), "\n";
print chisquare([20, 20, 20, 30, 20, 20, 30 ]), "\n";
exit;
```

LIST 6.4.5. OUTPUT OF `CHI.PL`

- C:\ftp>perl chi.pl
- There's a <1% chance that these data are random.
- There's a >50% chance, and a <70% chance, that these data are random.

6.5. AVOIDING TYPE 4 ERRORS WITH RESAMPLING

Statistics often boils down to this: Is there a difference between two populations, or are they indistinguishable? In biomedicine, the two populations are often the treated group and the untreated group, maybe the patients with the positive test results and the patients with the negative test results, and so on. The case in which the compared populations are statistically indistinguishable is referred to as the null hypothesis (e.g., the treatment did not have any effect). There are at least four different types of statistical errors (List 6.5.1).

LIST 6.5.1. TYPES OF STATISTICAL ERRORS

- Type 1—rejecting the null hypothesis when the null hypothesis is correct (i.e., seeing an effect when there was none)
- Type 2—accepting the null hypotheses when the null hypothesis is false (i.e., seeing no effect when there was one)
- Type 3—rejecting the null hypothesis correctly, but for the wrong reason, leading to an erroneous interpretation of the data in favor of an incorrect affirmative statement
- Type 4—erroneous conclusion based on performing the wrong statistical test

The type 4 error is the most embarrassing and the least excusable. You cannot blame a type 4 error on the data. It is all on you. Considering the rich variety of exotic statistical tests available to the novice, the opportunities for type 4 errors are endless. One way of avoiding type 4 errors is to have a dedicated statistician analyze your data. For those informaticians who have access to the services of a trustworthy statistician, this may actually be the best and most practical solution. There is, however, an alternate approach: resampling. Resampling is a type of statistical analysis that uses computers to model experiments and then repeats the experiments thousands or millions of time to determine the occurrence frequencies for particular sets of data. This area of statistics was popularized by Bradley Efron (67), and may have particular interest for readers of this book (List 6.5.2).

LIST 6.5.2. REASONS WHY RESAMPLING STATISTICS IS OF INTEREST TO BIOMEDICAL INFORMATICIANS

- Does not require any knowledge of statistical tests
- Applicable to a wide range of problems, including clinical trial design and decision analyses
- Easy to understand
- Easy to program with Perl

The next sections will discuss the simple programming techniques used in resampling statistics.

6.6. USING RANDOM NUMBERS

Many simulation programs rely on a random number generator. The random numbers are used to simulate probabilistic events.

Let us imagine that you are not exactly a whiz at probability. You have a pair of dice and would like to know how often you might expect each of the numbers (from one to six) to appear after you have thrown one die.

The essence of the Perl script is in the following line, which uses Perl's pseudorandom number generator, `rand()`:

```
$one_of_six = (int(rand(6))+1);
```

This command will randomly assign a number between 1 and 6 to the variable *$one_of_six*.

How does it work? `Rand(EXPRESSION)` returns a random fractional number greater than or equal to 0 and less than the value of EXPRESSION. If EXPRESSION is omitted, then the value 1 is used.

We are not interested in decimal fractions, so we use the integer, function `int()`, on the output of the `rand()` function to produce a 0, 1, 2, 3, 4, or 5. Because we want our output to be an integer that is 1, 2, 3, 4, 5, or 6, we simply add 1 to the output number.

`Randtest.pl` simulates the results you may encounter when you throw a die 600,000 times, checking each time to see what number came up (Lists 6.6.1–6.6.3).

LIST 6.6.1. RANDTEST.PL, **A PERL SCRIPT THAT SIMULATES 600,000 CASTS OF A DIE**

```
#!/usr/bin/perl
$count = 0;
while ($count < 600000)
{
$count++;
$one_of_six = (int(rand(6))+1);
$hash{$one_of_six}++;
}
while(($key, $value) = each (%hash))
{
print "$key => $value\n";
}
exit;
```

LIST 6.6.2. OUTPUT OF FIRST TEST OF RANDTEST.PL

- C:\ftp>perl randtest.pl
- 1 => 100002
- 2 => 99902
- 3 => 99997
- 4 => 100103
- 5 => 99926
- 6 => 100070

LIST 6.6.3. OUTPUT OF SECOND TEST OF RANDTEST.PL

- C:\ftp>perl randtest.pl
- 1 => 100766
- 2 => 99515
- 3 => 100157
- 4 => 99570
- 5 => 100092
- 6 => 99900

Randtest starts by setting a loop simulating 600,000 casts of the die. Each loop uses the rand function. The Perl function rand(number) yields a pseudorandom number of value less than 6. We integerize the result using Perl's int() function, which truncates anything past the decimal point. This produces pseudorandom integer values of 0, 1, 2, 3, 4, or 5. We add one to the value to produce pseudorandom integers as they might appear on a throw of a die.

We make a hash of the frequency of occurrence of the different integer outcomes for all of the 600,000 simulations.

The results are as one might expect. Each number "came up" about 100,000 times. Just for fun, we repeated the script output, with much the same result.

There are many uses of random numbers, particularly in the fields of cryptography and probability. Another example of a simple use of a random number generator is demonstrated in the ranfile.pl script (Lists 6.6.4 and 6.6.5). A random number generator can save you from ever inventing the name of a file by producing a name randomly. The ranfile subroutine can easily be pasted into any Perl script that generates a filename. The chances that you will ever see two files with the same randomly chosen filename is very remote (unless you are dealing with a huge number of files). If filename collisions are a problem, then you can always use Perl to do a directory search to ensure that the filename does not already exist.

LIST 6.6.4. RANFILE.PL, A PERL SCRIPT THAT ASSIGNS RANDOM NAMES TO NEWLY CREATED FILES

```perl
#!/usr/bin/perl
#Makes 10 randomly named files, with 8 leading characters,
#a period and three trailing characters
while ($count < 10)
{
$count++;
&ranfile; #Tells Perl to skip the ranfile subroutine
}
sub ranfile
{
my @listchar;
my $count;
for ($count = 1; $count <= 12; $count++)
{
push(@listchar, chr(int(rand(26))+65));
}
$listchar[8]= ".";
my $randomfilename = join("",@listchar);
print "Your filename is $randomfilename\n";
return $randomfilename;
}
exit;
```

LIST 6.6.5. OUTPUT OF `ranfile.pl`

- C:\ftp>perl ranfile.pl
- Your filename is EKDUFKBR.YNX
- Your filename is QVDKUVBY.QUI
- Your filename is FNZXNKEE.MLV
- Your filename is NRTXEHQI.VFX
- Your filename is GWMOLKMX.AYU
- Your filename is LZAKZQDW.RYR
- Your filename is PRUAONQQ.OSJ
- Your filename is XDEDHLKD.GAY
- Your filename is RUSLNSXI.XVR
- Your filename is IEPGAWDP.LEH

The `ranfile.pl` script loops ten times, each time incrementing the *$count* variable and calling the ranfile subroutine.

The ranfile subroutine picks a random number between 0 and 25 and adds 65 to the result (65–90). The `chr()` function produces the ASCII character corresponding to a number. Numbers 65 to 90 correspond to uppercase A through Z. This function is repeated 12 times, producing a twelve-character array that will serve as a twelve-character filename. We want the ninth character to be a period, so we simply reassign the ninth member of the array (array element 8 when you start counting with zero) with the "." character. Joining them all, we have a random filename with an 8-character prefix and a 3-character suffix. We could have expanded our filename space by using digits, if we wished. I use this Perl routine frequently within other scripts when a new file is created by the script and I want a new filename assigned for each execution of the script.

6.7. RESAMPLING AND MONTE CARLO STATISTICS

Random numbers are used in many artificial life programs. In many instances, these programs are based on simulating objects that obey certain rules of behavior (move one square in any direction, duplicate yourself, disappear, etc.) and events that are triggered by probabilistic outcomes occurring at specified times.

In these simulations there are many outcomes that could result from a small set of initial conditions (i.e., number of objects, probability of certain events). It is much easier to write simulation programs and observe their outcomes than to directly calculate outcomes in a set of governing equations.

In a series of papers by William Moore and me, we developed Monte Carlo simulations for tumor cell growth, simulating cell replication and cell death and attributing different probabilities of cell death for each replication cycle. The simulations demonstrated that very small changes in a tumor cell's death probability (per replication generation) profoundly affected the tumor's growth rate. This suggested that chemotherapeutic agents that can incrementally increase the death rate of tumor cells may have enormous clinical benefit. Furthermore, we showed that if you simulate the growth of a cancer from a single abnormal cancer cell, most simulations result in the spontaneous extinction of the tumor—a somewhat unexpected finding that helps us to understand why tumors occur much less frequently in humans than one might expect from observations on the spontaneous occurrence of mutations in our growing cells.

This leads us to the purpose of this section: Biological simulations can be modeled with a few lines of Perl and can be used to predict outcomes that would be intractable to any direct mathematical analysis (Lists 6.7.1 and 6.7.2).

LIST 6.7.1. AI.PL, A PERL SCRIPT THAT SIMULATES CLONAL TUMOR GROWTH

```perl
#!/usr/bin/perl
print "Enter the death probability for your simulation\n";
print "Number must be between zero and one.\n";
print "Most realistic numbers are .45 to .50\n";
$value = <STDIN>;
$value =~ s/\n//o;
if ($value > 1)
    {
    print "Exiting... you must pick a number between zero
and one\n";
    end;
    }
print "THE PROVIDED CELL DEATH PROBABILITY IS $value\n\n";
my $roundnumber = 1; #initiate the generation counter
&cycle; #Tells Perl to skip to cycle subroutine


    sub cycle
    {
my $total = 0;
my $count = 1;
if ($roundnumber > 10)
```

```
        {
      print "I've seen enough!";
      end;
        }
$roundnumber++;
print "\nStarting with a single malignant cell,";
print "let's watch the clonal growth.\n";
$sum = 1;
while($sum > 0)
        {
      my $i = 1;
      while ($i < $sum +1)
        {
        $i++;
        $randnum = int( rand(100) ) + 1;
        if ($randnum > (100 * $value))
          {
          $sum = $sum + 1;
          }
        if ($randnum < ((100 * $value) -1))
          {
          $sum = $sum—1;
          }
        }
    if ($sum < 1)
      {
      print "Tumor terminated...good!\n";
      &cycle;
      }
    if ($sum > 5000)
      {
      print "\nBad news. Let's stop watching this
malignancy.\n";
        &cycle;
        }
      if ($sum > 0)
        {
        if (length($total) < 60)
          {
          print "$sum ";
          $total = $total . $sum;
          }
          else
          {
          print "\n$sum ";
```

```
        $total = "$sum ";
        }
      }
    }
  return 1;
  }
exit;
```

LIST 6.7.2. OUTPUT OF AI.PL

- C:\ftp>perl ai.pl
- Enter the death probability for your simulation
- Number must be between zero and one.
- Most realistic numbers are .45 to .50
- .46
- THE CELL DEATH PROBABILITY IS .46
- Starting with a single malignant cell, let's watch the clonal growth. Tumor terminated...good!
- Starting with a single malignant cell, let's watch the clonal growth. 1 Tumor terminated...good!
- Starting with a single malignant cell, let's watch the clonal growth. 2 1 4 2 1 1 1 Tumor terminated...good!
- Starting with a single malignant cell, let's watch the clonal growth. 2 1 5 6 8 8 8 12 15 18 18 20 19 27 32 30 31 20 14 16 23 30 30 36 38 34 50 52 67 75 97 114 133 143 150 156 159 178 200 254 302 292 329 336 382 441 489 603 630 701 770 862 923 1056 1084 1210 1369 1473 1664 1776 1959 2196 2475 2862 3098 3327 3740 4095 4634 Bad news. Let's stop watching this malignancy.
- Starting with a single malignant cell, let's watch the clonal growth. Tumor terminated...good!
- Starting with a single malignant cell, let's watch the clonal growth. Tumor terminated...good!
- Starting with a single malignant cell, let's watch the clonal growth. 3 1 3 5 3 1 1 Tumor terminated...good!
- Starting with a single malignant cell, let's watch the clonal growth. 4 6 5 6 3 3 1 Tumor terminated...good!
- Starting with a single malignant cell, let's watch the clonal growth. 2 2 5 3 2 2 6 5 6 5 4 2 1 Tumor terminated...good!
- Starting with a single malignant cell, let's watch the clonal growth. 3 5 3 7 6 3 3 1 1 Tumor terminated...good! I've seen enough!

The script produces ten simulations and outputs the results of each simulation. The algorithm that simulates tumor growth only takes a few lines of Perl (List 6.7.3).

LIST 6.7.3. PERL SNIPPET SHOWING THE ALGORITHM THAT REPEATEDLY ASSIGNS PROBABILITIC OUTCOMES TO AN EVENT

```perl
while ($i < $sum +1)
{
$i++;
$randnum = int( rand(100) ) + 1;
if ($randnum > (100 * $value))
{
$sum = $sum + 1;
}
if ($randnum < ((100 * $value) -1))
{
$sum = $sum-1;
}
}
```

In this snippet, Perl picks a random number between 1 and 100:

```perl
$randnum = int( rand(100) ) + 1;
```

Perl then compares that number with the preassigned (model) probability that an event will occur. In this case, the event is the death of a dividing cell. Let us say that the preassigned probability that a cell will die during a growth cycle is 0.45. The variable $value is assigned 0.45 and multiplied by 100 to produce the number 45. If the number (from 1 to 100) that Perl has randomly chosen is greater than 45, then the model would let the cell live and increases the number of cells in the population by one (because the cell successfully divides if it survives):

```perl
if ($randnum > (100 * $value))
{
$sum = $sum + 1;
}
```

If the number (from 1 to 100) that Perl has randomly chosen is less than 46, then the model would kill the cell and decrease the number of cells in the population by one (because the dead cell dropped from the population):

```perl
if ($randnum < ((100 * $value) -1))
{
$sum = $sum-1;
}
```

Perl repeats this exercise for every cell in the population and for every cell cycle for the duration of the simulation. The model permits us to change the cell death probability over and over again, to see how perturbations in cell death rate may alter population growth. Does the model accurately predict the growth of tumor populations from single cells? Not at all. The model is based on unproven assumptions about how cell populations grow. The purpose of the simulation is to let us see how changes in a variable may possibly alter the outcome of complex events. Humans cannot, through any act of mentation, calculate the outcome of complex events. The model gives us some idea of the range of outcomes that might be expected under a set of assumptions. This knowledge can be used to build more sophisticated models based less on assumption and more on experimental evidence.

6.8. HOW OFTEN CAN I HAVE A BAD DAY?

Imagine this scenario. One of the pathologists on service has just made a diagnostic error on each of three consecutive reports. Luckily, the errors were detected in the pathology review conference and corrected before the reports were released.

The Chair of the department calls the pathologist to her office and berates her for a completely unacceptable error rate. No pathologist should be permitted to diagnose three consecutive cases incorrectly.

The pathologist defends herself, saying that a long-term review of her cases shows that she has a 2% error rate, which is the national average for pathology errors. She cannot explain why three errors occurred consecutively, but she supposes that if you sign on enough cases, you will eventually make three consecutive errors. The Chair is not persuaded by this analysis.

Who is right? A few lines of Perl can resolve the issue (List 6.8.1).

LIST 6.8.1. `RUN.PL`, A RESAMPLING SCRIPT IN PERL THAT SIMULATES RUNS OF ERRORS

```
#!/usr/local/bin/perl
$errorno = 0;
while ($count < 100001)
    {
    $count++;
    $x = rand(100);
    if ($x < 2)
        #simulates a 2% error rate
```

```
        {
        $errorno++;
        }
    else
        {
        $errorno = 0;
        }
    if ($errorno == 3)
        {
        print "Uh oh. 3 consecutive errors\n";
        $errorno = 0;
        }
    }
exit;
```

The Perl script simulates 100,000 diagnoses, which is a fair estimate of the total number of diagnoses a pathologist might render in his or her entire career (at 4,000 diagnoses per year over 25 years of service). Each diagnosis is assigned a random number between 0 and 100. The "diagnosis" loop is repeated 100,000 times. In each loop, if the randomly assigned number is less than 2, then the pathologist's error number is incremented by 1. If the next diagnosis is randomly assigned a number greater than 2, then the error number is dropped back down to 0 (i.e., the next diagnosis is correct and the run of errors is broken). If an error occurs on 3 consecutive occasions, then the event is printed to the computer monitor (List 6.8.2)

LIST 6.8.2. OUTPUT OF RUN.PL

- c:\ftp>perl run.pl
- Uh oh. 3 consecutive errors
- Uh oh. 3 consecutive errors

In this trial of 100,000 diagnoses, using a 2% error rate, the modeled pathologist had two runs of three consecutive errors. Since 100,000 diagnoses represents the number of diagnoses rendered by a pathologist in her entire career, one can say that she can be permitted a 3-error day twice in her career.

6.9. ROUGH TEST OF THE BUILT-IN RANDOM NUMBER GENERATOR

Perl's built-in random number generator is not truly random. Eventually, the sequence of random numbers will repeat. When that happens, randomness is lost. For many purposes, such as simple Monte Carlo simulations, this will have no detrimental effect. For robust cryptographic work, a lame random number generator may be catastrophic.

Several tests for randomness have been proposed. Compression techniques all take advantage of the nonrandom nature of information (text, images, etc.). Compression algorithms fail completely when they encounter a truly random sequence of characters. If a file fails to compress (become smaller) with a compression utility, it is an excellent indicator that the file is composed of random characters.

A crude indicator of randomness is an unbiased distribution of randomly chosen items. After a billion random selections from the alphabet, one might expect an approximately equal number of selected a's, and b's, and c's, etc. A random selector producing a billion m's (and nothing else) would qualify as a very odd example of randomness.

The following snippet of code repeatedly selects integers from 1 to 100 and counts the number of times each integer is selected. A good random number algorithm should yield a near-equal number of selections of each integer (List 6.9.1).

LIST 6.9.1. SNIPPET OF PERL CODE TO DETERMINE UNBIASED RANDOM SELECTION

```perl
open (HOLD,">holder.txt")||die"cannot";
while ($n < 1000000)
    {
$x = int(rand(100)) + 1;
#pick a number between 1 and a hundred
#make a hash of the numbers picked and the
#number of times each is picked
$randhash{$x}++;
$n++;
    }
foreach $key (sort byval keys %randhash)
    {
    print HOLD "$randhash{$key} $key\n";
    }
sub byval
    {
    $randhash{$a} <=> $randhash{$b};
    }
```

6.10. THE MONTY HALL PROBLEM: SOLVING WHAT WE CANNOT GRASP

This is the legendary Monty Hall problem, named after the host of a televised quiz show where contestants faced a similar problem:

"The player faces three closed containers, one containing a prize and two empty. After the player chooses, she is shown that one of the other two containers is empty. The player is now given the option of switching from her original choice to the other closed container. Should she do so? Answer: Switching will double the chances of winning."

Marilyn vos Savant, touted by some as the world's smartest person, correctly solved the Monty Hall problem in her newspaper column. As a result, she received thousands of responses, many from mathematicians, disputing her answer.

Basically, this is one of those rare problems that seems to defy common sense. Personally, whenever I have approached this problem using an analytic approach based on probability theory, I come up with the wrong answer.

In desperation, I decided to forget about logic and simply perform Monty Hall's game. It can be done with a two-person model. One person randomly chooses a place to hide the prize, and the second person goes through the steps of picking the container. You can repeat this a few thousand times, accumulating sufficient data to confirm or invalidate Marilyn vos Savant's solution.

Or, you can model the game with Perl, using Perl's built-in random number generator to hide the prize in one of three places (List 6.10.1).

```perl
#!/usr/bin/perl
#Monty Hall simulation when you switch boxes, montesw.pl
$count = 0;
$winner = 0;
while ($count < 10000)
    {
    @box_array = (1,2,3);
    $full_box = (int(rand(3))+1); #this determines the actual full box
    $guess_box = (int(rand(3))+1);
    #this is the box that you picked as first choice
    @empty_array = grep{$_ != $full_box} @box_array;
    #these are the two empty boxes
    @showbox = grep{$_ != $guess_box} @empty_array;
```

```perl
    #these are the empty box(es)
    #with the guess box excluded
    if (scalar(@showbox) == 1) #if the guess box was the wrong choice
      {
      $winner++; #we've decided that we'll switch
      }
      $count++;
      }
    print $winner;
    exit;
    #!/usr/bin/perl
    #Monty Hall simulation when you refuse to switch boxes, monteno.pl
    $count = 0;
    $winner = 0;
    while ($count < 10000)
      {
      @box_array = (1,2,3);
      $full_box = (int(rand(3))+1);
      #this determines the actual full box
      $guess_box = (int(rand(3))+1);
      #this is the box that you picked as first choice
      @empty_array = grep{$_ != $full_box} @box_array;
      #these are the two empty boxes
      @showbox = grep{$_ != $guess_box} @empty_array;
      #these are the empty box(es)
      #with the guess box excluded
      if (scalar(@showbox) == 2) #if the guess box was the wrong choice
        {
        $winner++; #we've decided that we won't switch
        }
    $count++;
      }
print $winner;
exit;
```

LIST 6.10.1. OUTPUT OF MONTESW.PL

- C:\ftp>perl montesw.pl
- 6598
- C:\ftp>perl monteno.pl
- 3408

The first script simulates the Monty Hall strategy where the player takes the option of switching her selection. The second script simulates the Monty Hall situation where the player declines to switch her selection. By taking the switch option, she wins nearly twice as many simulations as she would have won if she had declined the switch. The beauty of the resampling approach is that the programmer does not need to understand why it works. The programmer only needs to know how to use a random number generator to create an accurate simulation of the Monty Hall problem that can be repeated thousands and thousands of times.

How does the Monty Hall problem relate to biomedical informatics? Chapter 14 explores the nascent field of clinical trial modeling. Preliminary outcomes of clinical trials can be often so dramatic that the trialists choose to redesign their protocol mid-trial. A drug or drug combination may have demonstrated sufficient effectiveness to justify moving control patients into the treated group, or adverse reactions may necessitate switching patients off a certain trial arm. In either case, the decision to switch protocols based on mid-trial observations is a Monty Hall scenario.

6.11. INTERNAL AND EXTERNAL MATH MODULES FOR PERL

Perl contains abundant math primitives, the basic functions upon which advanced mathematical algorithms are built. These include arithmetic functions, trigonometric functions, the modulus operator, a built-in pseudorandom number generator, exponential operations, and logical (bit-based) operators. Perl also supports bit-vector operations (i.e., operations on arrays of bits). In addition to these internal Perl operations, Perl comes bundled with a host of Posix modules.

Posix is the ISO/IEC 9945-1:1990 and IEEE Std 1003.1 Portable Operating System Interface. It is a large, standard library of programming operations developed by the National Institute of Standards along with other organizations. About 250 functions are included in Posix and most are mathematical. The purpose of Posix is to provide a set of defined operations that will have the same name and function regardless of the programming language in which they are used. This provides significant interoperability between programming languages that adhere to the Posix specification. Perl comes bundled with a Posix module, providing direct access to these functions. To call a Posix function, you simply invoke the Posix module from your Perl script (Lists 6.11.1 and 6.11.2).

LIST 6.11.1. `CEIL.PL,` **CALLING A POSIX FUNCTION FROM A PERL SCRIPT**

```
#!/usr/local/bin/perl
use POSIX qw(ceil floor);
$num = 11.3;
print "Floor is ", floor($num), "\n";
print "Ceil is ", ceil($num), "\n";
exit;
```

LIST 6.11.2. OUTPUT OF `CEIL.PL`

- c:\ftp>perl ceil.pl
- Floor is 11
- Ceil is 12

In reality, it is virtually impossible for programming languages to implement the full set of Posix functions. The Perl interface to Posix, specifying functions that cannot be used in Perl, is available (68).

In addition, Perl users have developed and distributed a wide variety of advanced mathematical algorithms. Many of these algorithms, including Perl source code, can be found in "Mastering Algorithms with Perl," by Jan Orwant et al (69).

6.12. USING EXTERNAL MODULES—FAST FOURIER TRANSFORM

Jean Baptiste Joseph Fourier (1768–1830) gave us the Fourier transform. A transform is a mathematical operation that takes a function or a set of data and transforms it into something else. A reverse (or inverse) transform will take the product of the transform and produce the original function or dataset. For any transform, operations may exist that are much easier to perform on the transformed function than on the original (untransformed) function.

Although the Fourier transform has applications in many areas of science, its value to biomedical informaticians pertains mostly to signal processing (e.g., images, ultrasound waveforms). The transform takes a time series representation of a signal (signal amplitude variation over time) and maps it into a frequency spectrum (harmonics of different frequencies). Periodicity in a signal is easy to find in a Fourier transform. Operations on a Fourier transform can eliminate periodic artifacts, eliminate frequencies that occur below a selected threshold, distinguish different signals (e.g., voice and instrumental tracks), locate similarities between two signals, and so on. These activities are way beyond the scope of this book, and it is heartening to know that the Fast Fourier Transform can be easily called from a Perl script once the freely available module is installed from ActiveState or CPAN.

From the operating system prompt, the user enters "ppm" and the programmer's package manager interface comes to life (List 6.12.1).

LIST 6.12.1. USING THE ACTIVESTATE PROGRAMMER'S PACKAGE MANAGER

- c:\ftp>ppm
- ppm—programmer's package manager version 3.3.
- copyright (c) 2001 activestate corp. all rights reserved.
- activestate is a division of sophos.

- entering interactive shell. using term::readline::perl as readline
- library.

- type 'help' to get started.

- ppm> install math-fft

  =====================
- install 'math-fft' version 1.28 in activeperl 5.8.7.815.

  =====================
- downloaded 23541 bytes.
- extracting 9/9: blib/arch/auto/math/fft/fft.lib
- installing c:\activepl\site\lib\auto\math\fft\fft.bs
- installing c:\activepl\site\lib\auto\math\fft\fft.dll
- installing c:\activepl\site\lib\auto\math\fft\fft.exp
- installing c:\activepl\site\lib\auto\math\fft\fft.lib
- installing c:\activepl\html\site\lib\math\fft.html
- files found in blib\arch: installing files in blib\lib into architecture
- dependent library tree
- installing c:\activepl\site\lib\math\fft.pm
- successfully installed math-fft version 1.28 in activeperl 5.8.7.815.
- ppm>

Entering "help" at the prompt provides the user with the options. Using the search command yields a seemingly endless list of downloadable Perl Modules.

As an example of installing and using an external module, the Fast Fourier Transform is used.

The command for installing the module is: install math-fft. The package manager finds and installs the package in your Perl directory and lists the installation steps as they occur (List 6.12.1). The package manager indicates when the module is installed successfully. Occasionally, operator system incompatibilities, lack of prerequisite modules, or even Perl version mismatches will prevent a successful installation.

LIST 6.12.2. SIMPLE EXAMPLE SCRIPT FOR THE FAST FOURIER TRANSFORM MODULE

```
#!/usr/local/bin/perl
use Math::FFT;
my $PI = 3.1415926539;
my $N = 8; #N can be any power of 2, such as 4,8,16,64
$series = [1,2,3,4,5,6,7,8,9,10,11,12,13,14,15,16];
#could be anything
print "series" .join(" ",@$series). "\n";
my $fft = new Math::FFT($series);
my $coeff = $fft->rdft();
print "coefficients \n @{$coeff}\n\n";
my $spectrum = $fft->spctrm;
print "spectrum \n @{$spectrum}\n";
exit;
```

LIST 6.12.3. OUTPUT OF FAST FOURIER TRANSFORM SCRIPT

- C:\FTP>perl fft.pl
- series 1 2 3 4 5 6 7 8 9 10 11 12 13 14 15 16

- coefficients
- 136 -8 -7.99999999999999 -40.2187159370068 -8 -19.3137084989848 -8
- -11.9728461013239 -8 -8 -8 -5.3454291
- 0335439 -8 -3.31370849898476 -8 -1.59129893903726

- spectrum
- 72.25 13.1370711845441 3.41421356237309 1.61991440442178 1
- 0.723231346085845 0.585786437626905 0.5197830
- 6494829 0.25

Our concept of a medical image is changing every day. Just a few years ago, a medical image was something that a radiologist or pathologist pondered for a moment before rendering a diagnosis. Perl has an abundance of modules that handle traditional medical images (70).

The challenge for biomedical informaticians will stem from new, mind-expanding definitions of medical images. Today, an image may be almost any kind of binary object that contains information related to a disease or physiologic process. Infrared spectroscopy, Doppler imaging, duplex scans, tissue microarray whole-slide scans, and multispectral analysis are just some examples of techniques that organize data into image objects when the native representation of the data is nonvisual. Biomedical informaticians are likely to use transforms (Fourier transforms, wavelet transforms, fractal transforms) and other mathematical algorithms (including vector quantization) to find patterns of data that signify the presence of pathognomonic cellular events.

6.13. INDEXING TEXT

A concordance is a complete listing of all the words in a text, along with the locations in the text where they occur. Concordances are usually created for books of great significance, in which every word is deemed important. Not surprisingly, the Bible has been the subject of numerous efforts of scribes and scholars to create concordances for the many versions and translations of the new and old Testaments. It is difficult to imagine the enormity of creating a concordance by hand. Luckily, with Perl, a concordance can be constructed for any book in about a second, with under a dozen Perl command lines (List 6.13.1).

LIST 6.13.1. A FULL CONCORDANCE IN 10 COMMANDS

```perl
#!/usr/local/bin/perl
open (TEXT, "1DFRE10.TXT");
open (OUT, ">1DFRE10.OUT");
$line = " ";
while ($line ne "")
```

```
      {
    $cumline = "";
    for($i=0;$i<100;$i++)
      {
      $line = <TEXT>;
      $cumline = $cumline . $line;
      }
    $page++;
    $cumline = lc($cumline);
    $cumline =~ s/[^a-z\-\']/ /g;
    @wordarray = sort(split(/[\n\s]+/,$cumline));
    @concordance = grep { $marked{$_}++; $marked{$_} == 1;
} @wordarray;
    undef %marked;
    foreach $thing (@concordance)
      {
      $wordpage{$thing} = $wordpage{$thing} . " $page";
      }
    }
    #The concordance is finished. The next lines just
#display it on screen.
    foreach $key (sort keys %wordpage)
    {
    print OUT "$key \= $wordpage{$key}\n";
    }
exit;
```

Indexes are somewhat different from concordances. An index is composed of words and phrases from a book that hold particular interest to readers, followed by their locations in the book. An indexing script is nearly identical to a script that creates a concordance (Lists 6.13.2 and 6.13.3).

LIST 6.13.2. A FULL INDEXING SCRIPT IN 10 COMMANDS

```
#!/usr/local/bin/perl
open (TEXT, "1DFRE10.TXT")||die"cannot";
open (OUT, ">1DFRE10.OUT")||die"cannot";
$line = " ";
@indextermarray = ("gaul","roman
empire","emperor","village","england");
while ($line ne "")
```

```
      {
      $cumline = "";
      for($i=0;$i<100;$i++) #assumes 100 lines per page
        {
        $line = <TEXT>;
        $cumline = $cumline . $line;
        }
      $page++;
      $cumline = lc($cumline);
      $cumline =~ s/[^a-z\-\']/ /g;
      $cumline =~ s/ +/ /g;
      foreach $thing (@indextermarray)
        {
        if ($cumline =~ /\b$thing\b/)
          {
          $wordpage{$thing} = $wordpage{$thing} . " $page";
          }
        }
      }
#The index is finished. The next lines just display it
#on screen.
foreach $key (sort keys %wordpage)
  {
  print OUT "$key \= $wordpage{$key}\n";
  #prints to external file
  print "$key \= $wordpage{$key}\n"; #prints to monitor too
  }
exit;
```

LIST 6.13.3. AN EXCERPTED OUTPUT FOR THE INDEXING PROGRAM, LISTING ONLY THE TERMS "ENGLAND" AND "VILLAGE" AND THE PAGES ON WHICH THEY ARE FOUND

```
c:\ftp>perl indexer.pl
 .
 .
 .
england = 5 14 23 134 207 208 229 277
 .
 .
 .
village = 43 77 81 94 128 141 147 184 185 225 226 244
```

Most indexes are created by professional indexers who read through a text, noting the phrases that may be of particular interest to readers and jotting down the page number where the phrase was found. There are four problems with this approach (List 6.13.4).

LIST 6.13.4. PROBLEMS WITH HUMAN-BASED INDEXING

- Incredibly labor-intensive and time consuming
- The index cannot be built until the book is in final form and the page numbers are known, delaying the publication of the book until the indexing is completed
- If important phrases are omitted completely or if one or more of their locations are omitted, then no one will likely catch the error
- The indexing effort needs to be repeated if there are book revisions and pagination changes

It would be good to have an automated way of selecting index terms. Kim and Wilbur wrote a paper in which they describe six automatic methods for extracting candidate phrases-of-interest from text (71). The simplest method selects all commonly occurring two- or three-word phrases that lie between so-called stop words in the text. Stop words are short, high frequency words such as *a*, *and*, *but*, *if*, and *when* that almost never occur within index-worthy phrases (List 6.13.5). Stop words serve as barriers enclosing candidate phrases.

LIST 6.13.5. EXTRACTING CANDIDATE INDEX PHRASES FROM A TEST FILE

```
#!/usr/local/bin/perl
@stop = qw(
```

a about absent absence again all almost also although always among an
and another any are as at be because been before being between both but by can could cm did do does done due during each either enough especially etc for found from further had has have having here how however i if in into is it its itself just kg km made mainly make may mg might ml mm most mostly must nearly neither no nor observed obtained often on our overall perhaps present presence quite rather really regarding seem seen several should show showed shown shows significantly since so some such than that the their theirs them then there therefore these they this those through thus to upon use used

using various very was we were what when which while with within without would or can't doesn't not

```
);
open (TEXT,"1DFRE10.TXT")||die"Cannot";
open (OUT,">1DFRE10.OUT")||die"Cannot";
undef($/);
$phrase = <TEXT>;
$phrase =~ s/\n/ /g;
$phrase = lc($phrase);
$phrase =~ s/[^a-z \']/ /g;
foreach $stopword (@stop)
    {
    $phrase =~ s/ $stopword / \# /g;
    }
$phrase =~ s/[\s]+/ /g;
$phrase =~ s/ ?\# ?/\#/g;
@phraselist = sort (split("#",$phrase));
@phraselist = grep {$i{$_}++;(($i{$_}==2)&&(scalar(split("
",$_))>1));}@phraselist;
print OUT join("\n",@phraselist);
exit;
```

First 9 lines of output from phrase extraction script.

abate fortis
abbe foucher
abdication of diocletian
abilities of
able leader
abolition of
absolute power
abuse of
academy of inscriptions

6.14. SEARCHING LARGE TEXT FILES

This enormously useful script uses everything you have learned so far. The more you know about how to use Regular Expressions, the more uses you will find for this simple but powerful script (Lists 6.14.1–6.14.3).

LIST 6.14.1. SCRIPT ALGORITHM FOR REGULAR EXPRESSION SEARCHES OF THE MRCON TEXT FILES

1. Asks you for a regular expression to search a file. If you are not adept at regular expressions, just enter any word. Remember, a word or phrase is always the simplest regular expression. In the output example, we will search for the word "adenocarcinoma."
2. If you enter the return key without entering a regular expression, it simply exits the script.
3. Asks Perl to give you the current epoch time (number of seconds passed since some point in history).
4. Opens an enormous publicly available file named MRCON (we will learn a lot about this file in Biomedical Perl).
5. Reads every line of MRCON (several million of them), testing each line to see if it contains a substring that matches the regular expression that you provided (step 1).
6. If it finds a match, then it adds the line number and the line to an external file named regexout.txt.
7. When it is finished reading the file, it asks Perl again for the epoch time, and determines the script execution time by subtracting the script's end time from the script's beginning time.
8. It prints to the monitor the time spent executing the script, as well as the filename containing the output of all the lines from the MRCON file that matched your provided regular expression.

LIST 6.14.2. PERL SCRIPT FOR REGULAR EXPRESSION SEARCHES OF TEXT FILES

```perl
#!/usr/bin/perl
#this will pull out all the matching lines for a prompted
#regular expression from any text file. This short script is
#incredibly
#powerful, but it requires the user to have facility creating
#regular expressions.
open (OUT, ">regexout.txt")||die"Can't open file $value";
$filename = "regexout\.txt";
print "What's your search regex?\n";
$regex = <STDIN>;
$regex =~ s/\n//o;
if ($regex eq "")
    {
    close TEXT;
```

```
        close OUT;
      print "\nYou didn't give a regex...Goodby\n";
      }
$start = time();
&searchsub; #Tells Perl to skip to searchsub subroutine
$end = time()—$start;
print "Retrieval time is $end seconds.\n";
print "Your search results are in file $filename.";


sub searchsub
{
open (TEXT, "c\:\\umls\\mrcon")||die"Can't open file
$value";
$line = " ";
while ($line ne "")
   {
   $line = <TEXT>;
   if ($line =~ /$regex/oi)
      {
      print OUT $. . "\|" . $line;
      }
   }
}
exit;
```

LIST 6.14.3. OUTPUT OF REGULAR EXPRESSION SEARCH

- C:\ftp>perl perlfind.pl
- What's your search regex?
- adenocarcinoma
- Retrieval time is 5 seconds.
- Your search results are in file regexout.txt.

There is a problem with this approach to text searching. In order to find the lines matching an expression, Perl must open the file and sequentially examine every line in the file. Luckily, Perl is very fast. Perl can search a 138 megabyte file (a file the size of about 138 novels!) on a 1.8 MHz computer in just five seconds! We actually could have done the search even faster using the qr operator, available in Perl 5. The qr operator permits a regular expression to be compiled once, and then matched again and again without recompilation. This is very useful in scripts that loop over millions of lines, recompiling and rematching the regular expression at each loop cycle. We chose not to include the qr operator in our script to achieve algorithmic simplicity.

6.15. FINDING NEEDLES FAST USING A BINARY-TREE SEARCH OF THE HAYSTACK

It is very easy for Perl to find a specific item in an ordered list, no matter how long the list. If the list is ordered, then it can be gigabytes in length and Perl can find any record almost instantly (List 6.15.1).

What is an ordered list? Examples are an index, an alphabetized list such as a dictionary, or a numbered array.

LIST 6.15.1. A SHORT SCRIPT THAT PERFORMS A BINARY SEARCH ON A FILE

```perl
#!/usr/bin/local/perl
open (TEXT, "find_bin.txt");
seek(TEXT, 0, 2);
print "What word would you like to find?\n";
$findword = <STDIN>;
$findword =~ s/\n$//o;
$filesize = tell (TEXT);
for($i=1;$i<129;$i++)
    {
    $portion = int(($filesize * $i)/128);
    push(@portionarray,$portion);
    }
seek(TEXT, 0, 0);
$arraynumber = 64;
foreach $division (4,8,16,32,64,128)
    {
    $place = $portionarray[$arraynumber-1];
    seek(TEXT, $place, 0);
    $line = <TEXT>;
    $line = <TEXT>;
    $line =~ /^([a-z]+) /;
    $estimate_word = $1;
    if ($estimate_word gt $findword)
        {
        $arraynumber = $arraynumber-(128/$division);
        }
```

```
        else
        {
        $arraynumber = $arraynumber + (128/$division);
        }
    }
undef ($/);
seek(TEXT,($place-10000), 0);
read(TEXT,$holder,20000);
if ($holder =~ /\n($findword)[0-9\= ]+\n/)
    {
    print $&;
    }
    else
    {
    print "Sorry. Couldn't find $findword in the index.\n";
    }
exit;
```

Binary searches can be performed on any ordered list of any length, at great speed. Because this trick works on files with ordered content, programmers may prefer binary searches on files rather than database programs for rapid record look-ups.

6.16. CLUSTERING: ALGORITHMS THAT GROUP SIMILAR OBJECTS

A common task in biomedical informatics is to group items based on their similarity. This may involve grouping histopathologic images based on similar patterns, organizing documents based on content, or clustering samples of diseased tissues based on shared genetic or proteomic profiles. This is particularly useful when a sample is characterized by a multiplex profile consisting of hundreds or thousands of individual measurements (e.g., gene expression levels, protein levels, wave amplitudes, physical attributes, etc.).

DeHoon and coworkers have prepared a library of programs that will cluster sets of data based on a variety of similarity algorithms.[72] They provide a Perl implementation that can be easily installed with the ActiveState Perl packet manager.

```
c:\>ppm install http://bonsai.ims.u-
tokyo.ac.jp/~mdehoon/software/cluster/Algorithm-Cluster.ppd
```

An example that uses their Perl module, Algorithm::Cluster, is shown (Lists 6.16.1 and 6.16.2).

LIST 6.16.1. CLUSTER.PL, A PERL SCRIPT DEMONSTRATING A CLUSTERING ALGORITHM

```perl
#!/usr/local/bin/perl
use Algorithm::Cluster;


$row0 = [ 3, 4, 1, 3, 4, 7, 5];
$row1 = [ 1, 2, 32, 15, 60, 76, 87];
$row2 = [ 1, 2, 32, 13, 60, 80, 87];
$row3 = [ 5, 6, 3, 2, 5, 9, 2];
$row4 = [ 5, 6, 3, 99, 5, 9, 2];
$row5 = [ 5, 6, 3, 115, 5, 9, 2];
$data = [ $row0, $row1, $row2, $row3, $row4, $row5 ];
my %param = ( nclusters => 3, data => $data, mask => ",
weight => ", transpose => 0, npass => 10, method => 'a',
dist => 'e', initialid => [ ], );
my ($clusters, $error, $found) =
Algorithm::Cluster::kcluster(%param);
$i = 0;
foreach my $thing (@$clusters)
    {
    print "Row" . "$i" . " => Cluster $thing\n";
    $i++;
    }
exit;
```

LIST 6.16.2. OUTPUT OF CLUSTER.PL SCRIPT

- c:\ftp>perl cluster.pl
- Row0 => Cluster 1
- Row1 => Cluster 2
- Row2 => Cluster 2
- Row3 => Cluster 1
- Row4 => Cluster 0
- Row5 => Cluster 0

The script created three clusters from the test set of six data arrays.

Cluster 0:

$row4 = [5, 6, 3, 99, 5, 9, 2];
$row5 = [5, 6, 3, 115, 5, 9, 2];

Cluster 1:
```
$row0 = [ 3, 4, 1, 3, 4, 7, 5];
$row3 = [ 5, 6, 3, 2, 5, 9, 2];
```

Cluster 2:
```
$row1 = [ 1, 2, 32, 15, 60, 76, 87];
$row2 = [ 1, 2, 32, 13, 60, 80, 87];
```

The script clustered six arrays of data into three groups based on the similarity of their contained data elements. This script was written to conform with the usage syntax included in the distributed Perl module, Algorithm::Cluster. Readers will notice some unfamiliar syntax in the script. Arrays of data are enclosed by straight brackets (instead of parentheses) and an array variable has a strange prefix, (@$cluster). The module makes liberal use of Perl references, which are variables that contain the location in which data resides. References have their own syntax by which they are created and from which their referred data can be retrieved. We will not be explaining Perl reference syntax for two reasons: 1) the syntax for reference calling will change in the next version of Perl, and 2) **object-oriented programming** techniques can eliminate the need to directly de-reference encapsulated object data. A casual inspection of the row data should convince the reader that the script successfully clustered arrays of numbers based on their similarities.

6.17. RETRIEVING INFORMATION FROM THE INTERNET

Virtually all scripting languages have modules that permit users to retrieve and parse data using Internet protocols. In many cases, these modules are bundled with the standard distributions of the language interpreters. All the user needs to do is to invoke the module at the top of the script, and all the methods contained in the modules become accessible to the script. List 6.17.1 shows how to print a Web page directly through Perl.

LIST 6.17.1. EXAMPLE OF A VERY SIMPLE PROGRAM USING THE LWP (LIBRARY FOR WWW IN PERL)

```perl
#!/usr/bin/perl
use LWP::Simple;
print (get "http://www.nih.gov");
exit;
```

There are numerous books that explain the intricacies of finding, downloading, parsing, and transforming data residing on the Internet. A good resource is Clinton Wong's Web Client Programming with Perl (73).

6.18. GENE SEQUENCE PARSING: FINDING PALINDROMES IN A GENE DATABASE

Parsing gene sequences is a lot like parsing text, only easier. If you have access to gene sequence databases, then you can use your Perl skills to search and find patterns of interest, to compare two or more sequences for similarities, or to align sequences with relative or absolute locations in the genome. Dozens of books and thousands of journal articles cover this subject (List 6.18.1).

LIST 6.18.1. SOME PERL BOOKS IN BIOINFORMATICS (A VERY DIFFERENT FIELD FROM BIOMEDICAL INFORMATICS)

- Beginning Perl for Bioinformatics, by James Tisdall
- Mastering Perl for Bioinformatics, by James Tisdall
- Genomic Perl: From Bioinformatics Basics to Working Code, by Rex A. Dwyer
- Perl Programming for Biologists, by D. Curtis Jamison
- Developing Bioinformatics Computer Skills, by Per Jambeck and Cynthia Gibas
- Bioinformatics Biocomputing and Perl: An Introduction to Bioinformatics Computing Skills, by Michael Moorhouse and Paul Barry

---

Because bioinformatics has enjoyed exhaustive coverage, it will not be reviewed to any great extent herein. However, it would be remiss to exclude any examples of Perl sequence parsing in support of biomedical research. Palindrome matching is a gene parsing technique available to biomedical informaticians who can program in Perl. A word palindrome is a string of alphabetic characters that reads the same forward or backward (a man a plan a canal panama). A DNA palindrome is a sequence for which the header bases are the reverse complement of the tail bases. For instance GAATTC is a palindrome. To understand why this is true, you must know that DNA is composed of sequences of four bases, Guanine (G), Adenine (A), Thymine (T), and Cytosine (C), and that each strand of DNA is matched by a complementary second strand in which G on either strand is always coupled with C on the other strand, and A on either strand is always coupled with T on the other strand (List 6.18.2).

LIST 6.18.2. A SIMPLE DNA PALINDROME, GAATTC

- G at front couples with C at end
- A, following G, couples with T preceding C
- A, following A, couples with T preceding T

Notice that the sequence GAATTC is the same as its complementary strand read backwards. Other examples of short DNA palindromes are AAG_CTT, and GCCC_GGGC. Another type of DNA palindrome allows for spacer regions with one or more nonpalindromic bases separating the reverse-complement sequence. Spacer-separated reverse-complement sequences would permit looped strand self-annealing. By any definition, DNA palindromes are unusual sequences characteristic of a given gene.

Palindromes may have medically significant roles. Large DNA palindromes are associated with gene amplification and genetic instability in tumors. A recent study has shown that palindromes occur frequently in cancers (74). The authors of this study have suggested that genome-wide analysis of palindrome formation is a new approach to identify structural chromosome aberrations associated with cancer (74).

A biomedical informatician may wish to quickly locate and identify the palindrome sequences in cancer DNA. The researcher may wish to test the hypotheses that specific palindromes found in a cancer provide diagnostic information or provide predictive information relating to a specific tumor's treatment response.

A Perl script can easily find computationally complex palindromes, including reverse-complement nonrepeating palindromes with an intervening spacer region. The example `sample.pl` script operates on a given uninterrupted sequence of CAGT combinations, held in the file "sample" (List 6.18.3). This algorithm can be modified to find any type of DNA palindrome, parsing through gene sequence data of any length (Lists 6.18.4 and 6.18.5).

LIST 6.18.3. PERL SCRIPT FOR FINDING PALINDROMES IN A GENE SEQUENCE

```perl
#!/usr/bin/perl
$filename = "sample";
open (TEXT, "sample")||die"Cannot";
$line = " ";
$count = 0;
for $n (5..20)
```

```perl
      {
      $re = qr /[CAGT]{$n}/;
      $regexes[$n-5]= $re;
      }
   NEXTLINE: while ($count < 1000)
      {
      $line = <TEXT> ;
      $count++;
      foreach my $value (@regexes)
         {
         $start = 0;
         while ($line =~ /$value/g)
            {
            $endline = $';
            $match = $&;
            $revmatch = reverse($match);
            $revmatch =~ tr/CAGT/GTCA/;
            if ($endline =~ /^([CAGT]{0,15})($revmatch)/)
               {
               $start = 1;
               $palindrome = $match . "*" . $1 . "*" . $2;
               $palhash{$palindrome}++;
               }
            }
         if ($start == 0)
            {
            goto NEXTLINE;
            }
         }
      }
   close TEXT;
   while(($key, $value) = each (%palhash))
      {
      print "$key => $value\n";
      }
   exit;
```

LIST 6.18.4. EXCERPTED INPUT OF SAMPLE.PL (LINE-BREAKS OMITTED FROM ORIGINAL FILE)

- ATGAGCGAAGAAAGCTTATTCGAGTCTTCTCCACAGAAGATG-GAGTACGAAATTACAAAC
- TACTCAGAAAGACATACAGAACTTCCAGGTCATTTCATTGGC-CTCAATACAGTAGATAAA
- .
- .

- .
- .
- AAGATCAGAAGCGACCATGACAATGCTATTGATGGATTATCT-GAAGTTATCAAGATGTTA
- TCTACCGATGATAAAGAAAAATTGTTGAAGACTTTGAAATAA

LIST 6.18.5. EXCERPTED OUTPUT OF SAMPLE.PL

(* separates the spacer region from the flanking palindromic regions)

- C:\FTP>perl sample.pl
- CTTTG*TCAGGATGGGC*CAAAG => 1
- AGTAT*T*ATACT => 1
- GAAATC**GATTTC => 1
- AGTTT*GGCATCC*AAACT => 1
- CCTTA*CCCTGT*TAAGG => 1
- CTTCT*GGAGATTGAGA*AGAAG => 1
- .
- .
- .
- GATGG*ATTCAAG*CCATC => 1
- GTTTGG*CAT*CCAAAC => 1
- CTTCT*CCAC*AGAAG => 1

Palindromes can be found quickly in sequence datasets prepared from tissue samples. Finding palindromes is just one example of how a simple Perl script can find gene patterns of interest. Once found, the next step would be to associate a specific gene pattern with a clinical phenotype (i.e., the biological behavior of a disease or a lesion). This is one approach by which bioinformatics data (gene sequences) can complement medical data (clinical outcome or response to therapy).

6.19. WHY COUNTING IS NONTRIVIAL AND IMPORTANT

We are all taught to count in kindergarten. We all think we know how to do it. Nonetheless, the central activity of most biomedical informatics projects is "counting," and the most likely source of study design errors will relate to "counting."

A good illustration of the pitfalls of counting comes from our data on Korean War casualties. For decades after the Korean War, the U.S.

Defense Department had reported that approximately 54,000 U.S. soldiers died in the conflict. As late as 2000, the Defense Department issued a revised number, reducing the U.S. casualty number by 17,000. The original count had included U.S. soldier deaths occurring anywhere in the world during the Korean War. Nearly 50 years after the original count was taken, the official number of deaths in theater now stands at 36,616, of which 33,686 were battle deaths and 2,830 were nonbattle deaths. The original number of 54,000 was a good count of the number of service deaths occurring during a war, but it was a poor count of the number of Americans killed in Korean War battle.

Counting deaths would seem to be the most indisputable measurement in medicine, but confusion regarding the status of deceased populations is an intractable problem.

Richard Gordon describes an interesting development in England, where the simple act of counting the dead changed their perception of life (6). Beachy Head is a cliff in southern England facing the English Channel. Here the flat grassy earth abruptly gives way to a 532 foot drop. The vertical, chalky-white cliff face is a picturesque last stop for suicides. In 1975, the suicide rate dropped by half. What public health measures may have accounted for this dramatic improvement of the suicide rate? A new coroner had decided that bodies found at the foot of the cliff would be assayed for blood alcohol content. A body with alcohol in the blood would henceforth be labeled an accidental death. In order to be a suicide, the body would need to be dead and ethanol-free. The notion of someone bent on suicide taking a drink to fortify his or her resolve was not to be entertained. In essence, how you count things determines medical reality.

6.20. WHY YOU SHOULD WRITE YOUR OWN COUNTING PROGRAMS

We write our own counting programs because nobody else can do it for us. Simple counting routines are among the least generalizable computational tasks. This is because the manner in which you choose to count comes from a deep understanding of the data domain and a clear understanding of your study design. Neither of these can be preprogrammed into a general counting application.

The world is full of good software applications that will analyze data. There are very few software applications that will create your data for you.

Why is this? Data analysis can be generalized. If you provide a statistics program with a column of numbers, it will add them up, find the mean, calculate the standard deviation, and proceed to evaluate any complex statistical test you care to consider.

Because data counting is seldom generalizable, the biomedical informatician will design new counting protocols for every experiment and clinical study.

6.21. SOFTWARE UTILITIES VERSUS SOFTWARE APPLICATIONS

Software applications are usually large programs, with a sophisticated graphic user interface that permits the user to complete very specific tasks. Developers of software applications need in-depth knowledge of the tasks that their intended users will want to perform. They design their software to navigate the user through a logical sequence of choices leading to a certain type of functionality.

Software applications are nice, but software utilities are crucial. Utilities are typically small programs that perform a simple generalizable function. They often run from a command line (e.g., a command entered after a DOS prompt or a UNIX/LINUX shell prompt). They usually operate on files or on data provided in the command line (List 6.21.1).

LIST 6.21.1. EXAMPLES OF SOFTWARE UTILITY FUNCTIONS

- Archiving utilities
- Calculator utility
- Compression/decompression utilities
- Conversion utilities—Converts files (text, images, sound, video) to and from different formats
- Database utilities
- Directory searching
- Email service
- Encryption/decryption utilities
- File copying utilities
- File reading and parsing utilities
- FTP file retrieval
- Indexing utilities
- Sorting utilities
- Searching utilities
- Telnet remote computer access
- Text editing
- Web retrieval utilities

Many of these listed utilities are available at no cost and are described in the Appendix. Unix/Linux users will recognize that several of the listed utilities are available as simple shell commands (e.g., ls, bc, compress, uncompress, telnet, sort, cp, ftp, more pack, unpack, vi, and the highly esteemed grep).

If you are adept at using software utilities and if you know just a little bit of programming, then you can achieve a high level of software independence. Many utilities are available as commands or as software modules that can be built directly into programs that you write. Perl has thousands of utility-type modules freely available for download from the Comprehensive Perl Archive Network (CPAN) (66).

Remarkably powerful applications can be built using a few simple programming commands, one or more utility modules, and a graphic user interface. Many programming languages, including Perl, Python, and Ruby, come with graphic user interface modules that can be invoked from within scripts. Java uses Web browsers to provide a graphic user interface for Java applets. In many instances, biomedical informaticians will find it expeditious, if not vital, to create their own software solutions to suit their unique situations.

6.22. SOFTWARE EVALUATION

There is a world of difference between writing software for yourself and writing software for others. Basically, there are three categories of "others" that programmers may need to serve (in order of increasing fussiness): colleagues, buyers, and regulatory agencies. The regulatory agency that biomedical informaticians most often deal with is the FDA (Food and Drug Administration). The FDA's Quality System Regulation is described in section 520 of the Food, Drug and Cosmetic (FD&C) Act. The Quality System regulation helps ensure that medical devices are safe and effective for their intended use. Certain provisions of the medical device Quality System regulation apply to software (List 6.22.1).

LIST 6.22.1. TYPES OF SOFTWARE OF POSSIBLE INTEREST TO THE FDA

- Software used as a component, part, or accessory of a medical device
- Software that is itself a medical device (e.g., blood typing software)

- Software used in the production of a device (e.g., programmable logic controllers in manufacturing equipment)
- Software used in implementation of the device manufacturer's quality system (e.g., software that records and maintains the device history record)

Consumers tend to have very simplified and self-centered ways of evaluating software applications (List 6.22.2).

LIST 6.22.2. FEATURES OF SOFTWARE THAT BUYERS WANT

- Easy installation
- Simple instructions and documentation
- Friendly graphic user interface
- Functionality that supports the user's goals
- Transparency (no need for user to understand the underlying assumptions, algorithms, and data structures upon which the functionality of the software is based)
- Compatibility with operating system and other software residing on the user's computer
- Good user support services

Biomedical informaticians have responsibilities beyond their own personal interests. They have an obligation to conduct research that is scientifically sound, that uses methods that are understood and can be included in the "Methods" section of research papers, and that produces output that can be studied by their colleagues. Some features of software that might be important to biomedical informaticians are described in List 6.22.3.

LIST 6.22.3. FEATURES OF GOOD SOFTWARE (THAT SERIOUS BIOMEDICAL INFORMATICIANS NEED)

- Extensibility—the functionality of the software and the data can be modified and expanded
- Scalability—should work with any size of inputs
- Standardization of all data (input and output)
- Open source code
- Open access data
- Self-describing software

- Cross-platform functionality—software should operate in multiple operating systems
- Interoperability
- Availability of updates
- Full documentation of methods and algorithms

Regulatory agencies, funding agencies, and mission-critical applications (including medical care) may have a very different set of software requirements than buyers and biomedical researchers (48). These entities often require software to be rigorously validated (see List 6.22.4, modified from reference 48).

LIST 6.22.4. SOME PROPERTIES OF VALID SOFTWARE, MODELED ON FDA PRINCIPLES OF SOFTWARE VALIDATION

- Verified—"Software verification looks for consistency, completeness, and correctness of the software and its supporting documentation, as it is being developed, and provides support for a subsequent conclusion that software is validated."
- Tested—"confirm that software development output meets its input requirements." Includes testing at user site.
- Validated—"confirmation by examination and provision of objective evidence that software specifications conform to user needs and intended uses, and that the particular requirements implemented through software can be consistently fulfilled."
- Risk-assessed—"the safety risks posed by the software should be specified."
- Requirement-documented—"The software and system requirements must be fully documented(48)." The validation step requires an analysis of compliance with documented requirements.
- Controlled development process—"bugs are often introduced during the software development process. A controlled development process ensures that changes in the design of software are tracked and evaluated, documented and corrected when necessary."
- Design review—"Design reviews are documented, comprehensive, and systematic examinations of a design to evaluate the adequacy of the design requirements, to evaluate the capability of the design to meet these requirements, and to identify problems."

One of the more subtle distinctions in software performance is found in the related concepts of accuracy/reproducibility and predictability/validity. In the field of biomedical informatics, software can be used to yield a piece of data. If the data provides an accurate measurement of a biological quantity, and if repeated measurements of the same quantity provide the same quantitative result, then the software is accurate and reproducible.

A higher level of software function occurs when data are used to produce a conclusion. In the field of biomedical informatics, a conclusion often takes the form of an outcome prediction. If the software draws the same conclusion over and over with the same set of input variables, and if the conclusion reached can be shown to be correct in test after test of the system, then the software is valid and has high predictability.

Possibly the greatest challenge to the field of software evaluation comes from the increasing use of software whose constructions defy simple analysis (List 6.22.5).

LIST 6.22.5. CONDITIONS THAT CAN MAKE SOFTWARE DIFFICULT TO EVALUATE

- Intrinsic complexity of the software (75)
- Use of **off-the-shelf software**
- Use of external software components
- Withheld source code and poor documentation

Off-the-shelf software typically comes without source code, without documentation of contained algorithms, and without any way of modifying the software to suit a particular need or correcting bugs in the software.

Component-based and object-oriented software are popular approaches to software engineering because they permit the application designer to create software whose defined tasks are routed to prebuilt software components or objects. Problems may arise if the components or objects interact with each other in unpredicted ways. Nancy Leveson has written, "...software is allowing us to build systems with such a high level of interactive complexity that potential interactions among components cannot be thoroughly planned, anticipated, tested, or guarded against" (76). Software that is used in medical devices or that is used to make medical decisions or detect medical errors must meet high levels of reliability. Medical software must be used in a manner that permits bugs to be quickly detected and debugged with patches distributed to all the software users. The creation of high-quality software that is fully described and validated is a job for software developers. The task of constantly re-evaluating medical software is a job for biomedical informaticians.

Biomedical Nomenclatures

7.1. BACKGROUND

Modern nomenclatures are used to organize, index, and retrieve biomedical data. Most modern nomenclatures are prepared as a taxonomy (collection of the relevant items in a data domain), wherein synonymous terms are grouped together and assigned a unique concept code.

For instance, in the Developmental Lineage Classification and Taxonomy of Neoplasms (hereafter called the Neoplasm Classification), prostate cancer is assigned the unique concept code C486300, and all the term variants for this concept are attached to the same concept code (77–80) (List 7.1.1).

LIST 7.1.1. EQUIVALENT TERMS FOR THE CONCEPT IDENTIFIER C4863000

- C4863000 prostate with adenoca
- C4863000 adenoca arising in prostate
- C4863000 adenoca involving prostate
- C4863000 adenoca arising from prostate
- C4863000 adenoca of prostate
- C4863000 adenoca of the prostate
- C4863000 prostate with adenocarcinoma
- C4863000 adenocarcinoma arising in prostate
- C4863000 adenocarcinoma involving prostate
- C4863000 adenocarcinoma arising from prostate
- C4863000 adenocarcinoma of prostate
- C4863000 adenocarcinoma of the prostate

- C4863000 adenocarcinoma arising in the prostate
- C4863000 adenocarcinoma involving the prostate
- C4863000 adenocarcinoma arising from the prostate
- C4863000 prostate with ca
- C4863000 ca arising in prostate
- C4863000 ca involving prostate
- C4863000 ca arising from prostate
- C4863000 ca of prostate
- C4863000 ca of the prostate
- C4863000 prostate with cancer
- C4863000 cancer arising in prostate
- C4863000 cancer involving prostate
- C4863000 cancer arising from prostate
- C4863000 cancer of prostate
- C4863000 cancer of the prostate
- C4863000 cancer arising in the prostate
- C4863000 cancer involving the prostate
- C4863000 cancer arising from the prostate
- C4863000 prostate with carcinoma
- C4863000 carcinoma arising in prostate
- C4863000 carcinoma involving prostate
- C4863000 carcinoma arising from prostate
- C4863000 carcinoma of prostate
- C4863000 carcinoma of the prostate
- C4863000 carcinoma arising in the prostate
- C4863000 carcinoma involving the prostate
- C4863000 carcinoma arising from the prostate
- C4863000 prostate adenoca
- C4863000 prostate adenocarcinoma
- C4863000 prostate ca
- C4863000 prostate cancer
- C4863000 prostate carcinoma
- C4863000 prostatic cancer
- C4863000 prostatic carcinoma
- C4863000 prostatic adenocarcinoma
- C4863000 prostate gland adenocarcinoma
- C4863000 adenocarcinoma of the prostate gland
- C4863000 adenocarcinoma of prostate gland

- C4863000 prostate gland carcinoma
- C4863000 carcinoma of the prostate gland
- C4863000 carcinoma of prostate gland

When a nomenclature collects synonymous terms for unique concept iden-tifiers, medical text containing any of the terms corresponding to a single concept can be assigned the unique concept code. When all the terms in a medical database have been coded, they can be retrieved through a concept search that collects all synonymous terms by their unifying concept iden-tifier. A medical sentence can be coded many different ways. The follow-ing is a sentence that has been coded using a neoplasm nomenclature.

Sentence=Primary synovial sarcoma of the mediastinum a clinicopatho-logic immunohistochemical and ultrastructural study of 15 cases.

term="sarcoma of the mediastinum" code="C6606000"

term="synovial sarcoma" code="C3400000"

term="synovial sarcoma of the mediastinum" code="C6618000"

term="primary synovial sarcoma" code="C8826000"

The example provides a so-called exhaustive coding strategy. Terms were coded even when subsumed by larger terms (e.g., synovial sarcoma and primary synovial sarcoma). A parsimonious coding strategy for the same sentence may have coded only a single term that seemed to best represent the lesion (i.e., synovial sarcoma of the mediastinum). In this simple example, it becomes clear that there are different approaches to coding text, and the different approaches may produce different sets of coded terms for a single piece of text.

In the fields of medicine and biology, synonymy is common. Even rare tumors often have several synonymous terms. Consequently, medical vocabularies tend to be large datasets requiring fastidious curation (List 7.1.2).

LIST 7.1.2. SYNONYMS FOR THE RARE TUMOR, NASOPHARYNGEAL CARCINOMA

- Regaud tumor
- nasopharyngeal carcinoma
- lymphoepithelial carcinoma
- Schmincke tumor

7.2. BIG NOMENCLATURES AND SMALL NOMENCLATURES

There is considerable interest on the federal level to promote national and international standard medical vocabularies.[81] Standard medical nomenclatures have enormous advantages, ensuring that codified data collected from many different sources can be sensibly merged and integrated. They also ensure that a coded medical concept can be retrieved regardless of the particular term chosen to represent the concept.

Standard nomenclatures are created by committees composed of members of one or more large professional organizations. Standard nomenclatures typically have a vetting process whereby terms and definitions are reviewed by many people to ensure that the included terms harmonize with the sensibilities and interests of a range of stakeholder communities. The processes followed by standards development organizations all take time, but they serve to produce a widely accepted standard. Standardized nomenclature may have features that do not apply to small nomenclatures (List 7.2.1).

LIST 7.2.1. ADVANTAGES OF STANDARDIZED NOMENCLATURES

- Permanence
- Vetting—review and approval by experts and community stakeholders
- Wide use and universal recognition
- Comprehensive over a knowledge domain that extends over many specialized areas
- Mapping (between standards)
- Relationships between different domains
- Proven utility
- Development costs often transferred to users or to funding agencies

Despite their many advantages, general nomenclatures have limitations. Serious problems may arise when nomenclatures are incomplete, lacking relevant concepts and terms. If a relevant term is missing from the nomenclature, then data containing the term cannot be coded.

Because general nomenclatures are always incomplete, specialized nomenclatures have appeared to satisfy special interest groups.[82–87] Specialized nomenclatures tend to be written by a small number of people, but they have some features that general nomenclatures may lack (List 7.2.2).

LIST 7.2.2. ADVANTAGES OF SMALL, SPECIALIZED NOMENCLATURES

- Rapid addition of new terms
- Complete vocabulary for a narrow knowledge domain
- Immediate availability of frequently updated versions of nomenclature
- Data model appropriate for specialized uses of nomenclature
- Comprehensible by experts in the field
- Inexpensive to create and often available free to users

For decades, the approach to coding medical data has been to provide persistent and unchanging codes for medical concepts. Coding is intended to satisfy current and future data retrieval needs. If everyone uses the same nomenclature to code their data, then the data accumulated at different institutions can be electronically exchanged and integrated. The desire for unchanging medical codes to support future data integration efforts creates several problems. First, even standard nomenclatures change. Records coded with a 1995 version of SNOMED will have a different code set than records coded with the 2005 version of SNOMED. Second, different coding strategies may produce remarkably different coding results using the same nomenclature and the same dataset. For instance, one coder may prefer a parsimonious coding strategy producing the single best code for a diagnosis, whereas another coder may prefer a comprehensive strategy, providing codes for all terms in the text that match any terms in the vocabulary.

Finally, medical texts may have markedly different content and structure, making it impossible to sensibly combine coding results even when the same nomenclatures and coding strategies are used. For instance, a corpus of medical text may have poor orthography, or may represent many terms as nonstandard abbreviations, making it impossible for an autocoder to match terms from the medical records with terms from the nomenclature. If another set of medical records contains terms that are correctly spelled and eschews abbreviated forms, then the coding results will vary greatly, even when the same standard nomenclature is used to code both datasets.

In order to achieve coding uniformity between different datasets, the data must all be coded with the same nomenclature, using the same coding algorithm (whether the algorithm is conducted by humans or by machine), and there must be some determination that the coding algorithm provides comparable annotation for all the datasets. In reality, these conditions almost never hold. In later chapters, we will see that medical datasets must be recoded with different versions of a nomenclature and with different types of nomenclatures to suit the objectives of different types of data analyses. Autocoding large datasets can now be done quickly by using any nomenclature that associates terms with concept codes. We will demonstrate that thousands of surgical pathology reports can be autocoded in a fraction of a second using fast algorithms and powerful computers. When data sets are recoded, they can be recoded with more than one nomenclature, so long as the concepts are fully identified by their source nomenclature. Anticipated mandates to implement standard nomenclatures should accommodate dual-coding strategies that permit retrieval of data that has been coded by a general nomenclature and by one or more specialized nomenclatures.

7.3. CURATING NOMENCLATURES

Samuel Johnson defined a lexicographer as a "harmless drudge." The drudgery of the lexicographer's tasks is beyond dispute. In the domain of medical nomenclatures, however, the harmlessness of the lexicographer is far from certain.

Medical terminologies are replete with examples of minor term modifications that can result in treatment error. Carcinoma in situ of bladder is a very different lesion than non-invasive transitional cell carcinoma of bladder. The former is a widespread lesion associated with a high mortality. The latter lesion is a focal tumor that can be easily excised. However, both lesions are composed of words that mean the same thing ("in situ" and "non-invasive"). If the curator of a nomenclature is unaware of the distinction between the two tumors, then he or she may mistakenly assign the same code to both terms. In either case, mistaking in situ carcinoma of bladder with non-invasive transitional cell carcinoma of bladder could result in harm to the patient.

Subtyping concepts is one of the most difficult jobs for the curator. As an example, consider the common skin mole. A mole may come in many named varieties, such as: Achromic nevus, Balloon cell nevus, Blue nevus, Cellular blue nevus, Compound nevus, Dermal nevus, Dysplastic nevus, Epithelioid and spindle cell nevus, Epithelioid cell nevus, Fibrous papule of the nose, Giant pigmented nevus, Hairy nevus, Halo nevus, Intradermal nevus, Intraepidermal nevus, Involuting nevus, Jadassohn's blue nevus, Junctional nevus, Juvenile nevus, Magnocellular nevus, Melanocytic nevus, Mixed dermal and epidermal nevus, Naevus, Neuronevus, Nevus, Nonpigmented nevus, Pigmented nevus, Regressing nevus, Spindle cell nevus, and Spitz nevus.

The curator of a nomenclature must decide whether it is worthwhile to lump all the subtypes of a lesion under one concept number, whether to create separate concept codes for each variant term, or whether to reclassify terms that may not belong to their historically assigned class (e.g., is fibrous papule of the nose really a nevus?).

Many disease names can best be classified as nonsequiturs, with no predictable relationship to any particular attribute (List 7.3.1).

LIST 7.3.1. HOW NAMES OF DISEASES ARE CHOSEN

- As an expression of a characteristic pathologic process (e.g., muscular dystrophy)
- For the physical agent that produced the disease (e.g., plumbism)
- For a group of people who were at high risk for the disease (e.g., Legionnaires' Disease, named after a group of conventioneers who succumbed in an early outbreak)
- For a molecule found in diseased cells (e.g., amyloidosis, prion disease)
- For a geographic region in which the disease occurs (e.g., Tangier Disease from Tangier Island, Maryland)
- For a geographic region from which an epidemic emanated (e.g., Lyme disease from Lyme, New York)
- For a striking clinical feature of the disease (e.g., sleeping sickness)
- As a crude and insensitive comparison to an inanimate object (e.g., gargoylism)
- As a literary metaphor (e.g., Pickwickian syndrome, Mad Hatter's disease)
- For a striking microscopic feature (e.g., sickle cell anemia)
- For a patient who had the disease (e.g., Lou Gehrig disease)
- For a physician or scientist who treated, described, or researched the disease (e.g., Hodgkin disease, Cushing disease, Kaposi sarcoma)
- As a clueless acronym (e.g., CATCH 22, cardiac abnormality, abnormal facies, t-cell deficit due to thymic hypoplasia, cleft palate, and hypocalcemia all resulting from a deletion on chromosome 22)
- As a trope from any existing language (e.g., Moyamoya disease derives from "moyamoya" meaning "puff of smoke" in Japanese, for the characteristic tangle of tiny cerebral vessels seen on x-ray)
- As a paean to Greek and Latin scholarship (e.g., pityriasis lichenoides et varioliformis acuta)

- As inscrutable combinations of one or more of the above (My personal favorite inscrutable disease name is the wistful-sounding "floating-harbor syndrome." This disease was named by combining the hospital in which one of the first cases appeared, Boston Floating Hospital, and for a second hospital in which another case appeared, Harbor General Hospital in Torrance, California.)

Curators are sometimes arbiters of good taste. Some of the names used in medicine are pejoratives and many of these have been replaced by less offensive terminology (List 7.3.2).

LIST 7.3.2. EXAMPLES OF OFFENSIVE MEDICAL TERMS

- Gargoylism—the name invites comparison of a patient with a monster.
- Mongolism and Mongoloid idiot—The disease is named after the peoples that the doctor believes look most like the person with the disease.
- Monster—the name suggests that the individual is not human.
- Cretinism—the name links a patient with a pejorative term (cretin).

Curators are expected to understand the root origin of terms. A Schwannoma is not a tumor composed of pieces of Dr. Schwann. The better name would have been "Schwann tumor" or "Schwann's tumor" or, more accurately, "Schwann's cell tumor." Schwann was the person who studied the cell (Schwann's cell), not the tumor. Likewise, a Kaposiform hemangioendothelioma is not shaped like Dr. Kaposi.

Some common medical terms are highly misleading, and the curator must know how to winnow the chafe. For instance, the term "Kuttner tumor" is a misnomer. The so-called Kuttner tumor is chronic sclerosing sialadenitis (inflammation of a salivary gland). It is sometimes mistaken for a squamous carcinoma or a lymphoma. It is not a neoplasm. The term "fat necrosis" is misleading. So-called fat necrosis is a postnecrotic accumulation of macrophages containing the phagocytized (engulfed) fragments of lipocytes. Fat is a nonliving substance and cannot necrotize (die). Inflammatory tumor of breast is neither a tumor composed of inflammatory cells nor a carcinoma with a florid inflammatory component. Inflammatory carcinoma of breast is a carcinoma of breast that invades breast tissue, diffusely producing a gross appearance that mimics cellulitis.

Curators of nomenclatures need to decide whether they want to include obsolete or otherwise denigrated terms. Excluding an offensive term may enhance the political correctness of a nomenclature but does little to ensure that decades-old records can be coded and retrieved.

Curators do much more than simply collect terms. The many choices that curators make (e.g., what goes in, what comes out, what concepts have meaning, what concepts are redundant) endow nomenclatures with a conceived purpose and a human soul.

The tasks of ancient curators are different from the tasks of modern curators (List 7.3.3).

LIST 7.3.3. TASKS OF THE ANCIENT CURATOR

- Select canonical (best) terms for concepts
- Delete obsolete or otherwise denigrated terms
- Prepare precise definitions for the included terms
- Prepare revised versions of the nomenclature at intervals, perhaps once each century
- Prepare nomenclature in an academic language, such as Latin, that limits access to scholars

Modern curators work much like their ancestors, but they also toil under a growing list of informatics-related burdens. Because modern nomenclatures are used to annotate medical data so that clinical information can be merged with heterogeneous data sources (e.g., tissue bank records, research datasets, epidemiologic databases), the duties of lexicographers have broadened to include a range of informatics activities. For this reason, the modern curator is involved in codifying terms (providing a unique identifier to a term and all its synonyms) and mapping terms between different nomenclatures (List 7.3.4).

LIST 7.3.4. TASKS OF THE MODERN CURATOR

- Add new terms to the nomenclature when they occur in the domain literature
- Group synonymous terms under a unique concept code
- Determine the relationships among the different terms in the nomenclature and provide links or ontologic classes that express these relationships

- Comply with standards for representing the terms in a nomenclature that will support data integration with other nomenclatures
- Ensure the logical consistency of the nomenclature
- Update and release revised versions of the nomenclature at intervals, perhaps daily
- Develop methods for representing term variations
- Post the nomenclature to the Internet, as an Open Access document
- Prepare a legal "use" disclaimer
- Develop methodology for linking concept codes to annotative data on the Internet

The American Society of Testing and Materials (ASTM) Standard of Quality Indicators for Controlled Health Vocabularies has described curation practices that are recommended in a federal document issued by the U.S. Department of Health and Human Services (81) (List 7.3.5).

LIST 7.3.5. GOOD CURATION PRACTICES FOR MEDICAL NOMENCLATURES

- General characteristics relate to utility and appropriateness in clinical applications, including that concepts are not vague, ambiguous, or redundant; purpose and scope are clear; coverage is in-depth, explicit, and comprehensive; there are systematic and formal definitions of all concepts; and the concepts are built into a reference vocabulary.
- Structure of the vocabulary model determines the ease with which practical and useful interfaces for term navigation, entry, or retrieval can be supported.
- Maintenance characteristics provide the technical choices which impact the capacity of a vocabulary to evolve, change, and remain usable over time, including context-free identifiers, persistence of identifiers, and version control.
- Evaluation criteria address how a vocabulary should be evaluated and include a clear statement of purpose and scope, availability of tools for mapping, and usability.

7.4. AUTOMATIC EXPANSION OF A MEDICAL NOMENCLATURE

Adding terms to an existing vocabulary traditionally involved reading current literature and transcribing new terms when they are encountered. Today, it is impossible for curators to read all of the biomedical literature pertaining to a nomenclature's domain. In this section, we describe a simple method for automatically extracting candidate new terms from any large corpus of text. It is based on the empirical observation that terms in a nomenclature are almost always composed of phrases occurring in other terms from the same nomenclature. The method compares word doublets in a medical text against a list of word doublets found in a nomenclature (88) (List 7.4.1). Text phrases composed of sequences of word doublets found in an existing nomenclature are candidate new nomenclature terms. This general method can be used with any text and any existing nomenclature. This method permits curators to continually enhance their nomenclatures with new terms, which is an essential activity needed to ensure the proper coding and annotation of biomedical data.

LIST 7.4.1. DOUBLET METHOD FOR FINDING CANDIDATE TERMS FROM TEXT

1. Collect all the doublets that occur in the entire nomenclature (i.e., accumulate a list of the doublets from every term in the nomenclature).
2. Parse text from the medical literature into an ordered collection of overlapping doublets. As an example, "serous borderline ovarian tumor" would be parsed as "serous borderline, borderline ovarian, ovarian tumor".
3. Compare each consecutive text doublet against the array of doublets from the nomenclature to determine whether the doublet exists somewhere in the nomenclature.
4. If the doublet from the text does not exist in the nomenclature, then it can be deleted. If it exists in the nomenclature, then it is concatenated with the following doublet if the following doublet exists in the nomenclature. Otherwise, it is deleted. This process continues, concatenating doublets that exist somewhere in the nomenclature. Extraneous leading words (the, in, of, with, and) and trailer words, (the, and, with, from, a) are automatically deleted from the final concatenated sequence. Final concatenated sequences of two or greater consecutive doublets that match to doublets from the nomenclature are saved as candidate terms.

LIST 7.4.2. SNIPPET OF PERL CODE FOR THE DOUBLET METHOD

```
. . . . .
@hoparray = split(/ /,$line);
my $olddoublet = "";
for ($i=0;$i<(scalar(@hoparray)-1);$i++)
    {
    $doublet = "$hoparray[$i]$hoparray[$i+1]";
    if (exists $doubhash{$doublet})
```

```
        {
    if ($englishline ne "")
        {
        $englishline = $englishline . "$hoparray[$i+1]";
        }
    else
        {
        $englishline = $doublet;
        }
    }
```

The full Perl script for extracting candidate nomenclature terms from text is available as a supplemental file from an open access manuscript (89). The snippet of Perl shows the heart of the term extraction algorithm (List 7.4.2).

At the top of the snippet, a fragment of unpunctuated text is split at the space character between words, and the resulting list of consecutive words from the text is assigned to an array:

```
@hoparray = split(/ /,$line);
```

For the number of words in the array, each overlapping word doublet is assigned to a variable through a for-loop:

```
for ($i=0;$i<(scalar(@hoparray)-1);$i++)
{
$doublet = "$hoparray[$i]$hoparray[$i+1]";
```

An associative array of each doublet occurring in a reference nomenclature has been prepared in a prior segment of the script, and this associative array has been assigned the name %doubhash. Each doublet occurring in @hoparray is interrogated to determine whether the doublet exists in %doubhash:

```
if (exists $doubhash{$doublet})
```

If the doublet exists in %doubhash, then the second word of the doublet is added to the concatenation string of consecutive doublets occurring in @hoparray and found in the nomenclature ($englishline):

```
{
if ($englishline ne "")
    {
    $englishline = $englishline . "$hoparray[$i+1]";
    }
```

If the concatenation of consecutive doublets is empty, then the doublet starts the new concatenation string:

```
else
   {
   $englishline = $doublet;
   }
}
```

The purpose of the doublet phrase extractor is to parse through any corpus of text, extracting phrases that may contain new nomenclature terms. The phrases are chosen to meet two criteria (List 7.4.3).

LIST 7.4.3. CRITERIA FOR INCLUDING A PHRASE AS A CANDIDATE NEW TERM

- Candidate phrases in medical text are concatenated strings of word doublets that are contained in terms found in an existing nomenclature.
- Candidate phrases do not already occur in the nomenclature.

The doublet extractor works fast to produce a neat list of candidate phrases that can be conveniently reviewed by a curator. In a test case, a 31+ megabyte corpus was extracted in 2 seconds, to produce several hundred phrases that could be added to the reference nomenclature (requiring about 30 minutes of the curator's time) (88). We will learn more about the doublet algorithm in Chapter 9.

Misbehaving Text: Dealing with Poorly Written Medical Text

8.1. BACKGROUND

Medical informaticians dream of the day when all medical data will be captured by computers in a highly structured format that ensures data uniformity. In this utopian vision, only canonical forms of medical terms will be used. Medical reports will have a uniform format and will be computer parsable and human readable. Taxonomies will be small because biomedical staff will be constrained to use preferred terms for medical concepts.

Unfortunately, the current trend in medical reporting seems to favor unstructured narrative data entry. I can remember the early days of computers when data storage and memory constraints were at a premium. Years were entered as two-digit values (nobody worried about Y2K back in the 60s), and entry words were selected from lists and were typically represented by a single digit. Today, the storage and transmission of textual data are nonissues. Large vocabularies of millions of terms can reside in active memory. Physicians prefer narrative text to structured text (70), and most of the medical data entered by physicians appears in the form of free-text e-mails, memoranda, progress notes, hospital reports of every type, research publications, and so on. Free expression results in a seemingly unlimited way of describing a single thought, and large taxonomies are sometimes useful tools for organizing and retrieving the many terms found in narrative free-text.

In the next few chapters, we will deal with issues of free-text transformation, autocoding, scrubbing, metadata annotation, classification, and ontologies. All these efforts require an appreciation of medical free-text.

8.2. SPELLING ERRORS

Narrative medical text is replete with spelling errors. This is because narrative text is written by humans and humans are imperfect. Fortunately, the human brain is wonderfully fault-tolerant and can easily interpret misspelled words. The following lesson, entitled, "Our Amzanig Barnis," of unknown authorship, has made the rounds of many Internet blogs and user groups.

"Can you raed tihs? Olny srmat poelpe can. I cdnuolt blveiee taht I cluod aulaclty uesdnatnrd waht I was rdanieg. The phaonmneal pweor of the hmuan mnid, aoccdrnig to a rscheearch at Cmabrigde Uinervtisy, it deosn't mttaer in waht oredr the ltteers in a wrod are, the olny iprmoatnt tihng is taht the frist and lsat ltteer be in the rghit pclae. The rset can be a taotl mses and you can sitll raed it wouthit a porbelm. This is bcuseae the huamn mnid deos not raed ervey lteter by istlef, but the wrod as a wlohe. Amzanig huh? yaeh and I awlyas tghuhot slpeling was ipmorantt! If you can raed tihs psas it on!!"

Computers can be programmed to tolerate spelling errors. The following Perl script, spell.pl, will take a medical word and produce a list of words (selected from an external wordlist file) that have similar spelling to any provided word.

```perl
#!usr/bin/perl
use String::Approx qw(amatch);
print "What word would you like to approximate?\n";
$givenword = <STDIN>;
print "\nApproximate matches\n";
open(WORDLIST, "c:\\ftp\\word") or die "Cannot";
while(<WORDLIST>)
    {
    print if (amatch($givenword));
    }
close WORDLIST;
exit;
```

LIST 8.2.1. OUTPUT OF FUZZY SPELLING MATCH

- c:\ftp>perl spell.pl
- What word would you like to approximate?
- hemocromatosis
- Approximate matches
- haemochromatosis
- hemochromatoses
- hemochromatosis

Approximate word matching (sometimes called fuzzy matching) is useful for supporting database searches when the user is unsure of the exact spelling of their query term (List 8.2.1). Users of approximate word matching algorithms should be cautioned that, in medicine, there are many word pairs with similar orthography and dissimilar meaning (List 8.2.2).

LIST 8.2.2. ONE-LETTER (MOSTLY) DIFFERENCES AMONG PROPERLY SPELLED WORDS

- arteritis <=> arthritis
- auxiliary => axillary
- brachial <=> branchial
- callous <=> callus
- chlorpromazine <=> chlorpropamide
- chorionic <=> chronic
- coitus <=> colitis
- colic <=> colonic
- costal <=> coastal
- cygnet <=> signet
- diploic <=> diploid
- disc <=> disk
- disease <=> decease
- dyskaryosis <=> dyskeratosis
- ectatic <=> ecstatic
- enema <=> anemia
- facial <=> fascial
- facies <=> feces
- faeces <=> facies
- fascial <=> facial
- fetal <=> fatal
- firearm <=> forearm
- hallux <=> helicis
- helicis <=> hallux
- herpangina <=> herpetic
- herpetic <=> herpangina
- hydatid <=> hydatidiform
- hydatidiform <=> hydatid
- ileitis <=> iliitis
- ileum <=> ilium
- isotope <=> isotrope

- keratin => kerasin
- keratinocytic => keratinolytic
- keratosis <=> ketosis
- lipoma <=> lymphoma
- live <=> liver
- lover <=> liver
- malleolus <=> malleus
- milia <=> milium
- mucous <=> mucus
- myelofibrosis <=> myofibrosis
- oncology <=> ontology
- osteoblastoma <=> osteoclastoma
- paleontology => paleodontology
- palette <=> palate
- palpation => palpitation
- parental <=> parenteral
- penal <=> penile
- penicillamine <=> penicillin
- penile <=> penal
- perineal <=> peroneal
- pleural <=> plural
- porphyria <=> porphyruria
- prostate <=> prostrate
- protuberans <=> protruberant
- quinidine <=> quinine
- rachischisis <=> rachitis
- rachischitic <=> rachitic
- ret <=> rett
- rosacea <=>rosea
- semantic <=> somatic
- silicon <=> silicone
- taenia <=> tinea
- thecoma <=> thekeoma
- tinnitus <=> tinnitis
- trichinosis <=> trichosis
- ureteral <=> urethral
- vagitis <=> vaginitis

Medication errors occasionally arise when a drug is mistaken for a different medication with a similar name (List 8.2.3). This problem is compounded by the pharmaceutical industry's habit of assigning new drug names by their sound-appeal rather than by their clinical activity, chemical composition, or pharmaceutical category. Naming errors are most important in cases where drug allergies are common (e.g., sulfonylureas) and in life-threatening situations where the administration of the correct medication is crucial. Perhaps patients would benefit if drug names were not invented by marketing firms.

LIST 8.2.3. DRUGS WITH SIMILAR NAMES

- acetazolamide <=> acetahexamide
- ambien <=> amen
- amiodarone <=> amrinone
- cardene <=> cardizem
- chlorpropamide <=> chlorpromazine
- clonidine <=> klonipin
- clozapine <=> olanzapine
- feldene <=> seldane
- flomax <=> volmax
- flutamide <=> flumadine
- imipenem <=> omnipen
- lodine <=> codeine
- methadone <=> methylphenidate
- ms contin <=> oxycontin
- oruvail <=> clinoril
- penicillin <=> penicillamine
- prilosec <=> prozac
- quinidine <=> quinine
- retrovir <=> ritonavir
- zocor <=> cozaar

In any corpus of text, there will be words that are misspelled frequently, and usually a small number of misspelled words account for the bulk of errors. Many of the misspellings are transliterations (an exchange in the order of the characters that belong in a properly spelled word) (List 8.2.4).

LIST 8.2.4. COMMON MISSPELLINGS APPEARING IN PATHOLOGY REPORTS

- abcess (should be abscess)
- anastamosis (anastomosis)
- bissected (dissections are done with bisections)
- caricnoma (the most commonly occurring terms are commonly misspelled)
- cassett (both cassette and casette are permissible)
- debridment
- entirley
- formlain
- illeocecal (one "l" please)
- lymphnode (a lymph node is two words)
- malilgnant
- membraneous (the noun, "membrane," has an adjective, "membranous")
- mesentary
- negtive
- palmer
- spleenic (the noun is "spleen," but the adjective is "splenic")
- tannish ("ish" is a popular but unnecessary suffix)
- uretheral (ureteral is a word and so is urethral, but uretheral is not)

Sometimes variant spellings of a word are permissible (List 8.2.5). I spent most of my adult life unsure of the spelling of the color grey (grey or gray). Only recently was I informed that either spelling is correct. Other words are misspelled so often that few people bother to correct the errors. HIPPA and HIPAA are omnipresent in the biomedical literature, but only one spelling is correct.

LIST 8.2.5. PERMISSIBLE ALTERNATE SPELLINGS

- anonymization = anonymisation
- artifact = artefact
- cassette = casette
- catheterisation = catheterization
- dilatation = dilation

- exotropia = exotrophia
- preventative = preventive
- sulfate = sulphate
- sulfur = sulphur
- sulfuric = sulphuric
- travelling = traveling

I suspect that some of the terms in the Unified Medical Language System (UMLS) with variant spellings are actually misspelled (List 8.2.6). Even an authoritative nomenclature may contain errors. After all, UMLS was prepared by humans.

LIST 8.2.6. DUALLY OCCURRING ORTHOGRAPHIC VARIANTS IN UMLS THAT ARE PROBABLY NOT PROPER EQUIVALENCES

- neurilemmoma and neurilemoma
- sacroiliitis and sacroileitis
- costalchondritis, costochondritis, and costal chondritis
- azoospermia and azospermia
- Bartter's Disease and Barter's Disease
- in situ and insitu
- gall bladder and gallbladder

8.3. HOMONYMOUS TERMS

Homonyms are words or phrases that have multiple meanings (List 8.3.1).

LIST 8.3.1. DISEASE HOMONYMS

- cervical carcinoma (of neck or of uterus?)
- medullary carcinoma (can refer to medullary carcinoma of breast or thyroid, or of adrenal medulla)
- Paget's disease (can refer to different diseases involving either breast or bone)
- Bowen's disease (can refer to different diseases in skin and nipple)

In addition to homonyms, there are examples of nearly identical terms with different meanings. Many of these are eponyms. Carney has a syndrome and a complex with his name. Cushing has a syndrome and a disease. Both men were outdone by Kaposi, who has a sarcoma, a disease, and an eruption that carry his name.

8.4. ABBREVIATIONS THAT ARE SOMETIMES BOTH ACRONYMS AND SHORTENED FORMS

Acronyms are usually concatenations of the first letters of a phrase. Abbreviations are usually compressed or short forms of words. The letter L (for the word left) is both an acronym and a shortened form. This is true for almost all single-letter abbreviations. Another term that is difficult to assign as either acronym or short form is DNA (deoxyribonucleic acid). DNA may well be an acronym, because the D is the first letter of deoxyribonucleic and the A is the first letter of acid, but the N comes up in the middle of a deoxyribonucleic. The letter N is the first letter of a word that could stand as an individual word (nucleic), even though it does not in this case. DNA can also be thought of as a simple shortened form of a long word, the same way that "cmpd" is a shortened form of the word compound. In both, the letters are pulled from their order of appearance in the full word but are chosen from scattered sites within the word. An example of a mixed acronym/abbreviation is "dsv," representing the "dermatome" of the fifth sacral nerve. Here a preposition, an article, and a noun (of, the, nerve) have been dropped for the abbreviation; the order or the acronym components has been changed (dermatome sacral fifth); an ordinal has been changed to a cardinal (fifth changed to five); and the cardinal has been shortened to its roman numeral equivalent (v).

8.5. PREPOSITIONS AND ARTICLES RETAINED IN AN ACRONYM

When forming an acronym from a phrase, it is difficult to guess when to use or abandon prepositions. Many acronyms exclude prepositions and articles. "CAP" is the acronym for College of American Pathologists, snubbing the "of." Other abbreviations are not so snobbish (DOB = date of birth). The word NIH (National Institutes of Health) denies any generosity to its sole preposition. Sometimes both forms are accepted abbreviations (e.g., edd = estimated date of delivery and edod = estimated date of delivery).

8.6. SINGLE EXPANSIONS WITH MULTIPLE ABBREVIATIONS

Just as abbreviations can map to many different expansions, the reverse can occur. For instance, high-grade squamous intraepithelial lesion can be abbreviated as "HGSIL" or "HSIL." Xanthogranulomatous pyelonephritis can be abbreviated as "XGP" or "XGPN." Angio-immunoblastic lymphadenopathy can be abbreviated as "ABL," "AIL," or "AIML."

8.7. NONSENSE ABBREVIATIONS

ANNL and ANLL represent the phrase acute nonlymphoblastic leukemia. It is impossible to imagine how the term ANNL ever became the abbreviation for a phrase that contains a solitary letter N, but this abbreviation appears occasionally in the pathology literature. The term PT-LPD represents post-transplantation lymphoproliferative disorders. The only location for a hyphen in the expansion is between the letters p and t. Why does the acronym move the hyphen? The term GNU (GNU is not UNIX) is an example of a self-referring acronym. Fully expanded, this acronym is of infinite length. Although the "N" and the "U" expand to words (not UNIX), the letter G is forever inscrutable.

The expansion for "OK" is simply "okay," the phonetic spelling of the sound made by the pronunciation of the abbreviation. Neither the abbreviation nor the expansion has any obvious entomologic derivation.

8.8. COMMON USAGE THAT CONFOUNDS MEANING

The term TREC is the acronym for "text retrieval conference." However, it seems that whenever TREC appears in a sentence, it occurs in the phrase "TREC conference" (trec.nist.gov/). Clearly, the word "conference" is redundant in this example. Apparently people would rather attend a "TREC conference" than either a "TRE conference" or a TREC.

8.9. SHIBBOLETHS (RESTRICTED SPOKEN MEANINGS)

Sometimes straightforward abbreviations adopt phonetic forms with features of shibboleths. For instance, the term peripheral neuroectodermal tumor is abbreviated as "PNET," but PNET sounds like "peanut," and peanut is now the abbreviated form used in conversation for these tumors. Examples of other phonetic expansions are "cabbage" for the phrase coronary artery bypass graft, and the term "tobasco," used for the phrase total abdominal hysterectomy and bilateral oophorectomy.

At times a word's abbreviation looks enough like an expansion to goad a spell-checker into action. The word "cameleon" is an abbreviation for the phrase cytosine arabinoside, high-dose methotrexate leucovorin oncovin. Spell-checkers should not replace the abbreviation with a "chameleon."

Though not a medical abbreviation, the following practice exemplifies the horrors of recursive abbreviations. The term SMETE is the abbreviation for the phrase science, math, engineering, and technology education. The term NSDL is the abbreviation for the term National SMETE Digital Library community (found at www.osti.gov/speeches/asist.html). Assuming that the term requires an abbreviation, wouldn't the form of the abbreviation holding a clue to the identity of the expansion be "NSMETEDL"?

8.10. PEJORATIVE ABBREVIATIONS

Pejorative or disrespectful terms should never appear in the medical record. When they occur, it would be better if they were not expanded: "flk" = "funny looking kid" and "gomer" = "get out of my emergency room."

8.11. LOCALE-DEPENDENT ABBREVIATIONS

Americans sometimes forget that most English-speaking countries use British English. Americans contribute a minor share of English free-text. So "TOF" makes no sense as an abbreviation of tracheo-esophageal fistula in Bethesda, Maryland, but this abbreviation makes perfect sense in London, where patients may have tracheo-oesophageal fistulas. The term GERD (representing the phrase gastroesophageal reflux disease) makes perfect sense to Americans, but it must be confusing to Australians.

8.12. CLASSIFYING ABBREVIATIONS BY THEIR EXPANSION ALGORITHMS

Different types of abbreviations create different types of interpretive problems. When a document is parsed into words, it is relatively easy to determine whether a given word string matches a term in a long list of abbreviation/expansion pairs. However, an algorithm is needed to determine whether the word string is correctly mapped to its intended expansion. The algorithm used to perform this task may depend on the context of the parsed document word and on the class or classes of abbreviations matching the parsed word. Sections 8.13 through 8.19 classify abbreviations by the algorithmic tasks required for their accurate selection and expansion.

8.13. EPHEMERAL ABBREVIATIONS

The most common form of abbreviation is the ephemeral abbreviation. The ephemeral abbreviation is invented on the fly by a writer and is intended to exist within a single document. These are the abbreviations that are usually found early in an article as an uppercase string within a parenthetical expression following the first appearance of the expansion. Elsewhere in the article they appear as stand-alone uppercase character strings. Ephemeral abbreviations are typically highly coordinated noun terms that appear sufficiently often within a particular document to justify their creation. For example, a pathology article may contain many references to an unidentified eosinophilic nodule of basement membrane-like material (abbreviated as "UENBMM"). The author probably has no intention of incorporating the abbreviation into the permanent medical literature. It is easy to build a parser that automatically extracts such terms from text because they are almost always introduced in a structured way (i.e., expansion immediately followed by parenthetical abbreviation). The ephemeral abbreviation exists only within a specific document. An algorithm might look for an uppercase string (often enclosed by parentheses) preceded by or following a text phrase, the first letters of which equal or approximate the uppercase string. This text phrase would be the expansion of the ephemeral abbreviation. Whenever the same uppercase "word" appears later in the same document, it could be tagged with a metadata tag, indicating that the uppercase string is an abbreviation and that its expansion is the previously determined text phrase. The abbreviation and its expansion would disappear at the end of the document.

8.14. HYPONYMOUS ABBREVIATIONS

The entity A is a hyponym or subordinate of B if A is a specific kind of B. So poodle is a hyponym of dog. The term HSIL (representing the phrase high-grade squamous intraepithelial lesion) is a hyponym of SIL. The phrase AIDH (representing the phrase atypical intraductal hyperplasia) is a hyponym for IDH (intraductal hyperplasia). In many instances, there are abbreviations for the hyponym, but no abbreviation for the more general term. For example, the term DVT expands to "deep vein thrombosis," but there is no medical abbreviation for the phrase venous thrombosis of undetermined depth (i.e., no "VT"). "PE" stands for the term pulmonary embolus, but "E" is not in use as an abbreviation for the word embolus. The most common hyponym examples relate to singular/plural forms. After all, every singular form is a hyponym of its plural. So, the term "rbc" represents the phrase red blood cell. Some people use "rbc" to refer to either the singular or the plural (because "c" expands to "cell" or to "cells"). But other people prefer to turn the abbreviation into a familiar plural form, "rbcs." In many cases, when a plural is added to an abbreviation, people will demarcate the plural form from the singleton by an awkward use of uppercase and lowercase characters. So, erythrocytes may be abbreviated as "RBCs." It is also common, but incorrect, to engage the possessive form when converting an abbreviation into its plural form (e.g., RBC's). Occasionally, the plural form of an abbreviation is used, even when it defies rational analysis. So, a man with withdrawal symptoms may have the "DTs," even though he is only suffering from one case of "delirium tremens." What do you do when the single form properly ends with a word that begins with "s"? The abbreviation for the phrase Hospital Information System is "HIS." If you wish to refer to multiple systems, is the plural "HISs," "HIS," or "HISes"? One may surmise that all three forms occur in nature.

Unfortunately, unless the plural abbreviation comes in the form of an uppercase acronym followed by a lowercase "s," confusion may arise with acronyms whose last expanded word is "syndrome." So, how would you otherwise distinguish "Lesch-Nyhan Syndrome" (LNS) from the plural of the abbreviation of the phrase lymph nodes (LNS)? Expanding single hyponyms of plural forms that do not end with an "s" is really not a problem. Nobody will care whether a parser expands "rbc" to "red blood cell" when the intended expansion was "red blood cells." There may be some minor annoyance when "TIA" is expanded to "transient ischemic attack" when it should have been expanded to "transient ischemic attacks." A smart parser can take its contextual cues from the word preceding the abbreviation. "Three TIA in 24 hours" should be mapped to the plural form, while "a TIA" should be mapped to the singular.

How do you deal with parsed abbreviations that end with the letter "s"? Abbreviation hyponyms that have a plural form ending with "s" can all be put into a single list. If the parser determines that the abbreviation was optimally formatted, with uppercase letters for the abbreviation and a lowercase "s" at the end, then the parser should only match against the singular hyponym (i.e., match TIAs against TIA). In other cases, the parser algorithm may choose to determine from the context of the sentence whether the abbreviation is a plural form. If so, it can look for a match among the list of abbreviations whose plural form ends with an "s." If there is a match, then that may be sufficient. If there is not a match, then the "s" can be truncated and matches should be sought in the large list of abbreviations not ending with a plural form designated by "s."

8.15. MONOSEMOUS ABBREVIATIONS

The monosemous abbreviation has a unique expansion. Therefore, it is relatively simple to write algorithms that correctly match expansions of monosemous abbreviations against abbreviations parsed from medical text. Fortunately, about half of abbreviations seem to be monosemous. In general, the longer the abbreviation, the more likely it will be to have a unique expansion.

8.16. POLYSEMOUS ABBREVIATIONS

Polysemy is the condition whereby a single term has multiple related meanings. The most polysemous medical abbreviation is "PA," which has at least 41 different expansions. There are many different algorithmic approaches to the problem of assigning a correct expansion to a polysemic abbreviation. An algorithm can simply use a "frequency of occurrence" list for the different possible expansions, choosing the most often-encountered expansion as the "correct" expansion for any abbreviation. The term "PA" appearing in a radiology report is much more likely to expand to "posterior-anterior" than to "propionic acid." However, a good algorithm may need to reckon with "pulmonary artery" as a reasonable alternative. Another algorithm may use the nonabbreviated words found in the paragraph or sentence containing the abbreviation as clues to the abbreviation's intended expansion. UMLS contains long lists of concepts that relate to other concepts. Choosing one expansion (from a list of expansions matching an abbreviation) based on its relationship to terms found in the text flanking the abbreviation, is a reasonable approach to dealing with polysemous abbreviations.

8.17. ABBREVIATIONS MASQUERADING AS WORDS

Particularly irksome are abbreviations that map to often-used general words, such as the phrases axillary node dissection (AND), acute lymphocytic leukemia (ALL), optic neuritis (ON), and acanthosis nigricans (AN). The most difficult abbreviations map to commonly used medical terms, such as Bornholm Eye Disease (BED), and Expired Air Resuscitation (EAR). Many acronyms will almost always appear as uppercase strings or as strings internally punctuated by periods. For instance, the phrase United States is often abbreviated as "US" or as "U.S.," thus distinguishing it from "us." But health professionals will not always play by the rules. A pin sometimes lurks in a diaper and sometimes lurks in a prostate (prostatic intraepithelial neoplasia).

If a word appears in all uppercase letters in a sentence (that is otherwise lowercase), it seems reasonable to assume that the word is an abbreviation. Abbreviations can be matched directly against a list of expansions for the abbreviations that masquerade as words. If a word parsed from medical text matches an abbreviation from the list of abbreviations that masquerade as words, and if the word has no distinguishing format, then an algorithm may be designed to consider the frequency of occurrence of the expansion compared to the frequency of occurrence of the nonabbreviated word. For instance, "and" will appear more often than "axillary node dissection," although "ash," the abbreviation for "atrial septal hypertrophy," may occur more often than "ash," the crumbly black material in the tray.

As in the algorithms created for the polysemous abbreviations, it is feasible to look for relatedness between the considered expansion and the words and concepts found in the vicinity of the parsed word.

8.18. FATAL ABBREVIATIONS: INNOCENT VICTIMS OF ABBREVIATION DRIFT

It is tempting to assume that abbreviations can be expanded whenever their context is known. For instance, the term CEA would expand to the phrase "carcinoembryonic antigen" in a blood test for a patient who is status post colectomy for colon cancer. The term CEA would expand to the phrase "carotid endarterectomy" in a patient whose carotids were being duplex-scanned for occlusive vascular disease.

Sometimes, even experts in a field cannot disambiguate a polysemous expansion (List 8.18.1). I call these "fatal abbreviations" because they cannot be interpreted with certainty and misinterpretations can lead to medical care errors. Such abbreviations probably devolved through imprecise use (a phenomenon I call abbreviation drift). In the case of the fatal abbreviation, it seems appropriate for algorithms not to try to pick the correct expansion but to display an output that lists all the possible expansions for the term. For example, "The patient has a history of AHA"; possible expansions are "acquired hemolytic anemia" or "autoimmune hemolytic anemia." Of all the abbreviations collected in the master list, the list of fatal abbreviations is the most important. Once a programmer has a list of these abbreviations and their alternate expansions, it is exceedingly easy to write a program that will parse the abbreviations from medical text and append a listing of all the possible abbreviations that might be applied.

LIST 8.18.1. FATAL PATHOLOGY ABBREVIATIONS

- abg—aortic bifurcation graft or aortobifemoral graft
- aha—acquired hemolytic anemia or autoimmune hemolytic anemia
- ascvd—arteriosclerotic cardiovascular disease or arteriosclerotic cerebrovascular disease
- chd—congenital heart disease or congestive heart disease or coronary heart disease
- doa—date of admission or dead on arrival
- edc—estimated date of conception or estimated date of confinement ("due date" means almost the opposite of "conception date")
- hzo—herpes zoster ophthalmicus or herpes zoster oticus
- ibd—inflammatory bowel disease, or irritable bowel disease

- lll—left lower lid or left lower lip or left lower lobe or left lower lung
- mcgn—mesangiocapillary glomerulonephritis or minimal change glomerulonephritis
- mvr—mitral valve regurgitation or mitral valve repair or mitral valve replacement
- nc—no change or noncontributory
- nkda—no known drug allergies or nonketotic diabetic acidosis
- pe—pulmonary effusion or pulmonary edema or pulmonary embolectomy or pulmonary embolism
- sk—seborrheic keratosis or solar keratosis
- uvf—ureterovaginal fistula, or urethrovaginal fistula

8.19. FORBIDDEN ABBREVIATIONS

The JCAHO (Joint Commission on Accreditation of Healthcare Organizations) has published a list of forbidden abbreviations that must not be used in medical records (List 8.19.1).

LIST 8.19.1. JCAHO "DO NOT USE" ABBREVIATIONS (MINIMUM LIST, EFFECTIVE JANUARY 1, 2004)

- U (for unit)—Reason: "U" visually mistaken as 0. Write "unit."
- IU (for international unit)—Reason: Mistaken as IV (intravenous or the number 4), or the number 10. Write "international unit."
- Q.D., Q.O.D. (Latin abbreviation for once daily and every other day)—Reason: Mistaken for each other. The period after the Q can be mistaken for an "I" and the "O" can be mistaken for "I." Write "daily" and "every other day."
- Trailing zero (X.0 mg), Lack of leading zero (.X mg)—Reason: Decimal point is missed. Never write a zero by itself after a decimal point (X mg), and always use a zero before a decimal point (0.X mg).
- MS, MSO4, MgSO4—Reason: Confused for one another. Can mean morphine sulfate or magnesium sulfate. Write "morphine sulfate" or "magnesium sulfate."
- mg (for microgram)—Reason: Mistaken for mg (milligrams), resulting in a 1000-fold dosing overdose. Write "mcg."
- H.S. (for half-strength or Latin abbreviation for bedtime), q.H.S.—Reason: Mistaken for either half-strength or hour of sleep (at bedtime). q.H.S. mistaken for every hour. All can result in a dosing error. Write out "half-strength" or "at bedtime."

- T.I.W. (for three times a week)—Reason: Mistaken for three times a day or twice weekly, resulting in an overdose. Write "3 times weekly" or "three times weekly."
- S.C. or S.Q. (for subcutaneous)—Reason: Mistaken as SL for sublingual, or "5 every." Write "Sub-Q," "subQ," or "subcutaneously."
- D/C (for discharge)—Reason: Interpreted as discontinue whatever medications follow (typically discharge meds). Write "discharge."
- cc (for cubic centimeter)—Reason: Mistaken for U (units) when poorly written. Write "ml" for milliliters.
- A.S., A.D., A.U. (Latin abbreviation for left, right, or both ears) O.S., O.D., O.U. (Latin abbreviation for left, right, or both eyes)—Reason: Mistaken for each other (e.g., AS for OS, AD for OD, AU for OU, etc.). Write "left ear," "right ear," or "both ears;" "left eye," "right eye," or "both eyes."

CHAPTER 9

Autocoding Unstructured Data (Narrative Text)

9.1. BACKGROUND

Medical autocoding can be considered a specialized form of machine translation (automated translation from one language into another). There are two approaches to machine translation. The first is to parse sentences into grammatical parts, permitting a program to reorder component parts of the sentence into a sequence of phrases that make grammatical sense in the target language. The sequential phrases of the transformed sentence can then be matched against a controlled vocabulary (in the target language), yielding translated text.

The problem with this approach is that it is computationally intensive (resulting in slow execution speed) and prone to errors when sentences are long or complex.

Many people live their lives thinking that grammatical sentences are always meaningful. This is not the case. Consider the following sentence: "I didn't say you lied to me." You probably think you understand the meaning of this short, simple statement. Actually, the sentence has at least seven different meanings, depending on which word is stressed (List 9.1.1).

LIST 9.1.1. SEVEN INTERPRETATIONS OF "I DIDN'T SAY YOU LIED TO ME."

1. "I didn't say you lied to me." Stressing "I," the sentence means that somebody else said that you lied to me.
2. "I didn't say you lied to me." Stressing "didn't," the sentence means that I had nothing to do with it.

---

3. "I didn't say you lied to me." Stressing "say," the sentence means that I didn't speak the assertion, but I may have made the assertion in a written or other nonverbal communication.
4. "I didn't say you lied to me." Stressing "you," the sentence means that someone else lied to me.
5. "I didn't say you lied to me." Stressing "lied," the sentence means that I said you did something to me (other than lying).
6. "I didn't say you lied to me." Stressing "to," the sentence means that you lied but not to my face.
7. "I didn't say you lied to me." Stressing "me," the sentence means that you lied to someone else.

Ambiguities that occur by varying the stress placed on words in a sentence are child's play compared to the chaos created by the indiscriminate use of pronouns. A pronoun is a short reference to a noun. The sentence, "He is here" only has meaning if the reader is informed who "he" is. When a sentence has more than one noun, the logical references between pronouns and nouns may become ambiguous. For example, "Dr. Payne told Mr. Pffeir that he had halitosis." Who had bad breath? Was Dr. Payne referring to himself or to Mr. Pffeir? Was the Dr. trying to convey that the halitosis was a past event, or does the halitosis continue into the present?

These potential sources of misunderstanding are common. Virtually every paragraph of biomedical text is replete with ambiguities. The worst offenders are long, complex sentences that contain several pronouns and that include words that have multiple meanings. The reason that machine translation fails has much more to do with the inadequacies of composed text than with the inadequacies of software (List 9.1.2).

LIST 9.1.2. COMMON PROBLEMS THAT REDUCE THE MEANING OF NARRATIVE TEXT

- Complex or run-on sentences
- Inscrutable use of negations
- Polysemous words and terms
- Idiomatic phrases
- Indiscriminate use of abbreviations
- Ambiguous pronouns
- Misspellings

It is not difficult to find examples of poorly written text (List 9.1.3).

LIST 9.1.3. THE FOLLOWING HAVE BEEN WIDELY DISTRIBUTED OVER THE WEB AND PURPORTEDLY CAME FROM REAL MEDICAL CHARTS

- "The baby was delivered, the cord clamped and cut, and handed to the pediatrician, who breathed and cried immediately."
- "The patient had waffles for breakfast and anorexia for lunch."
- "The patient lives at home with his mother, father, and pet turtle, who is presently enrolled in day care three times a week."
- "Bleeding started in the rectal area and continued all the way to Los Angeles."
- "Coming from Detroit, this man has no children."
- "Examination reveals a well-developed male lying in bed with his family in no distress."

Idiomatic expressions, almost by definition, convey a meaning that is not determined by the content of the expression. Consider the common assertion of insouciance, "I could care less."

If I could care less, that means that my level of caring is sufficiently high that lesser levels of caring would be feasible. This implies that I care about the subject. So why is the expression used to signify that someone does not care at all about the subject?

Consider the mind-boggling query, "Wouldn't you like me to erase your file?" Is the question an assertion that the responder would like to have the file erased? If that were the case, a reply of "yes" would result in the erasure of the file. Or does the questioner want to know if the responder would not like to have the file erased? In that case, a reply of "yes" would result in the file not being erased.

9.2. MACHINE TRANSLATION

Machine translation is a large field that covers direct translations between different languages (e.g., Russian to and from English), the interconversion of language modes (e.g., spoken words to and from narrative text), the interpretation of signals (e.g., military SIGINT, deriving intelligence from the analysis of intercepted signals), the annotation of text through the extraction of terms and concepts (i.e., medical autocoding), and the transformation of text into desired data structures (i.e., converting narrative text to tagged XML).

Translation between languages has been an active area of research that is made unnecessarily complex through the proliferation of overly specialized translation devices. If four monoglots speaking English, French, German, and Russian were to exchange information, then they would require 4 × 3 or 12 translators. If 100 monoglots speaking 100 different languages were to convene, they would need 100 × 99 or 9,900 different translators.

- English to French

- English to German

- English to Russian

- French to English

- French to German

- French to Russian

- German to English

- German to Russian

- German to French

- Russian to German

- Russian to French

- Russian to English

Are all these really necessary? Esperanto was invented in 1887 by L.L. Zamenhof as an easy and flexible language that could be used worldwide as everyman's "second" language. Esperanto has a vocabulary derived from Romance and Germanic languages and a relatively simple grammar. Esperanto has never achieved universal popularity, but it is used today by several million people and is a reasonable approach to reducing some of the problems created by a multitude of different languages. In the realm of machine translation, Esperanto could serve as an "exchange" or intermediate language. All translation between languages would proceed by first translating the source language to Esperanto and then translating from Esperanto to the target language. In the case of the four monoglots, the number of machine translators would be eight. If 100 monoglots speaking 100 different languages were to convene, they would need 100 × 2 or 200 different translators.

- English to Esperanto

- French to Esperanto

- German to Esperanto

- Russian to Esperanto

- Esperanto to English

- Esperanto to French

- Esperanto to German

- Esperanto to Russian

By using Esperanto as a intermediate translation language, the effort required to automatically translate between languages would be reduced geometrically. Despite the overwhelming advantage to using Esperanto as an intermediate language for machine translation, the field of machine translation is focused almost exclusively on direct translation between languages (e.g., English to and from Chinese). The reasons for this are many, but it may be worthwhile to recognize that machine translation is a much more complex task than directly substituting words from one language into the equivalent words from another language (List 9.2.1).

LIST 9.2.1. SOME STEPS IN MACHINE TRANSLATION

- Parsing sentences into grammatical structures
- Identifying idiomatic expressions
- Disambiguating polysemous terms (based on sentence context)
- Reordering terms based on grammar rules
- Providing gender, tense, and specialized language structures that may be absent in the source language
- Determining grammar rule exceptions existing for words and terms in the source and target languages
- Mapping between two different vocabularies

A software developer may choose to focus her efforts on specific vocabularies for which measurements can be made on the accuracy of automatic translations for source and target documents. The process of fine-tuning a translator for two languages may be much more practical than building a universal (Esperanto) translator. In fact, this argument makes sense if the problem of machine translation between languages is nongeneralizable (i.e., if the translation rules are dependent on the content of sentences and not on general properties of language).

Most machine translation software is replete with special exceptions that handle expressions that do not follow logical rules of grammar.

They are so many that translation errors are bound to occur. Professional (human) translators scoff at computer translations and collect lists of silly and misleading translations performed by computers. A favorite example is the English to Russian translator that took the idiomatic expression, "out of site, out of mind" and translated it to the Russian equivalent of "invisible idiot."

As discussed in the prior section, the problem with English is that common usage defies any consistent and logical description. Much of free-text is simply meaningless and cannot be reliably interpreted by humans or machine. We achieve an understanding of most written language based on shared cultural experience. Powsner and coworkers have shown that the contents of surgical pathology reports are variously interpreted many different ways by the various health professionals who read them (90).

It has been shown that free-text can be translated accurately by machine if the text is written in "Controlled English." Controlled English is a disciplined approach to sentence construction that avoids some of the intrinsic flaws in written language. Pogson has formalized rules for Controlled English (91) (List 9.2.2).

LIST 9.2.2. SOME CONTROLLED ENGLISH RULES (91)

- Each word in the text may convey only one meaning (e.g., if iris is an anatomic part of the eye, it cannot also be a flower).
- For each meaning, only one term may be used (e.g., if you use the term "tumor" you should not use the terms "neoplasm," "neoplastic growth," or "mass" when you want to convey the same conceptual meaning as "tumor."
- Each word is used in only one word class (e.g., if "report" is a noun, as in surgical pathology report, it cannot be used as a verb, as in "Please report the pathology results.")

Controlled English forbids **polysemy**. Words in Controlled English must have a single unambiguous definition, and this requirement places a restriction on the vocabulary that can be used in Controlled English text. Basic English is a list of about 850 words that have clear definitions and that convey more than 90% of the concepts commonly described in narrative text. Basic English was created by C.K. Odgen (1889–1957) (92). It has been championed by some very influential people, including Sir

Winston Churchill. The words of Basic English are available in pictorial form to facilitate comprehension of Basic English text by non-English speakers. Many books have been "translated" into Basic English, including the Bible.

Examples of text in regular English (List 9.2.3) and in Basic English (List 9.2.4) are shown.

LIST 9.2.3. REGULAR ENGLISH VERSION OF EXCERPT FROM WINSTON CHURCHILL'S ATLANTIC CHARTER

...They believe all of the nations of the world, for realistic as well as spiritual reasons, must come to the abandonment of the use of force. Since no future peace can be maintained if land, sea or air armaments continue to be employed by nations which threaten, or may threaten, aggression outside of their frontiers, they believe, pending the establishment of a wider and permanent system of general security, that the disarmament of such nations is essential. They will likewise aid and encourage all practical measures which will lighten for peace-loving peoples the crushing burden of armaments.

LIST 9.2.4. BASIC ENGLISH VERSION OF EXCERPT FROM WINSTON CHURCHILL'S ATLANTIC CHARTER

...it is their belief that all the nations of the earth, for material reasons no less than because it is right and good, will, in the end, give up the use of force. Because war will come again if countries which are, or may be, ready to make attacks on others go on using land, sea, or air power, it is their belief.

It is my opinion that neither the regular English nor the Basic English versions of the text are particularly well written. Both have multiple parenthetic expressions that would be virtually impossible for a machine translation device to interpret. Furthermore, the words of the Basic English vocabulary are deficient for the kind of specialized terminologies used in medical text. Perhaps these kinds of criticisms are responsible for the limited success of Controlled and Basic English. However, the fundamental observation that machine translation is accurate for text written in a disciplined, consistent, and simple style provides hope that it is feasible to achieve some meaning in medical free-text.

In the realm of medical free-text, a few modest recommendations would vastly improve efforts to parse and automatically code narrative text (93) (List 9.2.5).

LIST 9.2.5. SUGGESTIONS FOR CONTROLLING MEDICAL TEXT

- Sentences should be short and declarative, with an unambiguous sentence terminator.
- Negations should include the word "not" or "negative" and double negations should never be used.
- Abbreviations and acronyms should be represented as all-uppercase letters and should not contain periods, except when they occur at the end of a sentence.
- Abbreviations can be made plural by adding a lowercase "s".

Computer translators must be able to find the end of each sentence in order to separate distinct pathologic concepts. Unfortunately, the period is not an unambiguous marker for the end of a sentence. Periods appear all over reports in honorifics, abbreviations, numbers, and so on (Dr., Mr., Ph.D., P.I.N., $5.25, 4.2). Using the period as the sentence terminator would result in the abrupt separation and loss of terms that would otherwise be connected (e.g., P.I.N. of prostate would be parsed into four sentences: 'P.', 'I.','N.', and 'of prostate.'). I suggest a period followed either by a carriage-return or by a double-space.

It is important to distinguish negative assertions. The best way of making a negative assertion is in a noncompound assertion that uses the word "not." It is never advisable to combine an affirmative statement and a negative statement in the same sentence. For instance, the sentence, "The margins are positive for tumor, and the lymph nodes are negative for metastatic carcinoma," should be expressed as, "The margins are positive for tumor. The lymph nodes are negative for metastatic carcinoma." This also emphasizes the importance of accurate spelling. If "negative" is spelled "negtive", then the computer may code the sentence, "The lymph nodes are negtive for carcinoma," as a positive case. Negations should not be expressed as positive assertions. "Adenocarcinoma is absent" is a positive statement that has the same meaning as, "Adenocarcinoma is not present." The former requires the computer to understand the meaning of "absence," whereas the latter only requires the computer to recognize a common negation operator term ("not").

How can we use the general principles of Controlled English to retrieve meaning from meaningless sentences? Consider an example, "While sleeping in my tent, I was attacked by an elephant in my pajamas." The sentence meets the general requirements of a well-structured sentence, but its meaning is technically ambiguous. We understand the sentence only because we know that people wear pajamas, and elephants do not.

How might the sample sentence be rewritten? One way is to break the sentence up into two declarative statements:

While I slept an elephant attacked me.

While I slept, I was in my pajamas.

Both sentences refer to the same event (not to different occurrences of sleep), so maybe it would be preferable to rewrite the sentence as:

event

I slept

I wore pajamas

Elephant attacked me

end_of_event

This is better, but we still have the problem of pronouns that do not refer to a specific identified object. Who, exactly, is this "I" object? Who is the "me" object, and what does it mean to have "my pajamas"?

Consider an example of a ridiculously complex sentence.

Ann while Bob had had had had had had had had had had had a better effect on the teacher.

It looks a little better with punctuation.

Ann, while Bob had had "had", had had "had had"; "had had" had had a better effect on the teacher.

A clue may help.

Remember "had" is past perfect and "had had" is the conditional past perfect.

The meaning of the sentence becomes clear (maybe) if it is broken into assertions within an event with enclosing brackets separating distinct concepts:

event

Ann <had had> had had

Bob <had had> had

Teacher <prefers> had had

end of event

This exercise was intended to prepare readers for Chapter 12, in which we will see how RDF (Resource Description Framework) provides a semantic solution to representing textual meaning that can be deployed with standard, Web-based, markup languages.

9.3. AUTOCODING

As used in this manuscript, the term "autocoder" refers to a software program capable of parsing large collections of medical records (e.g., radiology reports, surgical pathology reports, autopsy reports, admission notes, discharge notes, operating room notes, medical administrative emails, memoranda, manuscripts, etc.) and capturing the medical concepts contained in the text.

The term "autocoding" should be distinguished from "computer-assisted manual coding." Health care workers may use a software enhancement of their Hospital Information Systems to code a section of text as they enter reports into the computer system. Typically, candidate terms and term codes are displayed on the same screen as the entered report. The person entering text is often given the option of editing the proffered codes. This process should not be confused with "autocoding" and is not equivalent to the fully automatic and large-scale coding required by biomedical informaticians.

Lexical parsers are a simple but somewhat brutish approach to machine translation. The lexical parser looks for exact matches between terms in text and terms in a nomenclature, and depends on terms existing in medical text without internal modifiers. For instance, the term "flat feet" extracted from the first record in the Online Mendelian Inheritance in Man (OMIM), would be missed by the lexical parser if it included an internal modifier, such as "flat erythemic feet." For this reason, much of machine translation work depends on the creation of elaborate grammar rules and exception lists to account for word-order variations in medical text.

Finding all the concepts in a corpus of text is a necessary and early step in all data mining efforts. Autocoded terms can be used individually as index terms for the document, on a record-by-record basis to produce a concept "signature" that is highly specific for each report, or collectively to relate the frequency of terms within records with the frequency of terms in the aggregate document (94).

Possibly the most useful type of dataset in the field of biomedical informatics are archived collections of surgical pathology reports. Surgical pathology databases offer several important features (List 9.3.1).

LIST 9.3.1. RESEARCH VALUE OF ARCHIVED SURGICAL PATHOLOGY DATA

- All biopsied disease entities are included in the database, representing every category of biopsied disease (e.g., metabolic/toxic, traumatic, genetic/congenital, neoplastic, degenerative, inflammatory, infectious).

- Specimens can be characterized not only by diagnosis but also by descriptive terminology that may relate to prognostic or treatment categories.
- Database entries correspond to archived material (glass slides and paraffin blocks) that can be recovered for research purposes.
- Preparing and coding reports is an established and required activity of surgical pathology departments.

De-identified databases consisting of diagnostic and demographic data collected from surgical pathology reports could be distributed and merged with the datasets collected throughout the world. Epidemiologists with access to such a merged database would be able to study the occurrence of hundreds of thousands of diseases. Individual institutions could use a merged database of coded surgical pathology reports to improve diagnostic performance. For instance, upon review of all neoplasm diagnoses, it may be noted that 50% of the adenocarcinomas of lung are designated as bronchioloalveolar type. Comparison with aggregate data from other institutions might indicate that bronchioloalveolar carcinoma should account for only 4–8% of lung cancers. This would prompt a histologic review of lung cancers. Specimen review might indicate that the diagnosis of bronchioloalveolar carcinoma is being overused, and that applying stricter diagnostic criteria would bring the incidence down to levels reported at other institutions. On the other hand, if a review of cases shows that the departmental diagnoses are accurate, then a high incidence of bronchioloalveolar carcinomas might be a valid public health issue.

In the past, the observation of a higher-than-expected incidence of a particular type of cancer has prompted important epidemiologic discoveries, in the cases of angiosarcoma of liver in tire plant workers (95) and clear cell carcinoma of vagina in women exposed in utero to DES (96). Aggregated surgical pathology databases provide a listing for every occurring pathologic entity, along with demographic information. The research value of such databases could be enormous, but first we must accurately extract and code the collected reports.

9.4. HUMAN FALLIBILITY AND THE LIMITATIONS OF HUMAN-COLLECTED DATA

We can all agree that humans are a fine species, capable of all sorts of laudable accomplishments (music, literature, architecture, science). But when it comes to collecting terabytes of data, humans always seem to come up a little short (93). Consider the field of vital statistics. Annual data for the entire U.S. population have been collected since 1935 by the Vital Statistics Program of the National Center for Health Statistics. The data are taken from death certificates and account for more than 99% of U.S. deaths (97). Death certificate data are notoriously error-prone, and the problems seem to extend beyond our national borders, as a similar set of complaints related to the low accuracy of death certificates have been voiced in the United Kingdom (98, 99). The most common error occurs when a mode of death is listed as the cause of death (e.g., cardiac arrest, cardiopulmonary arrest), thus nullifying the potential value of the death certificate. A recent survey of 49 national and international health atlases has shown that there is virtually no consistency in the way that death data are presented (100).

Humans are inconsistent, idiosyncratic, and prone to errors. Studies of coding accuracy show human coding error rates in the range of 10%–15% (101). Peter Hall and Lemoine have divided manual coding errors into five types (List 9.4.1).

LIST 9.4.1. FIVE COMMON CODING ERRORS IN HUMAN-CODED REPORTS

1. Factually correct but unhelpful codes (e.g., coding all benign lesions as "negative for tumor")
2. Inconsistent codes (coding "dysplasia" on Monday and "atypia" on Tuesday)
3. Idiosyncratic codes (using a mnemonic for a lesion, often inscrutable to other people, such as coding all fungal infections as "fungus ball," under the morphology axis, rather than taking the time to assign a specific code from the infection axis, and remembering that the now private code "fungus ball" must be used for any future fungal searches)
4. Entry errors (e.g., entering "lipoma" when one intends to enter "lymphoma")
5. Incomplete coding due to impatience or laziness

As discussed previously, translating a surgical pathology report into diagnostic codes is fundamentally equivalent to translating natural languages. A strength of computer generated coded databases is that the algorithms used to construct the databases can be tailored to the intended use of the database. For instance, if the intent of constructing a database is to produce an archive of retrievable cases, then the coding algorithms would be written to permit redundant coding so that cases of a particular kind would be included by almost any subsequent search strategy. A specimen of skin of face may be diagnosed as an actinic keratosis. For maximal inclusivity one would code under the topographies of skin, face, and head, and the morphologies of actinic keratosis, solar elastosis, dysplasia, atypia, and perhaps even squamous carcinoma and carcinoma in situ. On the other hand, if a database were being prepared to establish incidence data, then constructing an algorithm that chooses a best-match single topography and single morphology for each case might be preferable. The key point is that there is no single coding strategy that is optimal for all purposes. It is unthinkable to expect human coders to recode entire databases, whereas database recoding is a simple task for a computer.

By far, the most limiting factor in human coding is speed. Humans cannot keep up with the flood of biomedical data collected by hospital information systems. Machine translation is the only feasible way to transform gigabytes and terabytes of text. As long as clinicians, pathologists, radiologists, nurses, and scientists continue to type messages, reports, manuscripts, and notes into electronic documents, we will need computers to parse and organize the resulting text.

9.5. A FAST LEXICAL AUTOCODER

The doublet method is a novel approach to autocoding. It can autocode 0.8 Megabytes of text per second on a computer having a modest 1.6 GHz processor. This section describes the doublet method autocoding algorithm.

One of the many problems in the field of machine translation is that expressions (multi-word terms) convey ideas that transcend the meanings of the individual words in the expression. Consider the following sentence:

"The ciliary body produces aqueous humor."

The example sentence has unambiguous meaning to anatomists, but each word in the sentence can have many different meanings. "Ciliary" is a common medical word, and usually refers to the action of cilia. Cilia are found throughout the respiratory and gastrointestinal tracts and have an important role in locomoting particulate matter. The word "body" almost always refers to the human body. The term "ciliary body" should (but does not) refer to the action of cilia that move human bodies from place to place. The word "aqueous" always refers to water. Humor relates to something being funny. The term "aqueous humor" should (but does not) relate to something that is funny by virtue of its use of water (as in squirting someone in the face with a trick flower). Actually, "ciliary body" and "aqueous humor" are each examples of medical doublets whose meanings are specific and contextually constant (i.e., always mean one thing). Furthermore, the meanings of the doublets cannot be reliably determined from the individual words that constitute the doublet, because the individual words have several different meanings. Basically, you either know the correct meaning of the doublet, or you don't.

Any sentence can be examined by parsing it into an array of intercalated doublets:

"The ciliary, ciliary body, body produces, produces aqueous, aqueous humor."

The important concepts in the sentence are contained in two doublets (ciliary body and aqueous humor). A nomenclature containing these doublets would allow us to extract and index these two medical concepts. A nomenclature consisting of single words might miss the contextual meaning of the doublets.

What if the term were larger than a doublet? Consider the tumor "orbital alveolar rhabdomyosarcoma." The individual words can be misleading. This orbital tumor is not from outer space, and the alveolar tumor is not from the lung. The three-word term describes a sarcoma arising from the orbit of the eye that has a morphology characterized by tiny spaces of a size and shape as may occur in glands (alveoli). The term "orbital alveolar rhabdomyosarcoma" can be parsed as "orbital alveolar, alveolar rhabdomyosarcoma" Why is this any better than parsing the term into individual words, as in "orbital, alveolar, rhabdomyosarcoma"? The doublets, unlike the single words, are highly specific terms that are unlikely to occur in association with more than a few specific concepts.

Very few medical terms are single words. In the developmental lineage classification of neoplasms, there are 102,271 unique terms for neoplasms (77). All but 252 of these terms are multiword terms. Several innovative approaches to autocoding have used the higher information content of multiword terms (also called word n-grams) to match terms in text with terms in vocabularies (102).

The doublet method uses the higher term specificity of doublets (bigrams) to construct a simple and fast lexical parser. Lexical parsers are types of string-matching algorithms. In general, the overall speed of lexical parsers is determined by the speed with which the parser can prepare an array of all possible words and phrases contained in a block of text, coupled with the speed with which each of these phrases can be compared against all the terms in the nomenclature.

The doublet autocoder is too long to include here, but a public domain Perl script (doubcode.pl) is distributed with my previously published open access manuscript (88). The algorithm for the doublet method is described here (List 9.5.1).

LIST 9.5.1. ALGORITHM FOR THE DOUBLET AUTOCODER

1. Each phrase (term) in a nomenclature is converted into intercalated doublets, and each doublet is assigned a consecutive number.
2. Each nomenclature phrase is assigned the concatenated list of numbers that represent the ordered doublets composing the phrase.
3. Every text record is split into an array consisting of the consecutive words in the text record.
4. The text array is parsed as intercalated doublets. Intercalated doublets from the text that match doublets found anywhere in the nomenclature are assigned their numeric values (from the doublet index created for the nomenclature). Runs of consecutive doublets from the text that match doublets from the nomenclature are built into concatenated strings of doublet values. The occurrence of a text doublet that does not match any doublet in the nomenclature cannot possibly be part of a nomenclature term. Such text doublets serve as "stop" doublets between candidate runs of text doublets that match nomenclature doublets.
5. The runs of matching doublets are tested to see if they match any of the runs of doublets that compose nomenclature terms or if they contain any subsumed terms that match nomenclature terms.
6. The array of doublet runs extracted from the text that match nomenclature terms are cached in an external file.

Text doublets that do not match any doublets in the nomenclature are "skipped." Text doublets that match doublets from the nomenclature are concatenated to consecutive matching doublets until a nonmatching doublet is encountered. The algorithmic strength of the doublet method is achieved by eliminating the need to create and match (against a nomenclature) an array of all possible phrases of all possible lengths found in a textual record.

Developers of medical autocoders seldom publish manuscripts. It is my perception, based on many years of activity in this field, that most autocoders are proprietary products produced for a very specific type of job. I have never encountered autocoder software vendors who revealed the speed of their autocoders or shared any primary data that measures the performance of their autocoders. This is unfortunate because software developers may defer implementing brilliant ideas for autocoders if they are uncertain whether or not better autocoders already exist. Even if competing software developers were to share performance data, there are no widely accepted standards for measuring the performance of medical autocoders.

The most common cause of missed terms arises when text contains a modifying word that breaks the term into a phrase that no longer matches anything found in the nomenclature. For instance, "adenocarcinoma of the left lung," would be missed by a lexical parser if the nearest term in its terminology list is "adenocarcinoma of the lung." A rule-based parser or a semantic parser may have successfully teased out the "left" from the term and found the match. In this instance, the nomenclature failed the lexical parser because it did not list terms that indicated tumor laterality. Lexical parsers do not match terms that are absent from the text (i.e., no false positives). False-positive terms are possible in rule-based and semantic parsers if they create word patterns not present in the original text. Also, because lexical parsers strictly match phrases in text with phrases in nomenclatures, it is possible to achieve accurate results of dubious value. For instance, a lexical parser would parse "adenocarcinoma of the lung is not seen" and find a match against the neoplasm term "adenocarcinoma of the lung." The concept is present in the text, even if though it is absent from the patient. It is a misleading but "true" positive.

The doublet autocoder creates a string of words from a chunk of text, obliterating sentence boundaries. For fastidious developers who wish to ensure that their parsers respect sentence boundaries, it is possible to preprocess text into sentences with a sentence parser (14, 15). Lexical parsers can be further modified to provide an output that preserves the intended sense of the term as used in its context. For example, if the text includes the sentence, "Adenocarcinoma of the lung is not present," then the "sensible" lexical parser may be modified to tag the "adenocarcinoma of the lung" with a negation modifier, preserving the intended sense of the term.

9.6. EVALUATING AUTOCODERS: DEALING WITH PRECISION AND RECALL

Efforts to quantify the performance of autocoders have relied on precision and recall, two measurements that depend only on counting terms. Because counting is the most direct form of measurement, it is often assumed that the results of a counting exercise will yield unimpeachable data.

Precision and recall are widely used and widely vilified measures of autocoder performance. Hobbs has provided an elegant description of these two terms. "Recall is a measure of completeness, precision of correctness. When you promise to tell the whole truth, you are promising 100% recall. When you promise to tell nothing but the truth, you are promising 100% precision" (103). In the case of autocoded text, recall is the number of correctly autocoded terms divided by the total number of terms. Precision is the number of correctly autocoded terms divided by the total number of autocoded terms. Both of these measurements depend only on counting. Both of these measurements depend on the existence of an external judge who decides which terms are correct and which terms are incorrect. Some of the problems with measurements of precision and recall can be illustrated with the following snippet of autocoder output (List 9.6.1).

LIST 9.6.1. AUTOCODER OUTPUT ILLUSTRATING PROBLEMS WITH MEASUREMENTS OF PRECISION AND RECALL

```
<rdf:Description about="urn:PMID-15577676">
    <dc:title>
    paraganglioma-like dermal melanocytic tumor a unique
    entity
    distinct from cellular blue nevus clear cell sarcoma
    and cutaneous melanoma
    </dc:title>
    <v:autocode term="sarcoma" code="C9118000" />
    <v:autocode term="tumor" code="C0000000" />
    <v:autocode term="melanoma" code="C3224000" />
    <v:autocode term="cutaneous melanoma" code="C3510000" />
    <v:autocode term="nevus" code="C7570000" />
    <v:autocode term="clear cell sarcoma" code="C0000000" />
```

```
      <v:autocode term="blue nevus" code="C3803000" />
      <v:autocode term="paraganglioma-like dermal
   melanocytic tumor" code="C4228200" />
      <v:autocode term="cellular blue nevus" code="C4241000" />
</rdf:Description>
```

The PubMed citation appears between the enclosing metadata "<dc:title>...</dc:title>". The nine autocoded terms are each listed on separate lines beginning with "<v:autocode term". Notice that long terms are extracted along with smaller terms subsumed within the longer terms. Examples are "cellular blue nevus" and "blue nevus," "cutaneous melanoma" and "melanoma." The software operates through an algorithm that concatenates overlapping word doublets to produce the longest possible word-string matching a nomenclature term. Once the long term is matched, it matches fragments of the long term that are valid nomenclature terms. Matching small terms subsumed within larger terms is an important feature of the algorithm. It permits searches to be conducted over general concepts that would be missed when the more specific term is unfamiliar to the person conducting the query. A person who enters the query term, "blue nevus" would find all cases of "cellular blue nevus," even if unaware of this variant lesion at the outset of the query process.

Imagine that a human coder establishes the standard for precision and recall by coding four terms from the sample text:

- cutaneous melanoma

- cellular blue nevus

- clear cell sarcoma

- paraganglioma-like dermal melanocytic tumor

This human coder disdains the inclusion of small terms found within a large term, and does not include sarcoma, tumor, blue nevus, nevus, or melanoma in the list of correct terms.

The precision for the autocoder would be the number of correct autocoder responses (4) divided by the total number of autocoder responses (9), or 44%. However, if the human coder believed that subsumed terms should be included as valid terms found in the text, then the precision would be 9/9, or 100%.

The determination of recall is equally arbitrary, as shown in the following example that was also taken from the autocoded output file:

```
<rdf:Description about="urn:PMID-15070658">
   <dc:title>
   high-dose imatinib mesylate therapy in newly diagnosed
   philadelphia chromosome-positive chronic phase chronic
myeloid leukemia
   </dc:title>
   <v:autocode term="leukemia" code="C3161000" />
   <v:autocode term="chronic myeloid leukemia"
code="C3174000" />
   <v:autocode term="myeloid leukemia" code="C3172000" />
   <v:autocode term="chronic phase chronic myeloid leukemia"
code="C3175000" />
</rdf:Description>
```

Here, the human coder may find only one valid term in the text, "philadelphia chromosome-positive chronic myeloid leukemia." In this case, the autocoder found "chronic phase chronic myeloid leukemia" and the more general subsumed term, "chronic myeloid leukemia." It failed to match "Philadelphia chromosome-positive chronic phase chronic myeloid leukemia." If a human coder were to match only the longest term, ignoring the subsumed terms, then the autocoder's recall for this example would have been 0%, because the total number of correct terms would be one and the total number of the correct terms matched by the autocoder would be zero.

Precision and recall require a manual coding process to complement the autocoded output. Therefore, a determination of precision and recall requires the time and energy of domain experts who create the "gold standard" of human-encoded terms. The set of human-encoded terms is typically created with the expectation that it will be used throughout the development process and is typically produced as a one-time effort. Unfortunately, this approach cannot compensate for changes in the versions of the nomenclature or changes in the choice of nomenclature, which would directly affect the choice of human-coded terms. This approach also cannot compensate for inadequacies of human coding.

A development process using repeated comparisons of autocoded output measured against an unchanging, human-encoded output may result in a misleading sense of improved autocoding performance. If the development cycle is dedicated to creating an output that replicates one test set of human output, then it is unlikely that the final product will have the versatility to perform well against a wide variety of text, human coding preferences, or taxonomic variations.

The performance of autocoders is always a contentious issue. It would be a useful exercise to reexamine what autocoding performance means to different people in contrast to what autocoding performance means within the context of lexical parsers. First, every human coder is biased by his or her different perceptions of the knowledge domain. One coder may prefer "parsimonious" coding. In parsimonious coding, there is a "best" code that represents the ideas contained in a defined section of text. A review article on "liver cirrhosis" may contain many different terms, but the parsimonious coder may only preserve a single code for the entire article. Another coder, also a parsimonious coder, may not be so strict, but she may want only the best term from among a group of subterms. So if "adenocarcinoma of endometrium" appears in text, then she may want to preserve this term but omit the so-called atomic inclusive terms, "adenocarcinoma" and "endometrium." Another coder may want a complete listing of every matching term in a text, including terms that occur within larger terms. Still another informatician may want to include all ancestral terms for each term found in the text (i.e., terms not present in the original text but related to the textual concept). Finally, some coders seek to create "concept signatures" from text. A concept signature is the list of the concepts contained in a section of text. The relationship of one section of text to another section of text is determined by a quantitative representation of how closely their signatures match. Concept signatures are used to retrieve or organize related documents, not specific concepts (94).

9.7. OTHER PERFORMANCE ISSUES

The only thing that lexical parsers do is parse text by examining strings to see if they contain exact matches to terms from a nomenclature. There are no false positive matches (because the software does not extract terms that are not actually present in the vocabulary). When a lexical parser fails to extract a relevant term, it is always due to insufficiencies in the text (e.g., a misspelled term in a medical report) or in the vocabulary (e.g., the omission from the vocabulary of a legitimate term or concept). When discussing the performance of a lexical parser, such as the doublet method, speed is the only performance measurement that can be substantially improved by software. Coding accuracy is largely determined by the completeness of the nomenclature and the proper use of terminology within the text.

9.8. ON-THE-FLY CODED DATA RETRIEVAL WITHOUT PRECODING

Perhaps the most practical solution to data retrieval is with automatic recoding. It is now possible to recode large datasets very quickly. Data managers may find that they can recode their entire datasets when a user prefers a different vocabulary or when a new version of a vocabulary is issued. Recoding datasets may become impractical if the vocabularies are frequently modified or replaced. If the task of recoding large datasets is impractical, then there is another option. The purpose of this section is to describe a simple algorithm by which dataset records may be interrogated, quickly retrieving all the records that contain the concept-equivalents of a query term, using any biomedical nomenclature, and using datasets that have not been annotated with vocabulary codes (List 9.8.1). This algorithm achieves the functionality of a search over a coded dataset. Because the algorithm requires no precoding, it can eliminate the enormous expenditure of professional time and energy devoted to coding biomedical reports.

The algorithm for fast doublet matching is most easily understood by first describing a general approach to conducting code-based searches without precoding. Then, the specific method for fast doublet matching is described. Finally, a software implementation of the algorithm is provided.

LIST 9.8.1. ALGORITHM FOR CODE-BASED SEARCHES WITHOUT PREANNOTATION

- The user enters a query term.
- All the terms from a preferred nomenclature that are synonymous to the query term are collected into a list.
- Each term in the list is matched against the text corpus to determine the locations in the corpus where the term is found.

Any vocabulary is suitable, as long as the vocabulary consists of term/code pairs, where a term and its synonyms are all paired with the same code. For instance, the 2004 version of UMLS has 38 equivalent entries for the code C0206708, 9 of which are listed here:

- C0206708 | Cervical Intraepithelial Neoplasms

- C0206708 | Cervical Intraepithelial Neoplasm

- C0206708 | Intraepithelial Neoplasm, Cervical

- C0206708 | Intraepithelial Neoplasms, Cervical

- C0206708 | Neoplasm, Cervical Intraepithelial

- C0206708 | Neoplasms, Cervical Intraepithelial

- C0206708 | Intraepithelial Neoplasia, Cervical

- C0206708 | Neoplasia, Cervical Intraepithelial

- C0206708 | Cervical Intraepithelial Neoplasia

If the user had queried "Cervical Intraepithelial Neoplasms", then the query would be compared with the millions of terms included in the UMLS until a match is made against the exact-match term whose code is C0206708.

All of the terms in the vocabulary that are equivalent to the query term are collected from the nomenclature. Since we are dealing with term/code pairs, this means that all of the vocabulary terms with the same concept code are collected. In the example given, all 38 of the terms whose concept code is C0206708 would be collected.

One by one, the equivalent terms are matched against each record in the dataset to determine which record contains character strings that match any of the equivalent terms. In the case of the example, this would mean that all 38 UMLS terms equivalent to "Cervical Intraepithelial Neoplasms" would be matched against the entire set of data records. This is the rate-limiting step for the algorithm. This step could not be seriously contemplated prior to the advent of fast computers and fast search algorithms.

For each dataset record, if the record contains a character string that matches any of the equivalent vocabulary terms, then the record is retrieved. In the case of the example given, all records containing the term "cervical intraepithelial neoplasia" or any of the term equivalents found in UMLS would be merged into the query response and annotated with the common concept code C0206708.

The following algorithm describes a way to quickly achieve search results for the algorithm described previously and a sample text.

1. The doublet index for the dataset is prepared. The doublet index consists of each of the doublets (two consecutive words) in the datasets, along with all the locations in the dataset where each doublet occurs. In the sample dataset used for this manuscript, the doublet term "vancouver canada" happens to occur 95 times. Examples of 14 index entries for the "vancouver canada" doublet are:
   vancouver canada = 151198-17
   vancouver canada = 157354-8
   vancouver canada = 166770-13
   vancouver canada = 171565-8
   vancouver canada = 175470-11
   vancouver canada = 178127-8
   vancouver canada = 189527-11
   vancouver canada = 198094-8
   vancouver canada = 201139-11
   vancouver canada = 201398-12
   vancouver canada = 202037-8

vancouver canada = 204257-14

vancouver canada = 208131-8

vancouver canada = 223026-11

Each entry consists of the name of the doublet, the record number from the dataset in which the doublet occurs (e.g., record number 151198), and the offset position within the record at which the doublet occurs (e.g., word number 17). The index can be quickly compiled and, once created, never needs to change unless the dataset changes. This index will be used to locate terms composed of any number of words.

2. An associative array is prepared from the doublet index file, consisting of key/value pairs, where the keys are the set of all the different doublet terms present in the dataset, and the values are the byte location in the doublet index file where the doublet first occurs. The doublet index file is alphabetized. Knowing the first occurrence of a doublet in the index allows us to quickly find all the index entries for the doublet simply by going to the first location of the doublet and collecting successive line readings from the index file. The collection of all the index entries for the doublet specifies every record and every position in every record where the doublet occurs.

3. The nomenclature of interest is stored in memory as two associative arrays. One associative array consists of key/value pairs, with nomenclature terms as the keys and corresponding nomenclature codes as values. The other associative array consists of key/value pairs with nomenclature codes as the keys and the list of corresponding nomenclature terms as the values. These two associative arrays allow us to quickly match the user's query term against the entire nomenclature, identify the code number of the matching term (if it exists), and create an array of all the equivalent terms that match the code.

4. The arrays of vocabulary terms that are equivalent to the query term entered by the user are consecutively matched against all the records from the dataset (as described in steps 5, 6, and 7).

5. Each term in the array of equivalent terms is parsed as an array of doublet neighbors. In the case of terms composed of an odd number of words, an overlapping doublet at the end of the term is added. An example of a term composed of an even number of words would be "adenocarcinoma of the lung." The doublet array is "adenocarcinoma of", "the lung."

An example of a term composed of an odd number of words would be "refractory anemia with excess blasts." The doublet array is "refractory anemia," "with excess," "excess blasts."

6. For each term in the array of equivalent terms, entries are collected from the doublet index if they match any of the consecutive doublets that compose the term. The records that match a term are among the records that match every doublet in the term. For a record in this subset to match the term, it needs to contain the doublets that compose the term in the

same text order as the occurrences of the doublets in the term. The term "refractory anemia with excess blasts" is composed of three doublets that must occur in the following relative word positions: "refractory anemia" (position n) "with excess" (position n+2) "excess blasts" (position n+3).

To determine whether term doublets cooccurring in a record actually match a full term, one needs to test whether or not the doublets occur in relative positions corresponding to their positions in the term. For instance, a record may contain multiple occurrences of each of the doublets that compose the term "refractory anemia with excess blasts." Imagine that the doublets occur at the following word positions within the record: "refractory anemia" (locations 15, 92, 105, and 234) "with excess" (locations 17, 107, and 344) "excess blasts" (locations 18, 108, 992, and 1026).

We can be certain that the full term occurs twice in the record, beginning in positions 15 and 105. Only at these two offset positions for the doublet "refractory anemia" are there consecutive occurrences in the same record of the ordered doublets in the whole term (i.e., offsets n, n+2, n+3).

7. All of the dataset records containing all of the consecutively occurring doublets that compose the terms from the array of terms that are equivalent to the query term are collected from the dataset and annotated with the shared concept vocabulary code.

The following four Perl scripts and two vocabulary files are made freely available to the public from the Association for Pathology Informatics (80): `doub4.pl`, `bigsort.pl`, `doubdat2.pl`, `annotget.pl`, `neocl.xml`, and `neoself`.

The results of two trial runs of 100 randomly generated medical terms using two different medical vocabularies are shown. The trials were executed on a 2.89 GHz CPU.

1. `c:\>perl annotget.pl`

total time for 100 multi-word queries is 5 seconds
total time for 10 single words is 18 seconds

This software exercise used Snomed-CT as its source vocabulary and selected 100 terms at random from the nomenclature (104–107). This simulates a user entering 100 valid terms. For each term, the implementation created an array consisting of every term-equivalent for the original term. For each of these hundred arrays, all of the records in a 105+ Megabyte dataset were searched. Records that matched terms from the arrays were extracted and added to an external file. A special case arises when the term-equivalent of a multiword term is a single word term. For instance, nephroblastoma is a singlet equivalent of Wilms' tumor. Because the doublet index contains no singlets, the implementation creates an array of every doublet containing the word nephroblastoma, accounting for every possible occurrence of nephroblastoma. This means that for single word terms, a large array of doublets must be searched. This greatly lengthens the execution time for retrieving matches to singlets. In the first run of the software, there were 10 instances of single word terms occurring as term equivalents of randomly selected multiword terms. The speed of the program for 100 randomly chosen terms and all their term equivalents was 5 seconds for the multiword terms (e.g., 0.05 seconds per term). Eighteen seconds were required to search for 10 single words terms, or 1.8 seconds per singlet.

2. `c:\>perl annotget.pl`

total time for 100 multi-word queries is 438 seconds
total time for 3 single words is 5 seconds

This exercise used the default nomenclature, The Taxonomy for the Developmental Lineage Classification of Neoplasms, as its source vocabulary. As in the prior example, 100 terms were selected at random from the nomenclature, simulating 100 user-initiated searches. The average time for finding multiword terms is 4.38 seconds, approximately 100 times slower than the average time needed to find a search term using Snomed-CT as the source vocabulary. The reason for the slow execution speed is related to the disparate levels of synonymy in the two nomenclatures (108). The average number of synonyms for each term in the neoplasm taxonomy is 23. This means that a search of 100 randomly selected terms is expanded to 2300 term searches. Snomed-CT is a vocabulary with many terms (exceeding 295,000), but each term has, on average, fewer than two synonyms. This means that a search of 100 randomly selected Snomed-CT terms may expand to fewer than 200 term searches. The search for 100 randomly selected multiword terms in the neoplasm taxonomy yielded, after expansion, three single word terms, with an average search time of 1.66 seconds per singlet, which was nearly identical to the single-word search times for the Snomed-CT vocabulary.

9.9. DIFFERENT PHILOSOPHICAL APPROACHES TO TERM-BASED DATA RETRIEVAL

Advocates of data coding believe that raw textual data is poorly organized and needs to be interpreted, structured, and classified before it can be usefully interrogated as a database record. Coding has traditionally required human input. Humans do not code with great consistency or completeness. Humans also do not write narrative text without introducing ambiguities. This means that humans cannot consistently interpret narrative biomedical text. Although human coding can be improved with training and by hiring dedicated professionals whose primary responsibility is to maintain complete and well annotated records (e.g., Tumor Registrars), such efforts come at great expense.

Historically, standard nomenclatures such as ICD or Snomed-CT come out with new versions at least every decade. More importantly, it is virtually impossible to integrate the coded data in one dataset with the data in another dataset that has been coded with a different vocabulary or a different style of coding. After an institution has devoted thousands of professional hours to coding a large collection of biomedical records, it is impractical to ask professionals to go back and recode the data. In most cases, the cost of updating a legacy dataset with new codes has been prohibitive. When new nomenclatures emerge, institutions typically either ignore them or they deploy the new nomenclature prospectively, ignoring legacy data.

Manual coders are hopelessly outpaced by the avalanche of textual data collected by hospital information systems. Consider the narrative text produced or collected by health professionals: e-mail communications, progress notes, nursing notes, operation notes, surgical pathology reports, radiology reports, journal articles, white papers, data analyses, meeting summaries, and so on. Most of this data simply goes uncoded.

Automatic coding using natural language techniques holds enormous promise. A basic assumption of natural language parsing is that synonymous terms are closely related word phrases. For instance, the term adenocarcinoma of lung has much in common with alternate terms such as adenocarcinoma of the lung, adenocarcinoma of the lungs, lung adenocarcinoma, lung carcinoma, and so on. A program that takes into account minor variations in word order, grammatical constructions, word roots (stemming), syntax variation, or string similarities may be able to pull all the equivalent terms from a text automatically. A limitation of this approach is that term synonyms in medical vocabularies often have no etymologic commonality. Consider the term "renal cell carcinoma." The neoplasm taxonomy contains 54 synonyms, including adenocarcinoma of kidney, hypernephroma, and Grawitz' tumor. It would not be possible to discover these synonyms by employing a natural language parser. The only way of obtaining adequate synonymy is through a complete nomenclature. In the neoplasm taxonomy, synonyms for renal cell carcinoma are all coded as "C9385000." The 54 synonyms for "renal cell carcinoma" are: adenoca arising from kidney, adenoca arising in kidney, adenoca involving kidney, adenoca of kidney, adenocarcinoma arising from kidney, adenocarcinoma arising from the kidney, adenocarcinoma arising in kidney, adenocarcinoma arising in the kidney, adenocarcinoma involving kidney, adenocarcinoma involving the kidney, adenocarcinoma of kidney, ca arising from kidney, ca arising in kidney, ca involving kidney, ca of kidney, cancer arising from kidney, cancer arising in kidney, cancer involving kidney, cancer of kidney, carcinoma arising from kidney, carcinoma arising in kidney, carcinoma involving kidney, carcinoma of kidney, grawitz neoplasm, grawitz tumor, grawitz tumour, hypernephroid tumor, hypernephroid tumour, hypernephroma, kidney adenoca, kidney adenocarcinoma, kidney ca, kidney cancer, kidney carcinoma, kidney with adenoca, kidney with adenocarcinoma, kidney with ca, kidney with cancer, kidney with carcinoma, renal adenoca, renal adenocarcinoma, renal ca, renal cancer, renal carcinoma, renal cell adenoca, renal cell adenocarcinoma, renal cell ca, renal cell cancer, renal cell carcinoma, stage unspecified renal cell adenoca, stage unspecified renal cell adenocarcinoma, stage unspecified renal cell ca, stage unspecified renal cell cancer, and stage unspecified renal cell carcinoma.

Natural language parsing is computationally intensive and thousands of times slower than simple hash look-ups (such as those employed by the doublet method). Natural language parsing may be suitable for retrieving terms from a small corpus. When gigabytes or terabytes of information need to be processed, faster techniques are required.

The general problem of term identification in medical text is a central, unresolved issue in medical informatics. A recent review summarizes the different approaches and tools now available to informaticians (109). The following suggestions may be helpful when choosing a preferred method for querying medical datasets (Lists 9.9.1 and 9.9.2).

LIST 9.9.1. WHEN PREANNOTATION IS USEFUL

- When there is the need for a global analysis of the dataset (In a global analysis of a dataset, all the data elements are examined at once. Typically, the researcher is looking for relationships among the different data elements.)
- When the query response time must be very rapid
- When the expected number of queries may be very large

LIST 9.9.2. WHEN CODED SEARCHING WITHOUT PRE-ANNOTATION IS USEFUL

- When the dataset is typically searched one item at a time
- When the dataset does not change or changes only by the addition of records

- When the dataset is being searched using many different types of vocabularies
- When the dataset is searched with a single vocabulary that is constantly changing
- When one dataset needs to be integrated with another dataset, and the datasets have not been annotated with the same nomenclature

Nomenclature-based data retrieval without prior annotation, using the fast doublet method, can potentially eliminate much of the time and money now spent on **data coding**. The method supports retrieval with any version of any nomenclature, thus permitting researchers to integrate data among heterogeneous sources.

9.10. WHY IT IS IMPORTANT TO HAVE FAST AUTOCODING SOFTWARE

As an exercise in reality testing, it may be useful to estimate what the size of the data domain is when we are talking about surgical pathology reports.

There are about 25 million surgical pathology reports generated in the United States each year (and about 50 million cytology reports). The autocoder described in Section 9.5 handles 8,000 reports per second on a 2.8 GHz computer, and it does an incomparably better job than human coders! This means that it will code and scrub the 25 million surgical pathology reports in the United States in about an hour using a desktop PC.

If we had access to a supercomputer (operating more than 3,000 times faster than my desktop PC), then we could autocode and scrub every pathology report produced in the country in under 1 second.

When we discuss autocoding we should remember that coded datasets need to be continually recoded as nomenclatures and study designs change (List 9.10.1). Recoding large datasets requires computational speed.

LIST 9.10.1. WHEN YOU WILL NEED TO RECODE

- Whenever you want to change from one nomenclature to another (eliminates problem of brand-name loyalty)
- Whenever you introduce a new version of a nomenclature
- Whenever you want to use a new coding algorithm (e.g., parsimonious versus comprehensive, or linking code to a particular extracted portion of report)

- Whenever you add legacy data to your HIS
- Whenever you merge different pathology datasets (eliminates many mapping projects)

Computational tasks that take much time (more than a few seconds) tend to be shunned. The reasons for this are largely psychological. When a scientist runs a program and checks the output for mistakes, she will be naturally annoyed if she finds one. If it takes a few seconds to correct the error and run the software again, then a self-disciplined worker will repeat the exercise. But if finding an error means that the scientist must rerun a program that takes hours, days, or weeks to execute, then the level of annoyance rises. Biomedical programs often use large textual, data, or mixed data-textual sources. Finding errors in outputs is commonplace, and often requires multiple cycles of debugging, execution, and review. If the debug/execution/review cycle is short, then rapid progress often follows. If the debug/execution/review cycle is long, then projects are often abandoned or (worse) released without revision. Smart informaticians understand that program execution speed is very important (110).

Computational Methods for De-identification and Data Scrubbing

10.1. BACKGROUND

It is ironic that two of the most important technical tasks in the field of biomedical informatics are data identification and **data de-identification**. It would seem that the two jobs should cancel themselves, but they do not. The purpose of this chapter is to explain the close relationship between identification and de-identification and to suggest technical approaches to achieve either condition.

10.2. DE-IDENTIFICATION AND DATA SCRUBBING

Latanya Sweeney was an early proponent of technical approaches to medical record de-identification and has published extensively on the subject. Her work formed the foundation for current multistep approaches to de-identification, encompassing the following tasks (List 10.2.1):

LIST 10.2.1. MAKING MEDICAL RECORD DATA HARMLESS

1. De-identification of data fields that specifically characterize the patient (name, social security number, hospital number, address, age, etc.)
2. Free-text data scrubbing, removing identifiers from the textual portion of medical reports
3. Rendering the dataset ambiguous, ensuring that patients cannot be identified by data records containing a unique set of characterizing information
4. Free-text data privatizing, removing any information of a private nature that may be contained within the report

10.3. IDENTIFIERS

HIPAA specifies 18 types of data that can identify patients (List 10.3.1).

When these 18 identifiers are removed from a medical record, the record is minimally de-identified (under HIPAA).

The most difficult identifier is the last item on the list. It throws back into the HIPAA entity's court the problem of determining whether there are any uniquely identifying data in the record.

LIST 10.3.1. HIPAA SAFE HARBOR IDENTIFIERS

- Names
- Geographic subdivisions smaller than a state
- Dates (except year) directly related to patient
- Telephone numbers
- Fax numbers
- E-mail addresses
- Social security numbers
- Medical record numbers
- Health plan beneficiary numbers
- Account numbers
- Certificate/license numbers
- Vehicle identifiers and serial numbers
- Device identifiers and serial numbers
- Web URLs
- Internet Protocol (IP) address numbers
- Biometric identifiers, including finger and voice prints
- Full face photographic images and any comparable images
- Any other unique identifying number, characteristic, or code, except as permitted under HIPAA to re-identify data

10.4. STRIPPING IDENTIFIERS

A de-identification algorithm removes all patient identifiers from the patient records. Most hospital information systems (HISs) have a well-defined set of patient identifiers (name, social security number, medical record, etc.). These usually are accessed from reserved data dictionary fields in the HIS. Once these reserved fields are accessed, all other fields (including free-text fields) can be parsed and deleted of any identifier matches. So, if the patient's name (as found in the "name" field) is

Thomas Patterson, then any mention of Thomas Patterson can be deleted from free-text patient fields (such as admission notes, history notes, discharge notes). In addition, a robust algorithm should search and destroy any reference to Tom Patterson, or just plain Tom or the word Mr., Miss, Mrs., or Ms. followed by any name. It may be beneficial to have a list of all the names of patients registered in the hospital system and delete any free-text match (even if the name is not the name of the person attached to the record). It might be useful to remove all mention of staff doctor names or of any surname following the Dr. title. A similar process might be applied to the medical record number or social security number and would include all variations of presentation of a social security number (with or without hyphenation).

10.5. HOW GOOD IS GOOD ENOUGH?

The HIPAA regulations do not indicate that de-identification must be perfect. In addition, the precedent set in Southern Illinoisan v. Department of Health (see Chapter 2) (18), would indicate that confidential data may be used for research purposes even when de-identification is known to be imperfect. The issue for biomedical information is, "How good is good enough for de-identification software?"

10.6. SCRUBBING DATA

Many people in the biomedical informatics field define data scrubbing as the removal of identifying information from medical text. HIPAA permits medical data to be freely exchanged if the patient identifiers have been removed. Since the goal of many biomedical informaticians is HIPAA-compliancy, it would seem that the purpose of data scrubbing would be to remove identifiers. In my opinion, this is a very narrow way of thinking about the problem of data scrubbing. Biomedical informaticians who attempt to scrub medical records have an obligation to remove all private text contained in reports, even when the text does not identify a patient. What is "private" text? Private text is text that is nobody's business and that does not enhance the intended use of the de-identified patient record. In many cases, private text is written by hospital personnel with the expectation that it will be shared only among the persons directly responsible for the care of the patient. This may include notes documenting errors, misjudgments, warnings, and complaints. Most hospital personnel are expected to exclude information of an incriminating nature from the patient's medical records. Incident reports and quality assurance reports exist for this purpose. In reality, medical records often contain information that is best removed from shared data sets. An exception list of offensive terms that must be removed from medical records is a first-pass remedy.

There is a general understanding that when medical data are shared for the purposes of conducting research, there is an implied ethical obligation to share only that portion of the patient record that is actually needed to conduct the research. This is sometimes referred to as the **"minimum necessary provision."**

One method of data scrubbing is the subtractive method. In this method, the text is parsed, sentence by sentence, and the computer program determines whether any of the words need to be removed from the text.

Removing identifiers from text involves creating a list of patient names, physician names, geographic locations, street names, zip codes, components of dates (days, months, and years) expressed in different formats, and so on. When the parsing program encounters any words or phrases in the text that are also found in the list of identifiers, these words are removed.

Subtractive methods mimic the way that a human might censor a text. The human reads the text with a marker in-hand, prepared to strike out any words or phrases that she knows is offensive. In my opinion, subtractive methods for data scrubbing are ineffective and counterproductive (List 10.6.1).

LIST 10.6.1. DEFICIENCIES OF SUBTRACTIVE DATA SCRUBBING METHODS

- Requires the creation and continuous maintenance of an identifier list consisting of names of patients, staff, and medical centers as well as addresses and other geographic minutiae
- Requires the creation and continuous maintenance of rules for excluding text based on co-locations or patterns of expression that might signify a HIPAA identifier (e.g., a sequence of digits and slashes that might represent a date)
- Does not exclude private information that is nonidentifying but which may be incriminating or distasteful
- Does not satisfy the **"minimum necessary principle,"** holding that medical data convey only that information which is needed for research purposes.
- Slow. Each parsed sentence is typically evaluated through the entire list of pattern rules. This means that parsing a long corpus of medical text will take considerable time.

- Complex. Maintaining the rule list and the identifier list will add to the overall complexity of the software. Each institution that implements the software will need to maintain their own lists created for their patients and for their textual styles and formats.
- Inadequate. Subtractive scrubbers, under the best of circumstances, will occasionally miss an identifier. If a scrubber is 99% accurate, it may miss thousands of identifiers in a large text.

A far better strategy is to parse text, extracting every word except words from an approved list of non-identifying words. This is the concept-match algorithm (111). If you use the concept match method, then the implementation is simple and fast, and virtually foolproof. The algorithm steps through confidential text. When a medical term matching a standard nomenclature term is encountered, the term is replaced by a code and a synonym for the original term. When a high frequency "stop" word, such as *a, an, the,* or *for,* is encountered, it is left in place. When any other word is encountered, it is blocked and replaced by asterisks (List 10.6.2). This produces a scrubbed text. No identifiers will be present in the output because the only words in the output come from an approved list of terms.

LIST 10.6.2. ALGORITHM FOR THE CONCEPT-MATCH METHOD OF DATA SCRUBBING

1. Parse all input into sentences.
2. Parse each sentence into words.
3. Each stop word (high-frequency words, including prepositions and common adjectives) is preserved in its original place within each sentence.
4. Intervening words and phrases are mapped to a standard nomenclature. This step requires breaking phrases into all possible ordered concatenations of words. For instance, "Margins free of tumor" would become "margins free of tumor, margins free of, free of tumor, margins free, free of, of tumor, margins, free, of, tumor." Each member of the derivative list is matched against the entire database of Unified Medical Language System (UMLS) terms to determine whether a code exists for the term. Large terms subsume smaller substring terms.

5. Each coded term is replaced by an alternate term that maps to the same concept code, if an alternate term exists. For instance, the term renal cell carcinoma appearing in the text would be replaced by C0007134 (the UMLS Concept Unique Identifier for renal cell carcinoma) and by a different term that maps to the same code (such as rcc, hypernephroma, hypernephroid carcinoma, or Grawitz tumor). This step produces an output containing a different set of words than the original text (List 10.6.3).

6. All other words are replaced by blocking symbol consisting of an asterisk.

The concept-match algorithm is nomenclature-independent. Any controlled medical **terminology** that provides codes for medical concepts and synonyms for all the terms belonging to a medical concept can be used for the purposes of data scrubbing. The output of the scrubber consists of terms from a medical nomenclature, high frequency words, and asterisks (List 10.6.3).

LIST 10.6.3. SAMPLE OUTPUT OF THE CONCEPT-MATCH SCRUBBING METHOD

```
<rdf:Description about="urn:PMID-15832079">
  <dc:title>
primary synovial sarcoma of the mediastinum a
clinicopathologic immunohistochemical and ultrastructural
study of 15 cases
  </dc:title>
  <v:autocode term="sarcoma" code="C0000000" />
  <v:autocode term="sarcoma of the mediastinum"
code="C6606000" />
  <v:autocode term="synovial sarcoma" code="C3400000" />
  <v:autocode term="synovial sarcoma of the mediastinum"
code="C6618000" />
  <v:autocode term="primary synovial sarcoma"
code="C8826000" />
  <de_id>
  * primary synovial sarcoma of the mediastinum a * * and *
  * of * * * *
  </de_id>
</rdf:Description>
```

The output text can be hard to read and may consist predominantly of asterisks when the original records contains many words and terms that are not present in the "approved" word list.

A newer version of the concept-match method uses doublets (112). There is an external list of "approved" word doublets (about 80,000 of them). The doublet list is chosen to contain no identifying terms. The publicly available list of doublets was automatically compiled from two open source medical vocabularies (112). The list of doublets can be obtained from the Association for Pathology Informatics Web site:

http://www.pathologyinformatics.org/Resources/doubdb.txt

The algorithm is simple. The text is parsed, and all the doublets in the text that match a term in the approved list are retained. Everything else is replaced by an asterisk (List 10.6.4).

LIST 10.6.4. SCRUB.PL, **A PERL SCRIPT IMPLEMENTING THE DOUBLET VERSION OF THE CONCEPT-MATCH SCRUBBER**

```perl
#!/usr/local/bin/perl
open (TEXT, "doubdb.txt")||die"Can't open file";
$line = " ";
while ($line ne "")
    {
    $line = <TEXT>;
    $line =~ s/\n//o;
    $doubhash{$line} = "";
    }
close TEXT;
print "What would you like to scrub?\n";
$line = <STDIN>;
print "Scrubbed text.... ";
$line = lc($line);
$line =~ s/\'s//g;
$line =~ s/[^a-z0-9 \-//g;
@hoparray = split(/ +/,$line);
$lastword = "\*";
for ($i=0;$i<(scalar(@hoparray));$i++)
{
    $doublet = "$hoparray[$i] $hoparray[$i+1]";
if (exists $doubhash{$doublet})
{
print " $hoparray[$i]";
$lastword = " $hoparray[$i+1]";
```

```
      }
  else
     {
  print $lastword;
  $lastword = " \*";
     }
  }
  print "\n";
  exit;
```

This method works fast (1 Mbyte per second on my 1.6 GHz CPU) and does not permit any unlisted doublets to slip through (List 10.6.5). It retains more words from the text than the original concept match algorithm because it does not require concatenated doublets to match terms from the vocabularies that are the source of the doublets.

The value of the use of doublets (instead of approved words) is that a single seemingly innocuous word (like "No") can be a person's name ("Dr. No is in the hospital"). In this case, the inclusive doublets, "Dr. No" and "No is" are not found in the approved doublet list. The identifying text, "Dr. No is", will be excluded. On the other hand, accepted doublets containing the word "no", like "no tumor" or "no evidence" will be saved if they are included in the list of approved doublets.

LIST 10.6.5. FIVE SAMPLE OUTPUTS FROM SCRUB.PL

```
C:\ftp>perl scrub.pl
What would you like to scrub?
Basal cell carcinoma, margins involved
Scrubbed text.... basal cell carcinoma margins involved
C:\ftp>perl scrub.pl
What would you like to scrub?
Rhabdoid tumor of kidney
Scrubbed text.... rhabdoid tumor of kidney
C:\ftp>perl scrub.pl
What would you like to scrub?
Mr Brown has a basal cell carcinoma
Scrubbed text.... * * has a basal cell carcinoma
C:\ftp>perl scrub.pl
What would you like to scrub?
Mr. Brown was born on Tuesday, March 14, 1985
```

```
Scrubbed text.... * * * * * * * * *
C:\ftp>perl scrub.pl
What would you like to scrub?
The doctor killed the patient
Scrubbed text.... * * * * *
```

10.7. DE-IDENTIFICATION ALGORITHMS

One of the keystones of the de-identification process is the creation of datasets that contain no unique records. If every record has at least one additional record to which it is identical, then it becomes logically impossible to distinguish any one individual from any of the other individuals whose records contain the same data elements. Guaranteeing that any medical dataset contains only ambiguous records (i.e., records with multiple identical instances) is a feasible computational task. It may involve constantly revising the scope of certain data elements (such as using only the first few digits of zip codes, or using only the state to mark a patient's address) or even adding fake (ambiguating) records to the data. The method of de-identification would depend largely on the purpose of the data mining effort.

10.8. FEASIBILITY OF DE-IDENTIFICATION

Is it even feasible to de-identify medical records? Some informaticians believe that a database of unidentifiable patient records is impossible (113). The reason is that even when de-identified, medical records contain information that, when combined with data held in other databases, may uniquely identify patients.

Combinations of data in an unidentified medical record may apply to only one person in the population. Patient identification occurs when data values in a de-identified medical record are coupled with a public (identified) database. If a medical record contains an unnamed patient's birth date, gender, and zip code and a public database lists names of people in a zip code, along with their birth dates and gender, it is a simple step to ascertain the identity of patients whose data is contained in de-identified data records.

A story from the news may serve to clarify just how this may work (114). A 15-year-old boy was fathered using anonymously donated sperm. The boy wanted to know the identity of his biological father.

A private company had created a DNA database from 45,000 DNA samples. The purpose of the database was to allow clients to discover relatives by having their DNA compared with all the DNA samples in the database. The boy sent his DNA sample (a scraping of buccal mucosa) to the company, along with a fee. A comparison of the boy's Y chromosome DNA (inherited exclusively from the father) was compared with Y chromosome DNA in the database. The names of two men with close matches to the boy's Y chromosome were found.

The boy's mother had been provided (from the sperm bank) with the sperm donor's date of birth and birthplace. The boy used an online service to obtain the name of every man born in the two matching sperm donors' places of birth on the sperm donor's date of birth. Among those names, one name matched one of the two close matches from the DNA database search. The boy had (according to the news report) identified his biologic father. The boy used his own uniquely identifying information (i.e., his DNA) and complementary data from several databases. No single database source contained data that identified the biological father (114).

10.9. NONUNIQUENESS AND DE-IDENTIFICATION

One of the trickiest issues in database security is the issue of obtaining patient-specific knowledge through the use of cumulative query results. Basically, the problem occurs when the database being queried contains personal data, and multiple overlapping queries produce a dataset with enough data to make identification possible.

In retrospect, the sperm bank discussed in the prior section could have guarded the confidentiality of their sperm donors by concealing their dates and places of birth. Date and place of birth, along with gender, uniquely identifies a good portion of the U.S. population. An oft-cited observation by Latanya Sweeney is that 87% of the U.S. population is uniquely identified by date of birth, gender, and 5-digit zip code (41, 42). In the absence of information related to the biological father's date and place of birth, the boy would have learned only that two men from the DNA database had similar Y chromosomes to his. There may have been hundreds of thousands of other men (not included in the database of 45,000) who closely matched the boy's DNA.

In this example, the biological father was identified because one person was uniquely found to belong to two different databases. Had the database that supplied the names of people born on a given date and place been designed to ensure non-uniqueness, the boy's father would not have been identified.

As a logical rule, if two records in a database are exactly alike, they can never be distinguished. As a corollary, if no record in a database is unique, it is impossible to identify any of the records in the database.

The trick is to create databases in which all records have at least one other record with the same data elements.

For example, consider a database of seven items consisting of glucose levels obtained over a period:

glucose 98 100 94 106 93
glucose 98 100 94 106 93
glucose 98 100 94 106 93
glucose 96 98 90 91 88
glucose 96 98 90 91 88
glucose 75 80 70 75 75
glucose 75 80 70 75 75

No two records are unique. Because no single patient has a unique record, no patient can be identified uniquely. Now suppose we number the records (to distinguish one from another. Would this confer uniqueness on any record?

1. glucose 98 100 94 106 93
2. glucose 98 100 94 106 93
3. glucose 98 100 94 106 93
4. glucose 96 98 90 91 88
5. glucose 96 98 90 91 88
6. glucose 75 80 70 75 75
7. glucose 75 80 70 75 75

Not really. The numbers are arbitrarily assigned and provide no meaningful information. Now suppose that we assign a unique identifier to each record. Would this confer uniqueness to the records?

57203957204851. glucose 98 100 94 106 93
47473218465742. glucose 98 100 94 106 93
37311992230182. glucose 98 100 94 106 93
44232375637592. glucose 96 98 90 91 88
81492013636935. glucose 96 98 90 91 88
67827366252847. glucose 75 80 70 75 75
82729487019384. glucose 75 80 70 75 75

So long as the identifier does not serve as an identifier to another data record pertaining to the patient, the database maintains its nonuniqueness (even when the records are identified by a unique number).

But, imagine the following database:

57203957204851. john doe

47473218465742. frank smith

37311992230182. susan patient

44232375637592. sam public

81492013636935. larry carson

67827366252847. mary worthington

82729487019384. louis grant

With this information, we can easily attach a set of glucose values to each name. A unique number attached to a data record is potentially identifying if it is derived from or linked to identifying information.

10.10. LEVERAGING SOME CONFIDENTIAL INFORMATION TO LEARN MORE CONFIDENTIAL INFORMATION

Another type of problem in patient confidentiality arises when you have an identified person, you know that the identified person is included in a database, you have some confidential information about the person, and you want to learn additional information. This is a gray area because it begins with the assumption that confidentiality already has been breached. It really is not clear whether investigators have legal obligations extending to these situations. Regardless, a prudent investigator may choose to prepare a defense.

Let us say that there are two records of patients with rhabdoid tumor. We do not know which record applies to our patient of interest, but if both records are identical (have all the same diagnoses), then we can safely infer that our patient has all the diagnoses listed (for either record), and these may include items in addition to the diagnosis of rhabdoid tumor.

Let us say that there are 10 records with the diagnosis of rhabdoid tumor. We do not know which record belongs to the patient we are interested in. However, we notice that all 10 patients with rhabdoid tumor have in common a diagnosis of colon adenoma. Then we know that the patient of interest must have a colon adenoma.

Let us say that all 10 cases of rhabdoid tumor are in non-unique records (no two of the 10 records are exactly the same) and that there are no diagnoses common to all 10 patients (other than rhabdoid tumor). Nine of the 10 patients have prostate carcinoma as well as rhabdoid tumor. The patient we are interested in is a female. We can assume that the one record of rhabdoid tumor without prostate cancer belongs to the patient that we are interested in and all the diagnoses associated with the record also belong to that patient.

What could we have done to ensure anonymity of our patient (List 10.10.1)?

LIST 10.10.1. SUGGESTIONS OF NONUNIQUENESS IN DATABASE DE-IDENTIFICATION

1. No unique diseases are allowed (i.e., every concept in the database must be present in at least two records). Any record with a uniquely occurring tumor is expunged.
2. N-plicate records cannot contain values that are unique to the n-plicate set (if you have n identical records, then you should be able to look at all the diagnoses in the replicated record and find other records with the same diagnosis). If that is not the case, all such n-plicate records should be expunged from the public use database.
3. No value may be allowed to occur in every record from a set of records that share a common diagnosis. If that is the case, then every record containing the concept is expunged.
4. Every value that co-occurs in a record that contains a gender-specific tumor must occur in more than one additional record that does not contain a gender-specific tumor. Otherwise, all records containing the concept are expunged (NOTE: the same argument may be made for diseases that are highly age-specific, or ethnicity-specific, or possibly locale-specific).
5. No value-binned record can be unique to a second diagnosis (i.e., there may be 10 rhabdoid tumor cases, but only one case of rhabdoid tumor and basal cell carcinoma). Such cases are expunged.

Now, can someone learn something about their patient from reviewing the database after these precautions have been followed?

Yes. Let us say you know that a certain patient had rhabdoid tumor, and you check a database of 7 million cases and find no cases that could possibly match the patient you are interested in. You can infer that the case met an exclusion criterion. Now you know something you did not know before—that the case had the features of an excludable case. Is this a breach of confidentiality that can harm a patient? Probably not, but it does provide some information about a specific patient that would not have been available if the database had never existed.

Let us say you have a 7 million-case database published at a certain time, and you download the database again at a later time. You do a subtractive analysis of the two databases and extract the records that were present in the early file and absent in the later file. You also extract records that were absent in the early file and present in the later file. You might assume that cases that appear only in the later file are cases that occurred after the first file was created. This would tell you something about the newly appearing records. You may assume that the cases missing from the later file were records that needed to be expunged. This information could be exploited to acquire confidential information from the database. One way to get around this is to have a set of several thousand records of cases occurring at varying times that you plant or extract from different file versions.

Let us say that all 10 records of patients with rhabdoid tumor are unique and that there are no diagnoses common to any two of the 10 patients (other than rhabdoid tumor). But you happen to know that the particular patient that you have an interest in has rhabdoid tumor and basal cell carcinoma. You find one record in which rhabdoid tumor and basal cell carcinoma appears. You can be certain that this is the case record of interest. You now know all the confidential information contained in the record. In this instance, it is assumed that someone already has some confidential knowledge of a person's medical conditions. In general, if someone has obtained confidential information on a patient, then it can be very difficult to stop that person from acquiring additional information.

If you have been endowed with a clever but paranoid mind, it is possible to imagine all types of unlikely scenarios in which confidentiality can be breached. In Chapter 17, we will discuss the concept of "reasonableness" as a legal and ethical concept. A reasonable approach to confidentiality and privacy is all that can be expected from biomedical informaticians.

10.11. PERFORMANCE CONSIDERATIONS FOR DE-IDENTIFICATION SOFTWARE

No single de-identification method is likely to satisfy everyone. Published articles that describe a specific de-identification software product cannot account for the needs of every type of research effort (List 10.11.1).

LIST 10.11.1. PERFORMANCE ISSUES FOR DE-IDENTIFICATION SOFTWARE

1. Product availability—is the software product freely available and open source? Grant applications that propose proprietary data sharing solutions may receive disparaging reviews in study sections. Reviewers may expect large, multi-institutional efforts to implement open source de-identification algorithms. Conversely, proprietary solutions may be ideal for laboratory personnel who

lack the resources to implement and test published algorithms and who prefer turnkey applications.

2. Product speed—is the de-identification process fast? This becomes important when the research project involves millions of records or requires reprocessing records to satisfy research objectives that change over time or that serve different research protocols.

3. Product error rate—there is a trade-off between the accurate preservation of textual information and the successful elimination of all identifiers. If the research project requires the human review of de-identified reports, then it may be necessary to use a de-identification method that preserves as much of the original text as is feasible. De-identification methods that maximize the preservation of original text will tend to have the highest error rates.

4. Product integration and support issues—will the de-identification software work with heterogeneous data sources, or is it constrained to work with a specific data corpus? Will the software permit an interface to the researcher's preferred database, or will the researcher be required to transform the primary data structure to a secondary data structure? If so, will the secondary data structure conform to an **open standard**, or will it be a proprietary data structure? Will the software be upgraded and will the upgrades be freely available? Can the software be modified without violating license agreements?

5. Convenience—will the product require continual maintenance, staff training, and quality assurance? Sometimes simplicity and easy maintenance will justifiably outweigh performance.

10.12. DE-IDENTIFICATION AND DATA SHARING PATENTS

Somewhat alarming is the proliferation of patent applications covering fundamental processes in de-identification and data sharing. A visit to the U.S. Patent and Trademark Web site (http://patft.uspto.gov/netahtml/search-bool.html) indicates that (circa 2005) several medical de-identification protocols have been awarded patents and several dozen patent applications in the field of medical de-identification await review.

It would be unfortunate if the well-intentioned act of sharing data engendered legal reprisal. History would suggest that hospital laboratories tend to abandon methodologies encumbered by patent royalties (115).

The best way of ensuring an open environment for data sharing is by providing opportunities for the publication of data sharing methods. Establishing a wide assortment of published data sharing protocols as "Prior Art" will make it difficult for inventors to include fundamental data sharing processes in their patent claims.

Cryptography in Biomedical Informatics

11.1. BACKGROUND

The field of cryptography encompasses a variety of useful techniques in addition to encrypting and decrypting messages (116, 117) (List 11.1.1). In this chapter, we will look at a variety of cryptographic approaches in the field of biomedical informatics.

LIST 11.1.1. CRYPTOGRAPHIC METHODS VITAL TO BIOMEDICAL INFORMATICS

- Encrypting and decrypting messages
- Electronic signatures
- Message authentication
- Time stamping
- Creating unique identifiers
- Reconciling patients across institutions
- De-identification and re-identification
- Privatizing data sharing protocols
- Data referencing (with message digests)
- Watermarking and **steganography** utilities

11.2. ONE-WAY HASHING ALGORITHMS

One-way hashes, also called HMACs, were introduced in Chapter 6. One-way hashes can be used to anonymize patient records while still permitting researchers to accrue data over time to a specific patient's record (List 11.2.1).

LIST 11.2.1. EXAMPLE PROTOCOL FOR A ONE-WAY HASH DE-IDENTIFIED RECORD LINKAGE

1. John Q. Public arrives for the first time in your medical clinic.
2. John Q. Public has a glucose test ordered and receives a glucose value of 85.
3. Using the MD_5 one-way hash algorithm on the character string "John Q. Public", a hash value of "3f875ec450dfbb07-ed889e7b9c36da92" is generated.
4. In addition to John Q. Public's identified medical record, a de-identified record is prepared:

   3f875ec450dfbb07ed889e7b9c36da92^^glucose^^85

   A property of the one-way hash value is that it is a seemingly random collection of letters and numbers and no computational efforts applied to the one-way hash value can yield the patient's name. The de-identified record is given to a trusted database administrator who adds it to the database of de-identified records. The database administrator cannot identify any of the patients whose records are included in the database.
5. Ten years later, John Q. Public returns to the medical clinic and has another glucose test. This time, the glucose value is 95.
   A one-way hash is performed on the string "John Q. Public", yielding 3f875ec450dfbb07ed889e7b9c36da92, and a new de-identified record is prepared:

   3f875ec450dfbb07ed889e7b9c36da92^^glucose^^95

   The de-identified record is given to the trusted database administrator who adds it to the aggregate database. The database program finds a match to the one-way hash and concatenates the new record to the old record:

   3f875ec450dfbb07ed889e7b9c36da92^^glucose^^85^^glucose^^95

What has this accomplished? It achieves the seemingly impossible feat of accruing clinical data over time for de-identified data records. Every time John Q. Public comes to the clinic, his records are de-identified and the de-identified records are aggregated with all the records having the same, unique, de-identified hash value.

11.3. ONE-WAY HASH WEAKNESSES: DICTIONARY ATTACKS AND COLLISIONS

Insightful readers will notice that this approach has a flaw. Attacks on one-way hash data may take the form of hashing a list of names and looking for matching hash values in the dataset (so-called dictionary attack). Efforts to overcome this limitation include encrypting the hash or by hashing a secret combination of identifier elements, or both, or by keeping the hash value private (hidden). As in any privacy protocol, success is achieved by implementation strategies that minimize those risks that pertain to an institution's particular environment. Regarding implementation, problems arise when institutions have a flawed system for identifying patients. If a person is identified within a hospital system as Tom Peterson on Monday, and Thomas Peterson on Tuesday, then a system based on hashing names would fail. If the hash is performed on a unique, persistent patient identifier, then this system would have a better chance of success.

Technical problems may also arise. One-way hash collisions occur when two different strings yield the same hash value. Because hash values are pseudorandom character strings, the chance of a hash collision between two patients with different identifiers is very small. A variety of solutions have been suggested for large database implementations (where collisions may rarely occur). The most straightforward maneuver is to use a longer hash value. Secure Hash Algorithm (SHA) has different algorithmic forms (SHA-1, SHA-256, SHA-384, and SHA-512) with message digest (hash) lengths up to 512 bits. As the length of the message digest increases, the chance of having a digest collision becomes very small.

A 2005 paper by Faldum and Pommerening proposes a novel approach to assigning patient identifiers (118). They offer a mathematical algorithm that can distinguish 1 billion individuals without collisions, using a short, eight-character string that contains extra characters for error checking and correcting.

11.4. ZERO-KNOWLEDGE PATIENT RECONCILIATION

Biomedical informaticians in the United States who use one-way hashes to de-identify patient records have been challenged by HIPAA Privacy regulations (9) (List 11.4.1).

LIST 11.4.1. SECTION OF HIPAA REGULATION SPECIFICALLY ADDRESSING USE OF ONE-WAY HASH DE-IDENTIFIERS

- Comment: Several commenters who supported the creation of de-identified data for research based on removal of facial identifiers asked if a keyed-hash message authentication code (HMAC) can be used as a re-identification code even though it is derived from patient information, because it is not intended to re-identify the patient and it is not possible to identify the patient from the code. The commenters stated that use of the keyed-hash message authentication code would be valuable for research, public health and bio-terrorism detection purposes where there is a need to link clinical events on the same person occurring in different health care settings (e.g., to avoid double counting of cases or to observe long-term outcomes).

- Response: The HMAC does not meet the conditions for use as a re-identification code for de-identified information. It is derived from individually identified information and it appears the key is shared with or provided by the recipient of the data in order for that recipient to be able to link information about the individual from multiple entities or over time. Since the HMAC allows identification of individuals by the recipient, disclosure of the HMAC violates the Rule.

HIPAA's Final Rule on patient privacy places restrictions on the use of HMAC protocols for sharing research information. United States biomedical informaticians who want to use HMACs to de-identify and exchange patient data will have two options under HIPAA. Researchers may obtain a **Limited Data Use Agreement** permitting the exchange of research data between signatories. Researchers may also request waivers from their institutional review boards, permitting them to use HMAC protocols. These two remedies are provided by HIPAA to allow research using patient records that do not meet all of the de-identification measures described in the HIPAA Final (Privacy) Rule. For some researchers who wish to use HMAC protocols, one of these two remedies will suffice. However, U.S. researchers who wish to publicly share research data (i.e., who seek unlimited data use), or whose uses of data would require multiple submissions to their institutional review boards for waivers, may find these two remedies unsatisfactory.

Zero-knowledge protocols are techniques whereby a specific question is answered without actually sharing information (List 11.4.2). A safe, zero-knowledge protocol permits biomedical informaticians to compare two patient records to determine whether they belong to the same patient. This protocol can be performed without HMACs in such a way that no identifying information is shared between institutions (List 11.4.3).

LIST 11.4.2. STEPS OF THE PROTOCOL

- Step 1. Institution A and Institution B each create a random character string and send it to the other institution.
- Step 2. Each institution receives the random character string from the other institution and sums it with their own random character string, producing a random character string common to both institutions (RandA+B).
- Step 3. Each institution takes a patient identifier (a name, a social security number, a birth date, or some combination of identifiers) and sums it with RandA+B. The result is a patient random character string that is identical across institutions when the patient is identical in both institutions. This step may be implemented several different ways.
  - Step 3, implementation strategy 1. RandA+B is now destroyed at both institutions, and RandA and RandB are destroyed by the institutions that created each random string, leaving only the patient random character string at each institution. The destruction of these random numbers makes it impossible to recompute the original identifier from the patient random character string.
  - Step 3, implementation strategy 2. At this point, institutions may provide the patient random character string to a data broker. Having only the patient random character strings, the broker has no patient-related information.
  - Step 3, implementation strategy 3. The summation function can be any one of many logical operations on characters or strings or their constitutive bits, including logical or, x or, modulo addition, and so on.
- Step 4. Institutions A and B compare a subset of their patient random character strings.
  - Step 4, implementation strategy 1. Institution A sends the first character of the patient random character string to institution B. If the first character (or any subsequent character) is not identical in both institutions, then the protocol ends. The two patients are not the same person. If the first character is identical in both institutions, then institution B sends the second character of its patient random character string to institution A. If the second character held by institution B is the same as the second character held by institution A, then the process is repeated until a sufficient number of transactions have occurred, short of the length of the random character string, to convince the institutions that they have the same patient random character string. Implementing this optional strategy ensures that the patient random character strings are never actually exchanged between institutions.

LIST 11.4.3. ZERO-CHECK PROPERTIES

- No knowledge about the patient is transmitted across institutions. When institutions use an institutional broker to complete the transactions, the institutions themselves have no knowledge of the identity of the individuals.
- The protocol uses no encryption or one-way hash algorithm, and therefore, there is no need to protect the protocol from discovery.
- By destroying RandA, RandB, and RandA+B, the protocol can be implemented in a manner that makes it impossible to recompute the original identifier from the patient random character string.

The Zero-Check protocol has been simulated in a publicly available Perl script (15).

It is counterintuitive to think that the identities of two patients can be compared without any knowledge of the identities of either patient, but that is the exact purpose of the Zero-Check protocol. A physical analogy may clarify the essential feature of the protocol. Imagine two people each holding a box containing an item. Neither person knows the contents of the box that they are holding or the contents of the box that the other person is holding. They want to determine whether they are holding identical items, but they do not want to know anything about the items. They work together to create two identical imprint stamps, each covered by a complex random collection of raised ridges. With eyes closed, each one pushes his imprint stamp against his item. By doing so, the randomly placed ridges in the stamp are compressed in a manner characteristic of the object's surface. The stamps are next examined to determine whether the compression marks on the ridges are distributed identically in both stamps. If so, then the items in the two boxes are considered to be identical. Not all of the random ridges need to be examined—just enough of them to reach a high level of certainty. It is theoretically possible for two different items to produce the same pattern of compression marks, but it is highly unlikely. After the comparison is made, the stamps are discarded.

The physical analogy demonstrates the power of a zero-knowledge protocol. Neither party knows anything about his item, and neither party learns anything about his or the other party's item during the transaction. Yet, somehow, the parties can determine whether the two items are identical.

The idea is to replace a patient identifier with a random character string. The random character string is generated by a summation of a patient identifier with random character strings shared between two institutions. Once the random character string shared by the institutions is destroyed, each institution need only compare the product random strings. If they are the same, then the patients (whose identities are unknown) are the same person.

The Zero-Check protocol may be implemented using a wide variety of methods. If a RandA+B string is reused for multiple records, then a patient's random character string will become invariate and can be used to link a patient's record with additional records accruing over time. This creates a functionality equivalent to a one-way hash and may be preferred by institutions complying with the HIPAA proscription against one-way hash de-identification. However, institutions that implement a Zero-Check protocol that preserves the RandA+B string must take measures to ensure that the RandA+B string is kept secret.

In life, nothing is perfect, and any choice of implementation strategies will likely raise issues related to the balance of utility and security. If different RandA+B strings are created for a long list of patients, then the problem of identifier collisions (e.g., two different patients having the same patient random character string) arises. If a broker is used by institutions, then re-identification of patients may become impossible, depending on the "rules" created for brokered transactions. These general issues, familiar to anyone handling real-world implementations of abstract protocols, apply fully to the Zero-Check protocol.

Researchers who wish to share patient-related data across institutions need to have a way of determining when a single patient is included in multiple datasets. The Zero-Check protocol permits this kind of comparison. This protocol is just one example of those new methods that will permit researchers to comply with National Institutes of Health data-sharing policies and with HIPAA privacy laws.

11.5. THRESHOLD PROTOCOL

The purpose of this section is to describe and implement a threshold protocol that can render confidential medical records harmless while permitting the exchange of information for research purposes. A threshold protocol is a cryptographic technique that splits information into pieces, none of which contains sufficient information to recreate the original text (116). The protocol permits the original information to be reconstructed from some number of the derived pieces. Threshold protocols have been used since antiquity, commonly appearing as plot devices in adventure novels. A map to buried treasure is divided among the central characters, a puzzle is reconstructed when five missing pieces are assembled, measured turns of the combination lock are distributed to three untrustworthy co-conspirators, matching rings in a set are destroyed, and so on. A brief description of a threshold protocol for sharing medical records is shown in List 11.5.1.

LIST 11.5.1. THE BASIC THRESHOLD PROTOCOL

1. Text is divided into short phrases.
2. Each phrase is converted by a one-way hash algorithm into a seemingly random set of characters.
3. Threshold piece 1 is composed of the list of all occurring phrases, with each phrase followed by its one-way hash.
4. Threshold piece 2 is composed of the text with all phrases replaced by their one-way hash values, and with high-frequency words preserved.

A generalized confidentiality problem can be presented as a negotiation protocol between Alice and Bob. Bob has a file containing the medical records of millions of patients. Alice has secret software that can annotate Bob's file, enhancing its value many-fold. Alice will not give Bob her secret algorithm, but she is willing to demonstrate the algorithm if Bob gives her his database. Bob will not give Alice the database, but he can give her little snippets of the database containing insufficient information to infer patient identities.

Bob prepares an algorithm that transforms his file into two threshold pieces. Piece 1 is a file that contains all of the phrases from the original file with each phrase attached to its one-way hash value. Remember, a one-way hash value is a character string composed of a fixed number of seemingly random characters selected by a mathematical algorithm that cannot be reversed (116).

The one-way hash has two important properties:

1) A phrase will always yield the same hash value when it is operated on by the one-way hash algorithm.
2) There is no feasible way to determine the phrase by inspecting or manipulating the hash value. This second property holds true even if the hashing algorithm is known.

Bob will give Alice piece 1 (List 11.5.2).

Piece 2 is a file wherein each phrase from the original file is replaced by its one-way hash value (List 11.5.3). High-frequency words ("stop" words such as *the, and, an, but, if*, etc.) are left in place in piece 2. The use of "stop" words to extract useful phrases from text is a popular indexing technique. The list of "stop" words used in the threshold algorithm was taken directly from the National Library of Medicine's PubMed resource. Piece 2 will be used to reconstruct the original text or an annotated version of the original text, using Alice's modifications to piece 1.

The following is an example of a single line of Bob's text that has been converted into two threshold pieces according to the described algorithm.

Bob's original text:

"They suggested that the manifestations were as severe in the mother as in the sons and that this suggested autosomal dominant inheritance."

LIST 11.5.2. BOB'S PIECE 1

684327ec3b2f020aa3099edb177d3794 => suggested autosomal dominant inheritance

3c188dace2e7977fd6333e4d8010e181 => mother

8c81b4aaf9c2009666d532da3b19d5f8 => manifestations

db277da2e82a4cb7e9b37c8b0c7f66f0 => suggested

e183376eb9cc9a301952c05b5e4e84e3 => sons

22cf107be97ab08b33a62db68b4a390d => severe

LIST 11.5.3. BOB'S PIECE 2

they db277da2e82a4cb7e9b37c8b0c7f66f0 that the

8c81b4aaf9c2009666d532da3b19d5f8 were as

22cf107be97ab08b33a62db68b4a390d in the

3c188dace2e7977fd6333e4d8010e181 as in the

e183376eb9cc9a301952c05b5e4e84e3 and that this

684327ec3b2f020aa3099edb177d3794.

The author has placed in the public domain a Perl implementation that produces pieces 1 and 2 from a text and that reconstructs the text from pieces 1 and 2. The properties of piece 1 and piece 2 are shown in Lists 11.5.4 and 11.5.5 (170).

LIST 11.5.4. PROPERTIES OF PIECE 1 (THE LISTING OF PHRASES AND THEIR ONE-WAY HASHES)

- Contains no information on the frequency of occurrence of the phrases found in the original text (because recurring phrases map to the same hash code and appear as a single entry in piece 1)
- Contains no information that Alice can use to connect any patient to any particular patient record, and records do not exist as entities in piece 1
- Contains no information on the order or locations of the phrases found in the original text
- Contains all the concepts found in the original text (stop words are a popular method of parsing text into concepts)
- Bob can destroy piece 1 and re-create it later from the original file
- Alice can use the phrases in piece 1 to transform, annotate, or search the concepts found in the original file
- Alice can transfer piece 1 to a third party without violating HIPAA privacy rules or Common Rule human subject regulations (in the United States)—for that matter, Alice can keep piece 1 and add it to her database of piece 1 files collected from all of her clients

LIST 11.5.5. PROPERTIES OF PIECE 2

- Contains no information that can be used to connect any patient to any particular patient record
- Contains nothing but hash values of phrases and stop words, in their correct order of occurrence in the original text
- Anyone obtaining piece 1 and piece 2 can reconstruct the original text
- Bob can lose or destroy piece 2 and re-create it later from the original file

If Alice had piece 1 and piece 2, then she could simply use piece 1 to find the text phrases that match the hash-values in piece 2. Substituting the phrases back into piece 2 will recreate Bob's original line of text. Bob must ensure that Alice never obtains piece 2.

The negotiation between Alice and Bob:

Bob prepares threshold pieces 1 and 2 and sends piece 1 to Alice. Alice may require Bob to prove the authenticity of piece 1, but Bob has no reason to care if piece 1 is intercepted by an unauthorized party. Alice uses her software (which may be secret, or it may require computational facilities that Bob does not have, or it may require large databases that Bob does not have), to transform or annotate each phrase from piece 1. The transformation product for each phrase can be almost anything that Bob considers valuable (e.g., a UMLS code, a genome database link, an image file URL, or a tissue sample location). Alice substitutes the transformed text (or simply appends the transformed text) for each phrase back into piece 1, collocating it with the original one-way hash number associated with the phrase.

Let us pretend that Alice has an autocoder that provides a standard nomenclature code to medical phrases that occur in text. Alice's software transforms the original phrases from piece 1, preserving the original hash values. Phrases from piece 1 that occur in the UMLS now have been given code numbers by Alice's software:

684327ec3b2f020aa3099edb177d3794 => suggested (autosomal dominant inheritance=C0443147)

3c188dace2e7977fd6333e4d8010e181 => (mother=C0026591)

8c81b4aaf9c2009666d532da3b19d5f8 => manifestations

db277da2e82a4cb7e9b37c8b0c7f66f0 => suggested

e183376eb9cc9a301952c05b5e4e84e3 => (son=C0037683)

22cf107be97ab08b33a62db68b4a390d => (severe=C0205082)

Alice returns this coded phrase list from piece 1 to Bob. Bob now takes the transformed piece 1 and substitutes the transformed phrases for each occurrence of the hash values occurring in piece 2 (which he has saved for this very purpose).

The reconstructed sentence is now:

They suggested that the manifestations were as (severe=C0205082) in the (mother=C0026591) as in the (son=C0037683) and that this suggested (autosomal dominant heritance=C0443147).

The original sentence is now annotated with UMLS codes. It was accomplished without sharing confidential information that might have been contained in the text. Bob never had access to Alice's software. Alice never had the opportunity to see Bob's original text.

11.6. IMPLEMENTATION ISSUES FOR THE THRESHOLD PROTOCOL

Depending on the type of file that needs to be converted into threshold pieces, some data preparation may be useful. In particular, it may be useful to encrypt or delete specific identifiers found in the original file, such as surgical pathology numbers. The file that is actually used by the algorithm should itself be assigned a hash number by the algorithm, as should piece 1 and piece 2. These three hash numbers could be saved and used for authentication purposes in later stages of a data negotiation protocol. Issues of data space collisions arise when using very large files.

The original text has been converted into two pieces, neither of which contains any identifying information. There is sufficient information in piece 1 for Alice to annotate the text and return it to Bob (annotated piece 1). Bob can reconstruct his original text, including Alice's annotations, thus adding value to his original data, without breaching patient confidentiality. Bob can pay Alice for her services. Alice can keep piece 1 and use it for her own purposes. Alice can make a large database consisting of all the piece 1 files she receives from all of her customers. Alice can sell piece 1 to a third party, if she wishes. Alice can update or otherwise enhance her annotations on piece 1 and sell the updated files to Bob.

The same protocol could have been implemented in a three-party negotiation. Bob may have been a data supplier with no interest in using the data himself. Suppose Carol was interested in Alice's annotations of Bob's file. Bob may have given Alice threshold piece 1 and Carol threshold piece 2. Alice may have made her transformation of the phrases in piece 1 and sent the transformed version of piece 1 to Carol. Carol could use Alice's transformed version of piece 1 and her copy of piece 2 to create a transformed version of Bob's original text. This would only work, of course, if the transformed version of Bob's original file (produced by Carol), contains no confidential information. A variation may involve assigning Bob as the trusted broker, who uses piece 2 and the transformed version of piece 1 to create a file for Carol. In this variation, Carol receives nothing until the end of the negotiation, and Bob can take measures to ensure that the file that Carol receives is "safe."

The threshold negotiation need not be based on text exchange. The same negotiation would apply to any set of data elements that can be transformed or annotated. The threshold protocol has greatest practical value in instances when data elements inform on other data elements that reside in the same data record. The protocol teases apart the data records and substitutes one-way hash values back into the record (170).

11.7. ELECTRONIC SIGNATURES

The term "electronic signature" is very misleading. An electronic signature is not a digitized image of a handwritten signature, nor does it represent any transformation of a handwritten signature. Legally, though, it is equivalent to a handwritten signature and can be used in commerce and in medical practice. The FDA has defined the electronic signature, along with several other closely related terms (List 11.7.1).

LIST 11.7.1. FDA DEFINITIONS RELATED TO DIGITAL SIGNATURES

- Biometrics means a method of verifying an individual's identity based on measurement of the individual's physical feature(s) or repeatable action(s) where those features and/or actions are both unique to that individual and measurable.
- Digital signature means an electronic signature based upon cryptographic methods of originator authentication, computed by using a set of rules and a set of parameters such that the identity of the signer and the integrity of the data can be verified.
- Electronic signature means a computer data compilation of any symbol or series of symbols executed, adopted, or authorized by an individual to be the legally binding equivalent of the individual's handwritten signature.

The digital signature is a mathematical operation performed on an electronic document (or some derivative of the document, such as a one-way hash of the file) with the signator's private cryptographic key (that she never shares with anyone else). The resulting "signature" is a string of characters that can be appended to the document. This string of characters can be decrypted using a public key (a special string of characters created when the private key is created and made freely accessible to the public). If the decryption produces an agreed message (such as the document itself, or the authenticating one-way hash of the document) then the digital signature is said to be verified. The desired features of an electronic signature are shown (List 11.7.2).

LIST 11.7.2. QUALITIES OF AN ADEQUATE ELECTRONIC SIGNATURE

- Nonrepudiation—can the signator plausibly deny that she signed the document?
- Unique identification—does the electronic signature uniquely identify the signator?
- Universal—can the signature be used with other existing signature or biometric systems?
- User-friendliness—can the signature be signed incorrectly or misinterpreted?
- Non-obsolescence—will everyone be able to read the signature 10 years or 100 years from now?

- Security—can someone change the file that was signed, change the signature to someone else's, invalidate a valid signature, or steal the signature?
- Extensibility—can someone sign for the signator, sign with the signator, or notarize the signature with another electronic signature?

In a fascinating editorial, Bruch Schneier argues that digital signatures cannot substitute for handwritten signatures or for biometric signatures (119). Schneier persuasively argues that electronic signatures do not substitute for the usual purpose of a signature, which is to indicate agreement with the contents of a document or to acknowledge responsibility for the contents of a document.

When someone receives a digitally signed document that is successfully decrypted and authenticated with a public key, it is reasonable to assume that the holder of the private key has digitally signed the document. Unfortunately, that may be the most that can be assumed. The digital signature does not indicate the intent of the signator. It does not even indicate that the signator read the signed document. It does not impart any evidence that the person who held the private key was actually the person who claimed to be the private key holder. If the private key holder intentionally or unintentionally sends a copy of her private key to all of her friends and associates, then documents signed with her private key will not identify the signator.

Digital signature protocols are implemented by software residing on computers. Those who trust digital signatures should ponder several questions (List 11.7.3).

LIST 11.7.3 DO YOU TRUST DIGITAL SIGNATURES?

- Is your computer secure? Might someone have stolen your private key?
- Is your encryption software secure? Might it contain a trapdoor subprogram that sends your private key to a malevolent entity?
- Is your encryption software reliable? Might it produce the same private key for different customers?
- Can you be certain that the software "signed" the correct document? Might it have signed a different document by mistake during a signing transaction?
- Are you certain that you will not lose track of your private keys over time?

Everyone loves a good algorithm. In a sense, algorithms prove that humans understand their universe and have produced logical and step-wise methods for coping with reality. Unfortunately, algorithms must be sensibly implemented before they yield much benefit. The algorithm implementation phase is where life often goes awry. It is difficult to achieve trust and reliability from complex systems (and this would include any system where multiple computers share information). In the next two chapters, we will discuss methods for organizing data and concepts so that the complexity of reality can be somewhat mitigated.

CHAPTER 12

Describing Data with Metadata

12.1. BACKGROUND

Extensible markup language (XML) is an informatics technology that allows any data element (e.g., a gene sequence, the weight of a patient, a biopsy diagnosis) to be bound to the data that describes the data element (i.e., the metadata). Surprisingly, this simple relationship between data and metadata is the most powerful innovation in information organization since the invention of the book. The way that we choose to implement metadata annotation could have evolved through any number of different architectures. However, XML has emerged as the dominant technology for this purpose. Seldom does a new technology arise with all the techniques required for its success, but this seems to be the case for XML.

12.2. METADATA, XML, AND RDF (RESOURCE DESCRIPTION FRAMEWORK)

In XML, data descriptors (known as XML tags) enclose the data they describe with angle-brackets.

```
<birthdate>September 28, 1950</birthdate>
```

The XML tag is `<birthdate>`. The tag and its end-tag enclose a data element, which in this case is the unabbreviated month, beginning with an uppercase letter and followed by lowercase letters, followed by a space, followed by a two-digit numeric for the date of the month, followed by a comma and space, followed by the four-digit year. The XML tag could have been defined in a separate document detailing the data format of the data element described by the XML tag. **ISO-11179** is a standard that tells people how they should specify the properties of metadata (120). In this case, the metadata is the XML tag, `<birthdate>`. If we had chosen to do so, we could have broken the `<birthdate>` tag into its constituent parts.

```
<birthdate>
<month_of_birth>September</month_of_birth>
<month_day_of_birth>28</month_day_of_birth>
<year_of_birth>1950</year_of_birth>
</birthdate>
```

The value of XML derives (List 12.2.1) from six properties.

LIST 12.2.1. SIX EXTRAORDINARY PROPERTIES OF XML

- Enforced and defined structure (XML rules and schema)
- Formal metadata (through ISO11179 specification)
- Namespaces (permits sharing of uniquely identifiable common data elements [CDEs])
- Linking data via the Internet (through Unique Resource Identifiers)
- Logic and meaning (the Semantic Web and Ontologies)
- Self-awareness (**software agents**, **artificial intelligence**, embedded protocols and commands)

These properties of XML are powerful because they permit us to understand the meaning of data and because they permit us to reach data anywhere on the Internet.

12.3. ENFORCED AND DEFINED STRUCTURE (XML RULES AND SCHEMAS)

An XML file is well formed if it conforms to the basic rules for XML file construction recommended by the W3C (Worldwide Web Consortium). This means that it must be a plain-text file, with a header indicating that it is an XML file, and it must enclose data elements with metadata tags that declare the start and end of the data element. The tags must conform to a certain syntax (e.g., alphanumeric strings without intervening spaces) and must also obey the rules for nesting data elements.

Most browsers will parse XML files and will reject files that are not well formed. The ability to ensure that every XML file conforms to basic rules of metadata tagging and nesting makes it possible to extract sensible data structures from XML files.

A well-formed XML file must be structured according to either a DTD (document type definition) or to a schema before it can be considered a valid XML document. DTDs and schemas are blocks of descriptors that specify the structure and content of an XML file. Schemas are more pop-

Figure 4. XML is the father of all metadata.

ular than DTDs. A variety of schema languages are available.[121] Regarding schemas, when an XML file is described by a schema and parsed by a validating browser (or by a so-called XML parser), you can be certain that the data contained in the file conforms to a specified structure and content. Files using the same schema will have the same data organization, and this greatly facilitates data integration between files.

Examples of widely adopted schemas from the field of bioinformatics are MIAME (minimal information for the annotation of a microarray experiment) (122) and MIAME-compliant MAGE-ML (microarray gene expression markup language) (123).

12.4. FORMAL METADATA (THROUGH THE ISO.11179 SPECIFICATION)

The concept of formalized metadata is simple. Consider the seemingly obvious metadata tag, `<date>`. Does this designate a day in a calendar, or does it represent a type of fruit, or does it refer to a social event?

The International Standards Organization has created a uniform way of defining metadata. This standard, the **ISO 11179**, specifies that metadata should have a qualified name or identifier, an authority that registers the name, a versioning history (allowing for modifications), a language of origin, a statement relating to usage, a data typing statement, and a definition that is unambiguous (120) (List 12.4.1). XML files should always include pointers (i.e., links) to the Web addresses of the files that contain the definitions of the metadata tags appearing in the XML file.

Standard methods of organizing and describing data are essential. As an example, the creators of the **Tissue MicroArray (TMA)** Data Exchange Specification have prepared a file that lists each of the 80 XML tags used in the specification, along with the ISO 11179 descriptors for each tag. This metadata definition file for the **TMA data exchange specification** resides at:

http://www.pathology.pitt.edu/pdf/cpctr/tma_cde.htm

LIST 12.4.1. DESCRIPTORS FOR THE METADATA TAG
`<core_organism>`

Identifier: core_organism

Version: 1.0

Registration Authority: Association for Pathology Informatics

Language: English (en)

Obligation: Optional

Datatype: Character String representing taxonomy.dat identifier number followed by an allowable taxonomy.dat name for the identifier number

Maximum Occurrence: Unlimited

Definition: Organism name at species level for organism whose tissue is represented in the donor block

Comment: URI for taxonomy.dat is ftp://ftp.ebi.ac.uk/pub/databases/taxonomy/taxonomy.dat. The correct entry for human tissue is "9606 human"

Without fully defined metadata, XML data has no meaning or value.

12.5. NAMESPACES (SHARING METADATA)

Problems arise when data from different documents are merged. How can we be sure that XML tags in one document will always mean the same thing when found in another document? This is achieved with namespaces. Whenever you use an element taken from another XML document, you should declare the namespace origin of the element. For example,

```
<table xmlns="http://www.w3.org/TR/html4/">
```

This xmlns (XML namespace) attribute indicates that the `<table>` element is the same element that is described for the World Wide Web organization's HTML recommendation and provides the namespace specific for this meaning of the `<table>` element. Thus `<table>`, as it is used in the data element, has a meaning that cannot be confused with "kitchen table" or "periodic table." If we had multiple elements from the HTML specification, then we may have chosen to list the namespace near the top of the XML document and assigned a prefix specific for elements belonging to the HTML namespace. Consider the following snippet of XML from the Gene Ontology specification (124). Two different namespaces are declared using the xmlns attribute.

```
<go:go xmlns:go="http://www.geneontology.org/dtds/go.dtd#"
xmlns:rdf="http://www.w3.org/1999/02/22-rdf-syntax-ns#">
<go:version timestamp="Wed Jun 19 12:34:48 1974" />
<rdf:RDF>
<go:term
rdf:about="http://www.geneontology.org/go#GO:0003673"n_associ
ations="0">
<go:accession>GO:0003673</go:accession>
<go:name>Gene_Ontology</go:name>
</go:term>
```

In like manner, a single XML file can use a single metadata tag to mean many different things, so long as each use of a metadata element is prefixed with the correct namespace. The namespace prefix annotation is a powerful informatics tool, permitting XML creators to recycle metadata from different namespaces. When the same metadata is used by many different researchers, the contained data can often be shared among their databases.

12.6. LINKING DATA VIA THE INTERNET

XML comes with specifications for linking XML documents with other XML documents, or with any external file that has a specific identifier or web location. This means that there is a logical and standard method for linking any XML document or any part of any XML document (including individual data elements) to any other uniquely identified resource.

12.7. LOGIC AND MEANING

Although the technical methodologies associated with XML can be daunting, the most difficult issues always relate to the meaning of things. A variety of formal approaches have been proposed to reach the level of meaning within the context of XML. The simplest of these is the

Resource Description Framework (RDF) (125). The importance of the RDF model is that it binds data and metadata to a unique object with a Web location. Consistent use of the RDF model assures that data anywhere on the Web can always be connected through unique objects using RDF descriptions. The association of described data with a unique object confers meaning and greatly advances our ability to integrate data over the Internet (126).

Our ability to understand properties of data objects is always enhanced when the objects can be formally related to other objects in a knowledge domain. The term "pityriasis lichenoides et varioliformis acuta" may mean nothing to most people. If we were informed that this term is the name of a disease and that the disease is a condition of the skin, then we learn that the term shares the properties common to all diseases and, more specifically, to diseases involving the skin. Collections of defined objects and their relationships are called ontologies. RDF can be used to express relationships between objects, object properties, and object classes. RDF has been extended as an ontology tool for several initiatives, including OIL (the European Union's program for Information Society Technologies) and DAML (the U.S. Defense Department's Advanced Research Project Agency's Agent Markup Language) (127).

Relationships between different data elements allow us to make generalizations about classes of data. For example, if an adept XML biomedical informatician notices that several different tumors seem to respond to a certain new treatment (based on a query routed through many different clinical trial XML datasets), then the significance of the finding may be enhanced if the researcher determines that each of the responsive tumors belonged to the same tumor class, as designated in an XML file that provides the biological classification of every known tumor type (77–79). This finding might lead the researcher to ask whether other tumors of the same class share this treatment sensitivity. Furthermore, if the researcher had access to another XML file that annotates all cancer classes with experimental data collected from many different laboratories, then he or she may find a specific genetic marker common to the tumor class. This genetic feature may be responsible for the heightened sensitivity of the class of tumors to the treatment protocol. This may lead to the development of a new class of drugs with specific activity against a specific class of neoplasm. At this time, such a scenario is fanciful. This situation will improve when detailed and organized clinical trial data are made publicly available.

12.8. SELF-AWARENESS (EMBEDDED PROTOCOLS AND COMMANDS)

XML provides the methods for querying XML files. Because XML can be used to describe anything, it certainly can be used to describe a query related to an XML page. This is the basis for SOAP (Simple Object

Access Protocol), an XML syntax for exchanging messages containing queries that can be passed over the Internet to different types of applications (128). When XML protocols are capable of autonomous behavior, composing queries, merging replies, and transforming their own content, they are usually referred to as **software agents** (see Chapter 15, Distributed Computing) (129).

12.9. INTEGRATING HETEROGENEOUS DATA WITH RDF

XML is a simple but powerful method for creating files composed of data and the metadata that describes the data. The promise of XML is that annotated data can be combined or integrated over heterogeneous datasets. This promise has not been achieved despite (or because of) countless efforts to create standard XML files for many different kinds of data. There is a growing perception in the informatics community that the proliferation of XML standards has resulted in a complex and chaotic environment that demands an unrealistically high level of informatics expertise among intended users. Scientists are disinclined to invest the time, energy, and money on standards compliance for every technology at their disposal, and vendors may be reticent to adopt new standards that may never achieve widespread acceptance. The proliferation of standards seems to have the unintended consequence of stifling systems interoperability and data integration across heterogeneous data sources.

An underappreciated fact is that XML schemas tell us what data to include in a file and how to organize the data, but XML schemas do not enforce meaning onto the data. The distinction between data that has structure versus data that has meaning is a very important concept. Of all the XML technologies, only RDF operates on the level of meaning.

As previously discussed, RDF statements, also known as "triples," consist of a unique data object and a metadata/data pair that belong to the unique data object. RDF triples can be collected from many different XML databases and merged without loss of meaning. RDF triples provide an opportunity for conducting advanced data analyses on grouped unique objects that share common properties (i.e., ontologies).

When XML is written in simple RDF-triples using specified sets of well-defined metadata and typed data, the resulting files will be meaningful, self-describing, and convertible to other XML formats. Scientists who approach data annotation using an implementation of W3C recommendations for RDF will be achieving a standardized way of representing their data without having to actually create new data standards for every type of data object (e.g. images, reports, experiments, and so on).

12.10. MEANING REQUIRES A FULLY SPECIFIED SUBJECT

Let us consider the elephant attack first described in Chapter 9. This time, let us say that John Public was the victim of the attack:

```
event
John Public slept
John Public wore pajamas
John Public was attacked by elephant
end_of_event
```

The statements refer to an event, and the event was unique to a certain time and place. Because the event was unique, it should be distinguishable from all other events. We can give the event a unique identifying number. For this section, we will use a pseudo-XML annotation that is easy to read.

```
<event id=142984>
John Public slept
John Public wore pajamas
John Public was attacked by elephant
<end_of_event>
```

The event involved a specific person named John Public, who was wearing a specific set of pajamas and who was attacked by a specific elephant. They should be assigned unique identifiers as well. Also, we feel confident that the concept of ownership will be generally understood, so we put it back into the list of statements:

```
<event id=142984>
<John Public id=9238> slept
<John Public id=9238> wore <pajamas id=4321>
<John Public id=9238> owns <pajamas id=4321>
<John Public id=9238> was attacked by <elephant id=1234>
<end_of_event>
```

When we think of the event that occurred, we might want to classify it as a certain type of event that might share properties with other events of the same kind or that might, when aggregated with events of the same kind, lead to further knowledge about such events. So we can group the event as a type of "sleep":

```
<event id=142984>
event_type=sleep
<John Public id=9238> slept
<John Public id=9238> wore <pajamas id=4321>
<John Public id=9238> owns <pajamas id=4321>
<John Public id=9238> was attacked by <elephant id=1234>
<end_of_event>
```

The event might also be categorized along with other events that can be grouped as "attacks":

```
<event id=142984>
event_type=sleep
event_type=attack
<John Public id=9238> slept
<John Public id=9238> wore <pajamas id=4321>
<John Public id=9238> owns <pajamas id=4321>
<John Public id=9238> was attacked by <elephant id=1234>
<end_of_event>
```

To make any sense of this statement, we need to understand the meaning of the words in the statement. In this case, we need to understand the meaning of the unique objects. In the case of semantic sets, the unique objects are defined by their identifier number and by the properties bound to the object. John Public is an identified unique object (id=9238) and he slept, wore pajamas, owned pajamas, and was attacked by an elephant. This thoroughly sums up John Public's involvement in the event, but does it provide meaning to his life? Not yet. In order to provide John Public with meaning, we need to know what the properties "slept," "wore," "owns," and "was attacked by" actually mean. Luckily, we have dictionaries that explain the meaning of these words. So if you have a good dictionary, the statements provide meaning to John Public. The group of statements comprises an event. The event types listed are "sleep" and "attack." If we wanted to begin to collect event information, then we could aggregate the statements under the general category of events or under the more specific categories of sleep events and attack events. The group of statements has meaning because all of the objects are uniquely identified and all the properties of the objects are defined. The statements can be grouped with similar events to provide aggregate information not contained in any of the individual types of events. Now suppose a sleepwear clothier wanted to develop a database and had provided a standard schema for the data that was to be included to the database. The rules of the clothier's standard schema are:

> Begin each record with a record type indicating that the clothing is worn during sleep, and include the name of the person sleeping and the clothes worn during sleep. The choices of clothes can be restricted to pajamas, briefs, or nothing. Pajamas and briefs should be annotated with their unique id number. The schema would be:

```
sleep
name of person sleeping, with unique identifier
uniquely identified clothing worn while sleeping (pajamas,
briefs, none)
end_sleep_record
```

We are in luck because all the information required by the schema is already contained in our event statements, and it would be a simple matter to write a software program that would pick out the data required by the sleep wear schema and format it as specified:

```
<sleep>
<John Public id=9238>
<pajamas id=4321>
<end_sleep_record>
```

Here we have used our generically formatted statements to comply with an external standard. But suppose the standard required additional information not contained in our set of statements. Suppose the standard required a statement on the length of time slept. We may be out of luck, but maybe not.

Remember, the event had a unique id number. If another ardent researcher had been collecting data on the length of sleep events for a population of people, then there might exist a database entry that looks something like this:

```
<event id=142984>
event_type=sleep
<length_of_event> 2 hours
<end_of_event>
```

This record, existing in another database, need not be aware of the elephant attack. All it needs to have, in order to have meaningful information, is the unique identifier for the event and the length of the event. In this case, the short sleep cycle is explained by the interruption by the attacking elephant, but that is immaterial. The statements related to event duration and the unique identifier for the event are all we need to complete the standard schema created by the clothier. As long as we have access to the database with event durations, we can compose a valid sleepwear record:

```
<sleep>
<John Public id=9238>
<pajamas id=4321>
<length_of_event> 2 hours
<end_sleep_record>
```

The clothier's standard record seems somewhat incomplete. It lacks an identifier for the sleep record and the event record, and it does not formally categorize "sleep" as a type of event. But it is what the clothier demands, and that is all we need to worry about.

In summary, if you identify each unique object of a statement with a unique identifier AND if you carefully define all of your properties of the unique objects AND if you classify the kinds of information described in your statements, then you are left with a meaningful set of data with the following properties: 1) it can exist independently of any specific file organization, 2) it can be integrated with data in other files that use the same identifiers for unique objects, 3) it can be used to provide aggregate or specific information about the data statements, and 4) it can be transformed into external standard data representations (List 12.10.1).

LIST 12.10.1. STEPS TO CREATE DATA DOCUMENTS THAT CAN BE EASILY INTEGRATED ACROSS HETEROGENEOUS DATASETS

1. Find a simple way of describing biomedical data using a syntax that confers meaning onto data (i.e., RDF syntax).
2. Develop a simple approach to listing the unique objects relevant to the domain (e.g., surgical pathology report, specimen, block, stain, laboratory test, submission data, completion data) and a way to uniquely identify these objects that can be used by any laboratory without risk of losing track of unique objects and without risk of assigning nonunique objects the same identifier).
3. Develop a repository for metadata that defines each metadata element in the domain and describes the data constraints (if any) of the data elements described by the metadata.
4. Use general algorithms/software for integrating, aggregating, and transforming data held in RDF triple databases.

12.11. MEANINGFUL BIOMEDICAL DESCRIPTION WITH NOTATION 3

Consider the following free-text description of a pathology image:

"The image is a squamous cell carcinoma of the floor of the mouth. It was taken by Jules Berman, on February 2, 2002. The microscope was an Olympus model 3453. The lens objective was 40x. The camera was a Sony model 342. The image dimensions are 524 by 429 pixels. The microscope and camera were not calibrated. The specimen is Baltimore Hospital Center S-3456-2001, specimen 2, block 3. The specimen was logged in 8/15/01 and processed using the standard protocol for H&E that was in place for that day. The patient is Sam Someone, medical identifier 4357. The tissue was received in formalin. The specimen shows a moderately differentiated, invasive squamous carcinoma. The patient has a 30-year history of oral tobacco use. The image is kept in jpeg (Joint Photographic Experts Group) file format and named y49w3p2.jpg and kept in the pathology subdirectory of the hospital's server. Its URL is https://baltohosp.org/pathology/y49w3p2.jpg. The image file has an md_5 hash value of 84027730gjsj350489. The image has no watermark. Copyright is held by Baltimore Hospital Center, and all rights are reserved."

Every assertion in the image description can be described by a triple consisting of a specified subject followed by a property followed by a value. Notation 3 (N3) is an abbreviated form of **RDF**. The narrative description can be readily translated in N3 (List 12.11.1).

LIST 12.11.1. IMAGE DESCRIPTION USING RDF TRIPLES IN NOTATION 3 FORMAT

- file:image.n3 @prefix :
- <http://www.pathologyinformatics.org/image_schema.rdf#>.
- @prefix rdf: <http://www.w3.org/1999/02/22-rdf-syntax-ns#>.
- :Baltimore_Hospital_Center rdf:type "Hospital".
- :Baltimore_Hospital_Center_4357 rdf:type"Unique_medical_identifier".
- :Baltimore_Hospital_Center_4357 :patient_name "Sam_Someone".
- :Baltimore_Hospital_Center_4357 :surgical_pathology_specimen "S3456_2001".
- :S_3456_2001 rdf:type "Surgical_pathology_specimen".
- :S_3456_2001 :image <https://baltohosp.org/pathology/y49w3p2.jpg>.
- :S_3456_2001:log_in_date "2001-08-15".
- :S_3456_2001 :clinical_history "30_years_oral_tobacco_use".
- <https://baltohosp.org/pathology/y49w3p2.jpg> rdf:type "Medical_image".
- <https://baltohosp.org/pathology/y49w3p2.jpg> :surgical_pathology_accession_number "S3456-2001".
- <https://baltohosp.org/pathology/y49w3p2.jpg> :specimen "2".
- <https://baltohosp.org/pathology/y49w3p2.jpg> :block "3".
- <https://baltohosp.org/pathology/y49w3p2.jpg> :format "jpeg".
- <https://baltohosp.org/pathology/y49w3p2.jpg> :width "524_pixels".
- <https://baltohosp.org/pathology/y49w3p2.jpg> :height "429_pixels".
- <https://baltohosp.org/pathology/y49w3p2.jpg> :hash_value "84027730gjsj350489".
- <https://baltohosp.org/pathology/y49w3p2.jpg> :hash_type "md_5".
- <https://baltohosp.org/pathology/y49w3p2.jpg> :watermark "none".
- <https://baltohosp.org/pathology/y49w3p2.jpg> :camera "Sony".
- <https://baltohosp.org/pathology/y49w3p2.jpg> :camera_model "342".

- <https://baltohosp.org/pathology/y49w3p2.jpg> :capture_date "2002-02-02".
- <https://baltohosp.org/pathology/y49w3p2.jpg> :diagnosis "squamous_cell_carcinoma".
- <https://baltohosp.org/pathology/y49w3p2.jpg> :topography "floor_of_mouth".
- <https://baltohosp.org/pathology/y49w3p2.jpg> :has "Intellectual_property_restriction".
- <https://baltohosp.org/pathology/y49w3p2.jpg> :copyright "all_rights_reserved".
- <https://baltohosp.org/pathology/y49w3p2.jpg> :copyright_holder "Baltimore_Hospital_Center".
- <https://baltohosp.org/pathology/y49w3p2.jpg> :microscope "Olympus".
- <https://baltohosp.org/pathology/y49w3p2.jpg> :microscope_model "3453".
- <https://baltohosp.org/pathology/y49w3p2.jpg> :microscope_objective_power "40X".
- <https://baltohosp.org/pathology/y49w3p2.jpg> :photographer_name "Jules_Berman".

This file (`image.n3`) can be converted to proper RDF with a Perl script (Lists 12.11.2 and 12.11.3).

LIST 12.11.2. `RDFPARSE.PL,` **A PERL SCRIPT THAT CONVERTS NOTATION 3 INTO RDF**

```perl
#!/usr/local/bin/perl
use RDF::Notation3;
use RDF::Notation3::Triples;
$path = "image.n3";
$rdf = RDF::Notation3::Triples->new();
$rdf->parse_file($path);
$triples = $rdf->get_triples;
print @$triples->[0]->[0];
print "###\n";
use RDF::Notation3::XML;
$rdf = RDF::Notation3::XML->new();
$rdf->parse_file($path);
```

```
$string = $rdf->get_string;
print $string;
use RDF::Notation3;
exit;
```

LIST 12.11.3. PROPERTIES OF IMAGE.N3

- Every statement has a fully specified object followed by a property and a value (a triple).
- Every unique object belongs to a class.

We will see in Chapter 13 that conferring class identity on a unique object has great value. Members of a class share all the properties of the class and inherit all the properties of ancestral classes. This permits us to draw logical inferences about class members.

12.12. THE DAML EXTENSION OF RDF

RDF was designed as a model of simplicity and logic. Unfortunately, soon after the release of the RDF specification, people started to notice certain limitations. The most important limitation of RDF relates to data typing. RDF simply does not contain an easy method for explicitly restricting the permissible values of a data element. In addition, RDF lacks certain concepts that ontologists would like to include, such as class union and class intersection.

DAML is an expansion of RDF that provides a variety of class operations that are considered essential in the field of artificial intelligence. The underlying assumption is that logical inferences of the kind needed in the design of software agents will require these logical constructs.

A more prosaic feature of DAML is its ability to reach into XML schema to include metadata primitives describing data types (List 12.12.1).

LIST 12.12.1. A FEW EXAMPLES OF XML SCHEMA PRIMITIVES THAT CAN BE INCORPORATED IN DAML

- enumeration
- positiveInteger
- minInclusive
- integer
- pattern

An example of the use of "positive integer" as specified within XML schema, and assigned within a DAML declaration is:

```
<daml:DatatypeProperty rdf:ID="glucoseValue">
<rdfs:label>Glucose value</rdfs:label>
<rdfs:domain rdf:resource="#Test">
<rdfs:range
rdf:resource="http://www.w3.org/2000/10/XMLSchema#positiveInt
eger">
</daml:DataypeProperty>
```

From the Perl perspective, the most versatile XML schema primitive is "pattern," which permits DAML declarations to specify a data range for an element that is described with a regular expression (i.e., a pattern).

Though the development of DAML specifications is beyond the scope of this book, the reader can imagine that the power of RDF triples is enhanced when the structure of the allowed data is well-defined. Also, when the metadata used in an RDF document belongs to a rule-based ontology, it becomes possible to create software that draws logical inferences from classes of data included in the RDF document. Ontologies will be discussed further in Chapter 14.

12.13. OWL (WEB ONTOLOGY LANGUAGE) EXTENSION OF DAML

In the time-honored tradition of never leaving well enough alone, the DAML extension of RDF has itself been extended. Like DAML, OWL provides a set of classes and properties that have a specific meaning (within the OWL schema). OWL users are guaranteed a common semantic interpretation of those triples that instantiated the OWL schema.

For the most part, the OWL specification includes classes and properties that permit logical inferences to be drawn from formal ontologies (130).

Simplifying Complex Data with Classifications and Ontologies

13.1. BACKGROUND

In the past decade, I have written thousands of short programs for my own professional needs. Out of those thousands of programs, there have been maybe six or seven that might have some generalizable utility. In these cases, I have published papers describing the algorithm, explained why I think it may have some general utility, and included the source code of the software in the open access manuscript. Most of these programs are about one hundred lines of code in length. In all cases, I include a standard disclaimer with the distributed code:

"The software is provided "as is," without warranty of any kind, express or implied, including but not limited to the warranties of merchantability, fitness for a particular purpose and noninfringement. In no event shall the authors or copyright holders be liable for any claim, damages or other liability, whether in an action of contract, tort or otherwise, arising from, out of or in connection with the software or the use or other dealings in the software."

Much of the software that I use as a researcher has been collected from colleagues who have done more or less the same thing. Academic programmers live in a software Eden, where most of what they want is free for the taking.

In contrast, the world of commercial and large-scale software development is a harsh realm. Most commercial software projects fail. Planned projects are seldom started. Started projects are seldom completed. Completed projects are seldom free of bugs. Finished, de-bugged projects are seldom acceptable to the intended users. Finished, de-bugged, and acceptable software projects seldom acquire wide popularity.

The magnitude of the losses from failed software projects should not be underestimated. According to a publication from the Standish Group, on average, 16.2% of software projects are completed on time and on budget. In general, the larger-staffed, more complex, and more expensive projects tend to have an even lower success rate. In the same publication, it was reported that only 9% of projects in large companies come in on time and on budget (131).

Commercial software is complex (List 13.1.1). Complex systems have unpredictable behavior and are very difficult to design in a manner that will work properly in different settings.

LIST 13.1.1. COMPLEXITIES OF COMMERCIAL BIOMEDICAL SOFTWARE

- Must protect the confidentiality and privacy of patients.
- Must not produce errors. Patient lives are at stake.
- Must not crash. Patient lives are at stake.
- Must have graphic user interface that anyone can use. Staff training is an expensive proposition, and many clients hate to train their staff to use their computers.
- Must provide functionality to the user. Most user complaints relate to a misunderstanding between the user and the developer relating to the intended purpose of the software (132). Most software developers know nothing about the workflow of hospitals. Developers seldom know which functions of their software are vital to patient care. Hospital personnel have trouble understanding how anyone could NOT know these things.
- All functionalities must be scalable (able to accommodate unanticipated increases in usage demands).
- Must successfully interoperate with many other systems (hardware and software) throughout the hospital and over the Internet.
- Must anticipate future needs. Hospitals pay many millions of dollars for information systems. They would much prefer not to buy a new system every time their activities change.
- Must survive the demise of the company that produced the software. The death rate of commercial biomedical software developing companies is high. Hospitals have been left with virtually useless systems when their software vendors have vanished.
- Must not be vulnerable to malicious attack. There are actually very few programmers with the expertise to design software with principles of computer security. The likelihood that any piece of software has been written with the help of a computer security expert is quite low.
- Must not be vulnerable to the unintended consequences of exuberant users. Large systems have been known to crash when users strain computational resources with recursive queries.

13.2. THE VALUE OF HOSPITAL INFORMATION TECHNOLOGY

Hospital information systems (HISs) are among the most complex and most expensive software systems. Hospital information systems are used by many different staff professionals who have many different roles and many different expectations. It is widely accepted that despite the effort and cost, HISs have been of enormous benefit to patients. Is this sense of value based on any objective measurement? If HISs are so wonderful, then why does the cost of healthcare continue to rise? Has information technology eliminated the fragmentation of medical care or reduced the complexities of health payment plans?

A 2006 review by the Rand Corporation seems to indicate that institutions that adopt commercial information systems have demonstrated limited ability to adequately compare costs against benefits (133). Published evidence for the value of implementing complex health information technology in community hospitals is scant. Most of the credible reports of the benefits of HISs come from large institutions that have developed their own systems incrementally, over many years (133).

Much can be learned from documented technology disasters. A 2003 article in the British Medical Journal described a project to install a computerized integrated hospital information system in Limpopo (Northern) Province of South Africa (134). This cash-poor province has 42 hospitals and invested heavily to acquire their HIS. The article describes what went wrong and provides a list of factors that led to the failure of the system. This included a failure to take into account the social and cultural milieu in which the system would be used. There was an underestimation of the complexity of the undertaking and insufficient appreciation of the length of training required by the hospital staff.

Failed system implementations occur in the United States. The Veterans Administration (VA) spent hundreds of millions of dollars on a financial tracking system. The software implementation failed during trials at the Bay Pines VA in Tampa Bay, Florida. Plans for extending the system to other VA hospitals became the subject of congressional hearings (135).

One of the most challenging features of many HISs is computerized physician order entry (CPOE). The intent of CPOE is to eliminate the wasteful hand-written (often illegible) doctor's orders that may need to be transcribed by nurses, pharmacists, and laboratory personnel before they are finally entered into the HIS. Having the physicians directly enter their orders into the HIS has been a long-awaited dream for many hospital administrators. In a fascinating report, patient mortality was shown to increase after implementation of CPOE. In this study, having

CPOE was a strong, independent predictor of patient death. Somehow, a computerized service intended to enhance patient care seemed to put patients at increased risk (136).

Without commenting on this particular study, it may be useful to review some factors that can transform CPOE and other well-intended medical informatics efforts into destructive technologies (List 13.2.1).

LIST 13.2.1. REASONS WHY HOSPITAL INFORMATICS PROJECTS, SUCH AS CPOE, MAY FAIL

- Tasks that were traditionally accomplished through interpersonal communication may be replaced by solitary entry sessions with HIS computer terminals. Opportunities to share helpful explanations and patient status updates may be lost.
- Computer entry tasks may be tedious, time-consuming, and repetitive. Harried staff, under these circumstances, may do an incomplete or sloppy job.
- Computer orders, once entered, may have no mechanism for correcting entry errors, modifying existing orders, or withdrawing orders altogether.
- The asynchronous nature of multi-user entries into the HIS may cause havoc in a system that depends on coordinated workflow. For instance, a prescription may not be filled by a pharmacy until an order entered by a clerk-typist is released by a physician. If there is no system to ensure that each entry occurs in a timely and coordinated manner, then workflow is halted.

Beyond informatics issues lie all-important social issues. High-tech medical solutions seldom achieve a desired effect for low-tech medical staff. Introducing complex informatics services, such as CPOE, requires staff training. There needs to be effective communication between the clinical staff and the hospital IT staff, and between the hospital IT staff and the HIS vendor staff. Everyone involved must cooperate until the implemented system is working smoothly.

Hospitals and HISs are complex. It is my perception that complexity lies at the root of many of the seemingly intractable problems in biomedical informatics. The next section will serve as an introduction to biomedical complexity.

13.3. UNDERSTANDING COMPLEXITY

Some of the best things in life are complex. Human beings are a good example. Most of the complex activities of the human body ensue automatically, without conscious volition. If we were responsible for planning and executing our many physiologic processes, all human activity would instantly cease.

Life on earth became complex by adopting new functions over hundreds of millions of years. Undoubtedly, the vast majority of added activities were rejected by evolutionary processes. Today, though humans are a glorious product of evolution, we are still punished for our complexity. A small clot in the brain can bring an end to our lives. A few minutes of airway obstruction will kill us. A wide array of toxins can interfere with constitutive cellular processes, leading to a quick and certain death. Over a thousand genetic disorders have been cataloged, all caused by small mistakes in some fragment of DNA. Physicians now recognize a new class of diseases: diseases of complexity. These are multifactorial diseases for which environmental and genetic factors culminate in conditions whose specific cause cannot be described. Death itself may be considered the ultimate consequence of human complexity. Why are we mortal? I would suggest that we are mortal because we are complex, and all complex systems will eventually suffer an insult that shuts the system down. As a pathologist, I was trained to understand the sequences of events that can lead to death. At no time during my training was it explained why, once death occurs, we cannot be resurrected. Why can we not simply fix the causes of a person's demise and start the corpse up again (á la Frankenstein)? We cannot reanimate deceased bodies because we are too complex. Once death occurs, irreversible cellular events unfold that are simply too numerous to fathom. Mortal man is afflicted by many thousands of distinct diseases, and all of them take advantage of the delicate condition of life tempered by complexity.

Software, like humans, is complex. When it comes to software complexity, there are two choices: You either develop a method for dealing with complexity, or you design the system so that the level of complexity is reduced. It would be nice if we had an objective and facile measurement of the complexity of any system. After a point, the software developer could measure the complexity of the system. When she finds that some threshold value (let us say 250 complexomes) has been exceeded, then the complexity managers can be called in to assess the situation. Unfortunately, this has never been the case. We stumble forward, trying to create a finished software product, but we never really know when to stop. In my opinion, many software projects are designed with a level of complexity that is simply untenable. Society would be better off if these projects were never launched. But we fail again and again because we cannot gauge our own limitations.

What are some of the signs of overly complex software? The system seems to crash more often, and it takes longer and longer to get things running again. You make inquiries. The IT staff inform you that there are many ways in which a complex system may break. Upper management, after discussing the problem with the IT supervisor, determines that the users must be doing something wrong. A variety of training committees are formed to ensure proper use of the system by all employees. Questions raised during employee training sessions go unanswered. The instructors promise to get back to the group with an answer. IT staff members report that some of the dependent files and patches are missing. Nobody seems to be sure where they are. Several versions of these are available, but nobody is certain which to use. Interface applications and subsystems no longer operate. The IT staff informs you that they are too busy attending to core system problems to deal with the annoyances arising from department-owned applications. By now, everything seems to run more slowly. The technical assistance staff no longer answers their phones. Known hackers vehemently deny any role in the problem. They say that hacking the system would be too easy. Nobody can provide a rational explanation for the situation. Ritualistic measures are employed (e.g., turn the system off, wait five minutes, turn the system on) because they have worked in the past. Successes occur rarely and always seem to have a magical cause. Worried looks and furtive glances have permanently replaced warm smiles. Your keyboard seems abnormally cold to your touch. You hear a constant "buzz" sound in your head.

Often, when software implementation seems overcome by complexity, implementers will reflexively lock down the system with a variety of desperate and Draconian actions (List 13.3.1).

LIST 13.3.1. DESPERATE BUT FUTILE ACTIONS INTENDED TO COPE WITH COMPLEXITY

- Lock down your data. Restricting the variety of data permitted in the database can sometimes reduce complexity.
- Lock down your software components. Use the last software version that worked and stop trying to enhance any components.
- Lock down your operating system. Do not even try to offer cross-platform interoperability.
- Lock down your set of assumptions. Software built on a static set of assumptions about the user's world is often manageable. Changing these assumptions is asking for problems.
- Lock down activities. Reduce the number of people or services that are supported by the software.
- Hire specialized programmers. Each programmer should concentrate on a very small component of your software. Hire more pro-

grammers so that every software component is adequately staffed with developers, analysts, and technical support staff. There is strength in numbers.

- Stop thinking about fundamental approaches to problems. There is no going back once the juggernaut is launched.

- Replace system with a newer, more expensive, and more complex system. Ahh. The cycle of life is renewed!

How do competent software engineers cope with software complexity? Software engineers have a language that lets them describe the many interactions between parts of a software application. This language, **UML**, is now an ISO/IEC standard, "19501:2005 Information technology—Open Distributed Processing—Unified Modeling Language (UML) Version 1.4.2." By using UML, they can visualize a complex system and anticipate or track a range of problems. Other measures have proven utility (List 13.3.2). An intelligent and highly trained program analyst can successfully cope with complex systems. Sadly, the complexities of software will eventually exceed the limits of humans to cope. Ultimately, complex systems become unpredictable. Jaron Lanier has written a superb discussion of the future of complexity (137). At one point, he suggests that "we have already reached the complexity ceiling of software."

LIST 13.3.2. A FEW HELPFUL MEASURES TO COPE WITH SOFTWARE COMPLEXITY

- Write clean software code and use in-line documentation to explain the purpose of software commands.
- Provide detailed and clear documentation for all software components.
- Use object-oriented languages and follow standard techniques for good object design.
- Use UML.
- Use **refactoring** methodology to improve complex code.
- Continually test software and carefully document all modifications.

"It's not always about finding a simple solution to a complex problem, occasionally it's about simplifying the problem." This quotation has been attributed to Adam Bosworth, but has probably been stated by countless others through the years. It is often abbreviated as KISS (keep it simple stupid). To keep things simple, we need to have some idea of what components of biomedical informatics are intrinsically complex (List 13.3.3).

LIST 13.3.3. INTRINSICALLY COMPLEX COMPONENTS OF BIOMEDICAL INFORMATICS

- Ontologies. Ontologies permit multiclass inheritance.
- Hospital information systems. HISs accept asynchronous input from many different users.
- Data security. It is easy to make something a secret, but it is difficult to keep a secret.
- Data consistency. Users are typically allowed to modify data. The repercussions of thoughtlessly modified clinical data are immense. In addition, many hospital systems fail to maintain unique identifiers for patients. A single patient who changes her name or address can be re-entered under a separate identifier in many systems. Once this occurs, the integrity of the entire HIS is destroyed.
- Standards. Standards require consensus from many different people with many competing agendas, and this contributes to complexity. Different finished standards can apply to a single measurement or protocol (e.g., inches and centimeters).

We also need to know the components that are intrinsically simple (List 13.3.4).

LIST 13.3.4. INTRINSICALLY SIMPLE COMPONENTS OF BIOMEDICAL INFORMATICS

- Classifications. A class inherits properties in a direct lineage from a parent class. An object can occupy only a single class. Classifications are easy to understand and compute.
- Flat data files that can be extended but not rewritten. A telephone book is a close example. If people never changed their names, never died, and never changed their telephone numbers, then a telephone directory would be an ideal flat-file.
- The EMR (electronic medical record). The EMR is the digital equivalent of the patient chart. In this model, all new clinical reports pertaining to a patient are inserted into the patient's EMR. This is a simple data model that can work well as long as one and only one record is created for each patient.
- Small, self-contained specialized information systems. These applications are designed for a specific and narrow function (e.g., cytopathology information system). Complexity does not intervene until the specialized information system needs to interact with other systems in the hospital.
- Fundamental algorithms. Almost all important algorithms are simple and can be explained in a few steps.

- Simple protocols. Very simple protocols can support incredibly complex systems. TCP/IP (the Internet protocol) is a simple strategy for transferring packets of information over a network of computers.
- Elegant object oriented programming languages, such as Ruby. Though Ruby is a simple and elegant language, it can be used to create hopelessly complex software. Programmers need extensive training in design principles that minimize complexity.
- Specifications. Specifications are formal ways of explaining what you have done so that computers and humans can understand and replicate your work.
- Unique data identifiers. Computers are good at creating and tracking unique identifiers.
- Encryption. It is easy to make something a secret.
- De-identified public datasets, provided without software. Publicly released de-identified data have immense scientific value and, with remarkably few exceptions, have not hurt patients.

Are there instances when we can have unlimited complexity without suffering any negative consequences? Yes. Consider this book. It contains a lot of information: regulations, programming instruction, algorithms, lists, and detailed explanations of the complex world of biomedical informatics. This book may actually be much more complex than any hospital information system. But the book never crashes. Complexity is tolerable so long as it only serves to gather and hold information is some sort of organized manner that can be accessed. The negative consequences of complex systems come into play when subsystems interact with each other. At any given moment, millions of people perform Google searches. Luckily, I need not embark on a trip to Nepal when you choose to Google "Katmandu."

Managing complexity will likely become the most important task for biomedical informaticians as the quantity and variety of accessible biomedical data grows over the next few years. The biomedical informatician who has a keen sense of how software and data can be simplified will have an enormous positive influence on the field of biomedicine.

13.4. DATA SIMPLIFICATION WITH CLASSIFICATIONS

The unrestricted experience of reality is complex and chaotic. If we were simply to record all the things and events that we see when we take a walk on a city street or a country road, we would be overwhelmed by the magnitude of the collected data: images of trees, leaves, bark, clouds, buildings, bricks, stones, dirt, faces, insects, heat, cold, wind, barometric pressure, color, shades, sounds, loudness, harmonics, sizes and positions of things, relationships between objects, and so on.

The collected lifetime experiences of an individual can be envisioned as a database of enormous size and complexity and of interactions and consequences occurring on small and large scales, all unfolding as an unpredictable cacophony of simultaneously occurring events. It is amazing that we manage to function in the universe, and yet most of us would concede that our lives are dull and largely uneventful.

We manage our lives by classifying complex data into simple categories of things that have defined properties and roles. By classifying the members of our data streams, we can ignore details of the specific instances of class objects. We classify data instinctively, and much of our perception of the world derives from our individually created class structures.

Materia Medica was written in 60 AD by Dioscorides, providing one of the earliest and most influential taxonomies of botanical medicine (138). This scholarly work also contained thoughtful discussion on the topic of taxonomic organization. Dioscorides asked why his predecessors had organized their listings of herbs alphabetically. Doing so separated herbs that were closely related and made it difficult to understand the shared properties of related plants. These early musings are just as valid today as they were nearly two millennia ago.

In biomedical informatics, there are two constructs for organizing class information: classifications and ontologies. The principles of classifications have ancient roots (pre-dating Aristotle, history's most notable classifier) that have endured millennia and yielded today's modern classification of living organisms (139).

13.5. EXAMPLE CASE: A MOLECULAR CLASSIFICATION OF CANCER

Cancer is certainly one of the most important diseases of man. The CDC publishes summary data on the number of deaths in the United States attributed to leading causes of death (140) (List 13.5.1).

LIST 13.5.1. CDC REPORT OF ANNUAL NUMBER OF DEATHS IN THE UNITED STATES FROM LEADING DISEASES

- Heart disease: 696,947
- Cancer: 557,271
- Stroke (cerebrovascular diseases): 162,672
- Chronic lower respiratory diseases: 124,816

- Accidents (unintentional injuries): 106,742
- Diabetes: 73,249
- Influenza/Pneumonia: 65,681
- Alzheimer's disease: 58,866
- Nephritis, nephrotic syndrome, and nephrosis: 40,974
- Septicemia: 33,865

Unlike most other diseases, cancer can be subdivided into thousands of named types, each with their own unique biology. The occurrence of so many different types of tumors has caused some people to claim that cancer is not a single disease but a collection of thousands of related diseases. Because pathologists and oncologists must be prepared to diagnose and treat many thousands of different types of tumors, there is a need to have a clinically useful classification of tumors.

One of the purposes of this book is to discuss the generalizable principles of biomedical informatics, and this has meant that in-depth discussions of specific diseases have been avoided until now. Cancer provides an important example of the benefits of classifications and ontologies, and we will need to examine this disease in some detail.

13.6. CANCER NOMENCLATURES, TAXONOMIES, CLASSIFICATIONS, AND ONTOLOGIES

In January 1999, the U.S. National Cancer Institute (NCI) issued a challenge to the scientific community "to harness the power of comprehensive molecular analysis technologies to make the classification of tumors vastly more informative. This challenge is intended to lay the groundwork for changing the basis of tumor classification from morphological to molecular characteristics."

Not surprisingly, this has resulted in lively debate over the relative value of morphologic and molecular classifications (141).

A classification is an organization of everything in a domain by hierarchical groups, according to features generalizable to the members of the groups. Four terms with distinctly different meanings have been used interchangeably with "classification," leading to considerable confusion among biomedical informaticians. These terms are "identification," "discrimination," "taxonomy," and "ontology."

Identification (also known as diagnosing or naming) is the act of placing something into its correct slot within an existing classification.

Discrimination is the act of finding features that separate members of a group according to expected variations in group behavior. Examples of discrimination are "grading and staging." Grading and staging involve reporting additional morphologic features (grading) or clinical behavior (staging) that help predict a particular tumor's clinical course or response to therapy.

A **taxonomy** is a complete listing of all the members of a classification. In the case of neoplasia, a taxonomy would be the complete listing of all the different named tumors.

An ontology is a rule-based grouping of some portion of a taxonomy. Ontologies support queries and logical inferences pertaining to the (ontologic) group members. This definition will be elaborated later in this chapter.

Much of the current work in the molecular classification of tumors is actually discriminant analysis disguised as classification. In a typical **gene expression array** study, the researcher will look at a group of tumors of a specific type.

Cluster analysis of the gene expression array values will help separate the tumors into groups with common expression patterns. Some of these groupings will prove to have a specific biologic feature (e.g., increased tendency to metastasize, higher response to a chemotherapeutic agent, lengthened survival). The clustered groups seldom qualify as new classes if they merely represent variations in the expected biology of a type of tumor. Variant groups are disqualified as classes if it can be shown that a tumor of a certain type may progress from one variant group to another variant group over time (e.g., slow-growing variant at one stage in development and fast-growing variant at another stage). A key concept in a classification is that members of one class cannot transform into members of another class (i.e., a colon carcinoma does not transform into a colon lymphoma).

In the author's opinion, common misuses of the term "classification" form the greatest impediment to progress in the field of cancer genetics. It is impossible to create a molecular classification of tumors based solely on the separation of tumors by variations of molecular markers. Clustering by variation only identifies differences among tumors and is not sufficient to establish a classification.

Classification is the process of showing that certain differences reliably distinguish the members of a group from the members of all other groups, and that these differences apply to the group's hierarchical descendants. Therefore, the data that comes from the molecular analysis of tumors are only a first step in the long process of tumor classification.

A tumor classification serves as the "key" data structure that links the names of tumors to tumor-related data held in clinical and experimental databases. A good classification should help drive down the complexity of enormous databases and help us discover relationships among different data elements by assembling data under sensible group hierarchies (List 13.6.1).

LIST 13.6.1. PROPERTIES OF A CLASSIFICATION

- A classification is a grouped taxonomy (listing of all objects in a knowledge domain) with the following four properties:

  1. Inheritance: Hierarchical structure, with each class of tumors inheriting properties of its ancestors
  2. Uniqueness: Each tumor occurs in only one place in the classification
  3. Comprehensive: All tumors are included
  4. Class-intransitive: A tumor from one class does not change into a tumor from another class (e.g., an adenocarcinoma does not become a lymphoma)

Classifications are important because class properties are shared among the members of a class, and because members of a class inherit the properties of their ancestors. Simply knowing the class of a bacterium can provide a microbiologist with deep insights relating to the expected growth conditions for the organism and the types of antibiotics that may be effective against the organism. A classification can be thought of as the encapsulation of all knowledge related to a domain. In a modern classification, the elements of the classification (classes and instances) serve as annotation keys and are capable of relating all data to the classification, regardless of the source of the data. Using classed tumor names (from a standard nomenclature), a search of gene expression array databases might locate gene array data specific to the class. In the last few years, efforts have begun to characterize tumors based on molecular pathways that will serve as targets for new, nontoxic chemotherapeutic agents. There have been early successes with tumors sensitive to the inhibition of tyrosine kinases (gastrointestinal stromal tumors [GIST] and chronic myelogenous leukemia) with Gleevec. Both these tumors derive from nonendodermal/ectodermal embryonic layers, suggesting that molecular pathways (hence targets for chemotherapy) may be class-dependent.

At present, there is simply no comprehensive modern tumor classification. A practical, though disappointing, explanation for this situation is offered by Diamandopoulos: "Since there are almost limitless varieties of tumors, a complete table of classification would require many pages. Any shortened version is not only necessarily incomplete but also likely to be confusing." (142)

This dour judgment may actually represent the modern scientist's perspective. Current tumor classifications suffer from the following limitations, described in List 13.6.2.

LIST 13.6.2. LIMITATIONS OF CURRENT NEOPLASM CLASSIFICATIONS

- Classifications are created piecemeal for specific sites or organ systems. Nobody has published a comprehensive classification, although comprehensive taxonomies have been attempted.
- Classifications are often based on medical disciplines, rather than on any biologic principles (e.g., classification of dermatologic tumors).
- A given tumor will appear redundantly when subclassifications are merged.
- No tumor classification has been prepared in a standard format designed to exchange, merge, or analyze heterogeneous biological data.

The most widely used authoritative resources are the World Health Organization classifications, which list the tumors that occur at different body sites. The problem with an organ system approach to classification is that every organ contains organ-specific and organ non-specific cell types. The brain, for instance, contains connective tissue and lymphoid tissue, and therefore is prone to tumors of connective tissue and lymphoid tissue. A listing of tumors that occur in the brain must include osteocartilaginous tumors, lipoma, fibrous histiocytoma, hemangiopericytoma, rhabdomyosarcoma, melanoma, lymphoma and myeloma, among others. These same tumors will be included again and again in every site-specific classification. Although each term may occur only once in each site-specific classification, the same lesion may occur a virtually limitless number of times when the site classifications are combined into a comprehensive classification of tumors. Although cancer taxonomies are different from classifications, they usefully provide all the instances of tumors that must be grouped within a classification. Excellent tumor taxonomies are now publicly available at no cost.

The classification we will now describe is based on developmental histogenesis and is very similar to classifications described in the mid 1950s (143) (List 13.6.3). The reasons for this approach to tumor classification are:

1. Organs may have multiple embryologic derivatives (e.g., skin contains tissues of ectodermal, neuroectodermal, and mesodermal lineages), but any given cell has only one lineage. This means that a histogenetic classification can assign any tumor to a unique position within the classification.
2. For the most part, tumors have a cell developmental stage. For instance, blastomas are thought to arise from a cell type that precedes organ differentiation. Squamous cell carcinomas of skin are tumors that have features of a cell type that developed from one of the

embryonic layers (ectoderm). An embryologic approach permits us to assign a cell type and a developmental stage to tumors.

3. A classification based on developmental histogenesis is relevant to the behavior of tumors. Ectoderm- and endoderm-derived tumors metastasize via lymphatics. Mesenchyme-derived tumors tend to metastasize by hematogenous spread.

4. A classification based on developmental histogenesis is consistent with modern molecular analysis of tumors. Mesenchyme-derived tumors tend to be characterized by simple fusion genes. Ectoderm and endoderm-derived tumors tend to be genetically unstable and cannot be characterized by a single genetic abnormality.

The complete neoplasm classification developed by the author is available at: http://www. pathologyinformatics.org/informatics_r.htm

LIST 13.6.3. SCHEMATIC FOR THE DEVELOPMENTAL LINEAGE CLASSIFICATION OF CANCER

```
embryonic
primitive
        primitive_differentiating
                totipotent_or_multipotent_differentiating
                limited_differentiating
        germ cell
        primitive_non_differentiating
non_primitive
        endoderm_or_ectoderm
                endoderm_or_ectoderm_surface
                endoderm_or_ectoderm_endocrine
                endoderm_or_ectoderm_parenchymal
                odontogenic_epithelium
        mesoderm
                mesenchyme
                        connective_tissue
                                muscle
                                fibrous_tissue
                                vascular
                                adipose_tissue
                                bone_cartilage
```

```
                    heme_lymphoid
            non_mesenchymal_mesoderm
                coelomic
                        coelomic_ductal
                        coelomic_cavities
                        coelomic_gonadal
                    sub_coelomic
                            sub_coelomic_gonadal
                            sub_coelomic_endocrine
                            sub_coelomic_ nephric
            neuroectoderm_neural_plate
                neural_tube
                        neural_tube_parenchyma
                        neural_tube_lining
                    neural_crest
                        peripheral_nervous_system
                        neural_crest_endocrine
                        neural_crest_melanocytic
```

The specific rationale for each category of the developmental lineage classification of neoplasia is far beyond the scope of this book. The classification and its utility in reconciling fundamental problems in tumor biology have been discussed in open access publications (77, 79). The general rules of biological classification have been well described by Ernst Mayr (139). The features of the classification most relevant to biomedical informaticians are summarized here (List 13.6.4).

LIST 13.6.4. GENERAL FEATURES OF THE TUMOR CLASSIFICATION RELEVANT TO BIOMEDICAL INFORMATICS

- Instance uniqueness. Each tumor entity occurs only once within the classification.
- Comprehensive. The classification ensures that every tumor of man can be placed somewhere within the classification.
- Simplicity. One of the purposes of a classification is to drive down the complexity that exists when the domain taxonomy is large. The entire classification is described by under 40 classifiers.
- Principled. The classification is based on known principles of developmental biology, not on political or artifactual distinctions between tumors. A counterexample would be a tumor classifica-

tion based on medical specialty (e.g., dermatologic neoplasms, hematologic neoplasms, head and neck tumors, etc.)

- The classification has "competence." In the field of informatics, competence is the ability to answer questions related to the instances of a data group.

- Standard method of organization. The classification is represented as an XML document.

- Scalability. It is easy to expand the classification with new subclasses. This is important, as the molecular analysis of tumors is likely to provide new taxa.

- Modifiable. It is easy to move subdivisions of the classification. Classifications are hypothetical re-creations of reality and must be changed as information is accrued.

- Understandable. The classification is easily understood by developmental biologists. Developmental biologists are major participants in post-genomic science and need to have tools to relate basic research with clinical exigencies.

- Credible. The classification complements modern theories of the "stem cell" origin of tumors.

- Compatible with other visions of reality. The classification does not invalidate existing diagnoses found in pathology reports. The medicolegal importance of this feature cannot be exaggerated. This relieves pathologists from reviewing all their prior cases and re-diagnosing them in conformance with a new classification.

- Open access. The classification is an open access document that can be used or criticized freely by the biomedical community (80).

13.7. PRACTICAL LIMITATIONS OF CLASSIFICATIONS

The major drawback in all classifications is that they impose a specific worldview of the data domain that cannot simultaneously include alternate views.

As an example, a researcher might be doing a review of certain pancreatic neoplasms that she has studied. The pathologist might have collected a series of mucinous tumors of the pancreas. The researcher might want to be sure that she has collected all the relevant entities, so she does a nomenclature query on "mucinous tumors of the pancreas" and finds none. That is because the classification was not designed to collect all the tumors of an anatomic site. Furthermore, the taxon "mucinous" was not employed in the classification (i.e., the quality of having mucin was not a classifying principle). Therefore, there is no way of collecting all the "mucinous" tumors as a preassembled class of lesions. It is possible to do a search on "mucinous" and "pancreas" and to collect all the tumors with both words in their name. Once these lesions are collected, it would be possible to collect all the named neoplasms that are synonymous with the terms that contain "mucinous" and "pancreas" in their names. But this in no way guarantees that the results of the search will pull all the neoplasms of interest to the researcher.

A similar problem would arise if a zoologist were doing a search over taxonomy.dat, looking for animals that live in North America and weigh over 130 pounds. If the taxonomy does not use location and weight as organizing taxons (and it does not), then animals of a particular weight and location cannot be extracted from the taxonomy.

We shall see that ontologies solve this dilemma by allowing class objects to be organized many different ways, and all at once.

13.8. ONTOLOGIES: MULTICLASS INHERITANCE AND LOGICAL INFERENCES

Ontologies are rule-based systems operating on classes of instance objects. Ontologies differ from classifications on several key points (List 13.8.1).

LIST 13.8.1. DISTINCTIONS BETWEEN ONTOLOGIES AND CLASSIFICATIONS

ontology

1. An ontology does not need to provide a theoretic embodiment of a data domain. In fact, an ontology need not be comprehensive (i.e., an oncology does not need to include all the instances of a knowledge domain) and may extend over several different knowledge domains.
2. Ontologic classes are characterized by one or more logical rules and include object instances that behave in conformity to the class rules. The classes in classifications are determined by a set of features that are shared among the members of the class. The features that define a class within a classification are usually not logical rules.
3. Ontologies permit multiclass inheritance. Any ontologic class can inherit from any number of father classes. A class within a classification can have at most one father class.
4. An ontologic object instance may belong to more than one class, just as long as the object obeys the rules of the class in which it is a member. An object in a classification can belong to only one class.
5. An ontologic class inherits the rules of its superclass. However, an ontologic class is not required to have a superclass (i.e., an ancestor class) or descendant classes (i.e., subclasses).

In a sense, an ontology is a classification with freedom. Multiclass inheritance and class-specific logic (instead of class-specific features) are the chief features that distinguish classifications from ontologies. A classification constructed in a manner that restates its class features as rules would qualify as a simple, but domain-comprehensive, ontology. For example, the classification of all living organisms can be converted into an ontology by creating a general rule applied to all classes: a class evolves from its superclass.

There are several advantages of ontologies over classifications (List 13.8.2).

LIST 13.8.2. GOOD THINGS ABOUT ONTOLOGIES

- Ontologies are computable and fit neatly into the object oriented programming model.
- Ontologies are semantically sensible and can be described with standard RDF syntax.
- Ontologies have competence, meaning they can be used to draw a variety of inferences about class members based on class rules.
- Ontologies are extensible and can be integrated with other ontologies.
- When the same ontology is used by different researchers, concepts in common use will have the same meaning and properties.

With the good comes the bad. Ontologies create problems that are not encountered with classifications (List 13.8.3).

LIST 13.8.3. BAD THINGS ABOUT ONTOLOGIES

- Ontologies place no constraints on internal complexity and can quickly become incomprehensible to humans.
- Ontologic complexity may lead to unanticipated consequences (including paradoxes of self-reference).
- Ontologies are relatively new and there are very few examples where they have shown to have biomedical value. Classifications have proven their value over millennia.
- Ontologies work on the assumption that medically relevant domains have an intrinsic logic that can be described by rules. This assumption may be false.

Rule-based systems, such as ontologies, are easily victimized by the law of unintended consequences. An example from the realm of clinical laboratory testing will illustrate. The laboratory creates a rule that applies to all differential blood cell counts (an ontologic subclass of laboratory tests). When a white cell count falls below a certain number (e.g., 4,500, the lower range of normal in adults) the laboratory information system issues a reflexive alert to the patient's physician. In this example, an error would arise when a neonate presents with a white blood cell count of 5,500 without triggering an alert. The normal range of white blood cells in a neonate is 9,000 to 30,000. The normal white cell count in an adult is 4,500 to 10,000. A white cell count of 5,500 in a neonate is leukopenic and may be signal a life-threatening condition. The same white cell count in an adult would be perfectly normal. The rule system would have failed to make the proper inference (and would have failed the patient) in this specific instance. In an ontology with many classes, many rules, and complex relations between classes, it becomes extremely difficult to assess, describe, evaluate, or even fathom the system.

13.9. GO, THE GENE ONTOLOGY THAT IS NOT AN ONTOLOGY

Certainly, the most famous biologic ontology is the Gene Ontology (GO) (124). No discussion of biomedical informatics would be complete without a description of GO and an explanation of the potential uses of this remarkable open access resource. However, it must be stated that GO, despite its name, is not an ontology.

Most of the comments to follow in this section were inspired by Barry Smith and his colleagues, who have disregarded the world's ennui and have persevered to search for meaning and purpose in medical ontologies. Those who plan to use ontologies in their work are strongly advised to read Barry Smith's superbly written and indispensable manuscripts (144–146).

GO is an amalgam of three classifications: cellular components, biological processes, and molecular functions. It is not an ontology because it is not a logical construction of rules applied to classes. If GO had simply been constructed as three separate classifications, then it would not occupy its unique and perplexing status. The creators of GO decided to combine all three classifications into a single structure described with RDF syntax. Because a single biologic entity can reside in three classes at once (i.e., an entity can be a cellular component, a biological process, and a molecular function), it violates the rules for a classification. So, if GO is neither an ontology nor a classification, then what is it? GO is an hierarchical controlled vocabulary. This designation, however, does not do justice to GO's remarkably useful structure.

Consider the GO instance, GO:0000080.

```
<go:term rdf:about="http://www.geneontology.org/go#GO:0000080"
n_associations="0">
<go:accession>GO:0000080</go:accession>
<go:name>G1 phase of mitotic cell cycle</go:name>
```

```
<go:definition>Progression through G1 phase, one of two 'gap'
phases in the mitotic cell cycle; G1 is the interval between the
completion of mitosis and the beginning of DNA
synthesis.</go:definition>
<go:is_a rdf:resource="http://www.geneontology.org/go#GO:
0051318" />
<go:part_of rdf:resource="http://www.geneontology.org/
go#GO:0051329" />
<go:dbxref rdf:parseType="Resource">
  <go:database_symbol>Reactome</go:database_symbol>
  <go:reference>69236</go:reference>
</go:dbxref>
</go:term>
```

The GO entry has a simple RDF syntax that begins with a unique object (i.e., http://www.geneontology.org/go#GO:0000080) leading to a pairs of key/value (metadata/data) pairs.

The metadata/data pairs include:

```
accession => GO:0000080
name => G1 phase of mitotic cell cycle
definition => Progression through G1 phase....
is_a => rdf:resource="http://www.geneontology.org/
go#GO:0051318"
part_of => rdf:resource="http://www.geneontology.org/
go#GO:0051329"
```

By providing a name and a definition, GO provides adequate self-description of its object members to permit a curator to equate any GO term with its equivalent terms in other nomenclatures or even in other languages. The "is_a" and "part_of" metadata items associate the object with its ancestors (is_a) and neighbors (part_of). The relationships in GO, though helpful in classifying objects, do not provide the formal rigor expected from an ontology (144). In an ontology, relationships can only have one meaning that applies to all the members of an ontology. The meaning of "part_of" will change for different objects. A nucleus may be part_of a cell (i.e., cellular component), and a coenzyme may be part_of an enzymatic activity (i.e., molecular function) but the part_of relationship between a nucleus and a cell, and between a coenzyme and an enzyme, are very different.

Having hierarchical biologic domains for uniquely identified objects enables researchers to drive down the complexity of large datasets. Guo and co-workers have used GO to assign gene array substrates to functional domains determined by GO relationships (147). A gene expression value was computed that combined the gene expression measurements collected on all the members of a functional domain. The gene expression signature of a biological sample was transformed into a profile of the activities of functional domains in GO. Instead of having thousands of seemingly unrelated gene expression measurements, the array data was classified under a few functional domains. Likewise, within the domains, gene expression activities of descendant groups could be determined. This novel approach demonstrates how GO can be used to simplify complex data and to represent observations as shared properties of biological classes.

GO is an open access effort from a group of highly motivated and talented scientists that makes good use of RDF syntax and that has become a valuable scientific resource. GO is not perfect, lacking the rigor and competence (ability to draw logical inferences) of formal ontologies. One of the tasks of the next generation of biomedical informaticians is to develop a logical, integrative, and practical approach to medical ontologies.

Clinical Trials: The Informatician Lives in a Statistical World

14.1. BACKGROUND

An important source of biomedical data comes from clinical trials. Biologic discoveries have no value unless they are shown to have diagnostic or therapeutic efficacy in a well-designed clinical trial.

This has not always been the case. Prior to the latter half of the twentieth century, clinical trials were virtually unknown. Some of the early clinical trials were so poorly conceived that they serve as cautionary tales. Notable is the egregious Tuskegee Syphilis Study, conducted by the U.S. Public Health Service (PHS) between 1932 and 1972. This study observed the natural course of late stage syphilis in 399 black men. The men were poor Alabama sharecroppers who were never told that they had syphilis. Their doctors had no intention of curing them of syphilis. The data for the experiment was to be collected from autopsies. Some of the ravages of untreated late stage syphilis include heart disease, paralysis, blindness, insanity, and death (148).

In 1963, in a study at Memorial Sloan-Kettering Cancer Center, cancer cells were injected into hundreds of patients with cancer. The injections resulted in tumor nodules that grew for several weeks before regressing (149). The study was done without informed consent.

These sad and shameful stories demonstrate that through the 1960s, clinical trials were still evolving (149).

14.2. DO WE NEED CLINICAL TRIALS?

Today, the term clinical trial is virtually synonymous with prospective randomized clinical trial. Randomization refers to the random assignment of patients to the treated or to the untreated (or standard treatment) group. In addition to being randomized, many clinical trials are blinded so that neither the treating physician nor the patients know the assignment group during the trial.

Before there were randomized prospective clinical trials, there were major medical breakthroughs. Virtually every medical advance in human history was achieved without the use of randomized double-blinded prospective clinical trials (List 14.2.1).

LIST 14.2.1. SOME MEDICAL BREAKTHROUGHS THAT OCCURRED WITHOUT BENEFIT OF RANDOMIZED PROSPECTIVE CLINICAL TRIALS

- 1796: Edward Jenner successfully vaccinates 8-year-old James Phipps with unproven smallpox vaccine (prepared from cowpox).
- 1881: Louis Pasteur successfully vaccinates Joseph Meister with unproven rabies vaccine.
- 1900: Jesse Lazear demonstrates (on himself) that yellow fever is transmitted by mosquito bite. Lazear dies from successful inoculation.
- 1944, 1972, and 1992: Sudden Infant Death Syndrome observed to be associated with infants sleeping on stomach, on soft mattresses.
- 1985: Marshall infects himself with *H. pylori*, thus developing gastritis and demonstrating the bacterial origin of gastric ulcers.

Sudden Infant Death Syndrome (SIDS) is an example of a major breakthrough in patient care that has evolved into common practice without the use of a controlled randomized clinical trial. SIDS is the nightmare disease feared by every infant's parent. In a typical SIDS case, the baby is left to sleep. When the parents check the baby, they find that he or she is dead. Moments of temporary sleep apnea are common in babies and adults. In SIDS, it is as though the process of breathing simply stops and does not resume. Autopsies on SIDS patients have never shown any consistent conditions in organs that may have caused death.

The devastation rendered by SIDS cannot be adequately described. Many bright medical researchers have devoted their careers to SIDS. The obvious suspects (respiratory controls in the brain and lungs) were examined intensely in hundreds of studies, with little to show for the effort.

Simple observations of the circumstances made at the death scene were shown to have enormous import. As early as the 1940s, the observation was made that many victims of SIDS were found in prone position on pliant bedding, often in soft layers of bedclothes (150). Similar observations were made again and again, and by the 1970s, people began to wonder whether babies could breathe adequately under these conditions (151). The New Zealanders are credited with showing that infant mortality drops when infants sleep in a supine position on a firm mattress. Numerous population studies have confirmed these observations. The "back-to-sleep" campaign is now a worldwide effort that is expected to reduce the number of SIDS deaths by more than half. This was all accomplished without the benefit of a randomized clinical trial.

14.3. THE LENGTH AND EXPENSE OF CLINICAL TRIALS

Modern clinical trials are long and expensive. The process of testing a candidate new drug can take many years. In the realm of cancer trials, the Prostate, Lung, Colorectal and Ovarian Cancer Screening Trial (PLCO, NIH/NCI trial NO1 CN25512) serves as an example. The PLCO is a randomized controlled cancer trial. Between 1992, when the trial opened, and 2001, when enrollment ended, 155,000 women and men between the ages of 55 and 74 joined PLCO. Screening of participants and the collection of follow-up data will end around 2016. The purpose of the study is to determine whether cancer screening will reduce cancer mortality (152).

The Framingham Heart Study began in July 1948 and will be completed in September 2008. This 60-year study investigates factors that may influence the development of cardiovascular disease in humans (153).

Khufu built the Great Pyramid at Giza, (2589–2566 BC) with the assistance of an estimated 100,000 laborers. The Great Pyramid is still standing and is visible to astronauts orbiting the globe. Khufu managed to complete construction of the Great Pyramid in just 23 years (nearly 40 years faster than the Framingham study).

Though prospective trials are often considered the only way of determining the efficacy and safety of new treatments and diagnostic tests, the public may legitimately ask whether society has the time, money, and patience for these studies. Those engaged in clinical trials may well ask themselves the following questions (List 14.3.1).

LIST 14.3.1. QUESTIONS FOR CLINICAL TRIALISTS

- Are data from clinical trials made available to the public?
- Are we making the best use of data collected in clinical trials?
- How often do clinical trials fail to provide definitive answers to the question that motivated the trial?
- When a prospective clinical trial fails to answer the question that motivated the trial, is the trial data made available to the public?
- Are we using the best available methods to guarantee that clinical trials are designed properly?

- Might clinical trials be designed in a manner that enhances the scientific and medical value of the trials beyond the original hypothesis?
- Might some prospective clinical trials be replaced by cheaper, faster retrospective trials?
- Might some clinical trials be replaced by new, innovative models that produce clinically sound results in less time and for less money?

14.4. AN IMAGINARY CLINICAL TRIAL

The following "thought" experiment demonstrates how a prospective clinical trial may fail to correctly evaluate a hypothesis.

In a retrospective study, Dr. X demonstrated a "perfect" tumor marker that never failed to distinguish between two tumor variants (aggressive and indolent). The aggressive tumor variant grew 10 times as fast and metastasizes at 10 times the rate as the indolent variant. Without Dr. X's tumor marker, the two tumor variants could not be distinguished by any routine morphologic evaluation (i.e., indolent and aggressive tumors looked alike).

Dr. X's perfect tumor marker was received with great enthusiasm. For the first time, it looked as though patients would be treated in a manner appropriate to the biology of their tumors. Patients with aggressive tumors would have resection followed by intensive chemotherapy. Patients with indolent tumors would have resection and no chemotherapy.

Of course, Dr. X would need to wait until a prospective clinical trial confirmed the preliminary findings.

In a prospective trial of the same marker, 200 tumors are excised at the time of clinical detection (tumor size 2 centimeters). Dr. X finds that 100 of the tumors stain as "indolent variants" and 100 tumors stain as "aggressive variants." The prospective trial followed all 200 patients, determining survival at five years.

Here is the rub. At the end of the trial, there is no survival difference between patients with "indolent variants" and patients with "aggressive variants." The marker is considered a total failure, with millions of dollars wasted on the prospective trial.

How is this possible? Poorly designed prospective trials can lead to erroneous conclusions. The key to finding the error in this imaginary example lies in an understanding of why cancer patients may die after their tumor has been excised. Cancer deaths following primary tumor excision are almost always due to metastases that were seeded prior to the time that the primary tumor was excised. If the primary tumor had not metastasized before it was excised, then the patient is cured by the excision. If the primary tumor had metastasized before it was excised, then the patient is likely to die. This is true whether the tumor is an aggressive tumor or an indolent tumor. The survival advantage of indolent tumors (compared to aggressive tumors) is that indolent tumors are less likely to metastasize.

Consider the design of the prospective trial and the initial conditions of the trial. Two hundred tumors were excised. All excised tumors (whether indolent or aggressive) were 2 centimeters in diameter. We are told that the aggressive tumors have a growth rate 10 times that of the indolent tumors. So, if it took 1 month for an aggressive tumor to reach a 2 centimeter size, then it must have taken 10 months for an indolent tumor to reach 2 centimeters in size. We are also told that the rate of metastasis in the aggressive tumor is 10 times that of the indolent tumor. Because aggressive tumors had $\frac{1}{10}$ the growth history of the indolent tumors (for instance, 10 months compared to 1 month), both the aggressive and indolent tumors had the same number of metastatic cases at the time that the tumors were excised (i.e., at the moment when the prospective clinical trial began). Hence, there was no difference in the survival outcome between the tumor variants, because survival outcome is almost entirely determined by the presence or absence of metastases at the time of primary tumor excision.

Dr. X may have benefited from a simulation model designed to predict outcomes from a set of biological conditions and restraints. As we have seen in Chapter 6, it is easy to model tumor growth using Monte Carlo simulations. It is also easy to enhance the simulation with models of metastastic events.

14.5. MODELING A CLINICAL TRIAL

In Perl, tumor cell growth can be simulated, beginning with a single cell (List 14.5.1). Each cell in the simulation is provided with a characteristic chance of metastasizing that extends to every descendant of the cell. To simulate the imaginary trial, we might provide the following probabilities of a cell metastasizing in any cell generation.

For instance, we may provide an initial metastatic probability of 1 in 50 million for each cell in the aggressive tumor and 1 in 5 million for each cell in the indolent tumor.

Each cell in either tumor type has a very low likelihood of metastasizing, but the probability for the cells in the aggressive tumor are 10 times as high as the probability for the cells in the indolent tumor.

Both tumors begin their growth history with a single cell, and the cell number doubles with each generation. This is actually an inaccurate mathematical characterization of tumor growth. Real tumor growth is a balance between complex processes of cell growth and cell death. The model of Berman and Moore provides a set of outcomes consistent with a chosen set of initial growth conditions (154).

LIST 14.5.1. SNIPPET OF PERL CODE DEMONSTRATING HOW METASTASTIC EVENTS CAN BE SIMULATED USING THE MONTE CARLO TECHNIQUE

```perl
$badoutcome = "No mets for the bad tumor";
#begin with no metastases
$start = time();
while (1) #this will loop forever unless something in
#block prompts exit
   {
   $bad = 2 * $bad; #population doubles with each loop
   print "$bad\n";
   srand;
   for (1...$bad) #for each cell in population
      {
      $badchance = int(rand(5000)) +1;
      if ($badchance == 5000) #1 in 5,000
         {
         $badchance = int(rand(10000)) +1;
         if ($badchance == 10000) #multiplied by 1 in 10,000
            {
            $badoutcome = "$n $bad $badchance\n";
            print $badoutcome;
            exit;
            }
         }
      }
   $n++;
   if ($bad > 50000000) #population reaches 50 million
                        #without metastasizing
      {
      print "$badoutcome\n";
      $end = time();
      $totaltime = $end-$start;
      print "Time for execution is $totaltime seconds\n";
      exit;
      }
   }
```

14.6. WHAT DO MODELS TELL US?

Mathematical models are important because they provide us with some sense of the realm of possible outcomes for a clinical trial. If we can anticipate the kinds of outcomes that might occur in a clinical trial, then we may improve our trial designs to maximize the chance for a decisive outcome.

When a clinical trial is begun, everyone fears that the results will be negative, dashing the hopes for a new cure or test. If trialists were realistic, then they would acknowledge that the greater fear lies in a trial that is inconclusive. In an inconclusive trial, all the time, money, risk, and effort is wasted. At the end, nobody knows any more than they did at the start of the experiment.

The value of modeling is that it allows us to anticipate the range of possible outcomes that may result from a trial. With this information, we can design better trials and, hopefully, avoid inconclusive studies. At least for the moment, clinical modeling has limited value as an outcome predictor.

14.7. THE INFORMATICS OF CLINICAL TRIALS

Clinical trials are a huge industry. At any given moment, there are 40,000–80,000 randomized controlled clinical trials conducted worldwide at a cost that exceeds $10 billion (155). These trials generate an enormous amount of data. The Clinical Data Interchange Standards Consortium (CDISC) develops and supports global data standards for pharmaceutical clinical trials. Although discussion of the CDISC standard is beyond the scope of this book, biomedical informaticians should understand that clinical trials are probably the most massive enterprise undertaken in the realm of therapeutics research and development. All clinical trials should conform to a variety of industry standards recommended by private consortia (such as the CDISC) and federal regulators (such as the U.S. FDA). More importantly, biomedical informaticians have an opportunity to enhance the field of clinical trial-based translational research (List 14.7.1).

LIST 14.7.1. ROLE OF BIOMEDICAL INFORMATICIANS IN CLINICAL TRIALS-BASED TRANSLATIONAL RESEARCH

- Protecting human subject privacy and confidentiality (always the first responsibility of biomedical informaticians)
- Developing new approaches for clinical trials that reduce the cost and length of trials without sacrificing scientific value
- Choosing a primary hypothesis whose scientific importance will endure to the end of the study

- Expanding study designs to test multiple hypotheses during the course of the trial
- Capturing data that can complement other scientific efforts
- Designing the studies in ways that ensure that the primary hypothesis (i.e., the hypothesis that justifies the study) is adequately tested
- Organizing the data (using common standards such as CDISC)
- Ensuring that the analysis of data is conducted in a manner free from bias
- Reporting the conclusions of the study
- Distributing the data that support the conclusions of the study

14.8. CLINICAL TRIALS NEED TO BE VALIDATED BY POST-TRIAL EXPERIENCE

It is worth remembering that prospective randomized clinical trials are types of experiments and have all the vulnerabilities inherent in any scientific project. They can be poorly designed, misinterpreted, invalid for under-represented patient subpopulations, unrepeatable, and falsified. Because clinical trials often extend over many years, clinical reality may change in the interim. The treatment–response protocols tested in the trial may become irrelevant or may need to be modified. The only true validation of clinical trials will come from monitored clinical experiences in medical centers treating many different types of patients (male, female, different nationalities, different ages, concurrent diseases, multiple medications). Clinical trials need to be followed with short and long-term outcomes analyses to validate the original trial observations. The validation of clinical trials by post-trial experience is another job for biomedical informaticians.

Distributed Computing

15.1. BACKGROUND

Software agents are computer programs that can work with some auton-
omy, taking cues from the data that they encounter and adjusting their
behavior to perform a variety of tasks that they were not specifically programmed to perform. The Internet makes it possible to create useful software agents. Because data sources are identified (by uniform resource
locators) and accessible (through TCP/IP data transport protocols), it is
feasible to design software agents that seek out data throughout the
Internet. With the advent of RDF, data can now be "understood" on a
software level, as each identified object in RDF can be associated with
pairs of metadata and data, and each object can be associated with properties and other objects sharing a common ontologic class.

An example might be a software agent that schedules appointments for
biomedical informaticians (List 15.1.1).

LIST 15.1.1. PLAIN ENGLISH DESCRIPTION OF A SOFTWARE AGENT PROTOCOL

- You provide the software program with the following inputs: a list
  of people who you would like to make an appointment with, and a
  calendar file that contains your free dates and times as well as
  dates and times that have already been obligated.
- The software agent uses the standard http (Web) protocol to visit all
  the URLs of all the names on your list.
- At each Web site, the software agent searches for the class objects
  associated with the unique person name. If all goes well, the software agent finds a calendar object that belongs to the named person.

- The calendar object contains unique date-time entries associated with prior appointments. The agent matches a list of available dates and times from your calendar.
- The software agent enters appointments in the calendars of your associates and in your calendar.
- The software agent sends e-mail messages to you and your associates indicating the new appointments.

The vision of the "semantic web" proffered by Sir Tim Berners-Lee holds that data described in RDF triples can be understood by software agents.

15.2. REMOTE PROCEDURE CALLS, SOAP, WEB SERVICES, AND GRID COMPUTING

Until now, the emphasis of this book has been on self-reliance. Many informatics tasks can be done on an unconnected personal computer, if the user has access to relevant datasets.

Sometimes, the most effective way of advancing an informatics agenda is through networking. A succession of increasingly complex networking protocols characterize the evolution of network-based computational tasking (List 15.2.1).

LIST 15.2.1. INCREASINGLY COMPLEX TASK-SHARING NETWORK PROTOCOLS

1. FTP (file transfer protocol)
2. TELNET
3. HTTP (hypertext transfer protocol)
4. RPC (remote procedure calls)
5. XML-RPC (xml-based remote procedure calls)
6. SOAP (simple object access protocol)
7. P2P (peer-to-peer networking)
8. WEB Services
9. GRID computing

FTP (file transfer protocol) is an Internet protocol for transferring files between different networked computers. Files can be uploaded or downloaded.

TELNET is a network protocol for establishing command-line sessions on remote host computers.

HTTP (hypertext transfer protocol) is the familiar World Wide Web protocol that permits Web pages to be exchanged. Enhancements of server and client functionality (e.g., CGI [common gateway interface] scripts on the server side and applets on the client side) empower users to distribute computational tasks using the HTTP protocol.

RPC is the abbreviation for remote procedure calling. A client invokes a computational method and calls another networked computer to execute the method.

XML-RPC is an RPC call performed using XML configured commands.

SOAP is a formalized protocol that establishes uniform terms and methods for describing RPC transactions in XML syntax.

Web Services are resident server functionalities that accept client-initiated requests through an interface described by WSDL (Web services description language).

P2P is a protocol for distributing messages (queries and responses) through a network of peers. Peers are networked host computers that, for purposes of the P2P protocol, are somewhat autonomous and have properties that are neither client-type nor server-type).

GRID computing is a method for providing Web services by brokering client requests through a network of participating servers. In the most advanced grid computing architecture, requests can be broken into computational tasks that are processed in parallel on multiple computers and transparently (from the client's perspective) assembled and returned.

A discussion of these protocols would be beyond the scope of this book. Readers should know that the popular scripting languages provide open source modules for the less complex protocols (FTP, TELNET, HTTP, RPC, and SOAP). There is an enormous literature available on these topics. Several books are dedicated to describing available Perl modules (156, 73). Motivated readers are encouraged to implement these useful protocols.

Web Services, P2P, and GRID require complex architectures. Projects based on these technologies typically have participation by a group of computer scientists blessed with time and expertise.

15.3. DATA UTOPIA

Sir Tim Berners-Lee is the embodiment of a data utopia. As a principle inventor of the World Wide Web, he has improved our access to information and improved the manner in which information is created. The semantic web advances his vision, making it possible to understand and integrate information of many different types.

In the field of biomedical informatics, the hope is that medical progress will move much faster if we have free and open access to well-described, well-organized, and meaningful information. The technology for collecting and integrating biomedical data is already with us. The world is waiting for biomedical informaticians to start making sense of it all.

15.4. DATA DYSTOPIA

The ability to create, modify, limit, and distribute all of the data that people can access is an awesome power.

In the novel *1984,* George Orwell describes a totalitarian government that alters reality at will by modifying news items and historical documents to suit their own interests. Information sources that could not be changed (such as old books and other printed documents) were forbidden. A totalitarian government that controls Internet data can also control our perception of the past, the present, and the future.

The threat of a data dystopia is quite real. Everyone would agree that the Internet influences our vision of reality. The Internet provides an endless parade of zeroes and ones that, for some people, have replaced friends, family, and community. If the data that we receive over the Internet has been selected, or modified to influence our thinking, then a belated 1984 will descend upon us.

How does this relate to biomedical informatics? Biomedical informaticians will soon be in a position to control access to data that will influence what it means to be a human being in a world where cloning, parceled health care, emergent plagues, life-long medication regimens, eugenics, and euthanasia are options (not hypothetical concepts).

Woody Allen wrote, "More than any other time in history, mankind faces a crossroads. One path leads to despair and utter hopelessness. The other, to total extinction. Let us pray we have the wisdom to choose correctly." (157)

A Practical Approach to Ethics for Biomedical Informaticians

16.1. BACKGROUND

Biomedical informaticians are entrusted with personal data about people, and biomedical data can be used in ways that harm individuals and groups. The top priority for any biomedical informatician must be to protect human subjects from harm. Most of the ethical issues in biomedical informatics relate to this simple imperative, but the devil lies in the details. Because human subject protection must have the highest priority for every biomedical informatician, every book in the field should have a section that deals with ethical issues (List 16.1.1).

Biomedical ethics can be reduced to the Golden Rule: "Do unto others as you would have them do unto you." If you were enrolled in a study or trial, then you would hope that the researchers were doing everything in their power to protect you. Perhaps the most productive way of thinking about ethics is as an enabling methodology. If a researcher understands the ways that their research can harm patients, then a best effort application of the Golden Rule will almost always provide a practical way of protecting the patient and completing their research objectives.

As a tongue-in-cheek exercise, a set of commonly encountered ethical challenges are described, along with recommendations for dealing with them. As with any posed ethical situation, there is no single solution. A satisfactory decision depends on actual circumstances, the vicissitudes of human nature, community standards of conduct, accumulation of legal precedent, and the ingenuity of the legal profession.

LIST 16.1.1. SOURCES OF ETHICAL CHALLENGES FOR BIOMEDICAL INFORMATICIANS

- HIPAA regulations
- IRB approvals
- Flawed de-identification methods
- Problematic network security protocols
- Data sharing requirements from funding agencies
- Contractual IP arrangements with employer
- Conflicts of interest
- Hidden patent violations
- Unanticipated lawsuits

16.2. IS IT EVER OKAY TO LIE?

Everyone knows that it is wrong to lie, but lying seems to be a highly prevalent condition in biomedical circles. Several recent reports document alarmingly high rates of lying on fellowship applications. In one report by Sekas and Hutson in the Annals of Internal Medicine, about 30% of applicants for gastroenterology fellowships who listed published articles misrepresented their accomplishments (158). Misrepresentation included citations of nonexistent articles in actual journals, articles in nonexistent journals, or articles incorrectly cited as "in press." It can be noted that competition for Gastroenterology fellowships is keen, with many applicants for a small number of slots nationwide.

The U.S. Department of Health and Human Services sponsors the Office of Research Integrity. The Office of Research Integrity investigates complaints of scientific misconduct and releases their findings to the public. A recent study by Lawrence Rhoades for the Office of Research Integrity found that 98% of the top 50 funded institutions reported research misconduct activity during the study period (1992–2001) (159). The three sins constituting the bulk of misconduct deeds were fabrication of data, falsification of data, and plagiarism. Each sin can be considered a type of lie.

Why do people lie? People lie because it serves some selfish purpose and because they think that they can avoid detection and punishment. Lies are purposeful misrepresentations of truth. Much more common than lying, among clinical workers and researchers, are biased representations of the truth intended to support a particular opinion. Researchers often have much to gain by influencing a reader's interpretation of data. Research biases are found in virtually every manuscript. It is human nature for an author to stress information that supports her conclusions and to omit any information that is "negative." There are very few authors who seriously entertain the notion that their own conclusions may be incorrect. Even when scientific papers are free of blatant lies, no manuscript can be considered an objective embodiment of truth.

Are there any conditions when lying is ethical? Maybe yes. Throughout this book, the author has argued that the primary responsibility of all biomedical researchers is to protect human subjects. If the primary responsibility of a researcher is to protect human subjects, then all other research responsibilities have a lower level of importance. Therefore, when there is a conflict between protecting patients and preserving scientific honesty, patient protection must win. It is useful to list the set of conditions for which dishonesty may be a reasonable ethical choice (List 16.2.1).

LIST 16.2.1. CONDITIONS UNDER WHICH IT MAY BE OKAY TO LIE (ALL CONDITIONS MUST HOLD)

- The lie protects a human subject for which you have a fiduciary responsibility.
- You are certain that the lie will not harm another human subject.
- You do not personally benefit from the lie.
- The lie is not part of a plan to mislead people.
- There is no way to protect the patient that does not involve lying.
- The liar is willing to accept any negative consequences that may ensue.

In 2005, a situation arose wherein a highly respected scientist was caught in a lie (160). Dr. Hwang Woo-Suk, a South Korean scientist, was the first person to produce a stem cell line from a cloned human embryo and was the first person to successfully clone a dog. When allegations that two junior members of his scientific team had donated their own eggs for experiments, Dr. Hwang denied that the allegations were true.

The significance of the allegations rose from the general principle that junior members of a scientific team have a dependent relationship with their laboratory chief. A request from a laboratory chief to a junior scientist for body parts (in this case, eggs) would be considered coercive. For this reason, it is generally accepted that laboratory chiefs should not use body parts donated by their junior staff.

According to Dr. Hwang, as reported in The Times, his researchers donated their eggs without his knowledge using false names. When he learned the truth, the researchers asked Dr. Hwang to protect their privacy. Dr. Hwang agreed to protect their privacy. When he was asked if anyone in his staff had supplied eggs used in his research, he lied. According to Dr. Hwang, the lie was intended to protect his workers.

When the truth surfaced, Dr. Hwang confessed his errors and resigned from all his official posts. Had he behaved unethically? His lie served to protect the privacy of his staff, but it also served his own interests by defending his work. Because the lie was not a "selfless" lie, it did not fulfill all the requisites of an "ethical lie." To Dr. Hwang's credit, he accepted full responsibility for the consequences of his lie. Once scientists are caught in a lie, all their research results come under suspicion. At the time that this section is being written (March, 2006) Dr. Hwang's life seems to be playing out like a Greek tragedy.

The issue of "trust" in science is a long-embraced concept. It is my personal opinion that scientists try to be honest, but they are rarely able to be objective about their own research. Because medical science is vital to the future of mankind, the results of scientific research should be prepared in a manner that maximizes our ability to review the methods and data that are the basis of published scientific assertions. One of the primary roles of the biomedical informatician is to prepare and distribute research data. The implementation of a process that opens all scientific efforts to objective review requires great wisdom. This is one more reason why biomedical informaticians have a crucial role in medical science.

Are there any other circumstances when lying may be acceptable? Yes, it may be okay for a scientist to lie so long as the false statements are identified as lies by the liar. This seemingly ridiculous position has practical value. As discussed in Chapter 12, the de-identification of database records may hinge on the nonuniqueness of any single record in the database.[42] If all the records in a database are nonunique, then it is impossible to link any record to a specific person (because the nonunique record may belong to one of several different persons).

Suppose a researcher has a database that has some unique records. For the sake of argument, suppose a database contains a million de-identified patient records. Of those million records, 100 are unique (i.e., 100 records have no other records that contain the same set of data values). The researcher intends to use the database for epidemiologic studies. She knows that the 100 unique records, even though they have been carefully stripped of patient identifiers, are vulnerable to re-identification. She could ensure patient anonymity by "inventing" duplicate records for the 100 unique records. This would insure nonuniqueness for every data record. However, data fabrication is a type of lying and is a universally condemned action.

Suppose the researcher invented 100 duplicate records and released the database to the public with the caveat that a small percentage of the records were duplicated to protect the anonymity of all the participating subjects. Who would be hurt? One hundred duplicate records (from a million) would not greatly affect scientific analyses of the dataset. Though there was data fabrication, the researcher openly announced her action and provided fair warning to those who chose to use the data. Patients were protected from research harm. In the opinion of the author, no ethical violation was committed.

16.3. WHEN CAN YOU USE UNCONSENTED IDENTIFIED MEDICAL RECORDS?

In the United States and many other countries, a "person" is defined as someone who is alive. Deceased patients are not considered human subjects and do no qualify for regulatory human subject protections under the U.S. Common Rule. In the United States, HIPAA (Health Insurance Portability and Accountability Act) protections extend to deceased patients. HIPAA specifies the circumstances under which autopsy data and medical records collected prior to the patient's death can be used for research (List 16.3.1).

LIST 16.3.1. HIPAA: 164.512 USES AND DISCLOSURES FOR WHICH CONSENT, AN AUTHORIZATION, OR OPPORTUNITY TO AGREE OR OBJECT IS NOT REQUIRED

(I) STANDARD: USES AND DISCLOSURES FOR RESEARCH PURPOSES.

(1) Permitted uses and disclosures. A covered entity may use or disclose protected health information for research, regardless of the source of funding of the research, provided that: ....

(iii) Research on decedent's information. The covered entity obtains from the researcher:

(A) Representation that the use or disclosure is sought is solely for research on the protected health information of decedents;

(B) Documentation, at the request of the covered entity, of the death of such individuals; and

(C) Representation that the protected health information for which use or disclosure is sought is necessary for the research purposes.

Autopsy data is a remarkably underrated source of biomedical data. In 1760, Giovanni Battista Morgagni published "De Sedibus, et Causis Morborum per Anatomen Indagatis Libri Quinque," containing the results of 640 autopsies. This work marked the birth of scientific autopsies. Unfortunately, the past 250 years have not seen substantial advances in the way we collect and organize autopsy data. For the most part, autopsy reports are long, complex, idiosyncratic narrative tomes.

Although pathologists have recognized the importance of collecting autopsy data in a standard manner using well-described data elements, a popular standard for autopsy data has never emerged.

The lack of well-organized autopsy data is particularly unfortunate because aggregated autopsy reports have particular value in biomedical informatics. Autopsy data can be integrated with laboratory tests, radiology reports, pharmacy data, and clinical data collected through the patient's life. A medical research database keyed to autopsy data can be assembled directly from hospital information systems without obtaining patient consent for any of the data records. The purposes of such a database are many (List 16.3.2).

LIST 16.3.2. SUGGESTED RESEARCH PURPOSES OF AN AUTOPSY DATABASE INTEGRATED WITH THE ELECTRONIC MEDICAL RECORDS OF THE DECEASED PATIENTS

- Validating the sensitivity and specificity of new diagnostic tests, including imaging techniques and new medical devices
- Determining the extent of disease, at death, of persons enrolled in clinical trials, as a measurement of response to different treatment protocols
- Documenting adverse effects of medications administered during the patient's life
- Correlating autopsy findings with pharmacogenomic databases, attributing diseases found at autopsy with specific gene variations

Even though it may be legal, is there not something unethical about using autopsy results without consent? Is there not a fiduciary obligation that extends to the relatives of the deceased patient? Maybe not. With the exception of forensic autopsies conducted by medical examiners or through the authority of a coroner's office, all autopsies performed in the United States are performed at the request of the deceased patient's next-of-kin. The procedure for obtaining next-of-kin consent for all nonforensic autopsies guarantees that the interests of relatives are protected. The autopsy request form typically specifies that the autopsy will be used for teaching and research purposes. It follows that data from routine hospital autopsies can be used in research databases, without violating the wishes of the patients' next-of-kin relatives.

On rare occasions, reliance on the next-of-kin to make final and binding decisions regarding the autopsy may have unintended consequences. The most common problem occurs when the next-of-kin makes a decision against the wishes of other members of the patient's family. For instance, a Native American may be married to a woman who is not a Native American and who may not respect Native American beliefs. As next-of-kin, she may permit an unrestricted autopsy, knowing that this may deeply offend her husband's relatives. On occasion, the next-of-kin will be estranged from the deceased and may act in a manner contrary to the expressed wishes made by the patient prior to dying. On rare occasions, a person will dishonestly represent himself or herself as next-of-kin and sign the autopsy request illegally.

The biomedical informatician must be sensitized to the manner in which data is collected and should try her best to behave in a manner that is more than fair but less than perfect. In many cases, when a legal autopsy request is signed by the deceased patient's next-of-kin but challenged by other members of the family, the pathologist will try to defer to the family's wishes to the extent possible without violating the autopsy request form. This may mean performing a "minimally invasive" autopsy and ensuring that the organs stay in the body for burial. This may also mean excluding some autopsy reports from research databases and excluding some autopsy tissues from research tissue archives.

In the United States, once an autopsy record has been added to a research database, the patient's past medical records, past archived tissues, and the tissues obtained during autopsy can be used in scientific efforts that have an expected societal benefit. Perhaps an unintended benefit of the **Electronic Medical Record (EMR)** is that it automatically expands the content of an autopsy. When a patient dies, the EMR becomes a ready-made, time-stratified collection of research data and tissues that augments the autopsy report.

16.4. WHEN CAN YOU USE PROPRIETARY SOFTWARE AND STANDARDS?

People often think they have bought software when they have only bought a software license. In legalistic terms, buying software is an activity closely akin to procuring a fishing permit. A software license specifies the permitted and restricted uses of the software. The consequences of using licensed software for scientific works are sometimes highly problematic. Sometimes a software application produces files or data objects that can be viewed only with a licensed copy of the software. This may effectively consign those wishing to see derivative works (works produced using the software) to buying their own software license. Software license provisions that apply to the user and propagate to the user's users, are sometimes referred to as viral provisions.

Scientists must be able to review and replicate the works produced by their colleagues. Software should facilitate the process of sharing scientific knowledge. When software licenses serve as impediments to data sharing, researchers should consider alternate tools.

Researchers should ask themselves a number of questions before using licensed software in their research efforts (List 16.4.1).

LIST 16.4.1. QUESTIONS THAT RESEARCHERS SHOULD ASK BEFORE PURCHASING A SOFTWARE LICENSE

- Will colleagues who want to review my work be required to buy their own version of the software?
- Can the software be modified by the licensee?
- Will the software export data files in a standard format that can be exchanged with and used by colleagues who use other software applications?
- Will the software export data files that can be publicly distributed (as in supplementary files distributed with a manuscript), or publicly displayed (as on a Web site)?
- Does the software license contain reach-through clauses? A reach-through is a legal device through which licensees must pay royalties on intellectual property produced with the help of the licensed software.

Most people do not think of standards as intellectual property, assuming that the value of any standard is determined by its universal availability and by its wide adoption. This assumption is not always true. Creating a standard takes time, intellectual resources, and money. Organizations that develop standards are sometimes eager to recoup their investments, and there is no law that prohibits standards developers from turning a profit. Standards may be distributed under restrictive licenses. A reasonable and common provision in "standards" licenses is a prohibition against modifying the standard. Some provisions in "standards" licenses are just as restrictive as provisions in software licenses. Users of standards should ask themselves the same set of questions as users of commercial software. In particular, users will want to determine whether intellectual property annotated or organized in conformity with a licensed standard can be freely distributed to colleagues who have not purchased the standard.

Software and standards developers who restrict the use of their products, either through copyright, patent, or license, should explicitly list the "fair uses" of their products. It would be helpful if licenses were written to permit uses that have societal value.

16.5. WHEN IS IT OKAY TO HAVE CONFLICTS OF INTEREST?

A conflict of interest is a type of bias. A bias occurs when a person prefers one thing to another for reasons that have nothing to do with the qualities of either. This bias may be due to bigotry or some form of prejudice. If a person is acting for an entity and chooses one thing over another because she benefits by making the choice, then this is a conflict of interest. Her interest should have been confined to making the best choice for the institution or corporation she represents. By personally benefiting from the choice, her interests are in conflict.

Many people seem to think that conflicts of interest are allowable if the conflicts are disclosed. This is wrong. Disclosure never reverses a conflict. The purpose of a disclosure is to warn us when someone cannot provide an honest evaluation of topics for which conflicts exist. Ethical speakers will defer speaking on a topic for which they have a conflict of interest.

Disclosure applies to informed consent documents. Imagine a situation where an investigator has a financial interest in a human subjects study for which informed consent is required. The informed consent document discloses the scientist's financial conflict of interest, indicating that the scientist may profit from the study. Is the disclosure included in the consent form an adequate protection for patients? Does it satisfy an ethical requirement?

This is a very difficult question. Scientists often stand to benefit from a biomedical study when the outcome validates their hypothesis. This is true even when the scientists have no financial interest in the study other than continuance of their contracts or the likelihood of attracting future grants. Investigators and institutions have an ethical obligation to try their very best to mitigate the effects of conflicts of interest. A reasonable response may involve blinded studies in which the results are evaluated by an external group of statisticians with no financial interest in the study. Another option may involve following a strict policy to publish the raw data from studies, regardless of the study's outcome, so that unconflicted colleagues can draw independent judgments. Investigators, Institutional Review Boards, and institutions should document all conflicts and the actions they take to ensure that, despite conflicts of interest, a fair and safe study will be conducted.

16.6. WHEN IS IT OKAY TO REFUSE CONSENT?

In the realm of biomedical informatics, ethical obligations seem to apply exclusively to the investigator. The patients themselves seem to be insulated from any ethical rebuke. A cornerstone of human subjects ethics holds that patients should never be coerced into participating in studies.

The quality of care that a patient receives should not be influenced by her decision to participate in a study.

There is no prohibition against asking people to think about the their personal conduct. Though it is inappropriate to raise these issues any-time during the consent process, the ethics of biomedical research consent is fair game at any other time. I am surprised by the paucity of magazine articles, newspaper editorials, radio spots, and television interviews that deal with the subject of research consent. The public should be aware that biomedical research produces advances in medical diagnosis and treatment. These advances depend on patients consenting to the use of their records and archived tissues for research. For most research in the field of biomedical informatics, the only risks to the patient are loss of confidentiality and privacy. The public should know that scientists employ methods that greatly reduce any chance that confidentiality or privacy could be breached.

Some people oppose the use of their records and their archived tissues for any research, regardless of the risks. Sometimes they have an anti-scientific attitude toward life, and this is certainly their right. It would be simple justice if those who do not support science were excluded from the benefits obtained through medical research. New pharmaceuticals could come with a short note on the product insert indicating that human subjects were used to develop the drug. Those opposed to human subject studies could opt out of taking the drug. Of course, this is not how life works. However, patients should understand that human subject studies support research efforts that will eventually benefit themselves and their families.

16.7. IS IT ETHICAL TO PATENT BIOMEDICAL DISCOVERIES?

Imagine that you have been studying a large database of clinical laboratory data that is integrated with a medical encounter database, a pharmacy database, and a clinical outcomes database. To your delight, you find that the ratio of two commonly performed blood tests is a highly accurate predictor of clinical response to a hormonal treatment for prostate cancer. Using the ratio of two tests, you can predict which patients will benefit from the hormonal treatment and which patients will not benefit. Is it ethical to patent this discovery?

Patents make sense when you have developed a manufacturing process or a machine that will be of interest to some industrial concern. If you have done the work, then you should share in the profits that will be made by the manufacturer.

But if you have done something that is implemented by individuals (not manufacturers) and will have direct patient benefits and would be abandoned if the patent were enforced, then a patent is a very bad idea. So a patent for tying a new kind of knot used in a surgical suture would probably not be a good idea. A patent for PET imaging might be a good idea (because individuals do not make their own PET machines).

The U.S. Congress apparently agrees. In 1999, Congress passed 35 U.S.C. 287 specifying conditions that would limit the damages collected by patent holders from healthcare practitioners (161).

> "With respect to a medical practitioner's performance of a medical activity that constitutes an infringement under section 271(a) or (b) of this title, the provisions of sections 281, 283, 284, and 285 of this title shall not apply against the medical practitioner or against a related health care entity with respect to such medical activity.
>
> (2) For the purposes of this subsection:
>
> (A) the term 'medical activity' means the performance of a medical or surgical procedure on a body, but shall not include (i) the use of a patented machine, manufacture, or composition of matter in violation of such patent, (ii) the practice of a patented use of a composition of matter in violation of such patent, or (iii) the practice of a process in violation of a biotechnology patent."

A reasonable inference is that if a patent were held on a new knot, surgeons would be permitted to use the knot during their performance of surgical procedures on patients. This new law may indicate a growing reluctance to permit patent holders to harm patients through a dogged pursuit of patent rights.

Where there is medical progress, there is the opportunity for profit. Scientists must search for guidance when they are tempted with money and fame. Inspiration comes from the past. On November 8, 1895, Wilhelm Roentgen performed the experiment that marked the discovery of X-ray imaging. Just six years later, in 1901, Roentgen's effort was awarded with the Nobel Prize. Roentgen declined to seek patents or proprietary claims on his discovery and even declined, unsuccessfully, the eponymous appellative, "Roentgen ray."

16.8. THE ETIQUETTE OF FREE SOFTWARE USAGE

The software and data listed in the Appendix are all free. Many programming languages, word processors, databases, and so on are free. Of course, this free software was produced by intense efforts of people who need to feed, clothe, and shelter themselves and their families. Am I ethically obliged to pay these people for their work?

Free and open source programmers foster the ideal of a community of like-minded workers who contribute to and benefit from distribution of open source software. Those who use open source software may consider joining the open source community by participating in open source projects, distributing their own software products under an open source license, and donating money directly to open source organizations.

16.9. HOARDING RESEARCH DATA

Does all experimental data need to be shared? In 1909, Paul Ehrlich tested over 900 arsenical compounds for efficacy against *Trypanosome cruzi*. None of the test compounds were active. A colleague, Sahachiro Hata, found that compound 606 had unanticipated antitreponemal (i.e., anti-syphilis) activity. Ehrlich and Hata tested 606 on laboratory animals with syphilis and achieved a high rate of cure. In 1910 the drug was released to the world under the name of Salvarsan. The trial data collected by Ehrlich and Hata must have been immense, but there was no real need to distribute the data collected on hundreds of failed experiments. The data had only historical value once the clinical results confirmed Salvarsan's efficacy and safety on humans.

Scientists who prefer not to share their research data have no trouble finding historical precedent for which data sharing was unnecessary and, basically, a waste of everyone's time. It is easy to find plausible reasons for data hoarding (List 16.9.1).

LIST 16.9.1. COMMON EXCUSES FOR REFUSING TO SHARE RESEARCH DATA

- The data is confidential and it would be unethical to release the data to the public.
- Members of the public may misunderstand the data.
- Competitors may purposely misinterpret the data to dispute the validity of the work.
- Preparing the data in a format that can be distributed to the public (e.g., the Internet) requires time, effort, expertise, and money that could be better spent on research activities.
- The data owner wishes to control the direction of research in her specific area, and the data owner's control would be lost if everyone in the field had access to the data.
- The data owner is offended that anyone would question her integrity by asking to review the primary data.
- The data is integral to another manuscript that has not yet been published. Distributing the data would violate the publisher's ban on pre-publication release of research data.

Nonetheless, there are times when data sharing is essential (List 16.9.2).

LIST 16.9.2. WHEN IS DATA SHARING IMPORTANT?

- When the data contributes one piece of a planned multi-part research effort towards which many different laboratories contribute
- When the data has general value for many other research efforts
- When the validity of the assertions drawn from the data are doubted
- When the validity of the data itself is doubted
- When there is reason to believe that the data can be re-examined to yield additional results

The current recommendation for data sharing, issued by the National Academy of Sciences, is that researchers share the data that supports assertions contained in their scientific manuscripts (28). Only data that supports published assertions needs to be shared.

Every once in a while, scientists can be asked to work pro bono (for the good). De-identifying, organizing, and distributing research data is sometimes an ethical obligation. The only exception that may apply is when data has an evil purpose. For instance, the data on an anthrax experiment may be justifiably withheld if it could be used to maximize the lethal effect of spores. Exceptions notwithstanding, scientists who decline to share their data should likewise refrain from publishing assertions based on withheld data.

16.10. ARE THERE ETHICAL ALTERNATES TO HIPAA'S SAFE HARBOR DE-IDENTIFICATION METHOD?

In numerous conversations and lectures, I have heard the repeated assertion that unconsented research can be performed only on de-identified records AND that HIPAA specifies 18 so-called safe harbor identifiers that, if stripped from records, achieve de-identification.

This assertion is inaccurate and misleading. HIPAA actually provides two different options for de-identifying medical records. One option involves stripping medical records of the so-called safe harbor identifiers (List 16.10.1). Actually, HIPAA specifies that after all the safe harbor identifiers are removed, institutions must ensure that it "does not have actual knowledge that the information could be used alone or in combination with other information to identify an individual who is a subject of the information" (Section 164.514 of HIPAA). This last requirement imposes a significant burden beyond merely stripping identifiers from a patient record.

As an alternative to the safe harbor de-identification method, HIPAA permits institutions to use novel methods for de-identification, so long as the alternate method protects patient privacy.

LIST 16.10.1. EXCERPTED FROM 164.514: OTHER REQUIREMENTS RELATING TO USES AND DISCLOSURES OF PROTECTED HEALTH INFORMATION

(i) A person with appropriate knowledge of and experience with generally accepted statistical and scientific principles and methods for rendering information not individually identifiable:

(ii) Applying such principles and methods, determines that the risk is very small that the information could be used, alone or in combination with other reasonably available information, by an anticipated recipient to identify an individual who is a subject of the information; and

(iii) Documents the methods and results of the analysis that justify such determination;

The HIPAA provision that permits institutions to develop their own methods for record de-identification has created, in just a few sentences, a new area of investigative science within the field of biomedical informatics. It permits anyone to invent, and profit from, new methods of record de-identification.

When record de-identification is infeasible, the next option for biomedical informaticians is to acquire patient consent for the use of identified records. Unfortunately, biomedical informaticians typically require thousands or millions of patient records, and securing patient consent for each record is usually impossible.

HIPAA provides an opportunity to conduct research on identified medical records, without patient consent, under certain circumstances (List 16.10.2).

LIST 16.10.2. EXCERPTED FROM SECTION 164.512: USES AND DISCLOSURES FOR WHICH CONSENT, AN AUTHORIZATION, OR OPPORTUNITY TO AGREE OR OBJECT IS NOT REQUIRED

(ii) Waiver criteria. A statement that the IRB or privacy board has determined that the alteration or waiver, in whole or in part, of authorization satisfies the following criteria:

(A) The use or disclosure of protected health information involves no more than minimal risk to the individuals;

(B) The alteration or waiver will not adversely affect the privacy rights and the welfare of the individuals;

(C) The research could not practicably be conducted without the alteration or waiver;

(D) The research could not practicably be conducted without access to and use of the protected health information;

(E) The privacy risks to individuals whose protected health information is to be used or disclosed are reasonable in relation to the anticipated benefits if any to the individuals, and the importance of the knowledge that may reasonably be expected to result from the research;

(F) There is an adequate plan to protect the identifiers from improper use and disclosure;

(G) There is an adequate plan to destroy the identifiers at the earliest opportunity consistent with conduct of the research, unless there is a health or research justification for retaining the identifiers, or such retention is otherwise required by law; and

(H) There are adequate written assurances that the protected health information will not be reused or disclosed to any other person or entity, except as required by law, for authorized oversight of the research project, or for other research for which the use or disclosure of protected health information would be permitted by this subpart.

Members of Institutional Review Boards should know that they are expected to weigh the benefits and risks of research and should approve beneficial research proposals whenever permissible. Investigators should avail themselves of regulations that move their research forward so long as the research will benefit society and will be conducted without harming patients.

16.11. CAN YOU USE CONSENTED DATA FOR UNCONSENTED RESEARCH?

Informed consent documents typically contain a brief description of the proposed research, along with a detailed list of the possible harms that might result from participation in the research project. In the case of most biomedical informatics projects, human subjects' risks are confined to loss of confidentiality and loss of privacy.

Consented databases sometimes have research value that was unanticipated when the consented project was planned. Patients suffering from asthma may have consented to the use of their medical records and their DNA for a particular study. The study may have been designed to find a complex genetic profile for persons at risk of developing asthma. A large database with thousands of consented records may have been assembled over a decade, and at great expense. Following the study, another set of researchers may have interest in understanding the different drug responses among asthmatics to a commonly administered asthma drug. The second set of researchers (who we will call "the petitioners") may wish to examine profiles of DNA SNPs (single nucleotide polymorphisms) that will distinguish the responders from the nonresponders. The petitioners come upon a manuscript from the first set of researchers (who we will call "the caretakers") and instantly recognize that the existing database of medical records and DNA samples would be ideal for their study. If the petitioners had access to these materials, then it would save their team a decade of time and millions of dollars in funding costs.

The petitioners ask the caretakers for all their consented data and DNA. The caretakers express sympathy, but indicate that their hands are tied. The petitioner study was not included in the informed consent documents. In addition, the informed consent document expressly indicated that the research would be undertaken at the caretaker's institution. So there is no way in the world that they could oblige the petitioners.

The petitioners regroup and suggest another approach to the caretakers. Could the entire database and the included DNA samples be anonymized by the caretakers and delivered to the petitioners? The petitioners have no interest in knowing the identities of the patients included in the database, and both the Common Rule and HIPAA regulations permit the free use of anonymized data and tissues.

The caretakers are wary of this latest proposal. Though research on anonymized pre-existing records is exempted from U.S. regulatory restrictions, their institution requires IRB approval for all human subject research efforts. The caretakers and the petitioners draft a joint proposal sent to the IRBs of both the caretaker and the petitioner institutions. In the proposal, the methods of record anonymization are described. The methods of payment for services rendered by the caretaker institution are also explained in the proposal.

The caretaker institution swiftly rejected the proposal. The caretakers are informed that anonymizing the data is a transparent end-run around the informed consent process. The database was created for a specifically consented project. The DNA collection cannot be considered pre-existing material, as it was specifically collected for their study and was consented only for their study. Providing these materials to the petitioners would be a betrayal of the consenting patients and, if discovered, would undermine any future efforts to accrue participants in studies that require informed consent.

The petitioner institution also rejected the proposal. The IRB, after consultation with several geneticists, determined that DNA cannot be de-identified, as it uniquely determines the donor. The proposed study would involve identifiable material and would need to obtain prospective consent. In addition, the proposal indicated that the petitioner institution would make payments to the caretaker institution for receipt of the database and the DNA collection. The petitioner institution was concerned that a reputation for buying DNA might detract from the institution's reputation. The IRB feared that patron support for the institution may suffer if it were known that they paid money for human specimens in a scheme that circumvented the customary consent process.

This example is completely fictitious, but it is the author's perception that similar situations occur quite frequently. Ethics is a very personal decision, and the hypothetical decisions by the two imaginary IRBs should be respected because they both reflect sensitivity to the inherent rights of human subjects.

However, the author disagrees with both IRB decisions and would have approved the proposal without hesitation. In the opinion of the author, both IRBs have lost sight of their primary obligation, which is to approve research that can benefit society, if the research can be conducted without harming patients. Furthermore, rejecting the proposal, in this case, would result in millions of dollars of additional expense and the imposition of an additional decade of time spent accruing new patients into a second database. The time and money devoted to a second, duplicative database places a considerable burden on society, which should have been considered during the deliberations of both IRBs.

In the case of the hypothetical proposal, the caretakers would anonymize their collected data. Anonymized data can be used freely in research and is not subject (in the United States) to HIPAA or Common Rule regulations. So long as the consented data was collected for the purposes stated in the consent form, there is no reason to entertain the notion that the consenters were deceived. If the data is anonymized so that the identities of the database subjects are irreversibly lost to the petitioners, then no harm can come to any of the human subjects.

The objection made by the petitioner institution that DNA is unique for every person is true. The issue is whether the DNA samples, which are not associated with the names of patients, will be used to match against another database of DNA samples that are associated with the names of patients. What would be involved in re-identifying the patient who matches an anonymous DNA sample?

First, a malevolent person must have access to the caretaker's anonymized DNA collection. She would need to prepare the DNA specimen using advanced technology, such as CODIS (162), requiring access to a modern laboratory and scrupulous adherence to testing protocols. Once the CODIS profile is obtained for an unknown sample, she would need to gain access to a private and guarded database that links unique DNA profiles with names of people. If the patient from whom the DNA sample was obtained is included in the external database, then she may be able to attach a name to the experimental DNA sample. Finally, she would need to have a motive to justify this enormous effort and personal risk on her part. If she were discovered during any step in this elaborate process, then she would be liable to prosecution under HIPAA. It is difficult to imagine how a malevolent person would benefit from matching an anonymous DNA sample with a name. DNA specimens are ubiquitous in every medical center. Tissue biopsies, cytology specimens, body fluids, and sometimes blood samples, are archived for many years on the majority of patients who receive treatment. Malevolent persons intent on collecting DNA samples would have a much easier time if they directed their efforts toward samples routinely archived by pathology departments.

HIPAA regulations expect IRBs to use judgment to measure risks and benefits. From HIPAA Section 164.512, IRBs may determine whether "The privacy risks to individuals whose protected health information is to be used or disclosed are reasonable in relation to the anticipated benefits if any to the individuals, and the importance of the knowledge that may reasonably be expected to result from the research." In this case, there seems to be very little risk that anyone would use anonymized DNA samples to breach patient privacy. If the petitioner's IRB is really concerned, then they can solve the problem by having the DNA samples destroyed after they have been used in the study.

In the opinion of the author, IRBs overreach when they try to anticipate the unspecified desires and interests of patients. The job of the IRB is to protect patients from harm, not to protect the imagined interests of patients.

16.12. WHEN IS IT ETHICAL TO ENFORCE COPYRIGHT ON MEDICAL RESEARCH PUBLICATIONS?

Copyright is a legalistic invention that permits authors to retain rights on distributed works. The most important of these rights is that the copyright owner can prepare and sell copies of the work, and nobody else can do the same.

When a publication is a biomedical work, there may be instances when infringements of copyright would benefit society. For instance, a manuscript may include an improved procedure for extracting intact RNA from archived tissue samples. The author has not patented the procedure, but copyright applies to the text in the manuscript. The organizers of a scientific meeting would like to copy the methods section of the manuscript and distribute a free copy to each of the 5,000 attendees at the conference. The organizers are of the opinion that this action would fall under the Fair Use Provisions of the Copyright act, as the purpose of distributing the excerpted text would have an educational purpose. Their legal counsel cautions that the distribution of the method is intended to enhance the overall value of the scientific meeting. She suggests that the organizers obtain legal permission to reproduce the excerpted text. Because the text was published in a journal, and the author had transferred copyright to the journal publisher, permission must be obtained from the publisher.

Life would be so much simpler if copyright owners (publishers or authors) stipulate from the outset the fair uses of their copyrighted content. For instance, an author may stipulate that entities may freely republish up to two images and up to a total of 300 extracted words from the text without violating copyright, provided that full attribution of copyright ownership is attached. Attribution would typically require that the copied images and text would contain a short comment indicating the source of the material.

It is the opinion of the author that owners of copyright have an opportunity to clarify the allowable uses of their copyrighted materials. This ethical act will benefit society by enhancing data sharing.

16.13. IS IT OKAY TO PROFIT FROM TISSUE BANKING SERVICES?

In 1999, scandal broke in Alder Hey Hospital, Liverpool. A formal inquiry concluded that thousands of infant organs and other body parts had been removed from deceased children and stored by the hospital's pathology department, without consent from the parents (163).

Numerous instances of malpractice occurred, including the unethical and illegal retention of organs, falsifying research applications and postmortem reports, ignoring specified limitations on postmortem examination, and lying to parents about postmortem findings (164).

The Alder Hey scandal serves to remind us that tissues, once removed from patients, may follow a strange and sinister destiny.

One of the few precedents dealing with the rights of patients over their removed tissues is the strange case of Moore v Regents of the University of California. The basic facts of this case are that John Moore had hairy cell leukemia treated successfully by splenectomy in 1976, at UCLA. Mr. Moore was called back to UCLA between 1976 and 1983 for blood work that, according to his UCLA physicians, could only be done at UCLA. Suspecting something fishy, Moore discovered that his UCLA doctor had used Moore's spleen cells to create an immortalized cell line. The cell line was named Mo-line and was awarded a patent (patent number 4,438,032) that is reputed to have a value in the billions of dollars.

Moore sued the Regents of UCLA over a variety of issues, claiming that UCLA did not inform him that his spleen would be used to create a commercial product, and that he should be assigned some intellectual property rights to the cell line. In a somewhat controversial decision, the court rejected Mr. Moore's claim to the intellectual property derived from his spleen cells. In the court's opinion, Mr. Moore did not participate in the intellectual research process. The court did recognize that Mr. Moore's physician had a fiduciary obligation to inform Mr. Moore that his spleen would be used for a commercial purpose. The Court suggested that Mr. Moore might wish to pursue a subsequent case focused on his doctor's breach of proper disclosure.

The Moore case is controversial for several reasons. First, some people think that the California decision was made in error and exemplifies judicial insensitivity to the legitimate concerns of human subjects exploited in so-called "gene prospecting" ventures (165, 166). Secondly, few people seem to be agreed on the precedent, if any, established by the ruling. In my opinion, the Moore v Regents of the University of California ruling seems to at least imply that so-called preexisting tissues (remnants of tissues that were removed solely for the purpose of treating the patient) can be used for research purposes. The ruling does not seem to fully address the serious human subjects issue that emerges when scientists are accused of tricking patients into assisting in research aimed at producing a marketable project. The billions of dollars that may potentially derive from tissue-based research can cloud any scientist's judgment. Liz Douglas has written a provocative essay on human subject exploitation in the realm of genomic research (165).

Today, the value of human tissue samples is great. Virtually every large research organization (including federal funding agencies, pharmaceutical companies, and biotech research centers) creates tissue banks of frozen and paraffin-embedded human tissues along with clinical annotations abstracted from patient charts. Biomedical informaticians play a role in organizing large tissue databases and integrating tissue data with data derived from experimental tissue-based experimental studies. All of these activities result in intellectual property of commercial value. Questions relevant to the ethical conduct of biomedical informaticians who participate in tissue biorepositories follow (List 16.3.1).

LIST 16.13.1. ETHICAL QUESTIONS FOR BIOMEDICAL INFORMATICIANS BUILDING TISSUE BIOREPOSITORIES

- Does the use of the tissues for research purposes deprive patients of material that may have importance to their current or future medical care?
- Were the patients informed that their tissues may be used for research purposes that could result in commercial products, and that they (the patients) will not share in any resultant profits?
- Are patients fully protected from any harm that may result from the research on their tissues?
- Is the data collected from patient charts de-identified and is it compliant with the **"Minimum necessary" provision** described in HIPAA?
- Will drugs or treatments developed through this research be unaffordable to the patients who contributed to the repository (a common situation for research conducted on patients from developing countries)?

Of these listed questions, only the last needs explanation. It is possible that research resulting from the use of a patient's tissues may result in a new medication that the patient needs. The costs of the new medication may be enormous, and the profits to the scientist may also be enormous. In fact, the costs may be so great that patients whose tissues were used to develop the medication are priced out of buying the medication. When researchers use a patient's tissues to develop a new product that the patient cannot obtain, they clearly have acted in a manner that is not in the interests of the patient.

16.14. HOW LIKELY IS A HIPAA LAWSUIT?

Institutions seem to worry a lot about potential lawsuits. A popular view on this subject is that hospitals and medical academic centers are deep-pocket resources, ripe for megadollar legal assaults. HIPAA regulations, it may seem, threaten an onslaught of legal cases based on minor oversights.

The reaction to HIPAA in the medical community has been predictable. Many physicians deeply resent HIPAA as an intrusion into their professional lives and as a new legal burden. In a survey conducted by the Association of American Physicians and Surgeons, respondents were asked to complete the following: "I would describe the HIPAA Privacy Rule as:" The posted responses were largely negative (167) (List 16.14.1).

LIST 16.14.1. SOME PHYSICIAN REJOINDERS TO THE OPENING PHRASE, "I WOULD DESCRIBE THE HIPAA PRIVACY RULE AS:"

A disaster for future of medical practice and a windfall for trial attorneys

A disingenuous scam and a ridiculous waste of time and money

A further burden on physicians who are already having trouble surviving

A joke, not really privacy—maybe impossible to actually comply with

A major hassle; no protection for patients' privacy

A Trojan horse

A way not to pay doctors

A worthless but potentially damaging body of legislation

Another example of bureaucrats justifying their existence

Another governmental intervention to make medicine difficult

As noted, HIPAA comes equipped with civil and criminal penalties. The civil penalties are written in a manner to protect institutions that are trying their best to follow the rules and even provides an opportunity to avoid penalties by correcting violations. "HHS may not impose a civil money penalty under specific circumstances, such as when a violation is due to reasonable cause and did not involve willful neglect and the covered entity corrected the violation within 30 days of when it knew or should have known of the violation." (9)

Criminal penalties are reserved for purposeful disclosures of private information, with the stiffest penalties imposed when the disclosure is made with the intent to profit from the crime: "... $250,000 and up to ten years imprisonment if the wrongful conduct involves the intent to sell, transfer, or use individually identifiable health information for commercial advantage, personal gain, or malicious harm." (9)

Because the laws were written to avoid stiff penalties for unintentional lapses of HIPAA compliance, many people assumed that HIPAA prosecutions would be reserved for intentional violations, and for cases in which patients were actually harmed as a result of an intentional or unintentional violation and had complained to the Office of Civil Rights or to the Justice Department. In fact, this seems to be the case. The first punishment under HIPAA was reported by the Washington Post on Sunday, November 7, 2004 (approximately 20 months after the HIPAA Privacy Rule went into effect). A technician was sentenced to 16 months in prison for the wrongful disclosure of individually identifiable health information for economic gain. In the U.S. attorney's office press release, "This is the first criminal conviction in the United States under the health information privacy provisions of the Health Insurance Portability and Accountability Act (HIPAA) which became effective in April, 2003." The press release described the crime: "he obtained a cancer patient's name, date of birth and social security number.... he disclosed that information to get four credit cards in the patient's name.... he used several of those cards to rack up more than $9,000 in debt in the patient's name." (168)

This case met the expectations of many people (List 16.14.2).

LIST 16.14.2. EXPECTATIONS OF HIPAA PRIVACY ACT PROSECUTIONS

1. Prosecutions would not be frequent (the August 19, 2004 conviction was the first criminal conviction under the HIPAA regulations that went into effect 16 months earlier).
2. Criminal prosecutions would apply to cases where patients suffered actual harm as the result of a willful HIPAA violation (as in the first reported criminal prosecution).
3. Hospitals would not be subject to frivolous prosecutions for minor HIPAA violations that did not result in harm to patients.

16.15. BEING FAIR TO THE OUTRAGED PATIENT

Everyone who works with human subject data (which includes virtually every biomedical informatician) dreads the day when they are confronted by an emotional patient, face contorted with rage, who shouts, "You have destroyed my life! You took my confidential medical data and you used it without my permission to do awful terrible experiments. Now everyone knows everything about my problems, and I have lost my privacy and my dignity. Nobody at your medical center cares about me. I can't sleep at night thinking about what you have done to me. Nobody will help me. I will not rest until this stops and you are fired from your job and this medical center is shut down. Who gave you the right to destroy my life?!"

My perception is that dramatic encounters, such as this fictitious episode, are commonplace. The reflexive reaction of researchers to hostile patients is to label the patient as crazy and to dismiss the complaint as groundless. My own opinion is that such complaints usually have some basis in fact. I view these complaints as exaggerated reactions to commonly held (and sometimes accurate) perceptions that medical centers put their own interests above their obligation to protect patients.

Eric Drew is the young man who was the victim of the first crime prosecuted under HIPAA. His story is inspirational (169). He was diagnosed with acute lymphoblastic lymphoma. At the time of his diagnosis, he was told that, if left untreated, he would die in 5 days. His treatment involved chemotherapy (unsuccessful) and bone marrow transplants (from his half-sister, another hero in the story). During his treatments he was near death on several occasions.

But his illness was not his only problem. Shortly after his diagnosis, he became the victim of identity theft. He suspected that a hospital employee with access to his administrative records chose him as an easy mark because he was likely to die and nobody would try to solve the case. He asked for help from the police, from the FBI, from credit card companies, and from hospital administrators, and he received no assistance. Concurrent with his treatments, he pursued leads. Finally, a TV station aired surveillance tapes of a man making a purchase with one of the bogus credit cards. Once the tape was shown to a TV audience, the thief was identified as a hospital employee who worked just a few feet from where Mr. Drew was being treated.

Mr. Drew's struggles did not stop with the identification of the thief. Eric Drew had to navigate the judicial system and finally engineered the first criminal conviction under HIPAA, the landmark case described in the prior section. Mr. Drew's privacy was violated by a hospital employee. The hospital declined to help him find the culprit. A cynic may have concluded that the hospital was only interested in protecting itself.

Patients must believe that the top priority for everyone involved in biomedical research is patient care and protection. This means that the first responsibility of biomedical informaticians is to protect patients and to earn patient trust. In my personal opinion, every research document that reaches patients, every consent document, every institutional Web page that touches on the topic of research, every biomedical manuscript published, must convey the institution's commitment to protecting patients, and must describe research goals in a manner that emphasizes patient protections.

When patients protest that they do not trust hospitals and doctors, they must be reassured that their concerns are of the utmost importance to the hospital staff. The patient should be told that the staff is devoted to protecting the patient and that protecting her privacy is the first and foremost consideration of every member of the research team. A spokesman for the institution should explain, in detail, the measures taken to ensure that the data used in the study will always be held in the strictest confidence and that (assuming this is the case) even the members of the research team have no way of identifying the patients involved in the study. Most importantly, medical/research staff must live up to their promises.

Will this guarantee a career without remonstrations from irate human subjects? No, but it will probably reduce the frequency of these encounters.

16.16. WHEN CAN I BE WRONG?

Nobody is perfect, and nobody expects perfection from any human endeavor. Much of law is based on a standard of "reasonableness." Humans cannot be held to an unreasonable standard. The commented version of the final HIPAA ruling includes 390 occurrences of the string "reasonable" (List 16.16.1).

In life, if you try your best and think about how others view your efforts, then things will usually work out for you.

LIST 16.16.1. EXAMPLES OF "REASONABLENESS" STANDARD APPLIED WITHIN HIPAA

- Statutory Background… The security standard authority applies to both the transmission and the maintenance of health information, and requires the entities described in section 1172(a) to maintain reasonable and appropriate safeguards to ensure the integrity and confidentiality of the information, protect against reasonably anticipated threats or hazards to the security or integrity of the information or unauthorized uses or disclosures of the information, and to ensure compliance with part C by the entity's officers and employees.
- Sec. 164.502(g)… We proposed to define "individually identifiable health information" to mean information that is a subset of health information, including demographic information collected from an individual, and that:

  (1) Is created by or received from a health care provider, health plan, employer, or health care clearinghouse; and

  (2) Relates to the past, present, or future physical or mental health or condition of an individual, the provision of health care to an individual, or the past, present, or future payment for the provision of health care to an individual, and

     (i) Which identifies the individual, or

     (ii) With respect to which there is a reasonable basis to believe that the information can be used to identify the individual.
- Section 164.504(e)—Business Associates… A covered entity would have been in violation of this rule if the covered entity knew or reasonably should have known of a material breach of the contract by a business associate and it failed to take reasonable steps to cure the breach or terminate the contract."

Grantsmanship for Biomedical Informaticians

17.1. BACKGROUND

Many research policy analysts have asserted that the integration of biomedical data with clinical data is essential for medical progress. In the past several years, NIH has issued a variety of policies and grant solicitations to encourage the development of new methods for sharing experimental data and integrating heterogeneous biological and clinical datasets.

My own perception is that many of the grant applications in the field of biomedical informatics have been scientifically weak and have suffered from a higher-than-anticipated rate of rejection. Unresolved infrastructural issues have certainly contributed to the problem (List 17.1.1).

LIST 17.1.1. INFRASTRUCTURAL ISSUES THAT HAVE DELAYED ADVANCEMENT IN THE FIELD OF BIOMEDICAL INFORMATICS

- Lack of standards for acquiring, collecting, annotating, and exchanging all types of biomedical data
- Poor quality of clinical data in hospital information systems
- Inability of institutions to cope with HIPAA privacy regulations
- Reluctance of funded researchers to share data
- Questionable data analysis methodologies for new technologies
- Enormous administrative cost of obtaining and tracking the patient consent process
- High cost and complexity of privacy/security tasks related to prospective clinical studies
- Poor access to large clinically annotated banks of human tissue samples of a wide variety of diseases required to validate candidate diagnostic tests

These temporary problems should not discourage biomedical informaticians from seeking grant funding. To the contrary, infrastructural weaknesses should be viewed as important areas of future funding.

Funding agencies and study sections do not expect grant applications to be problem-free. They do expect grant applications to be written in a thoughtful manner that demonstrates that the investigators fully understand the fundamental problems inherent in their research. Applicants should have innovative and reasonable methods of coping with these problems.

The purpose of this chapter is to discuss approaches to writing grant applications in the field of biomedical informatics that will enhance the value of the research projects and that may increase the likelihood of getting funded.

17.2. INSTITUTIONAL RISKS FROM BIOMEDICAL INFORMATICS RESEARCH

To obtain aggregated records for the purpose of conducting medical research, a researcher must submit plans to an Institutional Review Board and/or Privacy Board. Institutional Review Boards are designed to protect patients from harms that may be associated with medical research. When research involves preexisting patient records (and does not put the patient at physical risk through a medical intervention), the risks to the patient are confined to issues of confidentiality or privacy.

The risks to the institution are violations of federal or state regulations that restrict the uses of patient records for research. The two federal laws that apply to this situation are the Common Rule and the HIPAA Privacy Regulations (9, 26). Both of these rules permit the unrestricted use of patient records when the records are de-identified (i.e., when the data in the record is disengaged from any links to the patient). A variety of technical approaches help researchers create and use large numbers of de-identified medical records (15, 21, 41–43, 111, 170–173).

De-identification protocols often have a "smoke and mirrors" quality conferred by their reliance on exotic mathematical constructions (e.g., one-way hash algorithms, prime number factorization, and zero-knowledge protocols). Institutional Review Boards tend to distrust methodologies that they cannot understand. It is my perception that reluctance to use available de-identification algorithms will fade after many institutions safely implement these protocols.

17.3. FUNDERS' RISKS FROM BIOMEDICAL INFORMATICS RESEARCH

Funding agencies do more than dole out taxpayers' cash to the top-scoring grant applications. One of the fundamental beliefs of large funding agencies is that productive research flows from planned initiatives conceived by leaders in the agencies. These agency initiatives are intended to steer scientists towards useful scientific endeavors. There is a trend at NIH and other medical funding agencies to invest more and more money in initiatives that reward translational efforts (i.e., efforts that can forseeably lead to improved medical care). It seems that in all translational initiatives, the role of biomedical informatics is stressed by the funders.

The CTSAs (Clinical and Translational Science Awards) are large grants for institutional translational science studies. The NIH hopes this program will become increasingly important. By 2012, the NIH expects to fund 60 CTSAs with a total of approximately $500 million per year (174). The NIH issued a strong statement on the role of biomedical informatics in CTSA projects (175) (List 17.3.1).

LIST 17.3.1. STATEMENT ON THE KEY FUNCTION OF BIOMEDICAL INFORMATICS IN CTSA FUNDING

"Biomedical Informatics is the cornerstone of communication within C/D/Is and with all collaborating organizations. Applicants should consider both internal, intra-institution and external interoperability to allow for communication among C/D/Is and the necessary research partners of clinical and translational investigators (e.g., government, clinical research networks, pharmaceutical companies, commercial vendors, laboratories, and equipment manufacturers). Biomedical Informatics support is expected to be flexible and innovative. Interoperability, security, workflow, usability and standards are essential areas of work. To facilitate the conduct of research in health care settings and the transfer of research findings into routine care, clinical and translational research must employ applicable standards (e.g., identifiers, vocabularies, transactions, security measures) adopted by the Department of Health and Human Services for use in U.S. health care and public health operations. All human subject data must be handled securely to ensure privacy and confidentiality. Biomedical informatics research activity should be innovative in the development of new tools, methods, and algorithms."

The NIH announcement stresses the same biomedical informatics fundamentals encountered again and again throughout this book: data interoperability, security, usability, standards, identifiers, vocabularies, transactions, privacy, security, tools methods, and algorithms. Funding agencies have reached the conclusion that without informatics infrastructure, there will be very little advancement in biomedicine. The best preparation for almost any biomedical grant involves working on the fundamentals of biomedical informatics and developing implementations that work within your own institution. In particular, institutions should develop ways of dealing with a set of common goals related to biomedical informatics (List 17.3.2).

LIST 17.3.2. SOME COMMON BIOMEDICAL INFORMATICS GOALS FOR INSTITUTIONS

- Develop a thoughtful approach to issues of human subjects protection, data organization, and data sharing. These may not be the focus of your research, but your research will suffer if you minimize their importance.
- Develop general protocols, approved by your IRB, for dealing with issues of confidentiality and data sharing. Experienced grant reviewers appreciate institutions that use a tested infrastructure to support their research staff.
- Develop collaborations with researchers outside your department and outside your institution. Translational research needs cross-disciplinary expertise, and biomedical informatics requires large datasets collected from multiple institutions. Funding agencies and grant reviewers understand this and will look favorably at innovative proposals that draw information and expertise from diverse sources.
- Train staff in the fundamentals of biomedical informatics. Hiring an informatics guru does not compensate for a staff of luddites (unless the guru can bring enlightenment to the entire staff).

17.4. SUGGESTIONS FOR BIOMEDICAL INFORMATICIANS WHO WRITE GRANT APPLICATIONS

Sadly, having a brilliant research idea is not sufficient to get a grant. It helps to have the following (List 17.4.1).

LIST 17.4.1. INGREDIENTS OF A GOOD GRANT APPLICATION IN THE FIELD OF BIOMEDICAL INFORMATICS (IN ORDER OF DESCENDING IMPORTANCE)

- A solid, credible set of specific aims (absolutely crucial)
- A known track record in the general area (usually determines who in the research team will be named the PI)
- Preliminary data
- A respected institutional infrastructure supporting the effort
- Collaborators who have the ability to provide a translational component
- Statistical expertise sufficient to convince the study section that the project is well designed and that the data analysis will be unimpeachable
- A clear understanding of data sharing and human subjects issues related to the project
- A sense of where the project will move after the initial funding period
- A sense of where the project complements other current efforts in the same field
- Good communication with a bright and competent program director (within the funding agency)
- An important idea

Everyone has heard stories of investigators who win funding with ridiculous hypotheses, ill-considered specific aims, no preliminary data, and no credible expertise in the field. Well, "time and chance happen to them all" (List 17.4.2).

LIST 17.4.2. AN ANCIENT OBSERVATION THAT SUCCESS FALLS OCCASIONALLY ON THE UNDESERVING

The race is not to the swift,

nor the battle to the strong,

nor bread to the wise,

> nor riches to the intelligent,
>
> nor favor to the men of skill;
>
> but time and chance happen to them all.
>
> —Book of Ecclesiastes 9:11

Life is not always fair, but investigators should not count on time and chance to bring funding to a poorly written grant. One of the most effective and practical ways of enhancing the likelihood of a grant award is to try your very best to write a thoughtful and clear description of your research plans and to consider the following suggestions (List 17.4.3).

LIST 17.4.3. SUGGESTIONS FOR RESEARCHERS

- When an investigator submits a work for publication, where the data is derived from patient records, the Methods section should include a description of the steps taken to minimize patient risks and should document that the IRB reviewed the research proposal. When these items are missing from a paper, editors and reviewers should feel free to ask authors to supply this information.

- When an investigator submits a grant application (particularly an application to a U.S. federal agency), a detailed strategy for protecting human subjects from research risks is required. Investigators should be aware that research using patient records is human subject research. Investigators should also be aware that current U.S. Federal Guidelines call for the inclusion of minorities, women, and children in clinical studies, unless there is a good reason for excluding them from the study population. For the purpose of satisfying federal inclusion guidelines, most agencies consider studies based on patient records to be clinical studies. A statement describing the inclusion of minorities, women, and children will be, in most circumstances, a requirement for biomedical informaticians who seek federal funding.

- Human subjects issues are a legitimate area of research for the biomedical informatician. Novel protocols for achieving confidentiality and security while performing increasingly ambitious studies (distributed network queries across disparate databases, extending the patient's record to collect rich data from an expanding electronic medical record, linking patient records to the records of relatives or probands, peer-to-peer exchange of medical data) will be urgently needed by the data mining community. Data miners would do well to stay abreast of regulations controlling the use of medical data so that they can develop regulation-compliant protocols for their activities.

- Anonymized data, by definition, cannot be linked to patients. Therefore, there is no legal or ethical reason to withhold anonymized datasets from the public. Quite the opposite. Anonymized datasets have enormous value to other researchers who can merge their data with yours, derive new ways of analyzing your data, or develop new questions that can be addressed by your dataset. Researchers who have created anonymized datasets should seriously consider publishing their data as a primary resource or as a secondary resource attached to any publication that results from the research project. Many journals and online publication services (such as PubMed Central and BioMed Central) encourage authors to submit their datasets as publication attachments.

- Funding agencies often have grandiose hopes for their research initiatives. They are sometimes willing to pay large sums of taxpayer money to support ambitious research projects. With few exceptions, large, complex, and expensive software projects will fail. Ironically, projects whose chief goal is to simplify data resources or reduce software complexity are seldom funded. I would encourage investigators to persevere. Complexity is an impediment to biomedical progress. A savvy study section may be receptive to a grant application that contains a credible set of goals for reducing complexity.

17.5. CLOSING PLATITUDES

It is vital for biomedical informaticians to approach their professional lives with a proper attitude. Can hackneyed advice help? Probably not. But it cannot hurt (List 17.5.1).

LIST 17.5.1. CLOSING PLATITUDES

- Insisting that something is true does not make it true. (Do not let people intimidate you into believing anything.)

- All biomedical informatics research is human subjects research and all human subjects must be protected from harm. (This feature distinguishes biomedical informatics from bioinformatics and reminds us that biomedical data comes from patients who place their trust in us.)

- Get funded so that you can do research; do not do research so that you can get funded. (Getting funded is not an achievement. Funding is a societal contract in which the investigator promises that he or she will achieve something.)
- The good fight is the fight that you lose and lose and lose until you win. (Do not worry about losing. Just worry about working toward an important goal.)
- Life is short but art is long. (This was written by Hippocrates around 400 BC and refers specifically to the art of medicine. Fundamental advances in biomedical informatics will endure beyond our short lives.)

References (Commented)

1. Innovation or stagnation: Challenge and opportunity on the critical path to new medical products. U.S. Department of Health and Human Services, Food and Drug Administration, 2004. http://www.fda.gov/oc/initiatives/criticalpath/whitepaper.html. Comment: The FDA explores the apparent slowdown in the release of new and innovative medical products.

2. Anderson NL, Anderson NG. The human plasma proteome: History, character and diagnostic prospects, *Mol Cell Proteomics*, 1:845–867, (2002). Comment: The Andersons have been leaders in the field of proteomic diagnostics for many years and have written a very useful review of blood-based protein diagnostics.

3. Benowitz S. Biomarker, Boom slowed by validation concerns. *J Natl Cancer Inst* 96:1356–1357, 2004. Comment: Realistic assessment of the slowdown in translational science in the cancer field.

4. Personalised medicines: Hopes and realities. The Royal Society, London, 2005. http://www.royalsoc.ac.uk/displaypagedoc.asp?id=15874. Comment: The Royal Society assessed the likely role of pharmacogenetics in clinical care and came to an unenthusiastic but realistic conclusion. "It is unlikely therefore that there will be an immediate change in clinical practice based on pharmacogenetics. Rather, there is likely to be a gradual increase in its clinical applications; its true potential may not become apparent for 15–20 years, during which time a great deal more information may become available about the practicalities of applying information derived from complex multifactorial systems in the clinic."

5. Strathern P: *A Brief History of Medicine from Hippocrates to Gene Therapy.* New York, Carroll and Graf Publishers, 2005, pp 169–171. Comment: This is a well-written and fascinating history of medicine.

6. Gordon R: *Great Medical Disasters*. New York, Dorset Press, 1986, pp 155–160. Comment: Lively essays on the history of medical catastrophes, including the black death, influenza, the long history of scurvy, yellow fever, and others.

7. Porter R: *The Greatest Benefit to Mankind*. New York, Norton, 1997, pp 304–347. Comment: A well-written and concise history of medicine.

8. Lipsett PA, Swoboda SM. Handwashing compliance depends on professional status. *Surg Infect* (Larchmt) 2(3):241–245, 2001. Comment: Physicians washed their hands much less frequently than nurses. Surprise!

9. Department of Health and Human Services. 45 CFR (Code of Federal Regulations), Parts 160 through 164. Standards for Privacy of Individually Identifiable Health Information (Final Rule). Federal Register, Volume 65, Number 250, Pages 82461–82510, December 28, 2000. http://aspe.hhs.gov/admnsimp/final/PvcPre01.htm. Comment: This is the much-feared HIPAA rule for protecting patient privacy.

10. Data Protection Act 1998. http://www.hmso.gov.uk/acts/acts1998/19980029.htm. Comment: The United Kingdom's Data Protection Act has many similarities to the U.S. HIPAA regulations. In particular, the Act applies exclusively to personal data, and personal data is defined as "data which relate to a living individual who can be identified-(a) from those data, or (b) from those data and other information which is in the possession of, or is likely to come into the possession of, the data controller."

11. Rosenthal DL. Cervical disease screening and detection: Emerging techniques in molecular diagnostic assays *Medical Laboratory Observer*, September, 2004. http://www.findarticles.com/p/articles/mi_m3230/is_9_36/ai_n6213176. Comment: Reports that approximately 50 million cervical cytology specimens (Pap smears) are screened each year in the United States.

12. Stranahan SQ. "Want a job?" *AARP Bulletin* 46:3–4, 2005. Comment: Reports that U.S. pharmacists fill 3.27 billion prescriptions each year.

13. American Hospital Directory. http://www.ahd.com/. Comment: The American Hospital Directory prepares a database from public and private sources, including Medicare claims data (MedPAR and OPPS), hospital cost reports, and other public use files obtained from the federal Centers for Medicare and Medicaid Services (CMS).

14. Fast Facts on U.S. Hospitals, 2005. www.aha.org/aha/resource_center/fastfacts/fast_facts_US_hospitals.html. Comment: Some useful statistics on U.S. hospitals.

15. Berman JJ. Zero-check: A zero-knowledge protocol for reconciling patient identities across institutions. *Archives of Pathology and Laboratory Medicine* 128:344–346, 2004. Comment: Large, multi-institutional studies often involve merging data records that have

been de-identified to protect patient privacy. Unless patient identities can be reconciled across institutions, individuals with records held in different institutions will be falsely "counted" as multiple persons when databases are merged. This paper describes a protocol that can reconcile individuals with records in multiple institutions.

16. Vista Monograph. 2005–2006. May 2005. Department of Veterans Affairs Health Administration. Office of Information. May, 2005. http://www.va.gov/vista_monograph/docs/vista_monograph2005_06.pdf. Comment: Monograph describing the U.S. Veteran's Administration free hospital information system. Includes instructions for obtaining the latest software distribution.

17. Malakoff D. Peer-review critic gets NIH rejects. *Science* 294:1255–1257, 2001. http://www.sciencemag.org/cgi/content/summary/294/5545/1255. Comment: Recounts the saga of George M. Kurzon, the physician who fought NIH through a FOIA claim and obtained the names of unfunded grant applicants.

18. LSU Law Center's Medical and Public Health Law Site. Cancer Registry Data May Be Available Through FOIA. http://biotech.law.lsu.edu/cases/adlaw/southern_illinoisan_brief.htm. Comment: A judicial ruling permitted a newspaper to receive cancer registry data through a FOIA (Freedom of Information Act) request. Though the data was not identified, the Illinois Department of Public Health argued that there was sufficient information in the records to permit a determined individual to discover the identities of some patients. The court ruled in favor of the newspaper, finding "Public health data collection is a worthwhile cause in the name of reducing morbidity and mortality. Although the strict confidentiality of health data is a noble cause and is worthy of statutory protections, ultimately a balance must be struck between public health concerns and privacy concerns."

19. Patent Infringement Lawsuits: By the Numbers, 2002. http://www.pearlltd.com/content/pat_inf_law.html. Comment: This fascinating site provides some amazing statistics related to the lucrative field of intellectual property rights. Did you know that the value of intellectual property owned by S&P 500 companies is approximately $3 trillion and that the amount spent on legal fees to litigate patent infringement lawsuits in the United States in 2000 was $4.2 billion?

20. The Digital Millennium Copyright Act of 1998. U.S. Copyright Office Summary. http://www.copyright.gov/legislation/dmca.pdf. Comment: The Digital Millennium Copyright Act (DCMA) became law on October 28, 1998. This legislation deals with international copyright protections for recorded works, particularly works that have been theft-protected by some technological device. Under most circumstances, the legislation prohibits users from engineering devices to counteract theft-protections added by the copyright holder

(there are exceptions). Interestingly, users are specifically permitted to make copies of copyrighted works, as specified in the following excerpt prepared by the U.S. Copyright Office: "Section 1201 divides technological measures into two categories: measures that prevent unauthorized access to a copyrighted work and measures that prevent unauthorized copying of a copyrighted work. Making or selling devices or services that are used to circumvent either category of technological measure is prohibited in certain circumstances, described below. As to the act of circumvention in itself, the provision prohibits circumventing the first category of technological measures, but not the second." Further, "This distinction was employed to assure that the public will have the continued ability to make fair use of copyrighted works. Since copying of a work may be a fair use under appropriate circumstances, section 1201 does not prohibit the act of circumventing a technological measure that prevents copying. By contrast, since the fair use doctrine is not a defense to the act of gaining unauthorized access to a work, the act of circumventing a technological measure in order to gain access is prohibited."

21. Berman JJ. Racing to share pathology data. *Am J Clin Pathol* 121:169–171, 2004. Comment: Patents are being sought on some of the basic methods for sharing biomedical data.

22. Jensen K, Murray F. Intellectual property enhanced: Intellectual property landscape of the human genome. *Science* 310:239–240, 2005. http://web.mit.edu/fmurray/www/papers/JensenMurray_SciencePolicyForum.pdf. Comment: This paper contains a fascinating graph of the human "patome." Four thousand three hundred and eighty-two of 23,688 human genes in NCBI are patented. The authors of the study mapped the patents to their location on human chromosomes Some of the human genes host more than one patent. For example, BMP7, an osteogenic factor, and CDKN2A, a tumor suppressor gene, both have more than 20 claims to patents.

23. To: Dr. Oliver Smoot, President, International Organization for Standardization, 2003. http://lists.w3.org/Archives/Public/www-international/2003JulSep/0213.html. Comment: A copy of correspondence from Tim Berners-Lee and to the President of the International Organization for Standardization, asking that the ISO not charge for ISO language codes, country codes, and currency codes.

24. Copyright Law of the United States of America and Related Laws Contained in Title 17 of the United States Code. http://www.copyright.gov/title17/92chap1.html#107. Comment: Describes fair use in the context of the Copyright Act. "The fair use of a copyrighted work, including such use by reproduction in copies or phonorecords or by any other means specified by that section, for purposes such as criticism, comment, news reporting, teaching (including multiple

copies for classroom use), scholarship, or research, is not an infringement of copyright."

25. Madey v Duke. http://www.ll.georgetown.edu subdirectory /federal/judicial/fed/opinions/01opinions/01-1567.html. Comment: The 2002 Madey v Duke court decision challenged the long-held belief that educational institutions and their academic faculty serve the public, without commercial motivations and without conflicts of interest.

26. Department of Health and Human Services. 45 CFR (Code of Federal Regulations), 46. Protection of Human Subjects (Common Rule). Federal Register, Volume 56, p. 28003–28032, June 18, 1991. http://www.hhs.gov/ohrp/humansubjects/guidance/45cfr46.htm. Comment: Although HIPAA (Health Insurance Portability and Accountability Act) privacy regulations seem to get all the attention, the Common Rule sets the basic principles for protecting patients from research risks, mandating the creation of Institutional Review Boards, and regulating the use of human tissues in support of medical research. It is essential reading for anyone involved in human subject research.

27. NIH Policy on Data Sharing, 2003. http://grants.nih.gov/grants/guide/notice-files/NOT-OD-03-032.html. Comment: This long-anticipated 2003 policy statement from the U.S. National Institutes of Health clarifies the important role of data sharing among scientists. It specifies that all grant applications to NIH requesting at least $500,000 in funds will need to have a section in the grant explaining how the investigators intend to share the data produced from grant-related research activities.

28. National Academy of Sciences Report: Sharing Publication-Related Data and Materials: Responsibilities of Authorship in the Life Sciences. The National Academies Press, Washington, D.C., 2003. Comment: This National Academy of Sciences Report, endorsed by many journal editors, clarifies that authors must submit to journals the primary data supporting their research conclusions.

29. CODATA Working Group on Archiving Scientific Data. http://www.nrf.ac.za/codata/. Comment: The CODATA working group tackles issues related to preserving and archiving scientific data.

30. Open Source Definition. http://www.opensource.org/docs/definition_plain.php. Comment: This definition is more akin to an open source "Bill of Rights." The first draft of the current definition is attributed to Bruce Perens, one of the principle players in the open source movement.

31. Open Source Initiative License Index. http://www.opensource.org/licenses/. Comment: The Open Source Initiative has an approval process for open source licenses. Software distributed under an

approved license can include a declaration that the software is "OSI Certified Open Source Software." The GNU copyleft licenses have been certified as open source software licenses.

32. Bethesda Statement on Open Access Publishing. http://www.earlham.edu/~peters/fos/bethesda.htm. Comment: Definition: an Open Access Publication meets the following two conditions: "1. The author(s) and copyright holder(s) grant(s) to all users a free, irrevocable, worldwide, perpetual right of access to, and a license to copy, use, distribute, transmit and display the work publicly and to make and distribute derivative works, in any digital medium for any responsible purpose, subject to proper attribution of authorship, as well as the right to make small numbers of printed copies for their personal use. 2. A complete version of the work and all supplemental materials, including a copy of the permission as stated above, in a suitable standard electronic format is deposited immediately upon initial publication in at least one online repository that is supported by an academic institution, scholarly society, government agency, or other well-established organization that seeks to enable open access, unrestricted distribution, interoperability, and long-term archiving (for the biomedical sciences, PubMed Central is such a repository)."

33. Public Library of Science (PLOS) Definition of Open Access. http://www.plos.org/about/openaccess.html. Comment: PLOS uses the Creative Commons Attribution License for its open access publications.

34. GNU Free Documentation License. http://www.gnu.org/copyleft/fdl.html. Comment: A GNU license for manuals, textbooks, and other documents.

35. What is Copyleft? http://www.gnu.org/copyleft/. Comment: The GNU organization publishes two licenses that are used for software produced by GNU and by anyone who would like to distribute their software under the terms of the GNU license. They are referred to as copyleft licenses, because they primarily serve the software users, rather than the software creators. One of the GNU licenses, the General Public License, covers most software applications. The GNU Lesser General Public License, formerly known as the GNU Library General Public License, is intended for use with software libraries or unified collections of files comprising a complex application, language, or other body of works.

36. Stallman R. Why "Free Software" is better than "Open Source." http://www.gnu.org/philosophy/free-software-for-freedom.html. Comment: In practice there is very little difference between the free software movement and the open source initiative. This essay by Richard Stallman, guru of the free software movement, stresses philosophic differences between these two related projects.

37. Contents: Volume 34, Database Issue. Nucleic Acids Research. January 1, 2006. http://nar.oxfordjournals.org/content/vol34/suppl_1/index.dtl. Comment: The yearly biology database issue lists over 800 databases. The descriptions of the different databases are available as open access articles.

38. Vermillion CO. Location of tumor diagnoses in a standard nomenclature punched-card disease index. *J Am Med Assoc* 165:2184–2185, December 28, 1957. Comment: This 1957 paper is perhaps the earliest description of a computerized index for medical diagnoses based on a standard nomenclature.

39. Wikipedia: Jesse Gelsinger. http://en.wikipedia.org/wiki/Jesse_Gelsinger. Comment: This Wikipedia article recounts the tragic death of Jesse Gelsinger, a volunteer in a gene therapy experiment conducted by the University of Pennsylvania.

40. Bren L. Human Research Reinstated at Johns Hopkins, with Conditions. U.S. Food and Drug Administration, FDA Consumer magazine, September–October, 2001. http://www.fda.gov/fdac/features/2001/501_john.html. Comment: On June 2, 2001, a 24-year-old healthy volunteer, Ellen Roche, died in an asthma study at Johns Hopkins Hospital. The investigation uncovered irregularities in the process by which human research subjects are protected from harm. For a short while, federally funded human research studies at Johns Hopkins were suspended.

41. Sweeney L. Guaranteeing anonymity when sharing medical data, the Datafly system. *Proc American Medical Informatics Association* 51–55, 1997. Comment: Latanya Sweeney was one of the first researchers to show that personal data extracted from different databases can be connected to identify patients whose names were removed from clinical research datasets.

42. Sweeney L. Three computational systems for disclosing medical data in the year 1999. *Medinfo* 9(Pt 2), 1124–1129, 1998. Comment: This is another contribution from Latanya Sweeney, who has pioneered computational methods for safely disclosing medical data without breaching patient confidentiality.

43. Malin B, Sweeney L. How (not) to protect genomic data privacy in a distributed network: Using trail re-identification to evaluate and design anonymity protection systems. *J Biomed Inform* 37:179–192, 2004. Comment: Latanya Sweeny was one of the first people to point out the difficulties in achieving de-identification of medical records. She has not published many papers, but each publication is worth reading.

44. Mars Climate Orbiter. Mishap Investigation Board. Phase I Report. November 10, 1999. ftp://ftp.hq.nasa.gov/pub/pao/reports/1999/MCO_report.pdf. Comment: Fascinating systems analysis of the Mars Climate Orbiter's crash onto Mars' surface on Sept. 23, 1999.

45. FIPS PUB 119-1. Supersedes FIPS PUB 119. 1985 November 8. Federal Information Processing Standards Publication 119-1 1995 March 13. Announcing the Standard for ADA. http://www.itl.nist.gov/fipspubs/fip119-1.htm. Comment: In 1995, ADA 95 was approved by ISO and ANSI, one of the earliest approved object-oriented languages. The U.S. NIST issued this publication indicating that ADA is suitable for use by Federal Agencies in systems that require very high reliability. Despite this, human programming error using ADA played a significant role in the crash of Ariane 5.

46. Ariane 5 Flight 501 Failure. Report by the Inquiry Board, July 19, 1996. http://homepages.inf.ed.ac.uk/perdita/Book/ariane5rep.html. Comment: On June 4, 1996, on the maiden flight of the French Ariane 5, about 40 seconds after flight initiation at a height of about 3700 m, the Ariane 5 veered off its flight path, broke up, and exploded. The report blames a software bug in the ADA program. From the report, "The reason why the active SRI 2 (Inertial Reference System 2) did not send correct attitude data was that the unit had declared a failure due to a software exception. The OBC (On-Board Computer) could not switch to the back-up SRI 1 because that unit had already ceased to function during the previous data cycle (72 milliseconds period) for the same reason as SRI 2. The internal SRI software exception was caused during execution of a data conversion from 64-bit floating point to 16-bit signed integer value. The floating point number which was converted had a value greater than what could be represented by a 16-bit signed integer. This resulted in an Operand Error. The data conversion instructions (in ADA code) were not protected from causing an Operand Error, although other conversions of comparable variables in the same place in the code were protected."

47. Therac-25, from Wikipedia, the free encyclopedia. http://en.wikipedia.org/wiki/Therac-25. Comment: Between 1985 and 1987, a software glitch in the Therac-25 radiation therapy machine resulted in massive radiation dosages for at least a half dozen patients.

48. General Principles of Software Validation; Final Guidance for Industry and FDA Staff. January 11, 2002. http://www.fda.gov/cdrh/comp/guidance/938.html. Comment: Software validation is a fascinating area. The FDA provides some guidance to medical device software developers who need to validate that their software really works as intended.

49. Booker D, Berman JJ. Dangerous abbreviations. *Human Pathology* 35:529–531, 2004. Comment: The Joint Committee for the Accreditation of Hospitals has banned the use of certain abbreviations that may lead to medical errors.

50. Patient Safety: Achieving a New Standard for Care. Board on Health Care Services (HCS), Institute of Medicine (IOM), 2004.

http://www.nap.edu/books/0309090776/html/. Comment: This report on patient safety emphasizes standardized reporting of patient information and of errors. Chapter summaries are available at the Web site.

51. Burke AP, Sobin LH, Federspiel BH, Shekitka KM, Helwig EB. Goblet cell carcinoids and related tumors of the vermiform appendix. *Am J Clin Pathol* 94:27–35, 1990. Comment: This paper describes the clinical biology of goblet cell carcinoid of appendix, which happens to be completely different from the clinical biology of plain old carcinoid tumor of appendix. The lesson learned is that small variations in the name of a tumor may have important clinical consequences. Therefore, nomenclatures must strive to include and distinguish all the variant names of clinically distinct neoplasms.

52. Johnsen K, Pugh N. NISTIR 6778 Guidelines for NIST Staff Participating in Voluntary Standards Developing Organizations' Activities. U.S. Department of Commerce, June 2002. http://ts.nist. gov/ts/htdocs/210/nttaa/ir6778.pdf. Comment: Excellent discussion of the standards development process.

53. Memorandum to Center for Regulatory Effectiveness, from Multinational Legal Services, September 11, 2000 re: Judicial Review of Technology Transfer Act Violations in Connection with The SEC's Proposed Rule on Auditor Independence. http://www.thecre.com/ watchlist/LegMemo_SEC_sViolate_NTTAA.html. Comment: The National Technology Transfer and Advancement Act of 1995 ("NTTAA"), Pub. L. No. 104-113, 110 Stat. 775 (Mar. 7, 1996), Section 12(d) of the NTTAA provides "(1) In General.—Except as provided in paragraph (3) of this subsection, all Federal agencies and departments shall use technical standards that are developed or adopted by voluntary consensus standards bodies, using technical standards as a means to carry out policy objectives or activities determined by the agencies and departments." In the opinion written at this Web site, there may be situations where the federal government can be brought to court if it tries to create new standards, bypassing private organizations.

54. Title 18. Crimes and criminal procedure. Part 1, Crimes. Chapter 95, Racketeering. Sec. 1951, Interference with commerce by threats or violence. http://frwebgate.acc.ess.gpo.gov/cgi-bin/getdoc.cgi?dbname= browse_usc&docid=Cite:+18USC1951. Comment: This section of the RICO Act deals specifically with conspiracies to interfere with commerce.

55. Life Sciences Identifiers Specification. OMG Final Adopted Specification, May 2004. http://www.omg.org/docs/dtc/04-05-01.pdf. Comment: There is a formal method for assigning unique identifiers to biological data, and this paper, prepared by OMG

(Object Management Group) shows how to do it using LSIDs (Life Science Identifiers).

56. Health Level 7 Home. http://www.hl7.org/. Comment: HL7 is a not-for-profit volunteer organization composed of healthcare experts and information scientists. HL7 creates standards for the exchange, management, and integration of electronic healthcare information.

57. American National Standards Institute. http://www.ansi.org/. Comment: Contains a link to their eStandards Store, which contains some of the best scientific standards that money can buy.

58. LSID Resolution Protocol Project. http://lsid.sourceforge.net/. Comment: Life Science Identifier (LSID) standard and resolution service Web site. On this page, the claim appears that "The amount of data generated in the Life Sciences field is estimated to be doubling every month."

59. Health Level 7 OID Registry. http://www.hl7.org/oid/frames.cfm. Comment: The HL7 uses a protocol for unique object identifiers that is a subset of the ISO unique object identifier system. Every HL7 unique identifier begins with the ISO identifier for HL7, "2.16.840.1.113883." HL7 assigns OIDs that all start with the HL7 unique identifier and end with additional numbers assigned by the HL7 registry service. HL7 assigns OIDs to users and vendors upon their request.

60. Kuzmak P, Casertano A, Carozza D, Dayhoff R, Campbell K. Solving the Problem of Duplicate Medical Device Unique Identifiers High Confidence Medical Device Software and Systems (HCMDSS) Workshop, Philadelphia, PA, June 2–3, 2005. http://www.cis.upenn.edu/hcmdss/Papers/submissions/. Comment: Discusses some of the difficulties in maintaining unique object identifiers. Provides the astonishing assertion that 1 in 1,000 of the in-use DICOM image identifiers are nonunique.

61. Requirement of DUNS number. Notice:not-od-03-055, National Institutes of Health (NIH), August 14, 2003. http://grants.nih.gov/grants/guide/notice-files/NOT-OD-03-055.html. Comment: Effective 2003, grantee organizations must have a registered Dun and Bradstreet Data Universal Numbering System (DUNS) number when applying for federal grants or cooperative agreements.

62. Leach P, Mealling M, Salz R. A Universally Unique IDentifier (UUID) URN Namespace. Network Working Group, Request for Comment 4122, Standards Track. http://www.ietf.org/rfc/rfc4122.txt. Comment: This Request for Comment (RFC) describes an in-use method for UUIDs (Universally Unique IDentifiers), also known as GUIDs (Globally Unique IDentifiers). A UUID is 128 bits long, and requires no central registration process. The UUID can serve as the name for an Internet resource.

63. Zipf's law. http://en.wikipedia.org/wiki/Zipf's_law. Comment: Excellent historical and technical discussion of the Zipf distribution.

64. Rivest R. Request for Comments: 1321, The MD5 Message-Digest Algorithm. http://rfc.net/rfc1321.html. Comment: Also found at http://theory.lcs.mit.edu/~rivest/Rivest-MD5.txt. Message-digest algorithms, also known as fingerprint algorithms or one-way hash algorithms, take a binary object, such as a file, and create a short, seemingly random string of characters (message digest) with the following properties: The same file will always produce the same message digest, if the file is changed in any way, then the algorithm will produce a different message-digest, and it is impossible to compute the original file from any manipulation of the message digest. MD-5 is an open algorithm with easily obtained software implementations. It is used to authenticate digital objects.

65. Secure Hash Algorithm (SHA-1), National Institute of Standards and Technology, NIST FIPS PUB 180-1, "Secure Hash Standard," U.S. Department of Commerce, April 1995. http://www.itl.nist.gov/fipspubs/fip180-1.htm. Comment: The Secure Hash Algorithm is an message digest algorithm approved by the U.S. Department of Commerce.

66. Comprehensive Perl Archive Network. http://www.cpan.org/. Comment: This site archives over 9,000 Perl modules that can be freely downloaded. These modules greatly extend the utility of Perl.

67. Efron B, Tibshirani RJ: *An Introduction to the Bootstrap.* Boca Raton, CRC Press, 1998. Comment: One of the most important books published in the area of resampling statistics.

68. Posix—Perl interface to IEEE Std 1003.1. www.fnal.gov/docs/products/perl/pod.new/5.00503/i686-linux/POSIX.html. Comment: Posix is a suite of fundamental commands, many mathematical, that any programming languages might include. The same Posix routine should perform identically in any conforming programming language, using the same name for the routine.

69. Orwant J, Hietaniemi J, Macdonald J: *Mastering Algorithms with Perl.* Sebastopol, California, O'Reilly, 1999. Comment: This is an excellent book that clearly describes commonly used algorithms. Working Perl scripts are provided.

70. Walsh SH. The clinician's perspective on electronic health records and how they can affect patient care. *British Medical Journal* 328:1184–1187, 2004. Comment: This well-written article provides a perspective on workplace computers shared by many physicians. Basically, physicians need to enter patient-related information quickly, without interruption of the normal clinical care workflow. They need to access patient data quickly and efficiently, and retrieve all the information that is relevant to the care of their patients.

Otherwise, physicians will be reluctant to adopt computers into their practice.

71. Kim W, Wilbur WJ. Corpus-based statistical screening for phrase identification. *J Am Med Inform Assoc* 7:499–511, 2000. Comment: Everyone appreciates a good index section in a textbook. In this thoughtful article, six methods for automatically selecting candidate index phrases from text are described and tested.

72. deHoon M, Imoto S, Miyano S. The C Clustering Library for cDNA microarray data. University of Tokyo, 2005. http://bonsai.ims.u-tokyo.ac.jp/~mdehoon/software/cluster/cluster.pdf. Comment: This open access suite of clustering algorithms can be extended to many types of multiplexed datasets. Instructions are included for implementing the algorithms from a Perl script.

73. Wong C: *Web Client Programming with Perl*. Sebastopol, CA, O'Reilly, 1997. Comment: This somewhat dated book provides a clear description of popular Perl methods for extracting data from the Internet.

74. Tanaka H, Bergstrom DA, Yao MC, Tapscott SJ. Widespread and non-random distribution of DNA palindromes in cancer cells provides a structural platform for subsequent gene amplification. *Nat Genet* 37(3):320–327, 2005. Comment: DNA palindromes contribute to chromosome instability and gene amplification, a hallmark of many human cancers.

75. Brooks FP. No silver bullet: Essence and accidents of software engineering. *Computer* 20(4):10–19, April, 1987. http://www-inst.eecs.berkeley.edu/~maratb/readings/NoSilverBullet.html. Comment: This early (1987) paper tackles the problem of software complexity, emphasizing the importance of software design. Brooks also suggests that one of the best ways for institutions to achieve computer productivity is to provide staff with basic applications (e.g., word processor, spreadsheet, statistical packages) and train them with simple programming skills.

76. Leveson NG: *A New Approach to System Safety Engineering*. 2002. http://sunnyday.mit.edu/book2.pdf. Comment: This incredible book describes how you can analyze large system breakdowns. After a disaster, there is a natural tendency to find the "one thing" that broke and led to everything that followed. Actually, disasters are always preceded by multiple systemic problems, and fixing the proximate event is just the beginning of a disaster prevention plan. Her discussion of the Bhopal tragedy is particularly engrossing.

77. Berman JJ. Modern classification of neoplasms: Reconciling differences between morphologic and molecular approaches. *BMC Cancer* 5:100, 2005, http://www.biomedcentral.com/1471-2407/5/100. Comment: A new classification can sometimes resolve certain questions that arise in alternate classifications.

78. Berman JJ. Tumor taxonomy for the developmental lineage classification of neoplasms. *BMC Cancer* 4:88, 2004. http://www.biomedcentral.com/1471-2407/4/88/abstract. Comment: A taxonomy is the list of domain instances that fill a classification. This paper describes the taxonomy for the Developmental Lineage Classification of Neoplasms.

79. Berman JJ. Tumor classification: Molecular analysis meets Aristotle. *BMC Cancer* 4:10, 2004. http://www.biomedcentral.com/1471-2407/4/10. Comment: Neoplasms can be classified by their developmental lineage, much as living species can be classified by their evolutionary lineage.

80. Association for Pathology Informatics Information Resources, 2006. http://www.pathologyinformatics.org/informatics_r.htm. Comment: This Web site contains the most current version of the Developmental Lineage Classification and Taxonomy of Neoplasms.

81. National Committee on Vital and Health Statistics. Report to the Secretary of the U.S. Department of Health and Human Services on Uniform Data Standards for Patient Medical Record Information. July 6, 2000. http://www.ncvhs.hhs.gov/hipaa000706.pdf. Comment: The Committee on Vital and Health Statistics recommends that the United States designate national healthcare vocabularies. The Committee indicated that such vocabularies would assure that data shared across systems would be comparable at the most detailed level.

82. Simmonds P, Bukh J, Combet C, Deleage G, Enomoto N, Feinstone S, et al. Consensus proposals for a unified system of nomenclature of hepatitis C virus genotypes. *Hepatology* 42:962–973, 2005. Comment: This is an example of a specialized nomenclature created by a group of experts in a narrow medical field.

83. Langlotz CP, Caldwell SA. The completeness of existing lexicons for representing radiology report information. *J Digit Imaging* 15(Suppl)1:201–205, 2002. Comment: No lexicon achieved greater than 50% completeness for any test set of imaging terms. Their report showed that no single lexicon is sufficiently complete to allow comprehensive indexing, search, and retrieval of radiology report information.

84. Fahy E, Subramaniam S, Brown HA, Glass CK, Merrill AH Jr, Murphy RC, et al. A comprehensive classification system for lipids. *J Lipid Res* 46:839–861, 2005. Comment: This paper demonstrates how experts in a narrow field can create a specialized vocabulary. The classification divides lipids into eight categories (fatty acyls, glycerolipids, glycerophospholipids, sphingolipids, sterol lipids, prenol lipids, saccharolipids, and polyketides) containing distinct classes and subclasses of molecules. The classification provides a 12-digit identifier for each unique lipid molecule.

85. Tenter AM, Barta JR, Beveridge I, Duszynski DW, Mehlhorn H, Morrison DA, Thompson RC, Conrad PA. The conceptual basis for a new classification of the coccidia. *Int J Parasitol* 32:595–616, 2002. Comment: This paper exemplifies the problems in general nomenclatures and classifications when they come up against the specialized requirements of experts who work in a small sub-field.

86. Campbell JR, Carpenter P, Sneiderman C, Cohn S, Chute CG, Warren J. Phase II evaluation of clinical coding schemes completeness, taxonomy, mapping, definitions, and clarity. *J Am Med Inform Assoc* 4:238–250, 1997. Comment: This is one of the few articles in the informatics literature that tries to thoroughly evaluate the adequacy of medical nomenclatures.

87. Berman HM, Westbrook J. The need for dictionaries, ontologies and controlled vocabularies. *OMICS* 7:9–10, 2003. Comment: The Macromolecular Information File dictionary was created under a mandate from the International Union of Crystallographers to support the Protein Data Bank, http://www.pdb.org.

88. Berman JJ. Doublet method for very fast autocoding. *BMC Medical Informatics and Decision Making* 4:16, 2004. http://www.biomedcentral.com/1471-2407/5/108. Comment: The doublet method is a lexical parsing algorithm that permits rapid autocoding with any nomenclature.

89. Berman JJ. Automatic extraction of candidate nomenclature terms using the doublet method. *BMC Medical Informatics and Decision Making* 5:35, 2005. Comment: This paper describes a fast computer program that will scan a corpus of text (of any size) and extract potential new terms for any given nomenclature.

90. Powsner SM, Costa J, Homer RJ. Clinicians are from Mars and pathologists are from Venus. *Arch Pathol Lab Med* 24:1040–1046, 2000. Comment: The authors showed that the pathologist's intended meaning is commonly misinterpreted by clinicians. In this study, the authors observed that surgeons misunderstood pathology reports 30% of the time. Furthermore, attempts to streamline the reports only made matters worse.

91. Pogson G. Controlled english: Enlightenment through constraint. *Language Technology* 6:22–25, 1988. Comment: Complex text seldom yields to accurate machine translation. If the text is written in short, simple declarative sentences, then machine translation becomes practical. Pogson describes rules of controlled English that facilitate computed natural language parsing.

92. Ogden's Basic English. http://ogden.basic-english.org/basiceng.html. Comment: The idea behind Basic English is that 90% of the concepts in English can be represented with 850 words. This Web site provides abundant information on this interesting approach to language simplification.

93. Berman JJ, Moore GW. SNOMED-Encoded surgical pathology databases: A tool for epidemiologic investigation. *Modern Pathology* 9:944–950, 1996. Comment: Encoded surgical pathology reports can be used to create epidemiologic databases.

94. Grivell L. Mining the bibliome: Searching for a needle in a haystack? *EMBO Reports* 3:200–203, 2002. Comment: Grivell describes a technique for creating a signature of text composed of a combination of terms and concepts extracted from the text, and serving as a metric against which other documents can be compared to determine the similarity between different documents. Similar documents can be retrieved based on relationships between their document signatures.

95. Hill RB, Anderson RE. Pathologists and the autopsy. *Am J Clin Pathol* 95:(Suppl)42, 1991. Comment: The authors extoll the virtues of autopsies.

96. Herbst AL, Ulfelder H, Poskanzer DC. Association of maternal stilbestrol therapy and tumor appearance in young women. *New Engl J Med* 284:878–881, 1971. Comment: This landmark paper linked an observed cluster of young women having an unusual cervical cancer with a common risk factor, in utero exposure to DES (diethylstilbestrol). This discovery could not have been made without access to surgical pathology reports and associated archived histologic slides.

97. Frey CM, McMillen MM, Cowan CD, Horm JW, Kessler LG. Representativeness of the surveillance, epidemiology, and end results program data: Recent trends in cancer mortality rate. *JNCI* 84:872, 1992. Comment: The Surveillance, Epidemiology, and End Results (SEER) project collects cancer-related incidence and mortality data collected from residents in geographically defined populations, representing about 10% of the U.S. population.

98. Ashworth TG. Inadequacy of death certification: Proposal for change. *J Clin Pathol* 44:265, 1991. Comment: A British perspective on the importance of the death certificate.

99. Kircher T, Anderson RE. Cause of death: Proper completion of the death certificate. *JAMA* 258:349–352, 1987. Comment: Though every physician is expected to write death certificates, surprisingly few physicians understand how to do the job correctly. As a consequence, death certificates are notoriously inadequate records of the cause of death. The authors explain the differences between the underlying and immediate causes of death, and between the mechanism and manner of death. They also describe how to complete the medical certification section of the death certificate.

100. Walter SD, Birnie SE. Mapping mortality and morbidity patterns: An international comparison. *Intl J Epidemiology* 20:678–689, 1991. Comment: This survey of 49 national and international health atlases has shown that there is virtually no consistency in the way that death data are presented.

101. Hall PA, Lemoine NR. Comparison of manual data coding errors in 2 hospitals. *J Clin Pathol* 39:622–626, 1986. Comment: This paper shows that diagnostic codes assigned by humans are often incorrect.

102. Heja G, Surjan G. Using n-gram method in the decomposition of compound medical diagnoses. *Int J Med Inf* 70:229–236, 2003. Comment: Some words appear frequently in combination with other words. The occurrence frequencies of 2-word, 3-word, n-word phrases can be used to infer the intended meaning of text.

103. Hobbs JR. Information extraction from biomedical text. *J Biomed Inform* 35:260–264, 2002. Comment: Useful review article. Includes a discussion of precision and recall.

104. SNOMED Clinical Terms. http://www.connectingforhealth.nhs.uk/technical/standards/snomed/. Comment: From the site: "The National Programme for Information Technology depends on having a common language for gathering and sharing medical knowledge. SNOMED CT will be the language of the NHS Care Records Service and will cut down the potential for differing interpretation of information and the possibility of errors resulting from traditional paper records. If clinical information is to be transferred and exchanged electronically, a standard clinical terminology is a necessary component of clinical systems. There would be problems in exchange of information for clinical or managerial purposes if several vocabularies and terms for the same topic were used within the NHS. SNOMED CT is, therefore, maintained and updated centrally. There will, however, be opportunities to submit requests for terms to be amended or introduced at a 'submission request' area on the NHS Terminology Service website."

105. National Library of Medicine. FAQs: Inclusion of SNOMED-CT in the UMLS. U.S. National Institutes of Health, 2003. http://www.nlm.nih.gov/research/umls/Snomed/snomed_faq.html. Comment: This FAQ explains encumbrances that apply to U.S. and non-U.S. users of SNOMED terms included in the UMLS Metathesaurus.

106. National Library of Medicine. SNOMED license agreement. U.S. National Institutes of Health, 2003. http://www.nlm.nih.gov/research/umls/Snomed/snomed_license.html. Comment: This is the agreement between the U.S. National Library of Medicine and the College of American Pathologists for the right to include SNOMED within the UMLS.

107. National Library of Medicine. SNOMED Clinical Terms (SNOMED-CT). U.S. National Institutes of Health, 2004. http://www.nlm.nih.gov/research/umls/Snomed/snomed_main.html. Comment: This is the only statement that I have found, issued by the National Library of Medicine, that plainly states that SNOMED is in fact a standard, "for use in U.S. Federal Government systems for the electronic exchange of clinical health information."

108. Berman JJ. Specialized cancer nomenclatures. Submitted, Cancer Informatics, Dec. 27, 2005. http://www.pathologyinformatics.org/Resources/special.htm. Comment: General nomenclatures may lack terms and concepts found in nomenclatures that focus on a narrow subdomain included in the general nomenclature. This means that for certain types of studies, particularly those that need to retrieve rare entities or uncommon variants of common entities, medical coding using standard nomenclatures will need to be supplemented with codes from specialized nomenclatures.

109. Krauthammer M, Nenadic G. Term identification in the biomedical literature. *J Biomed Inform* 37:512–526, 2004. Comment: All text is a mixture of valid medical terms (phrases like "hepatocellular carcinoma") embedded in everything else (phrases like "they also throw javelins"). To index the medical concepts in text, it is necessary to find the medical terms that lie within. There are a wide variety of software tools to do this, and to a large extent, the choice of tool is determined by the purpose of the analysis. This excellent review article describes some of the different approaches to identifying the medical terms in free-text.

110. Liu M, Grigoriev A. Fast parsers for entrez gene. *Bioinformatics* 21:3189–3190, 2005. Comment: The authors needed a publicly available fast **Entrez** Gene parser. They tested four Perl parsers for speed. The fastest parser processed the entire human Entrez Gene annotation file in under 12 minutes on a 2.4 GHz CPU.

111. Berman JJ. Concept-match medical data scrubbing: How pathology datasets can be used in research. *Arch Pathol Lab Med Arch Pathol Lab Med*, 127:680–686, 2003. Comment: Medical data scrubbing involves the removal of words from free text that can be used to identify persons or that contain information that is incriminating or otherwise private or information that does not meet the "minimum necessary" directive under HIPAA. This article describes a general algorithm that scrubs pathology free text quickly and without error. Essentially, all words in text are blocked out unless they are high frequency words (such as "of," "it," "the," "when") and words that match terms within a medical nomenclature. The scrubbed output preserves the sense of the original sentences.

112. Berman JJ. Comparing de-identification methods. March 31, 2006. http://www.biomedcentral.com/1472-6947/6/12/comments/comments.htm. Comment: A simple data scrubbing method that combines the Concept-Match method and the fast doublet method is described.

113. Behlen FM, Johnson SB. Multicenter patient records research: Security policies and tools. *J Am Med Inform Assoc* 6:435–443, 1999. Comment: Behlen and Johnson argue that it is impossible and probably unethical to scrub medical records clean. "However, aside from

the issues raised above, a database of unidentifiable patient records is infeasible. The extrapolation of the exemption rule from simple specimens to complex records ignores the strong identifying effect of linking even a small number of independent facts. Each fact identifies a subpopulation, and the linkage of facts defines the intersection of those sets. Each additional linked fact reduces the size of the intersection. When the intersection has only one element, an individual has been identified."

114. Stein R. Found on the Web, with DNA: A Boy's Father. The Washington Post. Sunday, November 13, 2005. Comment: A 15-year-old boy was fathered using anonymously donated sperm. The boy discovered the identity of his biological father through an ingenious and legal use of genetic databases. This article chronicles the story.

115. Cho MK, Illangasekare S, Weaver MA, Leonard DGB, Merz JF. Effect of patents and licenses on the provision of clinical genetic testing services. *J Mol Diag* 5:3–8, 2003. Comment: When a clinical test is encumbered by a patent, clinical laboratory directors may be reluctant to provide the test in their laboratories. In a telephone survey, 53% said that they decided against developing a new clinical genetic test because of a patent or license issue.

116. Schneier B: *Applied Cryptography: Protocols, Algorithms and Source Code in C.* New York, Wiley, 1994. Comment: Bruce Schneier is one of the most influential and creative thinkers in the field of cryptography and computer security. This book provides an excellent discussion of the mathematical and technical aspects of the field.

117. Schneier B: *Secrets and Lies: Digital Security in a Networked World.* Indianapolis, Wiley, 2000. Comment: This book delves into the social and human aspects of computer security. This is a very good companion to the same author's earlier book, *Applied Cryptography.*

118. Faldum A, Pommerening K. An optimal code for patient identifiers. *Comput Methods Programs Biomed* 79:81–88, 2005. Comment: Without collisions, the authors propose a hash for distributing every patient of a billion patients using eight characters, two of which can be used for error detection/correction.

119. Schneier B. Why Digital Signatures Are Not Signatures. Crypto-Gram Newsletter. November 15, 2000. http://www.schneier.com/crypto-gram-0011.html. Comment: The digital signature is a mathematical operation performed on an electronic document (or some derivative of the document, such as a one-way hash of the file) that is performed with a private cryptographic key. The product of the mathematical operation is a string of characters that can be decrypted using a public key. If the decryption produces an agreed message (such as the document itself, or the authenticating one-way hash of the document), then the digital signature is said to be verified. Schneier persuasively argues that this process does not substitute for the usual

purpose of a signature, which is to indicate agreement with the contents of a document or to acknowledge responsibility for the contents of a document.

120. ISO/IEC 11179. http://en.wikipedia.org/wiki/ISO-11179. Comment: ISO 11179 is a "specification and Standardization of data elements." It has been thought of as an unnecessary meta-metadata standard and is often ignored in the XML community. However, ISO 11179 is a crucial and fundamental part of any informatics effort. It provides a formal mechanism for creating unique identifiers for standard data elements and provides uniform guidance for developing and describing data elements. If all metadata had formal descriptions conforming to ISO11179, then standardized data could be exchanged between different organizations and the enormous redundancy of in-use data elements would be reduced or eliminated.

121. White C, Quin L, Burman L: *Mastering XML: Premium Edition*. San Francisco, Sybex, 2001. Comment: This book, as well as its updated editions, is an excellent review of XML principles and tools. It has an exceptionally useful section on Internet standards on pages 224–231.

122. Brazma A, Hingamp P, Quackenbush J, Sherlock G, Spellman P, Stoeckert C, Aach J, Ansorge W, Ball CA, Causton HC, et al. Minimum information about a microarray experiment (MIAME)—toward standards for microarray data. *Nat Genet* 29:365–371, 2001. Comment: Defines the content and structure of a minimal set of information needed to describe a microarray dataset.

123. Spellman PT, Miller M, Stewart J, Troup C, Sarkans U, Chervitz S, et al. Design and implementation of microarray gene expression markup language (MAGE-ML). *Genome Biol* 3:0046, 2002. Comment: This paper describes the gene expression microarray markup language and is one of the earliest and best examples of XML schema specifications for emerging biomedical technologies.

124. Harris MA, Clark J, Ireland A, et al. Gene Ontology Consortium. The Gene Ontology (GO) database and informatics resource. *Nucl Acids Res* 32:D258–D261, 2004. http://nar.oxfordjournals.org/cgi/content/full/32/suppl_1/D258. Comment: GO can be thought of as three classifications merged into an ontology: molecular functions, biological processes, and cellular components. "Molecular function" describes molecule-level activities such as a specific catalytic or binding action. An example is "kinase activity." "Biological process" describes coordinated cellular activities (e.g., respiration, cell death) that involve macromolecules. "Cellular component" describes subcellular locations of molecular activities and structures.

125. Resource Description Framework (RDF). http://www.w3.org/RDF/. Comment: This is an excellent source of information for the W3C RDF specification.

126. Ahmed K, Ayers D, Birbeck M, Cousins J, Dodds D, Lubell J, et al.: *Professional XML Meta Data*. Birmingham, Wrox Press Ltd., 2001. Comment: Metadata is the building block of XML, the semantic web, ontologies, software agents, and just about every projected web technology. Every informatician should have a deep understanding of metadata, and this book is an excellent resource.

127. DARPA Agent Markup Language Homepage. http://www.daml.org/. Comment: DAML is an extension of RDF that provides a way of specifying the constraints placed on data values. The DAML home page links to a wealth of documents and tutorials.

128. SOAP Version 1.2 Part 0: Primer W3C Recommendation. 24 June 2003. http://www.w3.org/TR/2003/REC-soap12-part0-20030624/. Comment: This is the W3C specification for **SOAP, Simple Object Access Protocol**.

129. Karasavvas KA, Baldock R, Burger A. Bioinformatics integration and agent technology. *J of Biomed Inform* 37:205–219, 2004. Comment: This is a clear, readable review article on software agents. The authors approach agent technology as a technique that supports data integration.

130. OWL Web Ontology Language Reference, W3C Recommendation, 10 February 2004. http://www.w3.org/TR/owl-ref/. Comment: This is the official W3C reference for OWL, a formal specification for a set of RDF triples that provide logical inferencing structures for ontologies.

131. The CHAOS Report, 1994. http://www.standishgroup.com/sample_research/chaos_1994_1.php. Comment: The Standish Group estimates that in 1995, $81 billion dollars was spent on canceled software projects.

132. Basili VR, Perricone BT. Software errors and complexity: An empirical investigation. *Communications of the ACM* 27:556–563, 1984. Comment: The authors found that most errors found by users in software are the result of difficulties in understanding the problem statement.

133. Chaudhry B, Wang J, Wu S, Maglione M, Mojica W, Roth E, Morton SC, Shekelle PG. Systematic review: Impact of health information technology on quality, efficiency, and costs of medical care. *Ann Intern Med* 144:E12–E22, 2006. Comment: Most of the credible reports of the benefits of HISs come from large institutions that have developed their own systems incrementally, over many years. Credible cost–benefit analyses of adopters of commercial HISs are rare.

134. Littlejohns P, Wyatt JC, Garvican L. Evaluating computerised health information systems: Hard lessons still to be learnt. *British Medical Journal* 326:860–863, April 19, 2003. http://bmj.com/cgi/content/full/326/7394/860. Comment: The authors report that about three

quarters of installed hospital information systems are considered failures.

135. Untangling the VA computer crash: How Bay Pines hospital went from guinea pig to paralyzed victim because of pressure to implement a new system. St. Petersburg Times Tampa Bay. March 28, 2004. Comment: The Veterans Administration spent nearly $500 million on a failed computer system.

136. Han YY, Carcillo JA, Venkataraman ST, Clark RS, Watson RS, Nguyen TC, Bayir H, Orr RA. Unexpected increased mortality after implementation of a commercially sold computerized physician order entry system. *Pediatrics* 116:1506–1512, 2005. Comment: Computerized physician order entry (CPOE) adds complexity to hospital information systems, and complexity can be detrimental to patient care. In this study, the mortality rate significantly increased from 2.80% to 6.57% (36 of 548) when CPOE was implemented.

137. Lanier J: The complexity ceiling. In Brockman J (ed): *The Next Fifty Years: Science in the First Half of the Twenty-First Century*. New York, Vintage, 2000, pp 216–229. Comment: This is a wonderful and thoughtful review article discussing the importance of complexity, and why complexity will be a dominant issue in computer science for many decades. The premise is simple: Computer systems can be designed with much more complexity than physical systems, and we have no available computational techniques that can predict the kinds of errors that can occur in a complex system.

138. Anderson FJ. An illustrated history of the herbals. *iUniverse*, 1999. http://books.iuniverse.com/viewbooks.asp?isbn=1583481141&page=15. Comment: Dioscorides wrote Materia Medica in 60 AD, one of the earliest and most influential taxonomies of botanical medicine. This scholarly work is recommended as an early source of thoughtful discussion on the topic of taxonomic organization.

139. Mayr E: *The Growth of Biological Thought: Diversity, Evolution and Inheritance.* Belknap Press, Cambridge, 1982. Comment: Ernst Mayr (1905–2005) wrote dozens of books and hundreds of papers on a variety of subjects in biology. His most enduring work has been on the subject of evolution and biological classification. This, in my opinion, is one of the most important books written in the field of biology. Its treatment of the subject of biological classification is brilliant and easily extends to the general area of medical ontologies.

140. Kochanek KD, Murphy SL, Anderson RN, Scott C. Deaths: Final Data for 2002. National Vital Statistics Report. 53:(5), October 12, 2004. http://www.cdc.gov/nchs/data/nvsr/nvsr53/nvsr53_05.pdf. Comment: Contains summary data for the leading causes of death in the United States.

141. Rosai J. The continuing role of morphology in the molecular age. *Modern Pathology* 14:258–260, 2001. Comment: Juan Rosai, a leading

pathologist, describes the clinical value of morphologic classification of disease.

142. Diamandopoulos GT, Meissner WA: Neoplasia. In Kissane, JM (ed): *Anderson's Pathology*. St. Louis, Mosby, 1985, pp 518–520. Comment: Diamandopoulos wrote, "Since there are almost limitless varieties of tumors, a complete table of classification would require many pages. Any shortened version is not only necessarily incomplete but also likely to be confusing."

143. Willis RA: *Borderland of Embryology and Pathology*. London, Butterworth, 1958. Comment: In the mid-twentieth century, many pathologists believed that neoplasms were a pathologic form of tissue embryogenesis. For instance, a Wilms' tumor was a disorganized growth arising from tissue recapitulating the genesis of the renal mesoderm (hence the descriptive name, "nephroblastoma"). This excellent and scholarly book discusses the similarities between embryologic growth and neoplastic growth.

144. Smith B, Kumar A. On controlled vocabularies in bioinformatics: A case study in the gene ontology", *BIOSILICO: Drug Discovery Today* 2:246–252, 2004. http://ontology.buffalo.edu/bio/Compositionality_in_GO.pdf. Comment: The Gene Ontology is an open access nomenclature and classification of macromolecules, cellular processes, and functions.

145. Smith B, Williams J, Schulze-Kremer S. The ontology of the gene ontology. *Proc Ann Symp Am Med Inform Assoc* 609–613, 2003. http://ontology.buffalo.edu/medo/Gene_Ontology.pdf. Comment: Barry Smith is one of the most important thinkers in the realm of biomedical ontologies. His comments on the Gene Ontology are particularly salient at this time, because they focus informaticians on some of the inherent complexities and unintended consequences of ontologies in general. In the particular case of the Gene Ontology, which can be thought of as three interleaved classifications (cellular components, biological processes, and molecular functions), the comments by Smith and colleagues are particularly valuable.

146. Smith B, Ceusters W, Klagges B, Kohler J, Kumar A, Lomax J, Mungall C, Neuhaus F, Rector A, Rosse C. Relations in biomedical ontologies. *Genome Biology* 6:R46, 2005. http://genomebiology.com/2005/6/5/R46. Comment: The relationships in ontologies that connect classes and instances (e.g., is_a, part_of, derived_from, located_in) need to be formally defined in a manner that permits their broad use in different biological ontologies. This paper discusses the importance of relationship terms in ontologies.

147. Guo Z, Zhang T, Li X, Wang Q, Xu J, Yu H, Zhu J, Wang H, Wang C, Topol EJ, Wang Q, Rao S. Towards precise classification of cancers based on robust gene functional expression profiles. *BMC*

Bioinformatics 6:58, 2005. Comment: The authors suggest a novel method of analyzing gene expression arrays of cancers by first grouping the expressed genes (in the array) into Gene Ontology functional classes.

148.   Tuskegee Syphilis Study. http://www.cdc.gov/nchstp/od/tuskegee/. Comment: This clinical study, conducted between 1932 and 1972, followed the natural history of untreated syphilis in 399 black men. It stands as one of the most shameful episodes in American medical history.

149.   Lerner BH. Sins of omission—Cancer research without informed consent. *NEJM* 351:628–630, August 12, 2004. Comment: A 1963 study at Memorial Sloan-Kettering involved injecting hundreds of patients with cancer cells. The study was done without informed consent.

150.   Abramson H. Accidental mechanical suffocation in infants. *J Pediatr* 25:404–413, 1944. Comment: To the best of my knowledge, this was the first report that linked crib deaths (SIDS) to the prone sleeping position and to soft bedding.

151.   Vennemann MM, Fischer D, Jorch G, Bajanowski T. Prevention of Sudden Infant Death Syndrome (SIDS) due to an active health monitoring system 20 years prior to the public "back-to-sleep-campaigns." *Arch Dis Child.* Jan 6, 2006. Comment: In the early 1970s, the East Germans had shown that the prone sleeping position was dangerous for infants.

152.   Prostate, Lung, Colorectal & Ovarian Cancer Screening Trial (PLCO). http://www3.cancer.gov/prevention/plco/. Comment: PLCO is an example of a large, long, and expensive clinical trial.

153.   Framingham Heart Study. Clinical Trials.gov. http://www.clinicaltrials.gov/ct/show/NCT00005121. Comment: This is the Web site for the Framingham Heart Study, one of the most expensive and longest clinical studies ever planned, extending from 1948 to 2008.

154.   Berman JJ, Moore GW. The role of cell death in the growth of preneoplastic lesions: A Monte Carlo simulation model. *Cell Proliferation* 25:549–557, 1992. Comment: Regression of precancerous lesions is common. This paper examines the hypothesis that early lesions operate under the identical growth kinetics of 'late' lesions (neoplasms), but that kinetic features favoring continuous growth in established lesions tend to favour extinction of lesions composed of small numbers of cells. Growth simulations of early lesions were produced using the Monte Carlo method. The model demonstrates that small increments in the intrinsic cell loss probability in even the earliest progenitors of malignancy can strongly influence the subsequent development of neoplasia from initiated foci.

155.   Calon F. Nonpatentable drugs and the cost of our ignorance. *CMAJ* 174:483–484, February 14, 2006. http://www.cmaj.ca/cgi/content/

full/174/4/483#R3-21. Comment: The pharmaceutical industry spends over $10 billion each year on randomized controlled clinical trials. The pharmaceutical industry funds about 90% of the 40,000–80,000 worldwide randomized controlled clinical trials.

156. St. Laurent S, Johnston J, Dumbill E: *Programming Web Services with XML-RPC.* Sebastopol, California, O'Reilly, 2001. Comment: This is a good book on remote procedure calling using XML syntax.

157. Allen W. My speech to the graduates. In: *Side Effects.* Ballantine, New York, 1981, p 81. Comment: Best line: "More than any other time in history, mankind faces a crossroads. One path leads to despair and utter hopelessness. The other, to total extinction. Let us pray we have the wisdom to choose correctly."

158. Sekas G, Hutson WR. Misrepresentation of academic accomplishments by applicants for gastroenterology fellowships. *Ann Internal Med* 123:38–41, 1995. Comment: About 30% of applicants for gastroenterology fellowships who listed published articles misrepresented their accomplishments.

159. Rhoades LJ. New Institutional Research Misconduct Activity: 1992–2001. U.S. Department of Health and Human Services, Office of Public Health and Science, Office of Research Integrity, 2004. http://ori.dhhs.gov/publications/studies.shtml. Comment: The U.S. Department of Health and Human Services Office of Research Integrity investigates scientific misconduct and publishes its findings.

160. Salmon A, Hawkes N. Clone 'hero' resigns after scandal over donor eggs. The Times, November 25, 2005. Comment: This is one of the early reports of irregularities in the laboratory of Dr. Hwang Woo-Suk, a South Korean geneticist.

161. Thirty-five U.S.C. 287 Limitation on damages and other remedies; marking and notice. http://www.uspto.gov/web/offices/pac/mpep/documents/appxl_35_U_S_C_287.htm. Comment: These important patent provisions provide a level of protection to healthcare practitioners. They permit healthcare practitioners to perform customary medical activities (e.g., surgical procedures), even when a patent claim may apply to the procedure.

162. Standards for Forensic DNA Testing Laboratories. http://www.fbi.gov/hq/lab/codis/forensic.htm. Comment: CODIS is the Combined DNA Index System. It serves as a forensic technology that enables federal, state, and local crime labs to exchange and compare DNA profiles electronically. Each profile in the database consists of 13 STRs (short tandem repeats), and this is enough to uniquely identify an individual. This paper describes standards for forensic labs that participate in CODIS.

163. Summary and Recommendations: The Royal Liverpool Children's Inquiry, 2001. http://www.rlcinquiry.org.uk/download/sum.pdf.

Comment: Official investigations of scandals are always fascinating reading. This report involves findings of unauthorized acquisitions of organs from deceased infants at the Alder Hey Hospital in the 1990s.

164. Hunter M. Alder Hey report condemns doctors, management, and coroner. *British Medical Journal* 322:255, 2001. Comment: The Alder Hey hospital, in Liverpool, was the site of long-term abuses of the tissue procurement system. This article comments on the investigation into the events surrounding the scandal.

165. Douglas L. Why the Human Genome Diversity Project is problematic for the indigenous community. http://homepages.wmich.edu/~bstraigh/AN490/LIZ.htm. Comment: In this thoughtful and provocative paper, Liz Douglas discusses several intellectual property issues pertaining to ownership of genetic information obtained from human subjects. She discusses Moore v Regents of the University of California and also discusses controversies arising from the Human Genome Diversity Project. Liz Douglas writes, "Officials of the Human Genome Diversity Project claim that their interest in the genetic information is purely academic, but research scientists in the past have already submitted patent applications on a handful of genes, gene products, cells and cell lines from the samples taken from indigenous communities ... It is not surprising that the indigenous communities are less than excited about this project." The Human Genome Diversity Project has been criticized as "business disguised as science," "gene prospecting," "genetic colonization," and another "trinket exchange" program.

166. Declaration of Indigenous Peoples of the Western Hemisphere Regarding the Human Genome Diversity Project. Phoenix, Arizona, February 19, 1995. http://www.tebtebba.org/tebtebba_files/susdev/bdv/iphgdp.html. and http://www.ipcb.org/resolutions/htmls/dec_phx.html. Comment: The Human Genome Diversity Project is an example of a scientific effort that has been denounced by many organizations. In this declaration, representatives from 18 organizations have strongly criticized the project. An excerpt: "We denounce and identify the instruments of intellectual property rights, patent law, and apparatus of informed consent as tools of legalized Western deception and theft."

167. Association of American Physicians and Surgeons. http://www.aapsonline.org/confiden/survcomm.htm. Comment: Humorus comments regarding HIPAA.

168. Seattle man pleads guilty in first ever conviction for HIPAA rules violation. United States Attorney's Office. Western District of Washington. Press Release, August 19, 2004. http://www.usdoj.gov/usao/waw/press_room/2004/aug/gibson.htm. Comment: The first criminal conviction under HIPAA.

169. Mankiewicz J. The lowest scam: An ID thief preyed on a cancer-stricken man. How Eric Drew fought back—and also fought leukemia. NBC News, December 25, 2005. http://www.msnbc.msn.com/id/10584944/. Comment: The is the inspiring story of a HIPAA violation victim who tracked down the hospital employee who stole his identity and won the first HIPAA prosecution case.

170. Berman JJ. Threshold protocol for the exchange of confidential medical data. *BMC Medical Research Methodology* 2:12, 2002. http://www.biomedcentral.com/1471-2288/2/12. Comment: Threshold cryptographic protocols divide messages into multiple pieces, no single piece containing information that can reconstruct the original message. The paper describes a novel threshold protocol that can be used to search, annotate, or transform confidential data without breaching patient confidentiality.

171. Berman JJ. Confidentiality for medical data miners. *Artificial Intelligence in Medicine* 26:25–36, 2002. Comment: This paper describes some of the innovative computational remedies that will permit researchers to conduct research and share their data without harming patients.

172. Bouzelat H, Quantin C, Dusserre L. Extraction and anonymity protocol of medical file. *Proc AMIA Annu Fall Symp* 323–327, 1996. Comment: This interesting paper uses the Standard Hash Algorithm (SHA) to replace identities by their message digests, while minimizing the hash collision rate and allowing the correct linkage of multiple records on any patient.

173. DeWaal AG, Hundepool AJ, Willenborg LCRJ. Argus: Software for statistical disclosure control of microdata. http://www.census.gov/prod/2/gen/96arc/iiawille.pdf. Comment: This unpublished, but open-archived paper, describes the Mu-Argus statistical algorithm used in the Netherlands to determine what de-identified data can be released without jeopardizing patient confidentiality.

174. NIH Record. November 4, 2005. http://www.nih.gov/nihrecord/2005/11042005Record.pdf. Comment: Translational medicine is a prime concern at NIH. Clinical and Translational Science Awards (CTSA) have been promoted as a way of accelerating translational research. "NIH expects to increase the number of awards annually so that by 2012, 60 CTSAs will receive a total of approximately $500 million per year."

175. RFA-RM-06-002: Institutional Clinical and Translational Science Award. National Institutes of Health, 2006. http://grants.nih.gov/grants/guide/rfa-files/RFA-RM-06-002.html. Comment: This is the formal announcement for CTSA, a major new initiative from NIH to support translational research.

176. Dublin Core Metadata Initiative. http://dublincore.org/. Comment: The **Dublin Core** is a set of basic metadata that describes XML docu-

ments. The Dublin Core elements were developed by a visionary group of library scientists who understood that every XML document needs to include self-describing metadata so that the document can be indexed and appropriately retrieved.

177. Dublin Core Metadata Element Set, Version 1.1: Reference Description. http://dublincore.org/documents/1999/07/02/dces/. Comment: This is the Web site for the Dublin Core elements.

178. Guidance for Industry, FDA Reviewers and Compliance on Off-The-Shelf Software Use in Medical Devices. September 9, 1999. http://www.fda.gov/cdrh/ode/guidance/585.pdf. Comment: Off-the-shelf software may be used in new medical devices as long as the device manufacturer follows FDA guidance to ensure that the included software is not hazardous.

179. Trithemius J. Steganographia (Secret Writing), by Johannes Trithemius. 1500. Comment: Early work on steganography. Cryptography is an ancient science.

180. Rivest RL. MIT Lab for Computer Science. March 18, 1998 (rev. April 24, 1998). http://theory.lcs.mit.edu/~rivest/chaffing.txt. Comment: This paper describes the brilliant winnowing and chaffing method of steganography.

Appendix

OPEN SOURCE PROGRAMMING LANGUAGES

19.1. THE C PROGRAMMING LANGUAGE

C is an ANSI standard programming language and is the favored language for most commercial software applications. As a testimony to C, most high-level programming languages (including Perl) are written in C.

If you are not a Linux user, a good way of installing GCC (GNU Compiler Collection, formerly the GNU C Compiler) is by installing Cygwin and then selecting GCC as one of the components you want to install during the setup dialog. Once installed, you can compile a C source code script from DOS or from the Cygwin window. If you do it from DOS, put your script in the subdirectory in which `gcc.exe` is kept or add `gcc.exe` to the PATH environment variable. If you do it from the Cygwin window, then you need to mount the directory that holds your source code, as in:
`mount -f -X c:/cygwin/bin /bin`

If your source code file is `sample.c`, then invoke:

`gcc sample.c` (assumes sample.c is in the same directory as `gcc.exe`)

This produces a file, `a.exe`, which you can execute by invoking `a` at the command prompt. You can change its name to any preferred filename.

If you've written a C++ script, give it a cc suffix and compile it by invoking g++ at the command prompt. For example, `g++ testcc.cc`

This produces `a.exe`, which you can change to any preferred filename.

19.2. THE JAVA PROGRAMMING LANGUAGE

Java can be downloaded from http://java.sun.com/j2se/1.4.2/download.html.

For non-Linux users, the Java programming language files are included in the J2SE Software Development Kit (SDK).

The self-installing `.exe` file produces directories, with the important files, `javac.exe` and `java.exe`, in the `/bin` subdirectory.

Write a test Java script, `script.java`, and put it in the `/bin` subdirectory.

Compile it with `c:\javac script.java`.

All java commands are case sensitive. If it compiles successfully, then it will produce the file Script.class. You can execute the script with the command `c:\java Script`.

19.3. PERL, OPEN SOURCE PROGRAMMING LANGUAGE

Perl comes bundled with virtually all Linux distributions. Versions of the Perl interpreter are available for just about every operating system from CPAN at www.cpan.org.

A very simple download for non-Linux users is available from ActiveState at www.activestate.com.

19.4. PYTHON, OPEN SOURCE PROGRAMMING LANGUAGE

Like Perl, Python comes bundled on Linux distributions.

A non-Linux version of Python is available from ActiveState at www.activestate.com.

19.5. RUBY, OPEN SOURCE OBJECT-ORIENTED PROGRAMMING LANGUAGE

Ruby was built to have many of the syntactic features of Perl but with the native object orientation of Smalltalk. Ruby is wildly popular in Japan. Some erstwhile Perl programmers have switched to Ruby, preferring the elegance and simplicity of object-oriented programming in Ruby.

Ruby can be downloaded from the Ruby home page: http://www.ruby-lang.org/en/20020102.html.

There are many online resources to help you begin programming in Ruby. A terrific online Ruby book, entitled "Programming Ruby: The Pragmatic Programmer's Guide," is available at http://www.rubycentral.com/book/.

An excellent site for technical documentation is http://www.ruby-doc.org/.

Here is a short Ruby script that reads lines from a file (List 19.5.1).

LIST 19.5.1. RUBY SCRIPT TO READ LINES FROM A FILE

```
#!/usr/local/bin/ruby
#READsome.rb, reads 300 lines from a big file
f = File.open "big"
outf = File.open("bigout.out", "w")
count = 0
while count < 300
    STDOUT.puts f.gets
    outf.puts f.gets
    count = count + 1
end
```

Notice that the general syntax of the script is much like Perl, but Ruby is a bit cleaner, avoiding the need for the "$" variable designator, the curly brackets enclosing loop blocks, and the ";" indicating the end of a command. Ruby statements are assertions of object methods.

The statement, `f = File.open "perlbig"` creates a new object instance of the File class, names it "f," associates it with the existing file named "perlbig," and uses the File method "open" to prepare the file for reading (parsing).

Here is a translation from Perl to Ruby for the script in List 10.6.4 (List 19.5.2).

LIST 19.5.2. RUBY SCRUB SCRIPT, EQUIVALENT TO SCRUB.PL

```
#!/usr/local/bin/ruby
f = File.open "doubdb.txt"
outf = File.open("scrub.out", "w")
```

```
doubhash = Hash.new
while line = f.gets
   line = chomp
   doubhash[line] = " "
end
f.close
puts "What would you like to scrub?"
line = gets.chomp.downcase
line = line.gsub(/\'s/, ")
line = line.gsub(/[^\w\s]/, ' ')
line = line.gsub(/ +/, ' ')
linearray = line.split
arraysize = linearray.length-2
lastword = "*"
for arrayword in (0 .. arraysize)
   phrase = linearray[arrayword] + " " +
            linearray[arrayword+1]
   if doubhash.key?(phrase)
     print " " + linearray[arrayword]
     lastword = " " + linearray[arrayword+1]
   else
     print lastword
     lastword = " *"
   end
   if arrayword == arraysize
     print lastword
   end
end
```

UTILITIES AND APPLICATIONS

19.6. SWIG, OPEN SOURCE GLUE TOOL

Interpreted scripting languages such as Perl, PHP, Python, Tcl, Ruby, and PHP are sometimes referred to as glue languages, because they permit programmers to glue compiled software (such as C routines) into scripts.

C excels at performing repetitive calculations very quickly, and the "perfect" scripting language has a simple and reliable method for importing C routines as needed.

SWIG is a software development tool that connects programs written in C and C++ with a variety of high-level scripting languages (such as Perl, Python, and Ruby).

SWIG may be freely used, distributed, and modified for commercial and non-commercial use.

SWIG can be downloaded at www.swig.org.

A SWIG tutorial is available at http://www.swig.org/Doc1.1/HTML/Contents.html.

19.7. OPEN MICROSCOPY ENVIRONMENT (OME)

The Open Microscopy Environment (OME) defines a data model and a software implementation to serve as an informatics framework for imaging in biological microscopy experiments.

The OME Data Model, expressed in Extensible Markup Language (XML), is extensible and self-describing. OME is an open source software project. All OME source code is available under the GNU library general public license.

The OME XML schema can be downloaded at http://www.openmicroscopy.org/XMLschemas/OME/FC/ome.xsd.

19.8. R, OPEN SOURCE STATISTICAL PROGRAMMING LANGUAGE AND BIOCONDUCTOR

R is an open source programming language for statistics. A free, easy-to-install version for non-Linux users can be found at http://www.stats.bris.ac.uk/R/bin/windows/base/.

A general R FAQ is available at http://cran.r-project.org/doc/FAQ/R-FAQ.html.

R is an example of a successful and sophisticated software project that was completed over several years by a group of dedicated experts scattered across the globe. The effort had virtually no funding.

Bioconductor is an open source software environment for computational biology and bioinformatics. It uses R extensively. The Bioconductor Web site is: http://www.bioconductor.org/.

19.9. OPEN SOURCE BIOPERL, BIOPYTHON, AND BIORUBY

Beginning with the venerable BioPerl organization, these language-specific bioinformatics efforts all provide open source environments supporting a range of bioinformatics tasks:

- http://www.bioperl.org/

- http://www.biojava.org/

- http://www.biopython.org/

- http://www.bioruby.org/

19.10. OPEN SOURCE ELECTRONIC LABORATORY NOTEBOOK, NEUROSYS

NeuroSys uses an open source ELN (**electronic laboratory notebook**) that was developed under grants from the NSF (National Science Foundation) and from the NIH Human Brain Project.

Registration is required, but software downloads are free at http://neurosys.cns.montana.edu/.

19.11. OPEN SOURCE GIMP IMAGE SOFTWARE

The GIMP is the GNU Image Manipulation Program. It is a popular, freely available software. It can be used for photo retouching, image composition, and image authoring. Versions of GIMP are available for most operating systems at http://www.gimp.org.

19.12. OPEN SOURCE NIH IMAGE

NIH Image is free image analysis software produced by the National Institutes of Health. It can be downloaded as easily installed packages made for a variety of different operating systems at http://rsb.info.nih.gov/nih-image/Default.html.

19.13. POV-RAY IMAGE RENDERING OPEN SOURCE SOFTWARE

POV-RAY is a free programming environment that allows users to render 3-D images from object primitives and virtual light sources. The results can be spectacular and can be used to enhance scientific presentations through visualized data projections. POV-RAY might be worth the effort for graphically adventurous or artistically gifted informaticians. It is found at http://www.povray.org/.

19.14. OPEN SOURCE COMPRESSION AND ARCHIVING UTILITIES (GZIP, GUNZIP, TAR, 7-ZIP, AND BUNZIP)

Gzip (short for GNU zip) is a compression utility designed as a surrogate for "compress," another popular compression utility that uses a patented algorithm. It has been adopted by the GNU project. Gzipped files are very popular among Linux users and are widely prevalent on Internet download sites.

Gunzip is the decompression utility that operates on gzipped files.

Gzip and gunzip are available for no-cost download from www.gzip.org.

TAR (originally Tape Archiver) has outlasted its original purpose (i.e., archiving tapes). TAR works on multiple platforms to archive multiple files into a single file for easy storage and transport.

Many people will compress TAR archives using gzip, and it is common to find files with a double suffix, such as *filename.tar.gz*.

When you consecutively decompress with gunzip and de-archive with TAR, you typically get a library of files distributed in a prenamed directory (and subdirectories). TAR can be found at http://www.gnu.org/software/tar/tar.html.

7-zip is a compression/decompression and archiving/de-archiving utility. It will decompress files created with commercial software. A download of this wonderful utility, distributed under a GNU LGPL license, is available at http://www.7-zip.org/.

Bunzip is a free implementation of the clever Burrows-Wheeler transform. For certain types of data, and with ample RAM memory, it can provide higher compression than many other algorithms. Most users of the algorithms use the newer bunzip2 version that can be found at http://www.bzip.org/.

19.15. CYGWIN, OPEN SOURCE UNIX/LINUX EMULATOR

Cygwin emulates many of the common Unix/Linux commands. It can be downloaded from http://www.cygwin.com/.

Download `setup.exe`. When the dialog box displays available components, expand the "development tools" box and check off all the gcc components. This will provide you with GNU's versions of C and C++.

19.16. GNUPG, OPEN SOURCE ENCRYPTION TOOL

GnuPG, the GNU Privacy Guard, is a complete and free replacement for PGP. PGP (Pretty Good Privacy) has a colorful history. Phil Zimmermann, who labored to develop PGP as a freeware encryption program, was accused by the U.S. government of exporting munitions. PGP and other encryption software were considered munitions in the 1990s. Though this seems strange to many, it should be remembered that for decades in the United States encryption algorithms were developed exclusively by mathematicians employed by the National Security Agency and possibly other intelligence agencies. The appearance and proliferation of innovative public encryption software was a shock to U.S. intelligence. The charges were eventually dropped. Today, PGP is a commercial software company.

Those who seek free and open source cryptography software may consider acquiring GNU's Privacy Guard. Because GnuPG does not use the patented IDEA algorithm, it can be used without any restrictions.

GnuPG is a RFC2440 (OpenPGP) compliant application. The RFC can be found at http://www.faqs.org/rfcs/rfc2440.html.

GnuPG can be downloaded from http://www.gnupg.org/download/.

GnuPG is available for several popular operating systems.

For those seeking simplicity, GnuPG can be used to produce a simple symmetric encryption of a file, using the -c command from the DOS command line, as shown:

```
C:\gpgdos>gpg -c outline.txt
```

Outline.txt is a sample file for encryption/decryption, and gpgdos is simply a created subdirectory containing the GPG files.

You will be prompted for a password. The encrypted output file produced by gpg is outline.txt.gpg.

The encrypted file can be decrypted with the -d decryption command and redirected to a preferred output file, for example:

```
C:\gpgdos>gpg -d outline.txt.gpg >c:\gpgdos\out.out
```

You will be prompted again for the same password that you used as the key for the encryption step.

19.17. WGET WEB SITE MIRRORING SOFTWARE

Wget is a free command-line utility that can be used to download Web pages or entire Web sites.

Wget is the non-Linux version of the Linux utility, "get."

Wget can be downloaded from ftp://sunsite.dk/projects/wget/windows/.

A tutorial on wget is located at http://www.gnu.org/software/wget/wget.html.

19.18. OPEN SOURCE INDEXING SOFTWARE (SWISHE-E AND LUCENE)

Swish-e is a fast, flexible, and free open source system for indexing collections of Web pages or other files. It is found at http://swish-e.org/.

Apache's Lucene is open source, Java-based indexing software. It is available from http://apache.osuosl.org/jakarta/lucene/binaries/.

19.19. OPEN SOURCE WORD PROCESSING SOFTWARE (ABIWORD AND OPENOFFICE WRITER)

AbiWord is a free, open source word processor. It is written to be compatible with many different operating systems and with many different languages. It will accept and create files of many different formats and has its own native XML format.

AbiWord can be downloaded from http://www.abisource.com/download/.

OpenOffice Writer, like AbiWord, is an open and free word processor. OpenOffice can be downloaded from http://www.openoffice.org/product/writer.html.

19.20. OPEN SOURCE EMACS TEXT EDITOR

Text editors (also called **ASCII editors**) are different from word processors. Text editors produce plain-ASCII files that use the basic alphanumeric characters found on standard keyboards. Text files have no formatting other than spaces, tabs, and line returns. Text editors are used to compose source code and can read many kinds of data files. Data files are often composed of sequential records, one record to a line, with each record consisting of data elements separated by a non-text character (such as "|" or a caret "^"). Such files are called flat files because they lack multi-dimensional data structures.

Word processors are not designed to load large files. The advantage of text editors over word processors is that they load large multi-megabyte files quickly. After opening a file, a text editor will close a file without converting the file to another format. When you want to browse through a 100 Megabyte file, use a text editor.

There are text editors available for every operating system. The most popular text editor is emacs, which is bundled into most Linux distributions. A free non-Linux version is available at http://ftp.gnu.org/gnu/windows/emacs/.

After decompressing the download file, install it by executing (running) `addpm.exe`, which you will find in the `/bin` subdirectory. This will provide an emacs icon for the desktop.

19.21. OPEN SOURCE SPREADSHEET SOFTWARE

OpenOffice Calc is a spreadsheet program that will open Excel spreadsheets. OpenOffice Calc can be found at http://www.openoffice.org/product/calc.html.

19.22. OPEN SOURCE PRESENTATION SOFTWARE

Presentation software permits users to make computer slide shows displayed by laptop projectors. OpenOffice Impress is free, open, and easy to use. It can be downloaded from http://www.openoffice.org/product/impress.html.

19.23. MUMPS, AN ANSI STANDARD PROGRAMMING LANGUAGE FOR MEDICAL INFORMATICS

MUMPS (Massachusetts General Hospital Utility Multi-Programming System) is a programming language that has special significance to the field of biomedical informatics. First developed in the late 1960s at the Massachusetts General Hospital, it is perhaps the only programming language specifically developed for biomedical databases. It became an ANSI standard programming language in 1977. The name "MUMPS" has been replaced with "The M programming language," but most people prefer the original term.

Some versions of MUMPS can be downloaded for free from http://www.hardhats.org/links/Mlinks.html.

The Veterans Administration File Manager Database and the Veterans Administration Vista Hospital Information System were written in MUMPS.

19.24. MYSQL, OPEN SOURCE DATABASE SOFTWARE

MySQL (pronounced "my sequel") is an open source database. A noncommercial version of MySQL can be downloaded at no cost from the developer's Web site at http://dev.mysql.com/.

19.25. PROTEGE, OPEN SOURCE ONTOLOGY EDITOR

Protege is a free, open source ontology editor and knowledge-base framework. Protege supports XML Schema, RDF, and OWL. It is available from http://protege.stanford.edu/.

19.26. VISTA, A FREE HOSPITAL INFORMATION SYSTEM COURTESY OF THE U.S. GOVERNMENT

Vista is the hospital information system used by nearly all 160+ Veterans Administration hospitals.[16]

As a product of the U.S. government, it has been made available to the public. Instructions for obtaining Vista are available from the Hardhats organization at http://www.hardhats.org.

Though available at no cost, installing, deploying, and troubleshooting a major hospital information system such as Vista requires considerable expertise. Several private companies now offer Vista installation services.

Commercial hospital information systems may cost upwards of $100 million. Those clever enough to install and implement the free VISTA software can potentially save their institutions a great deal of money.

19.27. CWM, A CLOSED WORLD MACHINE FOR RDF (IN PYTHON)

CWM (Closed World Machine) is a command-line Python program that will interconvert RDF and notation 3 (n3) files. It is available at http://www.w3.org/2000/10/swap/doc/CwmInstall.

CWM will convert an RDF file to n3, as shown in this command-line example:

```
C:\cwm-1.0.0>cwm --n3 sample.rdf
```

CWM supports a variety of routines designed to implement the semantic web.

FREE SERVICES AND DATA

19.28. PUBMED AND PUBMED CENTRAL

PubMed is the greatest and largest medical text resource in the world. Every human being can potentially benefit from this remarkable service provided by the United States National Library of Medicine. It contains abstracts of millions of medical articles extending back to the 1970s.

Each year, the value of PubMed increases as more and more journals provide open access to full-text articles from links embedded in PubMed search results.

19.29. RESOURCES FROM THE NATIONAL CENTER FOR BIOTECHNOLOGY INFORMATION

The public resources available from the U.S. National Library of Medicine's National Center for Biotechnology Information (NCBI) are of enormous importance to the field of bioinformatics. Besides the excellent online descriptions and tutorials provided by the NCBI, their many resources are described in virtually every popular book on bioinformatics.

Because this ground has been covered by so many other texts, the many NCBI resources will not be described here. Readers are referred to the NCBI Web sites at http://www.ncbi.nlm.nih.gov/.

19.30. DATABASE ISSUE OF NUCLEIC ACIDS RESEARCH

The most current database issue of Nucleic Acids Research is found at http://nar.oxfordjournals.org/content/vol33/suppl_1/index.dtl.

This issue describes hundreds of online biological databases.

19.31. LOCUSLINK AND ITS SUCCESSOR, ENTREZ GENE

The story of LocusLink illustrates some of the legacy-related difficulties encountered in the biomedical informatics community.

LocusLink was a database sponsored by the U.S. National Library of Medicine. It provided curated sequences and a range of descriptive information about genetic loci. Rich linkage to OMIM and to literature citations made it one of the few truly biomedical genomic databases (i.e., a database that associates biological data with clinical data).

LocusLink data was assembled in a large, curated data file, LL_TMPL, which is available by anonymous ftp from ftp.ncbi.nih.gov, at subdirectory /refseq/LocusLink/ARCHIVE.

The following is an abridged example of the first LocusLink record:

```
>>1

LOCUSID: 1

LOCUS_CONFIRMED: yes

LOCUS_TYPE: gene with protein product, function known or
inferred

ORGANISM: Homo sapiens

.

.

.
```

OFFICIAL_SYMBOL: A1BG

OFFICIAL_GENE_NAME: alpha-1-B glycoprotein

ALIAS_SYMBOL: A1B

ALIAS_SYMBOL: ABG

ALIAS_SYMBOL: GAB

ALIAS_SYMBOL: HYST2477

ALIAS_SYMBOL: DKFZp686F0970

PREFERRED_PRODUCT: alpha 1B-glycoprotein

SUMMARY: Summary: The protein encoded by this gene is a plasma glycoprotein of unknown function. The protein shows sequence similarity to the variable regions of some immunoglobulin super-gene family member proteins.

CHR: 19

.

.

.

ALIAS_PROT: alpha-1B-glycoprotein

LINK:
http://www.ncbi.nlm.nih.gov/UniGene/clust.cgi?ORG=Hs&CID=529161

UNIGENE: Hs.529161

OMIM: 138670

MAP: 19q13.4|RefSeq|C|

MAPLINK: default_human_gene|A1BG

LINK: http://www.ncbi.nlm.nih.gov/SNP/snp_ref.cgi?locusId=1

LINK:
http://www.ncbi.nlm.nih.gov/HomoloGene/homolquery.cgi?TEXT=1[loc]&TAXID=9606

LINK: http://www.gdb.org/gdb-bin/genera/accno?GDB:119638

LINK:
http://www.ensembl.org/Homo_sapiens/contigview?geneid=AK055885

LINK: http://genome.ucsc.edu/cgi-bin/hgTracks?org=human&position=AK055885

```
PMID:
15461460,15221005,14702039,12477932,8889549,3610142,3458201,25910
67

GO: biological process|biological process unknown|ND|GO:0000004|
GOA/IPI|na

GO: cellular component|extracellular region|IDA|GO:0005576|GOA/
IPI|3458201

GO: molecular function|molecular function unknown|ND|GO:0005554|
GOA/IPI|3458201
```

By linking sequences to standard nomenclature, to function, to Gene Ontology (GO) entries, to OMIM, and to PubMed citations, LL_TMPL was one of the richest public sources of integrated biomedical information in existence. A recently downloaded LL_TMPL file is 245,045,067 bytes in length.

In 2005, the NCBI transitioned LocusLink into Entrez Gene. The information that was contained in LL_TMPL is now distributed in a list of downloadable Entrez data files, also available through anonymous ftp: ftp.ncbi.nih.gov, at subdirectory /gene/DATA.

When a database transitions, new software is required to retrieve and integrate data from the new data sources. The skills needed to provide the new software are really simple: knowledge of the kinds of data available in the new dataset, knowledge of the manner in which the new dataset is organized and structured, a few simple methods for parsing through the new datasets to conduct data searches or data transformations (i.e., reorganizing or restructuring the data in a preferred format). As long as datasets undergo structural modifications and enhancements, biomedical informaticians will need to make adjustments.

19.32. TIME-STAMPING

The date of creation of intellectual property may have great importance. It is a crucial item in patent and copyright applications. When the precedence of a discovery is challenged, it is important to have a well-documented moment in time when the property was created.

To bind a specific time to a document, scientists may use a **time-stamp** service. If an electronic document is time-stamped by a reliable service, then no one will persuasively claim that the document came into existence at a later time. If a scientist religiously time-stamps her intellectual property without delay, then the time-stamp will correspond to the time of the creation of the intellectual property.

All biomedical informaticians should avail themselves of a time-stamp service for first versions of manuscripts, all breakthrough observations, even important e-mail exchanges. Researchers are cautioned not to rely on time notations appended to documents (e.g., e-mails) by network daemons. Though the time and data information included in e-mail headers is accurate in most circumstances, they can be altered easily.

A variety of time-stamping strategies have been used in the past. One popular strategy is as follows:

• Derive a one-way hash string from the created electronic document.

• Publish the hash value in classified section of a daily newspaper.

Only the hashed document has any reasonable likelihood of hashing to the published value, and the existence of the hashed value in a dated public work (such as a newspaper) ensures that the document must have been created prior to the publication date of the newspaper that contains the hash value.

Commercial time-stamping services are available. A free time-stamping service is available from PGP Digital Timestamping Service, which is found at http://www.itconsult.co.uk/stamper/stampinf.htm.

The user sends text to clear@stamper.itconsult.co.uk.

A return e-mail message will indicate the time that the text was received, and it provides an identifier number for the transaction and a pgp-signed digital certificate. The protocols for this service are well documented at the company Web site.

19.33. GOOGLE (AS IF YOU DIDN'T ALREADY KNOW)

As everyone knows, Google is one of the most innovative and useful services on the Web. The enormous volume of indexed information held in Google is a potential source of biomedical data and should not be overlooked by researchers.

The following are specific Google services that may be of interest:

• scholar.google.com (a Web citation search engine)

• Google earth (visualizing everything on the planet, and a potential resource for tracking emerging epidemics, visualizing the planetary distribution of diseases, and correlating the disease occurrence with geographic features)

19.34. SOURCEFORGE

Sourceforge is found at http://sourceforge.net.

Sourceforge describes itself as "the world's largest development and download repository of Open Source code and applications. Providing free services to Open Source developers."

It is a remarkable communitarian artifice that hosts thousands of active, cooperative open source efforts and provides public downloads of developed software. All software developed through SourceForge must be released under an open source license.

The group development process is managed with CVS, an open source tool that permits revision management on multi-authored software. The Sourceforge Web site has full documentation for development teams.

19.35. CVS, CONCURRENT VERSIONS SYSTEM

CVS is an open source tool that keeps track of changes in software or documents. With CVS, you can work with colleagues on a software project, with each developer contributing concurrent edits to the project. If a new version of the software is problematic, then the group can use CVS to revert to an earlier version of the software.

CVS is available for free download from http://www.nongnu.org/cvs/.

19.36. CPAN, THE COMPREHENSIVE PERL ARCHIVE NETWORK

CPAN is the Comprehensive Perl Archive Network. It consists of thousands of Perl modules contributed by volunteer programmers. All of the Perl software at the CPAN site can be freely downloaded at http://www.cpan.org.

19.37. REQUESTS FOR COMMENT

An RFC (Request for Comment) is a publicly available document that contains a proposal for an Internet-related protocol, specification, policy, or concept. The RFCs are archived at http://www.faqs.org/rfcs/ and at http://www.rfc-archive.org/.

A history of RFCs is available at ftp://ftp.rfc-editor.org/in-notes/ rfc2555.txt.

In general, these documents are scholarly works that provide a fascinating description of the ideas that formed the foundation of today's Internet. The RFCs are a valuable resource for techno-historians and for fastidious informaticians who prefer to understand the current state of information technology by understanding its formative evolution.

Examples of some available RFCs are:

- RFC 821—Simple Mail Transfer Protocol

- RFC 2396—Uniform Resource Identifiers (URI): Generic Syntax

- RFC 793—Transmission Control Protocol

- RFC 1034—Domain names—concepts and facilities

- RFC 2045—Multipurpose Internet Mail Extensions (MIME) Part One: Format of Internet Message Bodies

- RFC 1321—The MD5 Message-Digest Algorithm

- RFC 1738—Uniform Resource Locators (URL)

- RFC 1855—Netiquette Guidelines

- RFC 1591—Domain Name System Structure and Delegation

- RFC 1122—Requirements for Internet Hosts—Communication Layers

- RFC 1945—Hypertext Transfer Protocol—HTTP/1.0

- RFC 1155—Structure and Identification of Management Information for TCP/IP-based Internets

- RFC 791—Internet Protocol

- RFC 1661—The Point-to-Point Protocol (PPP)

- RFC 959—File Transfer Protocol

- RFC 2026—The Internet Standards Process—Revision 3

- RFC 1510—The Kerberos Network Authentication Service (V5)

19.38. OMIM, ONLINE MENDELIAN INHERITANCE IN MAN

OMIM is a listing of every known inherited condition in man. Each condition has biologic and clinical descriptions in a detailed textual narrative that includes a listing of relevant citations. There are nearly 17,000 conditions described, and the OMIM file exceeds 100 MBytes in length. The OMIM file can be downloaded from the National Center for Bioinformatics anonymous ftp site ftp://ftp.ncbi.nih.gov and subdirectory: /repository/omim/.

Additional information on OMIM is available at http://www.ncbi.nlm. nih.gov/omim/.

19.39. LOINC, LOGICAL OBSERVATIONS, IDENTIFIERS, NAMES, AND CODES

LOINC is a freely downloadable terminology available from http://www.regenstrief.org/loinc.

LOINC is registered to and copyrighted to the Regenstrief Institute. The intended purpose of LOINC is to provide a consistent method for describing clinical laboratory tests.

The LOINC file is about 13 MBytes in size and contains about 35,000 records.

19.40. HL7—HEALTH LEVEL 7

HL7 is a specification for transporting certain types of data that are typically collected by hospitals. Collections of HL7 data are called messages and are used to encapsulate information such as:

• Registration data—patient admissions, discharges, transfers

• Results/observations—laboratory tests, diagnoses, clinical observations, operative notes

• Orders—from pharmacy, laboratory, or nurse

• Billing/charges

Virtually any kind of information can be packaged into an HL7 message. All HL7 messages have a similar structure. The message begins with a header that contains a description of the message contents. The message header is typically followed by a Patient Identification (PID) segment containing patient demographics. This is followed by observations segments (OBR). The segment is composed of individual observations (OBX) and can be delimited by a vertical character, " | ". OBX segments typically specify the test identifier, description, value and code source, unit of measure, and observed value status for a test.

19.41. SEER

The Surveillance, Epidemiology, and End Results (SEER) Program of the National Cancer Institute is an authoritative source of information on cancer incidence and survival in the United States.

The SEER Public-Use Data include SEER incidence and population data associated by age, sex, race, year of diagnosis, and geographic areas (including SEER registry and county).

Public use Seer data are available at http://seer.cancer.gov/publicdata/.

Users must sign a public use Data Agreement before downloading SEER public use files. The Data Agreement is available at http://seer.cancer.gov/publicdata/access.html.

The public can download hundreds of MBytes of SEER data.

19.42. UMLS METATHESAURUS

The UMLS is the largest curated medical nomenclature in existence. The UMLS is available at no charge from the National Library of Medicine to U.S. and international users. Users must sign a License Agreement, available at http://www.nlm.nih.gov/research/umls/license.html.

Although the UMLS metathesaurus is made available to anyone, at no cost, there are restrictions on the uses of the vocabularies included in the metathesaurus distribution. The UMLS metathesaurus is composed of approximately 100 different vocabularies and thesauruses. Many of these vocabularies have very few restrictions on their use (the so-called Category 0 vocabularies), while other included vocabularies have policies that limit their uses.

The November 23, 2005 version of the UMLS metathesaurus can be downloaded in three zip-archived files. They are: 2005ac-1-meta.nlm 813,338,650; 2005ac-2-meta.nlm 609,100,058; and 2005ac-3-meta.nlm 748,339,684 bytes.

The file 2005ac-1-meta.nlm is a zipped archive file containing MRCON, the file that lists about 6 million UMLS terms. The November 23, 2005 version of MRCON is 714,357,612 bytes in length. It can be extracted from 2005ac-1-meta.nlm using a de-archiving, de-compressing utility program.

19.43. MEDICAL SUBJECT HEADINGS—MESH

MeSH (Medical Subject Headings) is a large, comprehensive, curated vocabulary created and maintained by the U.S. National Library of Medicine. It contains descriptors in a hierarchical structure (usually referred to as a MeSH tree) that allows searching at multiple levels of granularity.

Information on MeSH is found at http://www.nlm.nih.gov/mesh/meshhome.html.

The MeSH download page is http://www.nlm.nih.gov/mesh/filelist.html.

The Jan 10, 2006 downloadable MeSH flat file is named `D2006.bin` and is over 25 Megabytes in length. It contains nearly 23,886 records, and each record has a similar form.

19.44. GENE ONTOLOGY—GO

The GO Consortium Web site is http://www. geneontology.org/.

The GO Consortium distributes its products without a license, as long as users comply with its redistribution and citation policy, which can be found at http://www.geneontology.org/doc/GO.cite.html.

The latest versions of GO can be downloaded from http://archive.godatabase.org/latest-termdb/.

19.45. OBO (OPEN BIOLOGY ONTOLOGIES)

OBO is an open source collection of biological ontologies. Currently, most of the ontologies are devoted to animals (other than human animals). OBO can be found at http://obo.sourceforge.net/browse.html.

19.46. USHIK METADATA REGISTRY

The United States Health Information Knowledgebase (USHIK) is a metadata registry administered by the Health Informatics Standards Board (HISB) and composed of ISO-11179 compliant data elements contributed by numerous standard development organizations. It can be found at http://www.ushik.org/registry/x/index.html.

19.47. NEOPLASM CLASSIFICATION

The developmental lineage classification and taxonomy of neoplasms contains over 145,000 names of neoplasms and has been described in several open access publications (77–79, 89). It is the largest source of names of human neoplasms and is available as an XML file.

The latest public version is available from the Association for Pathology Informatics (80). The Web site for the gzipped XML-formatted nomenclature is http://www.pathology informatics.org/Resources/neoclxml.gz.

19.48. UNITED STATES CENSUS

The United States census can be found at http://www.census.gov/.

Public datasets can be downloaded from http://www.census.gov/popset/datasets.html.

Most of the datasets are in simple comma delimited ASCII format, with a key provided that lists the order and named data elements in each row (record) of the file.

Glossary

Abandonware—Software that was once shown to serve some useful purpose but which is no longer used. Almost all of the useful software ever written is now abandonware. In many cases, software loses its value if it is not continually de-bugged, enhanced, and aggressively marketed. The term "abandonware" is often applied to software created by graduate students as part of a funded research effort. Once the funding period ends and the students have moved to new pursuits, there is no support for marketing and distributing the software. Even when interest remains in the original software, it can be very difficult for a new programmer to understand the source code left by the original programmer. In addition, funding is typically rewarded for innovative ideas, and it is sometimes impossible to attract new funding to maintain a previously funded project.

ANSI (American National Standards Institute)—ANSI is a Standards Activities Organization. As such, ANSI does not itself develop standards. ANSI accredits standards developing organizations to create American National Standards. When something is described as an ANSI standard, it means that ANSI-accredited standards development organizations followed ANSI procedures and received accreditation from ANSI that all the procedures were followed. ANSI works with over 270 ANSI-accredited standards developers. ANSI coordinates efforts to gain international standards certification from the ISO or the IEC.

Anonymization (versus de-identification)—Anonymization is a process whereby all the links between a patient and her record are irreversibly removed, so that the record can be used freely for biomedical research. The difference between anonymization and de-identification is that anonymization is irreversible. There is no method for reestablishing the identity of the patient from anonymized records. De-identification, under HIPAA, permits records to be re-identified under a set of restricted conditions. The distinction between anonymization and de-identification is important because there are times when it would be advantageous to re-identify a research record. The problem with re-identification is that it provides an opportunity to harm the patient through loss of confidentiality or privacy. The choice of anonymization versus de-identification will depend on many factors that must be considered by the investigators and by the IRB committee.

Archived tissue blocks—All tissues removed from patients (e.g., by surgeons during operations, by dermatologists who sample small skin lesions, by phlebotomists who draw blood, by patients themselves when they collect urine specimens) go to the pathology department where they are examined. In many cases, samples of the tissues are fixed in formalin and then processed to produce a paraffin-infiltrated tissue encased in a block of paraffin. These blocks, sometimes referred to as cassettes (because plastic cassettes hold the paraffin block) are used as the source of thin tissue sections that can be mounted and stained on glass slides. Pathologists look at glass slides under the microscope and reach a diagnosis based on a correlation of clinical, gross, and microscopic features of the lesions. Unlike radiologists, who look at visual representations of physical lesions, pathologists look at the actual cells taken from the patient. In most cases, after some of the block has been used to produce tissue sections mounted on glass slides, the majority of the embedded tissue remaining in the block serves as a permanent sample of the biopsied tissue. Some laboratories have paraffin-embedded blocks that have been saved for over a century. Provided that the tissues were properly fixed after they were removed from the patient, these ancient paraffin-embedded tissues are perfectly suitable material for modern research studies. There are about 25 million surgical pathology specimens collected each year in the United States. The archived tissue blocks collected over the past century have enormous value for biomedical researchers.

Artificial intelligence—Also called AI. It is impossible to discuss futuristic concepts found in this book without some mention of artificial intelligence and so-called "thinking machines." In the opinion of some, formal knowledge specifications such as RDF, DAML, and OWL provide the ingredients for autonomous software agents that will perform intelligently and make complex decisions. I am of the opinion that biomedical informaticians will spend the next decade collecting, annotating, and merging large heterogeneous datasets. The methods for analyzing such data are still under development. For the short term, artificial intelligence will be confined to simple but important tasks, such as detecting errors in medication, and improving the quality of laboratory reports and physician orders.

ASCII Standard—ASCII is the American Standard Code for Information Interchange, ISO-14962-1997. The ASCII standard is a way of assigning specific 8-bit strings (a string of 0s and 1s of length 8) to the alphanumeric characters and punctuation. Uppercase letters are assigned a different string of 0s and 1s than their matching lowercase letters. There are 256 ways of combining 0s and 1s in strings of length 8, and this means there are 256 different ASCII characters. For some uses, the 256 ASCII character limit is too constraining. There are many languages in the world with their own alphabets or with their own accented versions of the ASCII romanized alphabet. Consequently, a new character code (Unicode) has been designed as an expansion of ASCII. To maintain facile software conversion (from ASCII to Unicode), ASCII code is embedded in the Unicode standard.

ASCII editor—see Text editor.

Autopsy—Also known as a post-mortem examination. The closely related term, "necropsy," is usually reserved for veterinary autopsies. The word autopsy comes from the Greek root terms auto (self) and opsis (sight), indicating that the autopsy is a method for mankind to inspect itself. A typical hospital autopsy consists of a systematic review of organs, cataloging the pathologic changes present in each organ and synthesizing a cause of death based on pathologic findings correlated with clinical history. Autopsies generally take a few hours to conduct, during which small samples of tissues are fixed in formalin, to be embedded in paraffin (wax). Thin slices of the paraffin-embedded tissues are mounted on glass slides and stained so that the cellular detail can be visualized under a microscope. Although the preliminary results of an autopsy are usually ready within a day, the final autopsy report, based on the examination of the microscopic slides, may take weeks or even months. The final autopsy report may be many pages in length, with detailed descriptions of clinical observations, laboratory studies, and post-mortem findings. Usually 20 to 100 paraffin-embedded tissues are collected in an autopsy, and these collected tissues are usually referred to as "tissue blocks" or "archived blocks." Most hospitals save these blocks indefinitely, and several academic institutions have archived blocks that date back to the American Civil War. The millions and millions of archived autopsy blocks distributed in hospitals throughout the world have enormous research value because they contain preserved cells and because they are annotated with clinical data (the autopsy reports). In the 1960s, it was common for hospitals to perform autopsies on 30–50% of hospital deaths. Worldwide, the rates of autopsies have plummeted. Today, in many hospitals, fewer than 1% of hospital deaths are followed by an autopsy.

Binary data—Technically, all digital information is coded as binary data. Strings of 0s and 1s are the fundamental units of all electronic information. However, when people use the term "binary data" they most often are referring to digital information that is not intended to be machine-interpreted as alphanumeric characters (text). Images, sound files, and movie files are almost always binary data files. So-called plain-text files, html files and xml files (consisting entirely of text characters) are distinguished from binary data files and referred to as text or **ASCII** files. Confusion arises in files that represent text but which have their own proprietary format for representing text characters and text display instructions. Though these files are intended to display text, they are usually referred to as binary word processing files.

Biomedical informatics—uses the data produced by research laboratories (sometimes called discovery data) and the data obtained from clinical repositories to obtain clinically useful results (e.g., new discoveries, tests, therapies, services, or procedures). Because biomedical informatics translates basic science into clinical reality, it is typically regarded as a translational or applied science. All fields of medicine collect biomedical data and often rely on professionals from other disciplines in their practice. Radiologists need physicists, image experts, programmers, software analysts, network administrators, and systems operators to support the complex and expensive tools at their disposal. Pathologists work with information systems managers and molecular biologists. The nursing profession has tackled many of the information management issues by acquiring a new set of skills involved in ward-based test ordering, outcomes assessment, and patient management; and by routinely preparing data that is reviewed by statisticians and hospital administrators. All of these activities have a common ingredient, biomedical data, which must be prepared in a way that humans and computers can evaluate.

Clinical validation—See Validation.

Classification—A hierarchical and comprehensive grouping of all of the instances of a well-defined knowledge domain.

Controlled Medical Terminology (CMT)—A medical terminology for which the curators limit the number of terms and concepts permitted in the domain of the vocabulary. A CMT may have a defined number of concepts (e.g., 1000) and may permit only a preferred subset of in-use terms. In general, CMTs impose a limited vocabulary in the expectation that users will confine their verbiage to the approved terms.

Curator—The word "curator" derives from the Latin, *curatus*, the same root for "curative" and conveys that curators "take care of" things. The curator must ensure that nomenclatures are comprehensive for their knowledge domain, and this can be quite difficult when the knowledge domain is growing rapidly. The modern curator must also ensure that the nomenclature is formatted and annotated in a manner that permits interoperability with a variety of data and software applications.

Data annotation—Data annotation is the act of supplementing individual data elements, descriptive data (metadata), and related data from external information sources (e.g., clinical or pathological details) for the purpose of enhancing the utility of the data records. Today, data annotation is usually accomplished with the help of **XML** (Extensible Markup Language).

Data de-identification—Large medical centers collect terabytes of clinical data every week, but none of this data are directly accessible for research purposes. To obtain aggregated records for the purpose of conducting medical research, a researcher must submit her research plans to an institutional review board and/or privacy board. Institutional review boards are designed to protect patients from harms that may be associated with medical research. In the case of research that uses pre-existing patient records, the risks to the patient are confined to issues of confidentiality or privacy. The risks to the institution are violations of federal or state regulations that restrict the uses of patient records for research. The two federal laws that apply to this situation are the so-called Common Rule and the HIPAA Privacy Regulations. Both of these rules permit the unrestricted use of patient records when the records are de-identified (i.e., when the data in the record is disengaged from any links to the patient). There is an intense and urgent interest in developing technical solutions (algorithms, software applications, standard protocols) that permit researchers to create and use large numbers of de-identified medical records.

Data integration—Occurs when information is gathered from multiple datasets, relating diverse data extracted from different data sources. Data integration is particularly important to biomedical researchers because data obtained from experiments on human tissue specimens has little applied value unless it can be combined with medical data (i.e., pathological and clinical information). In the past, research data was correlated with medical data by manually retrieving, reading, assembling, and abstracting patient charts, pathology reports, radiology reports, and the results of special tests and procedures. Manual annotation of research data is not feasible when experiments involve hundreds or thousands of tissue specimens, so the development of automatic methods for data annotation is a very important area of research.

Data-intensive biomedicine—Modern biomedical science is data-intensive. Gene, protein, and tissue microarrays allow us to look at changes in thousands of variables, all at once. Vast amounts of data are generated from single experiments. Likewise, large hospital information systems routinely collect and store terabytes of patient-related data. A human biopsy sample used in a high throughput array experiment is likely to have a wealth of clinical information stored in one or more hospital databases. Each biopsy has a surgical pathology report describing the specimen and listing pathologic findings. The surgical pathology report may contain an archived image of the lesion and a variety of special ancillary tests, including immunohistochemistry and cytogenetics findings. The biopsy used in the array experiment may be one of many different biopsies excised from the same patient, and these nonsampled biopsies may contain information pertinent to the experimental study. The patient's entire medical record, with demographic information (age, ethnicity, gender), history, physical examination, treatment, and outcome may reside in one or more hospital databases. The connected informational resources for an experiment can easily involve terabytes of data.

Data object—In the simpler past, it was easy to think of data as numbers or as a collection of numbers because databases imposed constraints on records and elements. Each record had a specific set of elements, and each element had a constrained datatype. Today, almost all information can be represented digitally, and any type of information can be annotated with other information. For instance, an EKG trace can be represented by a binary image, and the binary image can be annotated with information related to the format of the image, the EKG pattern of the image, the diagnosis rendered, a patient identifier, an EKG identifier, and so on. The data related to the EKG can be attached to the patient's EMR (electronic medical record) in whole or in part, and can also be linked to other reports generated in the hospital (e.g., billing records). Rather than thinking of the EKG as a record, it may be advantageous to think of the EKG as a data object, with a set of possible data elements belonging to the object, as well as a set of methods (software routines) that can be called upon to port sets of these data elements to other objects, and a set of general properties (list of methods) that are shared with other designated data objects. See also Object-oriented programming.

Data sharing—Data sharing involves one entity allowing data (whole datasets, specific records, or specific items from one or more records) to be accessed by another entity. This process may provide no-charge open access to the public; it can be performed on a fee basis, through contracts and other business arrangements; it may be performed to comply with administrative or regulatory requirements; or it may be performed under the duress of a subpoena. In all cases, medical data sharing transactions must protect patients from harm (i.e., without loss of privacy or breach of confidentiality).

Data scrubbing—see Scrubbing.

Dictionary—A vocabulary or a nomenclature with definitions for each entry.

Dublin Core Metadata—There is a fundamental difference between creating a document for oneself and creating a document for others. If you have created a document for yourself, then you do not need to include the name of the person who made the document, or the date that the document was created, or the purpose of the document, or restrictions on the use of the document, and so on. But if you have made a document that can be obtained and used by others, then you should include all of this information and more. Librarians understand the importance of having a set of information attached to every document that can be used to index documents for retrieval and that establishes the terms under which the document can be distributed and used. The Dublin Core is a set of metadata elements (XML tags) that were developed by a group of librarians who met in Dublin, Ohio. Every XML document should contain the standard set of annotations for the Dublin Core Metadata Element set (176, 177).

Electronic Laboratory Notebook (ELN)—ELNs are software applications that allow you to collect data in an organized manner that documents what you have done and when you did it (the kind of information that any experimentalist must produce on demand). ELNs can be used to standardize protocols, manage data quality, establish a convincing data trail, and facilitate data sharing between users. Most ELNs are proprietary software products. An exception is the open source NeuroSys (see Appendix). Despite claims to the contrary, ELNs are not particularly easy to master. Much of the functionality found in ELNs can be achieved by using common data specifications appropriate for the user's work (e.g., MAGE-ML), and an open source programming language to implement data capture and analysis (e.g., Perl).

Electronic Medical Record (EMR)—Also known as the electronic health record. The EMR is the digital equivalent of a patient's medical chart. A good EMR has all of the tests, reports, and documents for a patient collected in a database and keyed to the patient's unique identifier.

Entrez—The National Library of Medicine's text-based search and retrieval service that includes PubMed, Nucleotide and Protein Sequences, Protein Structures, Complete Genomes, Taxonomy, and other NCBI databases. An Entrez tutorial paper is available at http://www.ncbi.nlm.nih.gov/entrez/query/static/help/entrez_tutorial_BIB.pdf.

Gene expression array—Also known as gene chips, DNA microarrays, or DNA chips. These consist of thousands of small samples of DNA arrayed onto a support material (usually, a glass slide). Each sample of DNA is prepared by copying molecules of RNA of known sequence into fluorescently tagged sequences of complementary DNA, which are carefully placed on the array. When the array is incubated with cell samples, hybridization will occur between molecules on the array and single stranded complementary (i.e., identically sequenced) molecules present in the cell sample. The greater the concentration of complementary molecules in the cell sample, the greater the number of fluor-tagged hybridized molecules in the array. A specialized instrument prepares an image of the array and quantifies the fluorescence in each array spot. The greater the amount of fluorescence for each array spot, the greater the concentration of the molecule in the cell sample. The dataset comprising the fluorescent intensity of each post-hybridization array spot is a gene expression profile characteristic of the cell sample. By comparing individual gene expression levels in normal cells with those of diseased cells, researchers may discover candidate genes that play a causal role in disease processes. By comparing whole profiles of different tissue samples, researchers may identify subsets of genes having cellular pathways that distinguish one cell condition from another.

Grant—A grant is an award of money to a researcher in the hope that she will work productively. Most grants are awarded after reviewing a grant application, and in this case, the funders expect that the researcher will work on the project described in the application. The grantee's only real responsibility is to use the grant funds to support her work. The most important distinction between a research grant and a research contract is that the contract specifies a deliverable product, while the grant does not.

GRID computing—see Web services and grid computing.

Heterogeneous data—A pathology report and a histopathology image are very different types of data. One is a narrative text containing diagnostic terms along with clinical, demographic, and administrative information. The other is a binary file relating color and position to pixels. These are examples of heterogeneous data that are tied by a medical relationship. A digital representation of a bone X-ray may have a relationship to an operative note, to a bill for hospital services, or to an accident report. In these instances, the data are likely to have very different types of representations and formats and may have relationships that were not anticipated by the persons who created the data formats for each type of collected information.

HL7 (Health Level 7)—HL7 is an international data exchange specification for medical record data. The term "HL7" applies both to the data exchange specification and to the international group of health standards experts who work on the specification. The HL7 specification provides interoperability between the different devices and record types within a hospital and between different hospitals. For example, it may be used to share records between a laboratory information system (with blood test data) and the hospital's billing system. The latest version of HL7, version 3, permits data to be exchanged through XML, using an HL7 metadata vocabulary.

Human subjects research—Human subjects research is research that uses human subjects. This deceptively simple definition skirts two deeper questions: What constitutes a human subject, and What constitutes research? A human subject is a person or a part of a person or medical data pertaining to a person. This means that research conducted on archived tissue blocks or on medical charts is human subject research (even though no human is directly involved). Under the U.S. Common Rule, a person must be living to qualify as a human subject. Deceased individuals, along with their archived charts and tissues, are not considered human subjects. What is research? Research is a scientific study that seeks generalizable truth. If someone wants to know the number of patient encounters in a clinic in the past month, this would not be research, because the data is not generalizable and only pertains to a local situation. If a finding is published in a scientific journal, then it is almost always considered research, because it is assumed to have generalizable value of importance to the journal's readers. If an intern prepares a case report for a department's weekly morbidity and mortality conference, then the activity is probably not research because it only has local relevance. If the same case report leads to a generalizable finding and is published in a research journal, then it may have crossed the invisible line that separates a customary professional activity from a human subject research effort. When an activity is deemed "human subjects research," it automatically acquires the protections specified in the Common Rule and falls under the watchful eye of the IRB (126).

Intellectual property—Data, software, algorithms, and applications are products of intellectual effort and are potential sources of revenue. Data sharing can occur only in an environment that preserves the relationship between the owner and her intellectual property. This is sometimes achieved with material transfer agreements, a type of usage license that specifies how intellectual property might be used without violating or nullifying the value of intellectual property to an owner. Owners of intellectual property need successful strategies to share data while preserving the value of their intellectual property.

IRB—IRBs (Institutional Review Boards) are committees created under the Common Rule by hospitals and research organizations to ensure that human subject research is performed in a manner that protects human subjects. The most important activities of these committees in the realm of biomedical informatics involve ensuring the confidentiality and privacy of patients.

ISO/IEC 11179 (ISO11179)—XML data is flanked by metadata tags that describe the data, for instance, `<date>`October 1, 2005`</date>`. The metadata in this example is "date." But how do we know what the metadata "date" actually means? How do we know that it is referring to a day of the year and not to a type of dried fruit? Even metadata needs to be defined, and the ISO/IEC 11179 sets a standard for describing metadata. Well-defined metadata should be defined in an accessible document that includes the following defining information for the metadata tag: 1) Name—the label assigned to the tag, 2) Identifier—the unique identifier assigned to the tag, 3) Version—the version of the tag, 4) Registration authority—the entity authorized to register the tag, 5) Language—the language in which the tag is specified, 6) Definition—a statement that clearly represents the concept and essential nature of the tag, 7) Obligation—indicates if the tag is required to always or sometimes be present (contain a value), 8) Datatype—indicates the type of data that can be represented in the value of the tag, 9) Maximum Occurrence—indicates any limit to the repeatability of the tag, and 10) Comment—a remark describing how the tag can be used.

Limited Data Use Agreement and **Limited datasets**—Sometimes it may not be feasible to completely de-identify medical records. For instance, if the sender and recipient names were removed from an e-mail, this would serve to de-identify the e-mail from most readers. A determined individual may look for clues in the message or in the message header that could trace back to the names of the sender and receiver. A Limited Data Use Agreement permits the exchange of medical records between trusted signatories provided that the records cannot be easily identified, and that the IRB has reviewed and approved the proposed study and the Data Use Agreement and is satisfied that the process can be implemented without harming patients.

Medical vocabulary—see Vocabulary.

Middleware—An ill-defined realm of software development curiously described by middleware guru Ken Klingenstein as the "intersection of the stuff that network engineers don't want to do with the stuff that applications developers don't want to do." In more practical terms, middleware is software that operates over a network and supports interoperation between two or more different software applications. Closely related terms are mediators, wrappers, and agents. All these software tools function to merge, explain, or intelligently process diverse types of data dispersed through a network.

Minimum Necessary Provision—When using medical records for permitted purposes, HIPAA requires that only the minimal amount of information needed for the purpose is disclosed (see HIPAA excerpt). This may imply that information unrelated to research goals but included in medical reports must be removed prior to transferring the reports to external covered entities. The Minimum Necessary Provision applies to information other than identifying information.

> Section 164.514(d)—Minimum Necessary "covered entities must make reasonable efforts to use or disclose or to request from another covered entity, only the minimum amount of protected health information required to achieve the purpose of a particular use or disclosure."

Nomenclature—Comprehensive collection of the words contained in a specific and circumscribed knowledge domain.

Notation 3—Also called n3. A shorthand syntax for RDF providing a cleaner, less verbose format. CWM is a popular Python utility that inter-converts RDF and n3 and is available at http://www.w3.org/2000/10/swap/doc/CwmInstall.

Object-oriented programming—In object-oriented programming, methods (roughly equivalent to commands or to subroutines) belong to classes. The methods in a class are called by first declaring a variable to be a new object in the class. Once that is done, there is a syntax that allows the new class object to call upon any of the methods of its class or of the ancestor classes. In most object-oriented programming languages, there are hundreds of class methods that are built into the language. All of these methods can be immediately used in new programs. One of the difficult tasks in mastering an object-oriented language is learning what all the class methods do. This is sometimes referred to as learning the language's class library. Programmers can also create their own classes, class methods, instances of classes, and instance-specific methods. The easiest way of writing any object-oriented program is to declare a new instance of a class and then to invoke the class methods that can accomplish your computational goals. Object-oriented programs can be very short, because they often need to draw only on routines built into the language. If the programmer needs to create classes, then a much higher level of programming expertise is required. In practice, it is more difficult to master object-oriented programming technique than to master simple declarative programming. However, object-oriented programming has several advantages for the serious programmer: shorter, less complex programs, manageable software documentation, and reusable routines.

Off-the-Shelf Software (OTS software)—Defined by the FDA as a generally available software component used by a medical device manufacturer for which the device manufacturer cannot claim complete software life cycle control (178).

Ontology—An ontology is a rule-based grouping of members of a knowledge domain. Ontologies support queries and logical inferences pertaining to the (ontologic) group members. They can be used to test data for logical consistency and can be designed to discover relationships between different classes of data.

Peer-to-peer network—Sometimes data do not reside on a single server. To an ever-increasing extent, the data needed by scientists and healthcare workers reside on many different servers distributed over a wide geographic area and organized in a variety of data formats. When a group of data holders need to share their data without moving their data to a central repository, they may choose to create an Internet-based network of peer servers that can all respond to a client's request. The responses from the different peers can be collected into a single document and sent back to the client. As far as the client is concerned, the request for information and the reply might have been created by a single Web site (even though dozens of sites contributed to the reply). The peer-to-peer network is a strategy for data sharing that permits entities to maintain custody and control over their own data.

Open Access—Open access applies to documents in the same manner as Open Source applies to software. A formal definition of Open Access was drafted during a one-day meeting held on April 11, 2003 at the Howard Hughes Medical Institute in Chevy Chase, Maryland, and is available at http://www.biomedcentral.com/openaccess/bethesda/.

- "An Open Access Publication is one that meets the following two conditions: The author(s) and copyright holder(s) grant(s) to all users a free, irrevocable, worldwide, perpetual right of access to, and a license to copy, use, distribute, transmit and display the work publicly and to make and distribute derivative works, in any digital medium for any responsible purpose, subject to proper attribution of authorship, as well as the right to make small numbers of printed copies for their personal use."

- "A complete version of the work and all supplemental materials, including a copy of the permission as stated above, in a suitable standard electronic format is deposited immediately upon initial publication in at least one online repository that is supported by an academic institution, scholarly society, government agency, or other well-established organization that seeks to enable open access, unrestricted distribution, interoperability, and long-term archiving (for the biomedical sciences, PubMed Central is such a repository)."

Open standard—How could a standard not be "open"? Sadly, there are no prohibitions against imposing use and distribution restrictions on standards. Many standards are available only as copyrighted documents sold by the organizations that developed the standard. Some standards have restrictions on the distribution of the standard that may extend to all materials annotated with elements of the standard. Sometimes whole nations that have not paid a license fee to the standards development organization are prohibited from using the standard. An open standard should contain a license or a declarative language that specifies the unrestricted uses of the standard.

Polysemy—In polysemy, a single word, character string, or phrase has more than one related meaning. Polysemy can be thought of as the opposite of synonymy, wherein different words all mean the same thing. Polysemy is a particularly vexing problem in the realm of medical abbreviations. A single acronym may have literally dozens of possible expansions. In the context of this book, all the medical expansions of an acronym are related and polysemous. For instance, anterior–posterior and anatomic pathology are polysemous expansions of AP. Advanced placement and armor-piercing are not related polysemous terms because they are not medical terms.

Privacy Board—HIPAA created a mechanism (the Privacy Board) by which covered entities that have no IRBs may grant waivers to permit research using identified medical records (9). Privacy Boards are not permitted to review proposals that fall under the regulatory scope of the Common Rule (26). Covered entities with IRBs do not need to create Privacy Boards, because IRBs are authorized to grant HIPAA waivers.

Public domain—Not all data are owned. All copyrighted materials eventually exceed the term limits of copyright. Some people simply waive copyright on published materials. Data, documents, and books that are not owned by anyone fall into the public domain. Anyone can copy and distribute public domain materials without the permission of the author. Sometimes people neglect to provide proper citation to authors of public domain material. Public domain material must be cited just like any other original information source. To take false credit for another person's effort is plagiarism, even when the material is public domain. Authors who allow their works to be freely copied and distributed but who wish to retain some sense of attachment to their works might consider establishing copyright under the GNU free documentation license. The GNU documentation license is designed for textual information and can be found at http://www.gnu.org/copyleft/fdl.html.

Refactoring—Refactoring is a software method for taking complex code and introducing incremental improvements. The goal is to make the software easier to modify and enhance. Refactoring methods seem to be applied primarily to object-oriented languages, particularly Java. There are about 70 different kinds of improvements in the refactoring process, and some of them can be automated.

RDF—RDF (Resource Description Framework) is a special syntax within XML that constrains content to assertions that consist of a declaration of a specified object followed by a metadata/data pair of information pertaining to the object. These assertion triples (specified object, metadata, data pertaining to the specified object) are all that are necessary to bind data to subject and to create a statement of meaning. These statements of meaning can be aggregated with other statements from the same dataset or from other datasets, as long as they pertain to the same specified object. RDF is the foundation for the semantic web, in which logical inferences can be drawn from meaningful assertions (RDF triples) distributed throughout the Internet.

Scrubbing—Data scrubbing is a lot like any other kind of scrubbing. The purpose is to get rid of the dirt and to leave behind a clean product. When medical records are scrubbed, the most important component to remove are the patient identifiers, which is any information present in the text that may help determine the identity of the patient. These typically include the list of 18 HIPAA-specified identifiers (List 10.3.1). Beyond removing patient identifiers, an ideal record scrubber should remove identifiers of nonpatient individuals (e.g., nurses, doctors, staff), administrative entities (e.g., hospital names), geographic locations (e.g., addresses, cities), offensive remarks (e.g., "the patient is annoying"), incriminating remarks (e.g., that patient's doctor is incompetent), and any information that is not relevant to the intended purpose of the record.

Semantics—The study of meaning (Greek root, *semantikos*, significant meaning). Data can be structured and meaningless. Consider the assertion "Sam is tired." This is an adequately structured sentence with a subject, verb, and object. But what is the meaning of the sentence? There are a lot of people named Sam. Which Sam is being referred to in this sentence? What does it mean to say that Sam is tired? Is "tiredness" a constitutive property of Sam, or does it only apply to specific moments? If so, for what moment in time is the assertion "Sam is tired" actually true? To a computer, meaning comes from assertions that have a specific, identified subject associated with some sensible piece of fully described data (metadata coupled with the data it describes). As you may suspect, virtually all data contained in databases does not qualify as "meaningful."

SOAP—Simple Object Access Protocol. SOAP is an XML protocol for expressing Web Service requests and for encapsulating Web Service replies, using a syntax that is operating system and programming language independent.

Software agent—A computer program that can collect data, making logical inferences, and proceeding based on automated decisions. Though the definition of a software agent varies, most definitions convey the idea that software agents can interact with other software agents. This requires each software agent to contain instructions to describe itself using a standard data format that is understood by other agents. A special breed of software agent, the autonomous agent, proceeds without human supervision.

Software interoperability—It is not realistic to expect everyone to use the same operating system, the same programming language, and the same software applications. It is nonetheless often necessary to have software that can operate with other software regardless of differences in operating systems and programming language. There are a wide variety of methods by which this can be achieved. The topic of software interoperability has become complex, but it remains a fundamental issue in biomedical informatics.

Specification—A specification is a way of describing something using well-defined descriptors and well-defined units of measurement, and organizing the descriptive data in a manner than can be unambiguously understood.

Standards Development Organization—There are hundreds, and perhaps thousands, of organizations that develop standards. Standards Development Organizations may become members of a Standards Activities Organization, such as the American National Standards Institute, so that their product can become a National or International Standard.

Standards Activities Organization—There are only a few organizations that are devoted to facilitating the development of standards. These organizations mediate between Standards Development Organizations and Standards Organizations, providing guidance and procedures to move from a recommended specification to a certified new standard. ANSI (American National Standards Institute) is such an organization. ANSI has a Healthcare Informatics Standards Board (ANSI HISB) that facilitates the development and implementation of national and international medical informatics standards.

Standards Organizations—There are only a few organizations that certify new standards, and in the field of biomedical informatics, the two most important are ISO (International Organization for Standardization) and IEC (International Electrochemical Commission).

Steganography—A technique whereby a message is hidden within another object. Steganography has been around for centuries, with many of its methods described by Trithemious in 1500 AD (179). A common steganographic technique involves hiding a message within an image file. Most image files contain pixel values wherein the least significant bytes can be omitted or replaced without loss of image clarity. The bits of a secret message can be inserted into chosen pixel bits and extracted when needed. Rivest has described a clever method of hiding secret text in plain view using one-way hashes (180). Watermarking is closely related to steganography. Digital watermarking is a way of insinuating the name of the owner or creator of a digital object within the object as a mechanism of rights management.

String—In computer parlance, a string generally refers to a sequence of ASCII characters (i.e., a character string). All words are strings. All phrases are strings. All sequences of digits are strings. A variable in Perl typically holds a string.

Taxonomy—The list of instances in a knowledge domain. Taxonomies are used to fill a classification or an ontology.

Terminology—see Nomenclature.

Text editor—A text editor (also called an ASCII editor) is a software program designed to display and modify simple unformatted text files. Text editors differ from word processing software applications that produce files with formatting information embedded in the file. Text editors use the ASCII standard code that converts 8-bit binary sequences into alphanumeric characters. Text editors have certain important qualities lacking in word processors. Text editors, unlike word processors, allow you to inspect all the characters contained in a file. Text editors are much faster than word processors because they simply display the contents of files without having to interpret and execute formatting instructions. They can typically open files of enormous size with ease. Most word processing files choke on files that are hundreds of megabytes in length. Examples of free and open source text editors are Emacs and VI.

Thesaurus—a vocabulary that groups together synonymous terms.

Time-stamp—There are many times when it is important to know when a document was produced. Simply typing in a time and date does not suffice. You could be purposefully wrong, or you could provide wrong information inadvertently. Every computer can compute time and dates. The file systems of virtually all computer operating systems automatically add time and date information to every created file. Unfortunately, falsely setting the computer's time is a simple matter. In fact, the time and date for any file can be easily altered. Hospital information systems must have a dependable way of time-stamping patient transactions (e.g., when specimen was received, when report was generated, when physician was notified, when doctor orders were entered, when doctor orders were completed, when blood was received, when blood was typed and matched, etc.). This sometimes means regular checks of the computer clock against an external standard clock, saving time-stamped transaction data on an external medium that cannot be altered (so that later modifications to transaction times can be detected). In some instances, the use of a time-stamp service may be required (see Appendix 19.32).

Tissue blocks—see Archived tissue blocks.

Tissue microarray (TMA)—TMAs, first introduced in 1998, are collections of hundreds of tissue cores arrayed into a single paraffin histology block. Each TMA block can be sectioned and mounted onto glass slides, producing hundreds of nearly identical slides. TMAs permit investigators to use a single slide to conduct controlled studies on large cohorts of tissues, using a small amount of reagent. The source of tissue is only restricted by its availability in paraffin and ranges from cores of embedded cultured cells to tissues from any higher organism. In a typical TMA study, every TMA core is associated with a rich variety of data elements (image, tissue diagnosis, patient demographics or other biomaterial descriptions, and quantified experimental results).

Tissue Microarray Data Exchange Specification—Under ideal circumstances, a single paraffin TMA block can be sectioned into nearly identical glass slides dispensed to many different laboratories. These laboratories may use different experimental protocols. They may capture data using different instruments, different databases, different data architectures, different data elements, and immensely different formats. These laboratories could vastly increase the value of their experimental findings if they could merge their findings with those of the other laboratories that used the same TMA block. A key barrier to this process was the incompatibility between datasets produced in different laboratories. The TMA data exchange specification was developed jointly by industry and researchers. It is an open source method for conveying all of the data in a TMA experiment in a format that is understandable to both humans and computers. The TMA data exchange specification allows researchers to submit their data to journals and to public data repositories, and to share or merge data from different laboratories. The TMA data exchange specification is a well-formed XML document with four required sections: 1) Header, containing the specification Dublin Core identifiers, 2) Block, describing the paraffin-embedded array of tissues, 3) Slide, describing the glass slides produced from the Block, and 4) Core, containing all data related to the individual tissue samples contained in the array. Eighty CDEs (Common Data Elements), conforming to the ISO-11179 specification for data elements, constitute XML tags used in the TMA data exchange specification. A set of six simple semantic rules describes the complete data exchange specification.

Translational research—This term includes all biomedical research that attempts to find new therapies, devices, techniques, or tests that can be used in a clinical setting. Much of translational research is aimed at deriving benefit from the many advances in basic biomedical research archived in the past decade. Data sharing methodologies would be a type of translational research.

Web Services and **Grid Computing**—Web Services are server-based collections of data and software methods that operate on the idea that data and software can be accessed by remote clients. One of the features of Web Services is that they permit client users (humans or software agents) to discover the kinds of data and methods offered by the Web Service and the rules for submitting server requests. Grid Computing is a type of Web Services distinguished by greater flexibility and expanded capabilities. As both concepts mature, the two terms will be indistinguishable.

UML—Unified Modeling Language is a standard methodology, developed by the OMG (object management group) for specifying how a complex software application works. Properly specifying software using UML notation (or using UML diagramming techniques) requires significant expertise. For simple software scripts (the kind discussed in this book), UML is not necessary.

Unique Identifier—an elusive concept. A unique identifier serves to identify an object in a manner that distinguishes the object from all other objects. Three conditions should hold: 1) the unique identifier for an object can serve as the name of the object; 2) if two objects have the same unique identifier, then they must be equivalent (i.e., interchangeable) objects. In most instances (such as identifiers for people), two objects cannot have the same identifier; 3) if an object has more than one unique identifier (e.g., an LSID identifier and a DICOM identifier), then the object itself must contain, in an accessible form, all the unique identifiers that apply. The third feature needs some explanation. If an object does not contain all its different unique identifiers, then an object can be distinguished from itself. In the case of LSID and DICOM identifiers, the LSID identifier could (erroneously) distinguish the object from itself, identified by the DICOM identifier. There needs to be a way of knowing that the LSID identifier and the DICOM identifier both represent the same object. The only reliable way of accomplishing this is to have both pieces of data encapsulated by the object. Of course, the best approach is to forbid subsequent identifiers once the first identifier has been assigned.

Unique object—Objects that have immutable features that make the object different from all other objects. Every person is a unique object. Every moment in time is a unique object. The original Eiffel tower in Paris is a unique object. The class of "architectural towers" may not qualify as a unique object, but it can be a fully specified object, and it can be assigned a unique identifier representing its class.

Validation—One of the best uses of biomedical data is to validate assertions using existing data sources. You validate an assertion (which may appear in the form of a hypothesis, or a statement about the value of a new laboratory test, or a therapeutic protocol) by showing that you draw the same conclusion repeatedly whenever you analyze relevant datasets. It may be useful to compare reproducibility and validation. Reproducibility is when you get the same test result (i.e., an observed value) over and over. Validation is when you draw the same correct conclusion from the test result over and over. Biomedical datasets may contain millions of test observations, often annotated with clinical outcome data and epidemiologic data. Many people believe that a wide range of clinically important validation efforts could be performed quickly and cheaply if the data collected in hospitals were made available to researchers.

Variable—A variable in computer science is somewhat different than a variable in mathematics. You can think of a variable as a named container for a specified piece of data. In Perl, the command $thing = 5 is an assignment operation. The number 5 is assigned or put into the container named *$thing.* In Perl, a variable can hold any kind of character string (numeric, alphabetic, or alphanumeric), but the names of variables must be prefixed with a dollar sign (e.g., *$thing*).

Vocabulary—comprehensive collection of the words used in a general area of knowledge. A vocabulary is less focused than a nomenclature.

XML (Extensible Markup Language)—an informatics technology that allows any data element (e.g., a gene sequence, the weight of a patient, a biopsy diagnosis) to be bound to other data that describes the data element (metadata). Surprisingly, this simple relationship between data and metadata is the most powerful innovation in data organization since the invention of the book.

Index of Lists

Index